The *Past & Present* book series

General Editor
ALEXANDRA WALSHAM

Between the Devil and the Host

Michael Ostling received his doctorate in Religious Studies from the University of Toronto. Widely published on the topics of witchcraft, magic, other-than-human persons, and ethnobototany, he is co-editor of the internationally recognized journal *Magic, Ritual, and Witchcraft* and editor of the online *Database of Witch Trials in the Polish-Lithuanian Commonwealth, 1500–1800* (forthcoming). Ostling teaches interdisciplinary humanities in the Honors College at Arizona State University, where he attempts to practice a radical pedagogical approach inspired by Polish statesman and philosopher Jacek Kuroń.

Between the Devil and the Host

*Imagining Witchcraft in
Early Modern Poland*

MICHAEL OSTLING

Past and Present Publications

OXFORD
UNIVERSITY PRESS

OXFORD
UNIVERSITY PRESS

Great Clarendon Street, Oxford, OX2 6DP,
United Kingdom

Oxford University Press is a department of the University of Oxford.
It furthers the University's objective of excellence in research, scholarship,
and education by publishing worldwide. Oxford is a registered trade mark of
Oxford University Press in the UK and in certain other countries

© Michael Ostling 2011

The moral rights of the author have been asserted

First published 2011
First published in paperback 2024

All rights reserved. No part of this publication may be reproduced, stored in
a retrieval system, or transmitted, in any form or by any means, without the
prior permission in writing of Oxford University Press, or as expressly permitted
by law, by licence or under terms agreed with the appropriate reprographics
rights organization. Enquiries concerning reproduction outside the scope of the
above should be sent to the Rights Department, Oxford University Press, at the
address above

You must not circulate this work in any other form
and you must impose this same condition on any acquirer

Published in the United States of America by Oxford University Press
198 Madison Avenue, New York, NY 10016, United States of America

British Library Cataloguing in Publication Data
Data available

Library of Congress Control Number: 2023947968

ISBN 978–0–19–958790–2 (hbk.)
ISBN 978–0–19–886711–1 (pbk.)

Printed and bound by
CPI Group (UK) Ltd, Croydon, CR0 4YY

Links to third party websites are provided by Oxford in good faith and
for information only. Oxford disclaims any responsibility for the materials
contained in any third party website referenced in this work.

MIX
Paper | Supporting
responsible forestry
FSC® C013604

Dla Doroty, która wolałaby żebym został brzuchomówcą

Further Praise for *Between the Devil and the Host*

'an excellent monograph that faithfully reflects a regional history while offering important insights to the field as a whole . . . It will serve well as an assigned text in both graduate and undergraduate courses on the European witch hunts, and it should be read by scholars of witchcraft in general.'

Laura Stokes, *American Historical Review*

'In [Ostling's] brilliant analysis, the Polish witch stands at the crossroads of European and Slavic worlds, of high and low culture, of church and state, of formal court procedure and informal rites of reconciliation and counter-magic, of religion and 'superstition,' of reality and fantasy, and of culture and the individual.'

Valerie Kivelson, *Slavic Review*

'will be welcomed by specialists and more general readers alike as a useful and insightful contribution to early modern witchcraft studies.'

Hans Peter Broedel, *Church History*

'The author's religious-cultural approach to witches counters interpretations that tend to dismiss them as products of fantasy and superstition. An appendix, maps, and a table complement this stimulating book.'

L. B. Gimelli, *CHOICE*

'makes for fascinating reading . . . His framing of the wider question of what constitutes Christianity as an approach to reading witchcraft trials turns our attention to the margin between culture and self. His multidisciplinary approach (using comparative ethnology, folklore, and anthropology of religion) seeks to prove the very piety of the Polish Catholic peasant women accused of consorting with the devil through the motifs of diabolic copulation, host desecration, and invocation.'

Wanda Wyporska, *Magic, Ritual, and Witchcraft*

Preface to the Hardback Edition

On the first day of the course on witchcraft I teach at Central Michigan University, I hand out index cards and ask the students to draw unicorns on them. With varying levels of skill and detail, the students all draw the same thing: a horse with a long, spiraling horn growing from its forehead. I then ask the students how they know what unicorns look like, since (if we preclude the Indian Rhinoceros), such creatures do not exist. A brief discussion ensues in which, if all goes well, the class comes to realize that one *can* know all sorts of things about the unicorn: despite its imaginary status, one can trace the history of the unicorn from the Book of Job to the Irish Rovers; one can study the unicorn in art and poetry and folklore, one can theorize on its phallic symbolism and its predilection for virgins. We can know a great deal about unicorns, though nobody has ever seen one.

When I then ask the students to draw a witch, they take the point. Witches, like unicorns, do not exist. They are creatures of the imagination, and yet they can be studied through their representation in art and literature, theology and law. But witches differ from unicorns in one crucial respect: real women and men can be imagined to really possess the imaginary powers of witches. In Poland as in Europe and its colonies in the early modern period, people imagined their neighbors to be witches, with tragic results. This book tells the story of the imagined Polish witches, showing how ordinary village-women got caught in webs of suspicion and accusation, finally confessing under torture to the most heinous crimes. Through a close reading of accusations and confessions, the book also shows how witches imagined themselves and their own religious lives. Paradoxically, the tales they tell of infanticide and host-desecration reveal to us a culture of deep Catholic piety, while the stories they tell of demonic sex and the treasure-bringing ghosts of unbaptized babies uncover a complex folklore at the margins of Christian orthodoxy. Caught between the devil and the host, the self-imagined Polish witches reflect the religion of their place and time, even as they stand accused of subverting and betraying that religion.

The book is roughly organized into three parts, of several chapters each. Part I, 'History', focuses on the social, cultural, and legal context of Polish witch-trials and their change over time. Social and legal historians may find this section the most important part of the book: others might profitably skim Part I, moving on to the examination of religious and folkloric issues in Parts II and III.

Part II, 'Religion', traces the imagined practices of Polish witches, in the context both of the real practices of their accusers and of the normative teachings of the Catholic Church. Nobody was a witch, but everybody knew what witchcraft looked like. The imaginary spells and rituals attributed to witches modified or inverted the real charms, prayers, and counter-magical rites of ordinary Poles. Under torture, accused witches produced confessions through the imaginative elaboration of assumptions shared by all members of the society. When confessions included atrocity stories of the abused and desecrated Eucharist, these may be read in reverse: as inverted expressions of post-Tridentine Catholic piety, they provide a rare window into the Christian lives of early modern commoner women.

Part III, 'Demonology', explores the imagined relations between witches and devils. In witch-trials and confessions, indigenous Polish house-spirits and nature spirits came to take on the shape and form of the Christian devil. But interestingly, and to a degree not matched elsewhere in Europe, the process was reciprocal: while the house-spirit was diabolized, the devil was domesticated.

The final chapter considers wider questions of translatability, comparison, and the interpenetration of cosmopolitan and indigenous worlds: the imagined Polish witch is a crossroads figure, produced at the intersection of pan-European Christianity and local folklore, village politics and Roman law. Created in and through this babble of competing voices, the imagined witch was also a real woman, herself concrete and actual but also imagined—by the church and the magistrate; by her neighbors, by her enemies and her kin; by herself. I strain to hear her own voice (no less authentic and personal for being, like all voices, an artifact of the culture and religion and language through which it finds expression) in or behind the words of confession under torture. Like the multiple discourses of witchcraft, this book is ultimately an exercise in imaginative translation.

The book's many faults derive entirely from the shortcomings of its author. Whatever insight it contains must be attributed largely to the many people whose generosity and intelligence helped shape and guide the research and the writing. Thanks are due first to several careful readers of the long original manuscript: Jonathan Pearl, Janice Boddy, Juri Kivimae, Nick Terpstra, Lyndal Roper, Alexandra Walsham, Emily Hagen, and the anonymous readers of Past and Present Publications and OUP. Sarah King, David Perley, Małgorzata Pilaszek, Jacek Wijaczka, Tomasz Wiślicz, and Laurel Zwissler gave good advice, shared their own research, and offered encouragement. Of many helpful librarians and archivists I would like to particularly thank Candice Cheung, Ksenya Kiebuzinski, and Krystyna Klejn-Podchorowska. For other favors, large and small, I am grateful to William Burley, Ellie Cotton and her colleagues at Kaya, Alan Cottrell, Mark Crane, Kateryna Dysa, David Frankfurter, Stephanie Ireland, Kosma Jóźwiak, Agnieszka Karolczuk, Valerie Kivelson, Anna Kubicka, Karolina Kuczmierowska, Gisela Mutter, Jane Robson, Dorota Rogowska, and Briony Ryles. I received financial support during the research and writing stages of this book from the American Council of Learned Societies, the Fullbright Foundation, the University of Toronto Humanities Centre, and the Office of Research and Sponsored Programs at CMU. My family, and especially my wife Dorota, have endured my long hours and short temper with remarkable forbearance. The work is dedicated to her, and to my parents.

Preface to the Paperback Edition

Two decades ago, I had the good fortune to carry out research in Poland for several months, with funding from a Fulbright fellowship. When I explained to an assistant archivist in the Lublin archives that I was looking for the court records from witch trials, she appeared confused: "You mean like in your own country, in Salem?" she asked. This was significant: in Poland, a country in which several hundred women (at minimum) were burnt alive at the stake for the crime of witchcraft, the term "witch trial" invoked images of the panic in Salem, Massachusetts in 1692, where local authorities executed just 19 women and men for a similar crime. In the first years of the present millennium, witch trials were almost completely absent from the Polish historical imagination: they were something that happened elsewhere—in Western Europe or colonial America.

Twenty years later, the public imagination of witch trials in Poland has changed beyond recognition. In the village of Gorzuchowo there stands now a statue raised in 2015 to commemorate the ten women sentenced to the stake for witchcraft by the Kiszkowo town court in 1761. (Significantly, an accompanying plaque describes these women as *zielarki z Gorzuchowa*, "the herbalists of Gorzuchowo,"—thus reframing the targets of witchcraft accusation as bearers of traditional abilities, of secret pre-Christian female knowledge, for which they were punished with death.)[1] Meanwhile, during the massive Women's Strike protests across Poland in 2020, many women chose the witch as their symbol of resistance to patriarchal oppression: some marchers wore the stereotypical pointed black hat of the Hollywood witch, or painted their faces with Harry Potter's lightning-bolt scar. Borrowing a phrase from an American young adult fantasy novel, women carried plackards with the slogan *Jesteśmy wnuczkami czarownic których nie zdołaliście spalić*, "We are the granddaughters of the witches you couldn't burn."[2] Polish women (and people of all genders) fighting for reproductive rights and body autonomy, for the dignity of LGBTQ+ people, for a renewed connection to the natural world or for female-centered spiritualities or healing practices, all look to the history of the Polish witches for inspiration, and they are proud of the heritage of female power they understand themselves to

---

[1] Aleksandra Warczyńska, *Zielarki z Gorzuchowa*, https://wielkopolskaciekawie.pl/ciekawe-historie/zielarki-z-gorzuchowa-palenie-na-stosie/, accessed May 23 2023. See pp. 1–2 of the present volume for an account of the 1761 trial in Kiszkowo of the Gorzuchowo "witches" (or "herbalists").

[2] T. Thawer, *The Witches of BlackBrook*, Amber Leaf, Fort Collins 2015; F. Toon, "We Are the Granddaughters of the Witches You Couldn't Burn," https://www.penguin.co.uk/articles/2021/march/francine-toon-pine-inner-witch-violence-against-women.html (dostęp: 1.4.2022).

find in this history. When I gave an online talk about the Polish witch trials at the end of 2020, nearly a thousand people joined the livestream.

As will be clear from the chapters to follow, I argue against a romanticized vision of the early modern Polish witches as foremothers of present-day gender rebels. We have no evidence that the accused Gorzuchówo witches were herbalists in any sense—nor yet cunningwomen, enchantresses, fortune-tellers, cryptopagans, holders of secret or traditional women's knowledge in defiance of a patriarchal church and state.[3] The marchers in the *StrajkKobiet* certainly are, in some sense, "granddaughters of the witches you couldn't burn"—but only in the sense that they are the grand-daughters of ordinary early modern Polish women (mostly Catholic), women whose resistance to patriarchy took the form of everyday attempts to assert some autonomy over their own lives, everyday struggles for dignity or just survival. It is a central contention of this book—a contention strongly grounded in the evidence from the trials themselves—that the Polish accused witches were overwhelmingly drawn from this demographic of ordinary everyday women. With a few striking exceptions—the cunningwomand, vagabond, and prostitute Barbara of Radom; the healer Apolonia Porwitka; Dorota Gnieczkowa, who knew how to protect her clients against fire or storm—most Polish *accused* witches were not witches at all, on any standard definition of that word. They *became* witches only through suspicion and accusation, through confession coerced under torture, and conviction by a panel of male magistrates and jurymen. To insist otherwise is to unwittingly, unintentionally side with their accusers and judges, and more generally with the patriarchal system that ascribed to ordinary women a diabolical, demonic power.

This is not to say that I am unsympathetic to the contemporary feminist reimagination of the historical witch. Quite the contrary. I agree with the great British historian Ronald Hutton, who has done more than anyone else to debunk claimed connections between present-day Pagan or feminist-spiritualist practice and the actual behaviors of accused witches in past centuries. Nevertheless, Hutton expresses "delight" (a delight I share), that modern women have reclaimed the witch as "one of the very few embodiments of independent female power that traditional Western culture has bequeathed to the present."[4] Similarly, my colleague Laurel Zwissler, an anthropologist who studies modern Pagan feminism, teaches her students that the coven of witches at their sabbath is a fantasy, originating from *male* fears about women gathering secretly by night to plot against societal norms. Nevertheless, when a new feminist student club, inspired by her class, named itself a "witches' coven," "It was my turn to grin. I know that there were no Witches in the early modern witch trials; however [. . .] I cannot

---

[3] M. Ostling, "Witches' Herbs on Trial," *Folklore* 2014, vol. 125.
[4] R. Hutton, *The Witch: A History of Fear, from Ancient Times to the Present* (New Haven: Yale University Press, 2017), 279.

help but love that there are Witches now."[5] I agree. There were no witches in the early modern Polish witch trials, but I cannot help but love that there are witches marching in the Polish streets today.

The present edition of this book differs from the hardcover original (published a dozen years ago) in three important ways.

First, many small mistakes in the original edition have here been corrected. Reviewers of the first edition found a handful of minor errors of fact; others I discovered myself; still others came to light in the process of revision. No doubt errors remain, but these are fewer than there used to be.

Secondly, I have tried to clarify the argument in a number of places. Here too reviewers and colleagues have been of great assistance, if sometimes inadvertently: friends have gently pointed out passages they had found recondite or obscure, while occasional misconstruals of my point have helped me find other passages in need of more straightforward exposition. Early this century I still wrote like a graduate student; now, I hope, I write more like a teacher.

Third and most importantly, the current edition draws on a much larger database of trial records. There has been a great deal of good scholarship on the Polish witch trials since 2011, with major studies by Kateryna Dysa (on Red Ruthenia and Wołyń—both now regions of Ukraine), Wanda Wyporska (on Wielkopolska), and Jacek Wijaczka (numerous articles focused mostly on the towns and cities of northern Poland). Promising young scholars hare making their mark as well with detailed regional studies: Małgorzata Kowalska-Cichy (on Lublin), Marcin Moeglich (on Wągrowiec), and especially Łukasz Hajdrych (on Kleczew, "the Polish Salem"). Since 2017 I have been at work consolidating this recent research to create the Database of Witch Trials in the Polish-Lithuanian Commonwealth, 1500–1800, a digital resource scheduled to go online in Summer 2024, which will eventually make searchable the basic data for all known witch trials in the Commonwealth, updated as new scholarship comes in. Whereas the first edition of this book drew on materials from 254 trials involving 509 accused witches, the new edition, using materials collected in the making of this database, takes into consideration 526 trials and at least 892 accused witches. The beautiful new maps illustrate this much-expanded dataset, with trials now sprinkled right across the northern, western, and southern areas of the Polish Crown. All statistics, all tables, all figures in the present volume have been revised to reflect this new data as well: these revisions are especially noteworthy in the discussions of chronology, geography, and demographics in chapter 1. Surprisingly, however, this new data has only rarely required substantive adjustments to my interpretation of the history of Polish witchcraft in the chapters below. That analysis is now more deeply grounded in a larger evidential set—whereas in the first edition a given claim might be backed by two or three examples from the trial records, the

---

[5] L. Zwissler, "Witches Tears: Spiritual Feminism, Epistemology, and Witch Hunt Horror Stories," *The Pomegranate* 2016, vol. 18 (2), s. 199–200.

same claim now calls on five or six examples—but the arguments I made a decade ago still hold up in light of this new information.

The Database of Witch Trials in the Polish-Lithuanian Commonwealth, on which so much of the substance of this book is drawn and of which I am editor, is a team effort. The project has been enriched through the work of several research assistants at Arizona State University, among whom I must especially single out Max Strackbein-Bussey (for database management and for creating the maps in this edition), Hugo Crick-Furman (for translations from Belarussian and Ukrainian), and Katie Truong (for bibliographical assistance). Major contributors of trial record details include Bożena Ronowska, Jacek Wijaczka, Łukasz Hajdrych, Magdalena Kowalska-Cichy, and Kateryna Dysa. This revised English edition also benefits greatly from the readers and editors at Archiwum Kobiet (the Women's Archive) who took such great care with the Polish edition (Warsaw: Lupa Obscura, 2023) Emilia Kolinko, Monika Rudaś-Gródzka, Katarzyna Nadana-Sokołowska, Weronika Rychta, Olga Kowalczyk, and Iwona Misiak. I have been especially fortunate in my translator, Łukasz Hajdrych, whose expert knowledge of the topic has allowed for an especially accurate and sensitive rendering into Polish (and many hard-fought and detailed conversations about the interpretation of specific words or phrases—conversations that have improved the English revision as well). For inspiration, assistance, and advice, I must also thank Cristen Poynter, Jonathan Hadwen, Katarzyna Stańczak-Wiślicz, Laurel Zwissler, Tamar Herzig, Tomasz Wiślicz, Tricia Goffena-Beyer, the student-workers Collin Frank, Kirsten Terrill, Lindsey Schmidt, Marcellina Wiertek, Meghan Vaughn, and Pacey Smith-Garcia, and the students of my Magic and Modernity class at Barrett, the Honors College at ASU.

Finally, I would like to express my deep gratitude for the chance, once again, to bear witness on behalf of the Polish accused witches. We encounter these women and men through a tragic miscarriage of justice: they are wrongfully accused and (too often) wrongfully convicted of crimes they did not and could not have committed; even those who eventually went free had usually been tortured, humiliated, terrified. We cannot believe everything they say; neither can we ignore the testimony they offer about their lives: we must not neglect their fragmentary, mediated, but immeasurably precious voices. Probably none of them were witches in fact, but their bravery in unchosen resistance to a misogynistic and patriarchal system continues to inspire. I dedicate the revised edition of this book to the Polish women and men accused of witchcraft in the early modern period—both those that were burnt at the stake and those who "you couldn't burn"—as well as to their "granddaughters" rising up against misogyny and patriarchy in the 21st century.

Michael Ostling

June 2023

Contents

List of Figures and Tables

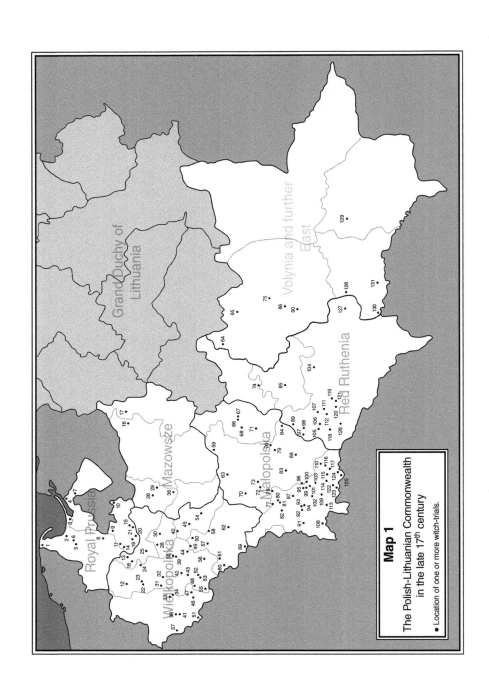

Map 1

The Polish-Lithuanian Commonwealth
in the late 17th century

• Location of one or more witch-trials.

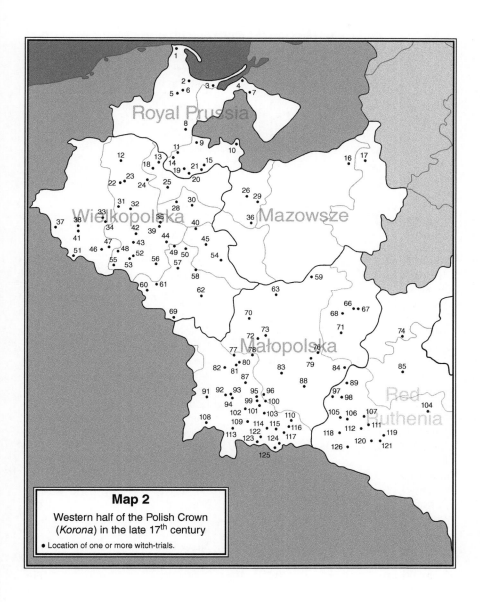

Map 2

Western half of the Polish Crown
(*Korona*) in the late 17th century

• Location of one or more witch-trials.

Index to Maps

1. IN ALPHABETICAL ORDER

2. IN NUMERICAL ORDER

Introduction

At the Crossroads

On the eve of Rogation Sunday, 1511 (May 24), '*vetula combusta* [*est*] *in campo extra oppidum Valischewo*'—a witch was burnt in the fields outside the town of Waliszew or Chwaliszewo, suburb of Poznań. Thus is described the earliest known execution for witchcraft in Poland. We have no record of the trial itself, and very few details of the accused witch's crime. We do know that she stood accused of having ruined several breweries through her craft—presumably by causing the fermenting mash to spoil. This information comes down to us through the records of a defamation suit in the Poznań ecclesiastical court: a citizen of Chwaliszewo had told a canon of the Poznań cathedral about the recent witch-burning; the clergyman responded that all the burghers of Chwaliszewo should be similarly burnt. In court, the canon explained that he had only been joking, and the case was closed (Chwaliszewo 1511).[1]

In 1761, two and a half centuries after the burning of the nameless Chwaliszewo woman, one of the last witch-trials in Poland paints a starkly different picture of witchcraft. The court of the tiny, privately owned town of Kiszkowo was invited to the village of Gorzuchów at the request of that village's owners, the noble Szeliski brothers. The Kiszkowo *wójt* or magistrate, three town-counselors, the court scribe, two executioners, and an apprentice executioner roomed and boarded in Gorzuchów, at the Szeliski brothers' expense, while they heard the accusations against five women of the village. By the end of the trial, *ten* women stood condemned of a long list of outrages and abominations, ranging far beyond maleficent magic. According to the court's verdict, the accused witches had 'forgotten the Fear of God', renounced their baptism, and 'bound themselves to the devil', with whom they engaged in 'association' (that is, sexual relations); they had met at 'Bald Mountain', had 'stolen the Most Holy Sacrament from various churches, burnt it to make a powder which they sprinkled in pig-sties and various dishonourable places, and had shed a second time that Most Holy

---

[1] Witch-trials included in my database (the great majority of the witch-trials discussed in this book) are cited by place and year of trial: e.g. Chwaliszewo 1511, Kiszkowo 1761. See the Appendix for the published and, where known, archival records of these trials.

blood, shed once for the ransom of the human nation by the Saviour of the world'; they had made bewitchments from the head of a mare, from vipers, snakes, the paw of a wolf, and buried these in various places to destroy people and cattle; they had, worst of all 'buried two Eucharist hosts in a mare's skull under the stairs of the manor, and another two under the threshold of the dining room', in order to destroy the health and household of their feudal masters. Accordingly, all ten were burnt at the stake at the border of the village (Kiszkowo 1761).

During the 250 years separating the Chwaliszewo trial of a single woman and the Kiszkowo trial of ten, the character of Polish witchcraft, and, more drastically, of Polish witch-*trials*, had changed. A rare crime in the early sixteenth century had become, by the mid-seventeenth century, a topic on everybody's mind: according to the polemical pamphlet *The Witch Denounced*, 'one hears about witch-trials more than about any other subject'.[2] From being a matter of divination, herb-craft, the preparation of amulets and love-charms, and at worst the magical spoiling of beer or milk,[3] it had become a much more nefarious business. Instead of semi-professional cunning-women whose power to heal implied power to harm, accused witches were now ordinary women in villages and small towns who came to be suspected of, and to confess to, the wildest crimes: spiteful and gratuitous malefice against cattle, humans, children; the raising of storms to destroy crops in the field and cause famine; feasts at Bald Mountain, with dancing to music played on a hoe or a plough or a foxes' tail; pacts with the devil consummated sexually; theft and desecration of that defining emblem of triumphant post-Tridentine Catholicism, the Body of Christ incarnate in the Eucharistic host. Instead of trials of a single woman for a specific crime of malefice, one finds trials of two or four or more: the crimes, the criminals, and the victims multiplying through the injudicious application of judicial torture. By the late eighteenth century, the carefully defined and circumscribed *vetula* of ecclesiastical-court procedure had been replaced, entirely it seems, by the terrifying *czarownica* of the popular imagination.

But these transformations of the imagined witch, and the attendant transformations in the consequences borne by those accused of witchcraft, should not blind us to deep and pervading continuities. In some contexts, such as the peasant-run village courts of southern Małopolska, trials remain similar over centuries: early and late, they mediate perennial anxieties about the health of children and cattle, the churning of butter, and brewing of beer (e.g. Wara 1582;

---

[2] *Czarownica powolana, abo krotka nauka y prestroga z strony czarownic* (Gdańsk: Jan Daniel Stoll, 1714 [1639]), f.3.

[3] Karol Koranyi, 'Czary i gusła przed sądami kościelnymi w Polsce w XV i pierszej połowie XVI wieku', *Lud*, 26(1927), 17; Stanisław Bylina, 'Magia, czary w Polsce XV i XVI w', *Odrodzenie i Reformacja w Polsce*, 35(1990), 41–2, 45; Joanna Adamczyk, 'Czary i magia w praktyce sądów kościelnych na ziemiach polskich w późnym średniowieczu (XV–połowa XVI wieku)', in M. Koczerska (ed.), *Karolińscy pokutnicy i polskie średniowieczne czarownice* (Warsaw: Wydawnictwo DiG, 2007).

Klimkówka 1702b). Even trials before town courts, which form the main subject of the present study, changed less in character than is sometimes appreciated: right through the whole period, most trials involved one or two accused witches, and most began with relatively straightforward accusations of malefice. In the eighteenth century as in the sixteenth, a witch was above all a woman who could harm through magic; above all, she stole milk and 'profit' from the udders of her neighbors' cattle. This close association of witches with milk-theft or milk-spoiling continued even into the twentieth century, when one still finds peasants driving milch-cows over a hatchet, whipping them with Easter palms, or hanging blessed herbs in their stalls to protect them from witchcraft.[4] Judicial practice has changed, but the fears, social interactions, and folk cosmology underlying witchcraft accusation have remained remarkably stable over time. The present study concerns itself with both the transformations and the continuities in this Polish imagination of the Polish witch—and in the judicial treatment of women to whom the label of 'witch' came to be ascribed.

In an insightful if polemic passage of his early exploration of Polish witchcraft beliefs, Ryszard Berwiński exploited the image of the crossroads—that place where the village meets the world, where you might encounter anyone and anything: a hanged criminal; the crucified Christ or the Virgin Mary in a roadside shrine; a fairy or devil peeking out from a hollow tree—to express his understanding of the Polish witch as a European import.

Witches are not characters developed from our own, national imagination; rather they are cosmopolitans, not born or raised in this or that country, but conceived at the cross-roads between this temporal and the everlasting world; their father the church militant, ignorance their mother.[5]

Like Berwiński's witch, this book stands at the crossroads: of Polish cultural and religious history; anthropology of religion and witchcraft; and the amorphous inter-discipline of witchcraft studies. But each of these fields, itself, is a crossroads discipline: each has been recently interested in the interplay between international and local, center and periphery, metropole and hinterland, cosmopolitan and indigene.

A trend of recent Polish historiography has stressed its reintegration with general European history, as against earlier emphases on Polish exceptionalism. Although some historians have wanted to maintain and highlight Polish differ-ence, others have worked to establish the basic comparability of Polish history to the history of Europe as a whole. Janusz Tazbir, long-time editor of *Renaissance and Reformation in Poland* (*Odrodzenie i Reformacja w Polsce*), stands as an ambivalent example of both trends: in monographs spanning a long career he

---

[4] See Jan Słomka, *Pamiętniki włościanina. Od pańszczyzny do dni dzisiejszych*, 2nd edn. (Kraków: Towarzystwo Szkoły Ludowej, 1929), 205; Urszula Lehr, 'Wierzenia demonologiczne we wsi Obidza (region sądecki) w świetle badań empirycznych', *Lud*, 66 (1982), 140.

[5] R. Berwiński, *Studia o gusłach, czarach, zabobonach i przesądach ludowych*, 2nd edn., 2 vols. (Warsaw: Wydawnictwo Artystyczne i Filmowe, 1984 [1862]), ii. 181.

champions particularly Polish achievements such as religious tolerance;[6] yet through numerous articles on the Polish reception of western notions and the western reception of Polish notions he has also sought to demonstrate inextricable links between Poland and Western Europe.[7] Within political and economic history, the late Antoni Mączak rejected traditional insistence on the unique trajectory of the 'noble democracy'. Instead, he consistently sought points of comparison between Poland and such states as Scotland or Denmark, and he developed pan-European models to understand systems of informal power.[8] Within religious history, a central theme of the publications associated with the East-Central Europe Institute has been the degree to which Poland, Lithuania, Bohemia, and Hungary were shaped by medieval Catholicism, Protestantism, and Counter-Reformation—experiences these regions shared with Western Europe but not with the Orthodox East.[9] In most of this recent work, the point has not been to insist on the identity of Polish historical trajectories with those of Western Europe; rather, it has been to resituate Polish history as a variation on a theme, as one of the many permutations of general Western European history, to be studied and taught alongside other such other permutations as the history of Spain or Scotland or Sweden. In other words, Polish and neighboring historians across a wide array of subdisciplines are beginning to concentrate on the ways in which local concerns, notions, and movements interacted with, integrated with, assimilated to, but also opposed or reacted to more general trends of European history.

Recent cross-cultural witchcraft scholarship displays a similar tension between the international and the local, and between the general and the particular. This tension inheres in the nature of the project: to what degree does the term 'witchcraft' denote a generalizable category made of commensurable practices and ideas across time and space? Within the anthropological literature, a tendency to reject the category of witchcraft as a colonial imposition[10] seems to be giving way to a renewed interest in commonalities and commensalities. An important trend of contemporary anthropological scholarship on witchcraft has been to move beyond the supposedly functional 'magical equilibrium' of tribal witchcraft beliefs, focusing instead on use of the imagined witch to negotiate between local

---

[6] e.g. Janusz Tazbir, *A State without Stakes*, tr. A. T. Jordon (New York: Kosciuszko Foundation, 1973).

[7] e.g. essays collected in Tazbir's *Sarmaci i świat* (Kraków: Universitas, 2001).

[8] Antoni Mączak, 'Jedyna i nieporównywalna? Kwestia odrębności Rzeczypospolitej w Europie XVI XVII wieku', *Kwartalnik Historyczny*, 100/4 (1993); *Money, Prices and Power in Poland, 16th–17th Centuries* (Brookfield, Vt.: Variorum, 1995); 'Patron, Client, and the Distribution of Social Revenue. Some Comparative Remarks', *Studia Historiae Oeconomicae*, 23 (1998).

[9] e.g. J. Bartmiński and M. Jasińska-Wojtkowska (eds.), *Folklor—Sacrum—Religia* (Lublin: Instytut Europy Środkowo-Wschodniej,1995); Jerzy Kloczowski (ed.), *Christianity in East Central Europe* (Lublin: Institut Europy Srodkowo-Wschodniej,1999); Hubert Łaszkiewicz (ed.), *Churches and Confessions in East Central Europe* (Lublin: Instytut Europy Srodkowo-Wschodniej, 1999).

[10] Berel Dov Lerner, 'Magic, Religion and Secularity among the Azande and Nuer', in G. Harvey (ed.), *Indigenous Religions* (New York: Cassell, 2000), provides a good brief overview of the issues at stake in exporting European notions of magic, witchcraft, and religion.

and international systems of power.[11] As happened in Europe in the early modern period, cosmopolitan, learned, and often textual imaginations of witchcraft have come together with local, usually oral understandings, and the results have often been an intensification of witchcraft fears and persecutions. However, as also in Europe, the results have also been intensely local, with major variations between regions; and they have been replete with unintended consequences. A suggestion coming out of this recent work is that intense witchcraft persecution occurs not at the center or the periphery but in the 'hinterland', the interactive and conflicting area—the spatial, social, economic, and conceptual crossroads—wherein a cosmopolitan, modern system comes into contact with local and traditional communities.[12] Although most of this recent work lacks a strong comparative element, it does provide a model for thinking about witchcraft beliefs as at once local and global, and about the problematic interaction between these two registers.

Within the field of European witchcraft studies more specifically, there has in recent years been considerable interest in the ways that 'canonical' assumptions about witchcraft and witch-trials played out on the margins of Europe. Since the publication of Ankarloo and Henningsen's influential *Early Modern European Witchcraft: Centers and Peripheries*,[13] historians of European witchcraft have also been taken up with problems of the interactions between center and periphery, metropole and hinterland. The studies in that volume from such marginal areas of Europe as Iceland, Sicily, Hungary, or Estonia challenged monolithic accounts of the witch-persecution by demonstrating extreme regional variety both in belief and practice: to mention just one example, they showed that a majority of the 'witches' in many of these areas were male. At the same time, the volume offered a unifying model of center and periphery, under which what we take to be typical of European witchcraft is, instead, characteristic of a central core (more or less France, Switzerland, and Germany), with greater and greater variation on theme as one proceeds into the political, cultural, and economic periphery. Moreover, these peripheral variations tend to decrease with time, so that, although they arrive late, 'typical' witch-persecution and 'typical' beliefs such as the *sabbat*-complex of devil worship and orgy do eventually make their appearance in the periphery. Witch-trials and demonology may be seen as part of a hegemonic

[11] Peter Geschiere, *The Modernity of Witchcraft* (Charlottesville, Va.: University of Virginia Press, 1997); Maia Green, 'Witchcraft Suppression Practices and Movements: Public Politics and the Logic of Purification', *Comparative Studies in Society and History*, 39/2 (1997); Paul Clough and Jon P. Mitchell (eds.), *Powers of Good and Evil* (New York: Berghahn Books, 2001).

[12] Jean Comaroff and John L. Comaroff, 'Occult Economies and the Violence of Abstraction: Notes from the South Africa Postcolony (The Max Gluckman Memorial Lecture, 1998)', *American Ethnologist*, 26/2 (1999); Bonno Thoden van Velzen and Imeka van Wetering, 'Dangerous Creatures and the Enchantment of Modern Life', in Clough and Mitchell, *Powers of Good and Evil*; David Frankfurter, *Evil Incarnate* (Princeton: PUP, 2006).

[13] Bengt Ankarloo and Gustav Henningsen (eds.), *Early Modern European Witchcraft* (Oxford: OUP, 1993 [1987]).

colonizing discourse that reaches out from the European center to influence the borderlands; but this discourse is also modified and indigenized in the process.

Ironically, it is sometimes difficult to decide at which level of discourse, the 'elite' or the 'folk', one finds a more uniform imagination of witchcraft. On the one hand, elite literary discourse shared assumptions drawn from a common heritage of classical texts. Stuart Clark's *Thinking with Demons*, an unparalleled inquiry into the pan-European discourse on witchcraft, has shown its surprising stability across confessional lines, legal systems, and political regimes. Polish elite demonology, though comparatively undeveloped, fits well into Clark's model, absorbing western tropes and topics with only minor changes. The anonymous Polish *Witch Denounced* is almost certainly independent of a work such as Friedrich Spee's *Cautio criminalis*, but its arguments are similar because its concerns, its assumptions, its theology are similar, and because it draws on the same western sources for its discussion.

On the other hand, local folklore could also exhibit strong uniformity at the folk level. One need not follow Carlo Ginzburg's tracing of the witches' *sabbat* to a pan-Eurasian shamanistic complex to note the very wide similarities in the cross-cultural motif of the witch. In Rodney Needham's useful phrase, the imagined witch is a 'synthetic image' drawing on pan-human fears, inverting pan-human values.[14] The imagination of the witch as a naked, night-flying, child-stealing corpse-eating insatiable over-consumer of limited goods ranges right across the world. Indeed, nearly every feature of the Polish imagined witch can be found elsewhere: desecration of the host, the preoccupation with milk, the attacks against children, the burial of vermin under the threshold to cause illness. The use of treasure-hauling demons to steal grain from neighbors explored in Chapters 9 and 10, which seems to be a typically Slavic or Balto-Slavic motif, was already reported by Virgil in his *Eclogues* a few decades before Christ, and receives discussion in Augustine.[15] Even so specific and local a practice as the use of fetus-ghosts for malefice or to find treasure, a practice and belief seemingly so dependent on Christian understandings of baptism, finds close parallels in the sorcery of present-day northern India.[16]

In this book, I have wanted to integrate discussion of the Polish imagination of the witch into the wider European and, indeed, world context. Against a historiography emphasizing Polish exceptionalism, tolerance, and 'mild' witch-hunts, I will show that the Polish village quarrels which led to accusations, the Polish trial process, and Polish sentencing habits were fully comparable to the rest of Europe. Against the countervailing assumption, that Poland experienced an exceptionally

---

[14] Rodney Needham, 'Synthetic Images', in *Primordial Characters* (Charlottesville, Va.: University of Virginia Press, 1978).

[15] Virgil, *The Eclogues*, tr. David Ferry (New York: Farrar, Strauss, & Giroux, 1999), 8.98; Augustine, *The City of God*, tr. Henry Bettenson (London: Penguin Classics, 2003), 8.19.

[16] Graham Dwyer, *The Divine and the Demonic* (London: RoutledgeCurzon, 2003), 63–4.

intense period of witch-trials and witchcraft fears, I intend to show that this too is incorrect: as elsewhere, most trials concerned malefice and turned on everyday concerns and fears. With the recent multiplication of excellent studies from all over Europe it is becoming increasingly difficult to point to any region as 'typical'. Nevertheless, it seems clear that the Polish state of affairs—with infrequent trials in most places, and a few areas of intense witch-persecution; with local persecution despite the attempts of central authorities to rein it in; with clerical misgivings about the abuses of witch-trials despite the Christian basis of the imagined witch—fits comfortably into trends found elsewhere in Europe.

A few words may be in order concerning the temporal and spatial scope of this study. In time, it covers what I have loosely called the 'witch-trial era', that is to say the two and a half centuries between the Chwaliszewo trial of 1511 and the abolition of witchcraft as a crime in 1776. Most of the material (both trials and texts) comes from the shorter period, approximately 1610–1750, which spans the height of witch-trials and of intellectual interest in witchcraft in Poland. However I have not hesitated, where necessary, to range far out of this temporal range. In Chapters 5 and 9 especially I have made considerable use of anti-superstition literature from the early and middle fifteenth century, while in several chapters I have supplemented the fragmentary evidence from witch-trials by making reference to folklore and ethnography from the nineteenth and twentieth centuries. This latter move has its dangers, but these are outweighed by the benefits. A passing reference to elderberry in a seventeenth-century trial (Turek 1652b), for example, can only be interpreted in the context of folkloric materials from the late nineteenth century and theological texts from the early fifteenth century. In this as in many comparable cases I have made the reasonable assumption that practices attested centuries before and centuries after the witch-trial era might have existed in similar form during that time-period itself.

In space, the study encompasses the territory of the Kingdom of Poland, the so-called *Korona* or Crown. From the late fourteenth century this kingdom was in dynastic union with the Grand-Duchy of Lithuania, while from 1569 until their partition and absorption into the empires of Russia, Prussia, and Austria, the two states were constitutionally joined together as the 'Most Illustrious Common-wealth' of Poland and Lithuania'. The territory of this vast country included, through most of the witch-trial period, the lands of present-day central and eastern Poland, Ukraine, Lithuania, and Belarus, and portions of Latvia. On the other hand, much of what is now western and north-western Poland (Silesia and western Pomerania) were not associated in any way with the Kingdom of Poland since medieval times. Despite the presence in these territories of large populations speaking Polish or related Slavic dialects, these territories are not considered in the present study.[17] Similarly, I do not consider the territory of Ducal or East Prussia, a fief of the Polish Crown through much of the sixteenth and seventeenth century which, however, exercised nearly total independence over most of this period.[18]

Recently Polish, Lithuanian, and Ukrainian scholars have rediscovered the history of the multinational Commonwealth as something distinct from and larger than the national histories which have dominated over the last two centuries.[19] Nevertheless, in this book I have concentrated on Poland alone, in isolation from Lithuania, and to a lesser degree, from Ukraine. Although the political culture of the Polish-Lithuanian nobility was singular, the legal history, and even more the social history and folklore, of the various regions remains distinct.[20] The legal history of witchcraft in the two nations of the Commonwealth really only comes together at the moment when witchcraft ceased to be a crime: the declaration of the Sejm in 1776 abolishing witchcraft as a capital crime in Poland was immediately extended to include Lithuania.[21]

Anthropologists have long been used to studying backwater communities of little international influence, assuming that the habits of any human group anywhere will be of interest to everyone everywhere. Historians are still expected to show that studies of peripheral regions will prove relevant to centers of culture or power. I find such an expectation disheartening—for me, at least, the imagined witches of early modern Poland are interesting in themselves, and my central task has been to understand them as themselves—nevertheless, I do think the findings of this book will be relevant to the understanding of witchcraft and magic in England and Germany, France and Spain. The crossroads where a Polish witch meets her devil leads both into her own village with its local folklore, and out into the whole wide world.

---

[17] On the witch-trials in Silesia, see Karen Lambrecht, *Hexenverfolgung und Zaubereiprozesse in den schlesischen Territorien* (Cologne: Bohlau, 1995). Poland experienced nothing comparable to the mass-panic at Neisse in Silesia in 1651–2, in which 188 people were executed in less than two years.

[18] On Ducal Prussia, see Jacek Wijaczka, *Procesy o czary w Prusach Książęcych/Brandenburskich w XVI–XVIII wieku* (Toruń: Wydawnictwo Uniwersytetu Mikołaja Kopernika, 2007). Wijaczka found 359 trials and a total of some 511 accused (of whom 86% were women), with a peak in intensity of witch-trials in the last quarter of the 17th cent. These proportions and this chronology, together with similar folkloric conceptions of the devil, demonstrate very considerable overlap between the Polish and Prussian trials.

[19] See esp. Andrzej Kamiński's programmatic account: *Historia Rzeczypospolitej wielu narodów 1505–1795* (Lublin: Instytut Europy Środkowo-Wschodniej, 2000).

[20] Although the Third Lithuanian Statute of 1588 listed witchcraft under noble palatinate-court jurisdiction, private manorial courts presided over most witch-trials in Lithuania. The literature on witchcraft in pre-partition Lithuania (which includes modern Belarus) remains scanty. For a survey of what little is known, see Malgorzata Pilaszek, 'Litewskie procesy czarownic w XVI XVIII w', *Odrodzenie i Reformacja w Polsce*, 46 (2002). Pilaszek found 97 trials between 1552 and 1771, 28 of which included death-sentences.

[21] Jerzy Michalski, 'Jeszcze o konstytucji sejmu 1776 roku 'Konwikcje w sprawach kryminalnych', *Kwartalnik Historyczny*, 103/3 (1996).

PART I

HISTORY

1

Contexts

HISTORIOGRAPHY

As elsewhere in Europe, the historiography of witchcraft in Poland has its roots in Enlightenment critique of an all-too-recent past. Simultaneously the most dramatic and most titillating example of a cruel, backward, and superstitious *ancien regime*, the 'great witch hysteria' justified present programs of reform and future dreams of the secular state: witch-persecution provided an inverted emblem for the ideology of progress. To adequately symbolize irrational fanaticism for liberal rationalists, witch-trials had to be pervasive, innumerable, and utterly lacking any rationality of their own; nineteenth-century historians had not yet learned to find social function in such primitive survivals of the Dark Ages. Accordingly, for a writer such as Jules Michelet, 'The clergy had not stakes enough' to execute the witches. 'They were brought to trial *en masse*, condemned on the slightest pretext. Never was such lavish waste of human life.'[1] This stereotype of massive, unmotivated, senseless cruelty was to prove remarkably long-lived.[2]

Poland produced no Michelet, but the mood of nineteenth-century scholars who touched on the Polish witch-trials was similar—with a twist. The Commonwealth of Poland and Lithuania disappeared from the map of Europe in the three Partitions of the late eighteenth century, and Polish historians of the long Partition era preoccupied themselves with searching for the causes of this catastrophe. A popular and not entirely unjustified theory placed the blame on the backwards, superstitious, unreformable ruling class of Poland-Lithuania, the *szlachta*, and on their doctrinaire Jesuit teachers.[3] Smugly secure in a xenophobic Catholicism which looked upon the Protestant West as decadent and on the Orthodox East as barbarian, the *szlachta* came to Enlightenment far too late.

---

[1] Jules Michelet, *Satanism and Witchcraft* (New York: Citadel Press, 1939 [1862]), pp. ix, xi.

[2] L. L. Estes, 'Incarnations of Evil: Changing Perspectives on the European Witch-Craze', *Clio*, 13 (1984), 136–9, traces this historiographical stance of rationalist disdain. See also the chapters by Peter Elmer and Christa Tuczay in J. Barry and O. Davies (eds.), *Palgrave Advances in Witchcraft Historiography* (New York: Palgrave, 2007).

[3] Andrzej Wierzbicki, 'Czarnowidztwo czy apologia? W poszukiwaniu prawdy historycznej', in *Przewrót umysłowy w Polsce wieku XVIII* (Warsaw: Państwowy Instytut Wydawniczy, 1979), 6; Władysław Smoleński, *Wiara w życiu społeczeństwa polskiego w epoce jezuickiej* (Warsaw: Ludowa Spółdzielnia Wydawnicza, 1951 [1882]).

Enamored of their medieval freedoms and noble privileges, they resisted the necessary reform of the state and allowed their homeland to be divided among the enlightened despots of Austria, Russia, and Prussia. Although witch-trials did not become the pivotal trope around which nineteenth-century Polish intellectuals organized their critique of the past, such discussion of witchcraft as did occur came filtered through the framing representation of a piously ignorant, superstitious, and cruel ruling class.

Thus Jósef Łukaszewicz, the great historian of Poznań and its environs, inveighed against 'the obscurantism of the Jesuit schools' thanks to which one finds witch-trials on 'nearly every page' of the early modern Polish court-records.[4] Thus, the didactic tone of Olszewski's study of witch-trials in central Poland, a work less of history than of admonition.[5] Thus, too, the earliest and most peculiar contribution to nineteenth-century scholarship on witchcraft: the anonymous, supposedly 'eye-witness account' of the last witch-trial in Poland, in 1775 in the village of Doruchów.[6] This riveting description—of the dunking of the witches in a nearby pond, where they fail to sink because of their full skirts; of the witches' imprisonment in the manor's grain cellar, immured in sauerkraut barrels; of the stakes for burning the accused, constructed even before magistrates had been summoned to the village from nearby Grabów; of the torture, by night, of the naked witches, by means of an iron rake or harrow, under which torture three alleged witches perished; of the lord of the manor presiding over the whole affair to ensure that harsh justice be done; of, finally, the mass burning of eleven women at the stake—this powerful story indicts the religious ignorance which made it possible, and which was finally disappearing 'under the benevolent rays of enlightenment'.[7] It is also fictitious. The supposed eye-witness account appears to have been the creation of Aleksy Rytter,[8] a parish priest who embroidered his own literary moralizing onto oral-historical materials recounting at least two separate trials (1762 and ca. 1770).[9] Many 19th century and indeed 20th-century scholars have accepted Rytter's sensationalized account without protest, because it fit so well with their preconceptions of what witch-trials were supposed to be like.

---

[4] Józef Łukaszewicz, *Krótki historyczno-statystyczny opis miast i wsi w dzisiejszym powiecie krotoszyńskim od najdawniejszych czasów aż po rok 1794*, 2 vols. (Poznań: Jan Konstanty Żupański, 1869–1975), 74–5; cf. Berwiński, *Studia o gusłach*, ii. 177–9.

[5] F. Olszewski, 'Prześladowanie czarów w dawnej Polsce', in *Album uczącej się młodzieży polskiej poświęcone J. I. Kraszewskiemu z powodu jubileusza jego pięćdsiesięcioletniej działalności literatckiej* (Lwów: Nakład Czytelni Akademii Lwowskiej, 1879).

[6] X.A.R., 'Relacja naocznego świadka o straceniu razem 14 tu mniemanych czarownic w drugiej połowie 18 go wieku', *Przyjaciel Ludu*, 2/16–18 (1835); repr. in Janusz Tazbir, *Cudzym piórem* (Poznań: Poznańskie Towarzystwo Przyjaciół Nauk, 2002), 104–9.

[7] Tazbir, *Cudzym piórem*, 109.

[8] We should now discount Tazbir's claim that the Grabów trial ws a literary hoax; Rytter's text is unreliable, but not intentionally falsified. Janusz Tazbir, 'Z dziejów fałszerstw historycznych w Polsce w pierwszej połowie XIX stulecie', *Przegląd Historyczny* 57/4 (1966).

[9] Michalski, 'Jeszcze o konstytucji', 93–4; Joanna Lubierska, 'Proces o czary w Doruchowie w 1775 r. w świetle nowych źródeł,' *Historia Slavorum Occidentis* 12/3 (2022): 30–63; Jacek Wijaczka, 'Proces o czary w Doruchowie w 1775 roku: Fakt czy mit?,' forthcoming.

Nineteenth-century Polish scholars made use of the image of the witch for rhetorical or admonitory purposes. However, with the partial exception of Ryszard Berwiński's mid-century *Studies of Superstition, Witchcraft, and Magic*[10]—a brilliant but idiosyncratic work of polemical folklore, intended to demonstrate that Polish folk culture derived entirely from elite, mostly western sources—no monograph devoted to Polish witchcraft existed until the mid-twentieth-century publication of Bohdan Baranowski's *Witch-Trials in Seventeenth and Eighteenth Century Poland.*[11] Baranowski deserves more recognition than he has recently been accorded by Polish authors, who have called his work 'worthless' and 'a failure'.[12] Approached with care, *Witch-Trials* remains a useful source of historical anecdote, and his publications of archival sources remain valuable.[13] But Baranowski's historical-materialist analytical framework led him to find an unholy alliance of church and *szlachta* behind every witchcraft accusation—a stance that involved him in a systematic pattern of exaggeration, misplaced emphasis, and tendentious interpretation. In this Stalinist version of nineteenth-century positivism, Polish witch-trials had found their historian.[14]

Witch-hunts, or 'the gloomy superstition' as Baranowski calls them, were a product of 'Popish politics and the Inquisition', but even more they represent the last raging battle of the church and of feudalism against emerging modernity.[15] Among the victims of witch-trials were to be found 'the bold fighters, male and female, for the rights of the peasant masses, people who entered into the futile battle against the power of feudal oppression';[16] while the spectacle of burning witches diverted 'the attention of the deluded populace from . . . their grievances

---

[10] Berwiński, *Studia o gusłach*; and see Adam Fischer, 'Ryszard Wincenty Berwiński (1819–1879)', *Lud*, 37 (1946), 141–59.

[11] Bohdan Baranowski, *Procesy Czarownic w Polsce w XVII i XVIII wieku* (Łódź: Łódzkie Towarzystwo Naukowe, 1952).

[12] Maria Bogucka, 'The Centre and Periphery of Witchcraze', *Acta Poloniae Historica*, 75 (1997), 187; Andrzej Karpiński, *Kobieta w mieście polskim w drugiej połowie XVI i w XVII wieku* (Warsaw: Instytut Historii Polskiej Akademii Nauk, 1995), 21.

[13] B. Baranowski (ed.), *Najdawniejsze procesy o czary w Kaliszu* (Lublin: Polskie Towarzystwo Ludowznawcze,1951); B. Baranowski and W. Lewandowski, *Nietolerancja i zabobon w Polsce w wieku XVII i XVIII: wypisy źródłowe* (Warsaw: Książka i Wiedza, 1987 [1950]).

[14] 'Stalinist' is not too strong a characterization of Baranowski's scholarship. In fact he helped popularize a conception of the Polish past that legitimated the new socialist regime by painting the system it replaced in the worst possible colors. In the early 1950s, he wrote or helped edit the following: a book exposing the Catholic Church as superstitious bastion of the feudal order (*Kontrreformacja w Polsce XVI–XVIII wieku*, 1950); a source anthology on 'intolerance and superstition' (*Nietolerancja i zabobon w Polsce*, 1950); and a source anthology on 'the collapse of culture in Poland in the age of Catholic reaction' (*Upadek kultury w Polsce w dobie reakcji katolickiej*, 1950). A third source-anthology on the 'situation of the peasantry at the end of the Noble Republic' (*Położenie chłopów u schyłku Rzeczypospolitej szlacheckiej*, 1953) helped set the groundwork for what Ślusarska has called the 'black legend' of the early modern Polish village: Magdalena Ślusarska (ed.), *Dwór, plebania i rodzina chopska* (Warsaw: DiG, 1998).

[15] Baranowski, *Procesy Czarownic*, 10–11.

[16] Ibid. 39.

and exploitation'.[17] Both witchcraft and witch-persecution were primarily instruments of class warfare in its feudal stage: *szlachta* used witch-accusation to get
rid of uppity serfs, while peasants used magic as part of their 'quiet battle' against
the feudal master.[18] As had been true in earlier Western European historiographies, witch-trials came to stand as the emblem for all that was wrong, cruel,
ignorant, and savage in the Polish past.

Historical accuracy is the first casualty of such a rhetorical orientation to the
past, not least because this orientation disregards the rhetorical nature of the
sources themselves. Baranowski and his precursors knew, but did not always
sufficiently appreciate, that they painted their dark portrait of the witch-trial era
using colors borrowed from satirical and polemical texts contemporary to the
trials. Ironically, considering Baranowski's own strongly anti-clerical stance, the
earliest and most vitriolic critics of the witch-trials were themselves mostly
churchmen, such as the probably Jesuit author of the *Witch Denounced*, who
denounces witch-trial judges as 'legal ignoramuses who can hardly recite the Lord's
Prayer'.[19] Similarly, the Franciscan friar Serafin Gamalski, in a text published by a
Jesuit press, called witch-trial judges 'analphabetic hillbillies' and, in an anticipa-
tion of Michelet's rhetoric, worried that 'our unhappy Poland will soon lack groves
and forests for stakes, and in Cities, Towns and villages, there will be too few
people left to serve as fuel for those fires'.[20] One can commend the acerbic
hyperbole of the seventeenth- and eighteenth-century polemicists; they painted
witch-trials in the blackest colors in order to awaken, in their readers, a sense of
urgency; in order to right what they saw as a terrible wrong. But such hyperbole is
no virtue in the historian. It has taken nearly half a century for the historiography
of Polish witchcraft to move beyond Baranowski's tendentious interpretations.

At the turn of the twenty-first century, the eminent legal historian Stanisław
Salmonowicz could survey the Polish scholarship on witchcraft and rightly
complain that little progress had been made since Baranowski's day.[21] Janusz
Tazbir had published a programmatic essay in 1978, critiquing Baranowski's
more extreme claims but adducing no new material;[22] while a handful of short
articles from the 1990s hinted at a renewal of interest in the subject.[23] But the

[17] Baranowski and Lewandowski, *Nietolerancja i zabobon*, 221.
[18] Baranowski, *Procesy Czarownic*, 35, 37; cf. G. Adamczewska, 'Magiczna broń i jej rola
w walce między wsią a dworem w Sieradzkiem w XVI XVIII w', *Łódzkie Studia Etnograficzne*, 5 (1963).
[19] *Czarownica powołana*, qu. 7, p. 52. See Michael Ostling, '"Accuser of Brothers": A Polish
Anti-Demonological Tract and its Self-Defeating Rhetoric', *Reformation and Renaissance Review*
22–23 (2020), 218–237.
[20] Serafin Gamalski, *Przestrogi Duchowne, Sędziom, Inwestygatorom, y Instygatorom Czarownic*
(Poznań: Drukarnia Akademicka, 1742), 7, 12–12ᵛ.
[21] Stanisław Salmonowicz, 'Procesy o czary w Polsce. Próba rozważań modelowych', in
G. Bałtruszajtis (ed.), *Prawo wczoraj i dziś* (Warsaw: 2000).
[22] Janusz Tazbir, 'Procesy o czary', *Odrodzenie i Reformacja w Polsce*, 23 (1978).
[23] E.g. Wacław Uruszczak, 'Proces czarownicy w Nowym Sączu w 1670 roku: Z badań nad
miejskim procesem karnym czasów nowożytnych', in E. Borkowska-Bagieńska and H. Olszewski
(eds.), *Historia Prawa: Historia Kultury* (Poznań: Printer, 1994); Krzysztof Szkurłatowski, 'Proces

radical reformulation of witchcraft scholarship initiated in the early 1970s, and the explosion of methodologically painstaking, theoretically sophisticated new studies which has followed this reorientation of Western European witchcraft scholarship in the last quarter of the twentieth century, had as yet found little echo in Poland.

Since the turn of the millenium, this situation has changed entirely. A steady stream of regional studies by the tireless Jacek Wijaczka has enormously increased our knowledge base.[24] Tomasz Wiślicz and Łukasz Hajdrych have provided invaluable case-studies of the largest witch-panic in Poland, a series of trials before the town court of Kleczew that led to the execution of forty-one accused witches in the last two decades of the seventeenth century.[25] Marian Mikołajczyk and Małgorzata Pilaszek have looked closely at matters of law and judicial practice, discovering, in general, that Polish witch-trials were run with more attention to procedure than had been generally supposed.[26] And monographic treatments have begun to appear: Joanna Adamczyk's survey of the trials before ecclesiastical courts in the fifteenth and early sixteenth centuries;[27] Kateryna Dysa's anthropologically informed analysis of the trials in western Ukraine;[28] Wanda Wyporska's important study of the trials in Wielkopolska;[29] and, above all, Pilaszek's pioneering synthesis of the entire phenomenon of Polish witch-trials—a massive study to which I am much indebted.[30]

The present work owes much to the recent spate of careful Polish scholarship. It departs from much of that scholarship, however, in treating witchcraft as a religious-cultural phenomenon with its own symbolic logic. There remains in the

inkwizycyjny przeciwko czarownictwu w praktyce sądow sołtysich województwa malborskiego na przełomie XVII i XVIII w. na tle rozwoju europejskiego prawa karnego', *Rocznik Elbląski*, 15 (1997); Malgorzata Pilaszek, 'Procesy czarownic w Polsce w XVI XVIII wieku: Nowe aspekty. Uwagi na marginesie pracy B. Baranowskiego', *Odrodzenie i Reformacja w Polsce*, 42 (1998).

[24] See the dozen or so studies by Wijaczka in the References—not counting his monograph on the trials in Ducal Prussia (Wijaczka, *Procesy w Prusach*).

[25] Tomasz Wiślicz, 'Społeczeństwo Kleczewa i okolic w walce z czartem (1624–1700)', *Kwartalnik Historyczny*, 111/2 (2004); in English, 'The Township of Kleczew and its Neighborhood Fighting the Devil (1624–1700)', *Acta Poloniae Historica*, 89 (2004). Łukasz Hajdrych, 'Proces o czary w Wąsoszach w 1688 r. Analiza procesu i problemy interpretacyjne', *Historyka. Studia Metodologiczne*, 51 (2021), 397–419.

[26] Marian Mikołajczyk, 'Przestępstwa przeciwko religii i Kościołowi w prawie miast polskich XVI–XVIII wieku', *Czasopismo Prawno-Historyczne*, 52/1–2 (2000); 'Jak obronić oskarżona o czary: Mowy procesowe z 1655 roku w sprawie Gertrudy Zagrodzkiej', in H. Dziewanowska and K. Dziewanowska Stefanczyk (eds.), *Z dziejów kultury prawnej* (Warsaw: Liber, 2004); Malgorzata Pilaszek, 'Apelacje w polskich procesach czarownic (XVII–XVIII w)', *Odrodzenie i Reformacja w Polsce*, 49 (2005); cf. Michael Ostling, 'Konstytucja 1543 r. i początki procesów o czary w Polsce', *Odrodzenie i Reformacja w Polsce*, 49 (2005).

[27] Adamczyk, 'Czary i magia'.

[28] Kateryna Dysa, *Istoriia z vid'mamy* (Kiev: Kritika, 2008). An English version of Dysa's work appeared recently, as *Ukrainian Witchcraft Trials: Volhynia, Podolia, and Ruthenia, 17th–18th Centuries* (Budapest: CEU Press, 2020).

[29] Wanda Wyporska, *Witchcraft in Early Modern Poland, 1500–1800* (London: Palgrave Macmillan, 2013).

[30] Małgorzata Pilaszek, *Procesy o czary w Polsce w wiekach XV–XVIII* (Kraków: Universitas, 2008).

current Polish treatment of witchcraft a trace of the old tendency to treat witchcraft beliefs and witch-trials as a pathology or sign of backwardness, and thus to refuse, as Robin Briggs has said of the older western scholarship, 'to accept that fantasy is a genuine experience'.[31] The merit of the present study, I would suggest, lies in its willingness to treat seriously witch beliefs, confessions, accusations, and behaviors: not indeed to treat them as 'true' but as sincere, coherent, and integrated with wider religious and cultural concerns.

NUMBERS

Discussion of the scale and scope of witch-trials in Poland tends to get mired in invidious comparisons. Scholars such as Janusz Tazbir and Maria Bogucka have been concerned to defend their vision of Poland as the 'state without stakes',[32] but even Baranowski believed that the Polish trials, numerous though he thought they were, paled beside the hundreds of thousands he mistakenly believed to have been burned in neighboring German lands.[33] Few have taken heed of Karłowicz's early admonition that, without a systematic archival survey, 'we have no right to adjudicate whether and to what degree the persecution of witches in Poland was greater and more zealous, or less and more mild, than elsewhere'.[34]

Unfortunately, the possibility of such a survey has all but disappeared since Karłowicz's day, due to the catastrophic losses suffered by Polish archives during World War II. As a punitive measure, the Nazis deliberately burned the Central Archives of Old Records (AGAD) and other archives: some 80 percent of its holdings were lost.[35] Whole regions, most notably Mazowsze, lost the greater portion of their recorded history, so that one now must rely on secondary sources, sometimes of dubious quality, published before the war. Both the massive losses and the fortuitous survivals of significant records doom any attempt at systematic statistics. The case of Kleczew, very thoroughly analyzed by Tomasz Wiślicz and more recently by Łukasz Hajdrych illuminates the problem well: between 1624 and 1738 the Kleczew court heard forty-seven witch-trials, with a total of 131 accused and at least 92 executed: by far the largest concentration of witch-trials known for any court in Poland.[36] All of these trials are recorded in a special criminal register or 'black book', kept separate from the ordinary judicial records

---

[31] Robin Briggs, *Witches and Neighbours* (London: Penguin Books, 1996), 38.
[32] Janusz Tazbir, 'Liczenie wiedźm', *Polityka,* 37 (2001); Maria Bogucka, 'Law and Crime in Poland in Early Modern Times', *Acta Poloniae Historica,* 71 (1995), 191.
[33] Baranowski, *Procesy Czarownic,* 9, 31, 169.
[34] J. Karłowicz, 'Czary i czarownice w Polsce', *Wisła,* 1(1887), 222.
[35] Andrzej Tomczak, *Zarys dziejów archiwów polskich* (Toruń: Uniwersytet Mikołaja Kopernika, 1980), ii.
[36] Wiślicz, 'Township of Kleczew', 67; Hajdrych, 'Wizja świata mieszkańców Kleczewa w świetle protokołów z księgi sądu wójtowskiego miasta Kleczewa (1624–1738)', (Poznań: Uniwersytet im. Adama Mickiewicza, 2022).

of Kleczew—which records are entirely silent on the subject of witchcraft. If this black book had not survived, fortuitously preserved in the collections of the Poznań Society of Friends of Science, our picture of witch-trials in the entire region would be radically different. Another Kleczew might be discovered at any time, or its intensive witch-persecution may indeed be the anomaly it appears to be in our current state of knowledge.

It will be recalled that the Franciscan friar Serafin Gamalski, writing in the mid-eighteenth century, warned that the endless Polish forests would soon not suffice for the production of stakes to burn witches.[37] Bohdan Baranowski's estimations of witches killed in Poland are equally hyperbolic. Baranowski systematically and intentionally exaggerated wherever he could, assuming death sentences where none were recorded, or treating denunciations as prima-facie evidence of further trials. This tendentious rounding upwards of all evidence led Baranowski to his most absurd claim, that in Poland some 10,000 accused witches were judicially executed during the late sixteenth through eighteenth centuries, with another 5,000 to 10,000 lynched.[38] While Polish historians have been voicing doubts for decades,[39] western scholarship has been surprisingly willing to accept this extremely high figure for witches executed in Poland—a figure that would put Poland at the center of the witchcraze.[40] However, these numbers are unquestionably wrong, as a brief evaluation of Baranowski's method makes clear.

The asserted mass lynchings may be dismissed out of hand.[41] The famous figure of 10,000 witches burned may be dismissed almost as quickly. Baranowski reached this figure through a process of tendentious extrapolation: he multiplied the number of towns in early modern Poland (around 1,250) by an arbitrarily derived four trials per town. The resulting figure (5,000) is then multiplied by two—this being the equally arbitrary, and unquestionably wrong, average number of witches executed per trial. Thus: 10,000 witches burnt in Poland. One is reminded of the methods and assumptions used by Gottfried Christian Voigt in

---

[37] Gamalski, *Przestrogi Duchowne*, 7.

[38] Baranowski, *Procesy Czarownic*, 30.

[39] Tazbir, 'Procesy o czary'; Pilaszek, 'Procesy czarownic w Polsce'.

[40] Eminent textbooks and works of reference have perpetuated Baranowski's figures: see e.g. Brian Levack, *The Witch Hunt in Early Modern Europe* (London: Longman, 1987), 20, 195 (corrected in the 3rd edn. of 2006); Robert Muchembled, *Le Roi et la sorcière* (Paris: Desclée, 1993), 75; Mark Greengrass, *The Longman Companion to the European Reformation: 1500–1618* (London: Longman, 1998), 277; P. G. Maxwell-Stuart, *Witchcraft in Europe and the New World, 1400–1800* (New York: Palgrave, 2001), 86.

[41] Lynching of suspected witches was extremely rare in early modern Poland. I am aware of just one clear case: when a delegation of townsfolk who had consulted a diviner about the suspected witch Prośka Kapłunka caught her fleeing the city of Krasiłów, they buried her up to the waist, piled wood around her, and burned her alive (Krasiłów 1720). However, lynching of witches did occur with fair regularity in 19th-cent. Russia and Ukraine, where judicial means for removing witches from the village were unavailable. See Christine D. Worobec, *Possessed. Women, Witches and Demons in Imperial Russia* (De Kalb, Ill.: Northern Illinois University Press, 2001).

the late eighteenth century to calculate nine million witches executed in Europe—a number we now know to be off by a factor of a hundred or more.[42]

So how many witches *were* executed in early modern Poland? Małgorzata Pilaszek has refused to speculate beyond her sources: her figure of 558 executed, out of 1,316 accused in 867 trials, may be taken as a minimum figure of known executions.[43] But it is unquestionably too low: though Pilaszek's study represents by far the largest survey of Polish archival sources attempted to date, it is far from comprehensive. My own estimate derives from my database of 526 trials between 1511 and about 1775, including at least 892 accused witches, of whom at least 362 were executed.[44] Taking under consideration only trials before town courts (village courts lacked the right to execute) I have evidence for 447 trials, 783 accused, and 360 known to have been executed: a ratio of approximately 0.8 defendants executed per trial. The trials come from 111 towns, giving an average of about four trials per town (although this average hides enormous variation: from just one trial in many towns to the very numerous trials in Braniewo, Chęciny, Fordon, Łobżenica, Nowe, Płońsk, Wągrowiec, or above all Kleczew). I will refrain from multiplying these averages by the total number of towns in Poland. But it is clear that many archives are destroyed, that the archives of many towns remain unexplored, and that many trials remain undiscovered. Given the large number of chartered towns in the early modern Polish Crown, a number of victims in the range of 2,000 over some 250 years is not at all unreasonable. Over so long a period and so large a territory, such a number would constitute a steady trickle of prosecutions, and would situate Poland, along with such countries as France or England, as a country profoundly affected by witchcraft fears without ever experiencing a 'witchcraze'.

However, these prosecutions are very unevenly distributed in space and time. Difficulties with the sources render a clear picture of regional variation impossible: recall that *all* records for Mazowsze were lost in World War II, so that the only trials known from that region come from a handful of pre-war studies. Nevertheless, a general trend is clear. Trials first appear in Wielkopolska in the west, an area in close economic and cultural contact with the Holy Roman Empire.[45] Of ninety-seven town trials before 1650, fully half are from this

---

[42] Wolfgang Behringer, 'Neun Millionen Hexen: Entstehung, Tradition und Kritik eines populären Mythos', *Geschichte in Wissenschaft und Unterricht*, 49/11 (1998).

[43] Pilaszek, *Procesy*, 266, 92.

[44] See the Appendix for the full list of trials, derived from archival research in Lublin and from a survey of the secondary literature from Łukaszewicz's pioneering work of 1838 through 2022. For practical reasons, I have not attempted to integrate Pilaszek's much larger, but overlapping, database of trials with my own. A long-planned online searchable database, (compiled in collaboration with Dysa, Hajdrych, Wijaczka, Wiślicz, and many others), will eventually collate all known witch-trials in Poland. A preliminary version of this database is set to launch in 2023.

[45] Baranowski consistently faults Germany as the source of the witchcraft trope in Poland (*Procesy*, 18; cf. Łukaszewicz, *Historyczno-statystyczne opis*, i. 76). While not untrue, this notion enabled Baranowski to leaven his critique of the Polish past with a pinch of xenophobic

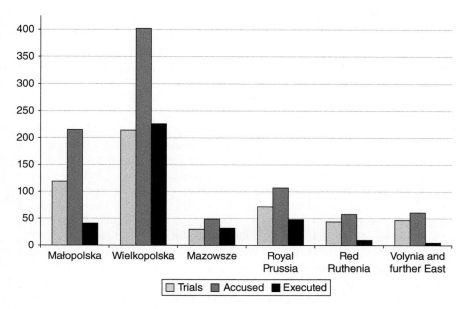

Figure 1.1. Witch-trials by region.

region. Though trials spread quite quickly east and south into Mazowsze and Małopolska, they remained most numerous in Wielkopolska and neighboring Royal Prussia.[46] Moreover, although the average number of *accused* witches per trial was very similar in Wielkopolska and Małopolska (just under two in both regions), the western region executed witches at a rate nearly three times as high (see Figure 1.1).

At the peak of witch-persecution in the last quarter of the seventeenth century, trials had become quite numerous in Małopolska, including its ethnically Ruthenian and religiously Uniate (Greek-Rite Catholic) and Orthodox eastern edge. But despite contemporary stereotypes whereby

> Poison and enchantment rule Ruthenia
> The Ruthenian lands swarm with witches[47]

the ethnically Ruthenian lands of the Commonwealth saw very few trials throughout the early modern period. Kateryna Dysa's study of witch-trials in

---

scapegoating and to indulge in the mandatory anti-German ideology of the immediate post-war. The tendentious tendency to blame Germany for Polish witch-trials continues even in the most recent, most careful Polish scholarship: e.g. Pilaszek, *Procesy*, 38–9, 128; for a critique of this tendency, see Salmonowicz, 'Procesy o czary w Polsce', 313–14.

[46] Pilaszek's archival survey found 183 trials in Royal Prussia, or about a fifth of the total (Pilaszek, *Procesy*, 509). My own survey suggests a smaller fraction of trials in Royal Prussia, but with a high execution rates similar to that of Wielkopolska.

[47] Sebastian Fabian Klonowic, *Roxolania, czyli ziemie Czerwonej Rusi,* ed. Mieczysław Mejor (Warsaw: Polska Akademia Nauk, 1996 [1584]), 112.

Podole, Wołyń, and right-bank Ukraine in the seventeenth–eighteenth centuries has found just thirteen executions in 189 trials: despite a very lively belief in witchcraft in the Ruthenian areas, magistrates were little interested in prosecuting the crime.[48] As recent work on witch-trials in Russia makes clear, the Orthodox Church and laity were far from indifferent to the crime of witchcraft.[49] Nevertheless, western concepts of the witch-cult and the *sabbat* found little purchase east of the Bug river; it is perhaps telling that several of the trials known from Ruthenian areas feature Polonized, Catholic noblemen as accusers.[50] Similarly, the bulk of the ninety-seven trials known to have occurred in Lithuania between 1552 and 1771 took place in the Catholic, ethnically Lithuanian areas of the Grand Duchy.[51]

Witch-trials were also unevenly distributed in time (see Figure 1.2). A graph of trials, accused witches, and executions, plotted by quarter-century from 1501 to the abolition of the witch-crime in 1776, describes a series of closely correlated bell-curves. From just a few trials in the sixteenth century, numbers rise sharply through the seventeenth century. By the 1630s, the author of the *Witch Denounced* was perhaps justified in saying that, at least in Wielkopolska: 'in these times Poland has become extraordinarily dense with the conflagration of Witches, either real or alleged, so that . . . one hears of no other subject than of Witches'.[52]

Numbers peaked in the last quarter of the seventeenth century, with 140 trials, 254 accused, and at least 108 executed (somwhat more than a quarter of the total in each category). Moreover, the half-century 1675–1725 saw nearly all of the really large cycles of trials before particular courts. There were sixty witch-trials in Fordon between 1675 and 1711,[53] and at least a dozen in Nieszawa between 1698 and 1722.[54] The court of Łobżenica sent some thirty-six convicted witches to the stake in the seventeenth century, most of these in the period 1675–1700.[55] In Grodzisk Wielkopolski, at least twenty witches from just five trials were executed between

---

[48] Kateryna Dysa, 'Witchcraft Trials and Beyond: Right-Bank Side Ukrainian Trials of the Seventeenth and Eighteenth Centuries' (Central European University, 2004), 40–7.

[49] Valerie Kivelson, 'Patrolling the Boundaries: Witchcraft Accusations and Household Strife in Seventeenth-Century Muscovy', *Harvard Ukrainian Studies,* 19 (1995); *Desperate Magic: The Moral Economy of Witchcraft in Seventeenth-Century Russia* (Ithaca: Cornell University Press, 2013); W. F. Ryan, 'The Witchcraft Hysteria in Early Modern Europe: Was Russia an Exception?', *Slavonic and Eastern European Review,* 76/1 (1998).

[50] e.g. Lublin 1681, 1732, 1737—all trials originating in far Ruthenia but referred to the Lublin town court via the noble Crown Tribunal in Lublin.

[51] Pilaszek, 'Litewskie procesy czarownic'. However, this preponderance of trials in ethnic Lithuania may be an artefact of Lithuanian scholarship (upon which Pilaszek depends), which has focused on this area.

[52] *Czarownica powołana,* 3.

[53] *Procesy,* 293, 345, 50. According to Pilaszek, the Fordon court executed witches at the extraordinarily high rate of 92%.

[54] Ibid. 353–6.

[55] Jacek Wijaczka, 'Mężczyźni jako ofiary procesów o czary przed sądem łobżenickim w drugiej połowie XVII wieku', *Czasy Nowożytne,* 17 (2004), 17–30; 'Procesy o czary w Polsce w dobie Oświecenia. Zarys problematyki', *Klio,* 17 (2005), 60.

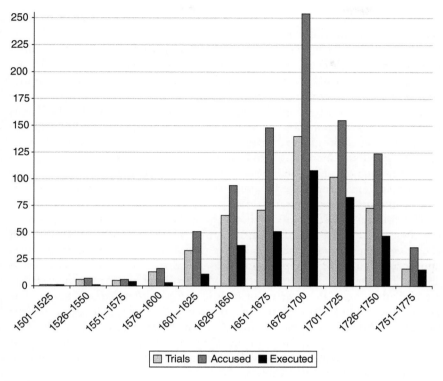

Figure 1.2. Chronology of witch-trials.

1700 and 1720;[56] while eighteen of the twenty-seven trials before the Nowe-nad-Wisłą court took place between 1701 and 1719.[57] The magistrates of Płońsk sent at least twenty-six of thirty-four accused witches to the stake in the short period 1699–1713.[58] Finally, as already mentioned, the largest and bloodiest cycle of trials known in Poland, before the court of Kleczew, accounted for 131 accused and at least ninety-two sent to the stake—forty-one of those deaths occurred between 1682 and 1700.[59] Although the eighteenth century saw a steep decline in trials from about 1725, there were still more accused and more executed for witchcraft in the period immediately prior to its abolition than in the first quarter of the seventeenth

[56] Mikołajczyk, *Przestępstwo i kara*, 36.
[57] Jacek Wijaczka, 'Witch and Sorcerer-Hunts in the Town of Nowe, the 17th and the First Half of the 18th Century', *Acta Poloniae Historica*, 98 (2008), 133; Pilaszek, *Procesy*, 293.
[58] Zygmunt Lasocki, 'Szlachta płońska w walce z czartem', *Miesięcznik Heraldyczny*, 12/1–3 (1933).
[59] Wiślicz, 'Township of Kleczew', 67; see now also Hajdrych, "Wizja świata." My own calculations of the executions in Kleczew are slightly lower, but my data is incomplete.

century—providing ample fuel for the Enlightenment polemic that led the Sejm to abolish the crime of witchcraft.[60]

In Chapter 2, I will trace the intellectual and legal contexts which made possible the growth of witch-trials in the seventeenth century. As we will see, the foundation for witch-persecution had been laid by the mid-sixteenth century. And yet trials begin in earnest only in 1620s, increasing in number and severity especially after about 1660. Although this book focuses on cultural and religious sources for the imagination of witchcraft, a brief account of the military, economic, and environmental disasters of the seventeenth century will help us to understand the increasing application of this imaginary construct to real women throughout that iron century. The picture that emerges is one of steady decline and increasing poverty, punctuated by periods of horrible violence, famine, plague, and even greater poverty.

The political and economic position of the Polish peasant declined throughout the early modern period.[61] Characteristic of the sixteenth and seventeenth centuries is the growth of the *folwark* or manorial farm, as noble landowners appropriated commons and purchased peasant-owned fields. These farms, geared above all to the export of grain for the Western European market via Gdańsk, established an agrarian economy of resource extraction and monoculture. The *folwark* labor supply came from the serf labor obligations (*pańszczyzna*) of the peasantry, who had to support themselves from the produce of their own lands, while also providing field labor to the demesne. These labor obligations grew from one day per week in the early sixteenth century to five days a week or even more in the late seventeenth century.

To furnish this labor while also working their own fields, land-holding peasants supported one or several *komornicy* (lit. 'chamberpersons', lodgers), who fulfilled the serf obligations on the manor fields in return for room and board. At the same time that their feudal labor obligations were increasing, propertied peasants found the size of their own fields, from which they had now to support both themselves and their lodgers, inexorably decreasing. The sixteenth-century 'typical' peasant holding of one *łan* (about 16 hectares) had shrunk, over the next centuries, to half that size or even less. An increasing proportion of the peasantry was made up of those whose land could not support them, and who had to supplement their income with wage labor at the manor or in the fields of a 'fully farming' peasant. These 'gardeners', 'cottagers', and the afore-mentioned 'lodgers' or *komornicy* lived in a hierarchy of poverty, at the very bottom of which were the landless laborers working on contract for a place to

---

[60] This chronology should be compared to those of Baranowski and Pilaszek. Expressed as percentages rather than as absolute numbers, they are in quite close agreement (Baranowski, *Procesy Czarownic*, 29; Pilaszek, *Procesy*, 507–8).

[61] I base the general description of peasant history offered here primarily on Wacław Korta, 'Okres gospodarki folwarczno pańszczyźnianej XVI XVIII wieku', in Stefan Inglot (ed.), *Historia chłopów polskich* (Wrocław: Wydawnictwo Uniwersytetu Wrocławskiego, 1992), 53–66.

sleep, board, and a tiny wage.[62] Even the best-off fully farming peasant was deeply poor, but the internal differentiation of the peasant estate provided ample opportunity for the jealousies and envy upon which witchcraft accusations depend.

Thus the peasants' plight worsened throughout the period of witch-trials in Poland. Peasants worked more, on less land, and with fewer options for improving their lot. With the stagnation of city and town development from the early seventeenth century, surplus peasantry had nowhere to go. Declining grain prices meant that even those who had something to sell could get less for it than previously. Meanwhile, spiraling inflation throughout the seventeenth century, combined with the *szlachta*'s absolute refusal to increase its own nominal tax burden, meant that the burden of paying for the central government which benefited them so little fell increasingly on the peasantry. By 1661 peasants paid fifty times the tax they had paid in the early sixteenth century.[63]

Grinding poverty, epidemic disease, spiraling inflation, and extortionary taxes made the peasants' plight increasingly desperate. But none of these more or less gradual problems can compare to the total disaster of the mid-seventeenth century: the cascading series of Cossack uprising, peasant *jacquerie*, Russian invasion, and Swedish occupation which nearly destroyed the country. Between 1648, when the Cossack leader Bohdan Chmielnicki rebelled against Polish Catholic overlordship, and 1660, when marauding Swedish armies were finally driven from the country, Poland experienced near-continual war, looting, famine, and disease. The *Potop* or 'Deluge', as the Swedish invasion is called, together with the other disasters of the period 1648–60, put a decisive end to an already declining era of relative prosperity.

Many small towns and cities never recovered. Several of the cities that later experienced large cycles of witchtrials were hit especially hard. Płońsk was reduced from 130 to just twenty-one buildings. From its peak at 327 houses in 1629, just thirty-four remained in Chęciny after the Deluge. Kleczew, a medium-sized town in the sixteenth century, had a population of perhaps 500 in 1673; Wyszogród, with a population of some 2,500 in 1550, shrank to some 600 souls after 1650.[64] Townspeople continued to enjoy the rights and privileges of Magdeburg Law; they continued to have their own courts and some measure of self-government. Nevertheless, with their wooden buildings, negligible trade and industry, low literacy, and a largely subsistence agricultural economy, small and

---

[62] By the late 17th cent., over half the inhabitants of peasant households were servants or lodgers of various kinds. M. Kopczyński, *Studia nad rodziną chłopską w Koronie w XVII XVIII wieku* (Warsaw: Wydawnictwo Krupski i S-ka, 1998), 205.

[63] Andrzej Wyczański, *Polska Rzeczą Pospolitą szlachecką* (Warsaw, 1991), 290–1.

[64] Maria Bogucka and Henryk Samsonowicz, *Dzieje miast i mieszczaństwa w Polsce przedrozbiorowej* (Wrocław: Zakład Narodowy im. Ossolińskich, 1986), 339–432; Wiślicz, 'Township of Kleczew', 66.

medium-sized towns came to differ little from villages; and townspeople, in their practices and mentalities, differed little from the surrounding peasants.

And these peasants were suffering as never before. Recent reservations about population loss during the Deluge only serve to emphasize the increased economic pressures brought upon those who survived it. Older mortality estimates, suggesting that as much as a third of the country's population died in the Deluge, have recently given way to much lower estimates: as low as 3 percent, at least for some areas.[65] However, the economic impact of the war and its aftermath was enormous: though the population remained relatively stable, the agrarian economy collapsed. The amount of grain sown between 1652 and 1661 dropped by more than half. Starving and desperate after looting by the Swedes and requisitions by their own armies, peasants sold their land to the nobility, thus participating in their own pauperization. Meanwhile, despite the decreased area of land under cultivation and the decreased productivity of cultivated land, the wheat export of 1662 was almost as high as in the best pre-war years.[66]

To sum up: after the disaster of the 1650s, there were nearly as many people in rural areas, but with less land available, in smaller plots; there was less grain sown and harvested, but about the same amount exported as previously. There was less money; but taxes had doubled. What had already been a precarious existence became nearly unbearable. The pressures and tensions in village life must have been enormous.

The disasters and hardships of the late seventeenth century meant that the people of Poland were more likely than at other times in their history to encounter the sorts of misfortune often attributed to witchcraft—children and cattle dying, fields ruined, milk spoiled, health destroyed. It also meant that such misfortunes were more disastrous than they had been in earlier times: a household with one cow is more strongly affected by its sudden death than is a household owning a dozen animals. The Deluge and its aftermath explain the statistical upswing in witch-trials over the next half-century, but not the character of those trials. Faced with misfortune, early modern Poles didn't always blame witches. When they did suspect a witch, they accused not just anyone, but specific sorts of people deemed, by their character, occupation, motive, and opportunity, to be particularly likely to practice witchcraft. In the next section, we explore this issue: who were the Polish witches?

---

[65] Wyczański, *Polska*, 290–1; Waldemar Kowalski, 'Ludność archidiakonatu sandomierskiego w połowie XVII wieku', in Jadwiga Muszyńska and Jacek Wijaczka (eds.), *Rzeczpospolita w latach Potopu* (Kielce: Wyższa Szkoła Pedagogiczna im. Jana Kochanowskiego, 1996), 257–70.

[66] Jadwiga Muszyńska, 'Straty demograficzne i zniszczenia gospodarcze w Małopolsce w połowie XVII wieku: Problemy badawcze', in *Rzeczpospolita w latach Potopu*, 284–7.

DEMOGRAPHICS

In his influential *Disquisitiones magicae*, the Spanish-Belgian Jesuit Martin Del Rio criticized Johannes Weyer for distinguishing scrupulously among such terms as *sagae* (wise women), *venefici* (poisoners), *malefici* (harmful magicians), *incantores* (enchanters), *striges* (night-flying witches), *and lamiae* (vampiric child-devouring witches)—as if these made a real difference.[67] Del Rio was right: by the seventeenth century, most of these terms and more had been absorbed into the general category of the witch, used by most authors of demonological or legal treatises as synonymous. Their literal meanings preserved clues to the building blocks from which the early modern witch had been constructed—she was a wise woman, a poisoner, an evildoer, an enchantress, a blood-sucking child-stealing night-demon associated with screech-owls. But a work of demonology, or a trial record, could refer to a woman as a *striga* without thereby implying vampirism or night-flight, and could speak of a *venefica* whose magical crime had not involved the use of poisons.

One finds in Poland a much narrower vocabulary of witchcraft. Clerical authors spoke of *guślarki* and *zabobonnice*—cunning-folk and 'superstition workers'—categorizations which they insisted must be kept distinct from *czarownice* or witches. Trial records, their formal sections usually written in Latin, speak mostly of *maleficae* and *veneficae*, although at least one trial document refers to a suspected witch as a *succubita* (Iwkowa 1602). In Polish, the suspect was simply a *czarownica*, more rarely a *guślarka* or a *baba*—a term that otherwise can mean 'old woman' or 'village woman'. Quite often records do not label the accused at all, but only speak of her crimes: *maleficium, veneficium, immissio daemonum*; or simply 'practicing witchcraft'.

In contrast to laconic trial records, early modern Polish lexicography displays an exuberant overabundance of terms for 'witches', often mixing them with demonic figures of various sorts: the witches thus become demonized quite literally. For example, the Jesuit lexicographer Grzegorz Knapiusz, in his massive *Thesaurus Polono-Latino-Graecus*, defines the female 'night-demon' *nocnica* as 'shade, night-groper, noon-tide demon, child's bogeyman, night terror'. This is a list of more or less synonymous supernatural creatures, all related to bad dreams. But if we follow Knapiusz's cross-reference to *przypołudnica* or 'noon-tide demon',[68] we find the synonym 'Czarownica', 'Wiedma seu Latawica', that is to say, 'witch, hag, flying demon'.[69] This last term, a rare female variant of the

---

[67] Martin Del Rio, *Disquisitionum magicarum libri sex* (Cologne: Petrus Henningius, 1633 [1608]), bk. 5 sect. 16.

[68] This is the *daemonium meridianum* of Ps. 91: 6, but also, in contemporary Slavic folklore, a female demon who brings sunstroke or headaches to field workers at their midday rest.

[69] Gregorz Knapiusz, *Thesaurus Polono-Latino-Graecus* (1643), quoted after Halina Wiśniewska, *Świat płci żeńskiej baroku zaklęty w słowach* (Lublin: Wydawnictwo UMCS, 2003), 242–3.

male *latawiec*, could be used as a translation of *succubus*, just as latawiec translated *incubus*, but it could also signify a being of almost bewildering variety, both witch and demon; a creature whose essence seems to lie in her very indeterminability:

> Sometimes I'm a bird, an animal, a cat, or an owl,
> At night a huge woman, who is called death.
> If you see me at noon, I'm a *przypołudnica*,
> But in the evening I'm a *wiedma* or a *latawica*.[70]

In other sources the *południca* or *przepołudnica* could translate Greek *ephialtes*—a term also usually understood to indicate a succubus/incubus and bringer of nightmares;[71] or the child-stealing *lamia*;[72] or, by metaphorical extension from both of these, a prostitute.[73] Similarly, Ursinus' early seventeenth-century grammar textbook equates the already-encountered *nocnica* to Latin *strix*, in all its meanings: screech-owl, vampiric night demon, and witch. In so doing, Ursinus assimilates local notions into a classical framework: 'Strix—the night screech-owl, *nocnica*, a bird as the ancients describe it: great, grey, with an owl's head and claws, with breasts like a bat. From this it is also a nickname for witches, who are called *wiedmy*, because they turn into such a bird and suck the blood of children. The people of Ruthenia aver this strongly to this very day, and by certain speeches drive *nocnice* away from women in labor.'[74] As a final example, the term *jędza* with which Jakub Wujek translated the *lilith* of Isaiah 34: 14[75] is otherwise a forest-demon and night-witch (cognate to the east-Slavic *baba yaga*), or, already in the seventeenth century, a 'very bad woman',[76] a meaning it retains today. Otwinowski used the same term to translate the classical *eumenides* or furies in his Polish rendition of Ovid's *Metamorphoses*.[77]

[70] Januarius [pseud.] Swizralus, *Peregrynacja dziadowska*, in *Dramaty Staropolskie*, ed. Julian Lewański (Warsaw: Państwowy Instytut Wydawniczy, 1961 [1614]), 173, vv. 858–61. I suspect that Knapiusz's dictionary entry (see previous note) is based on this passage: note the appearance in both of the rather rare form *wiedma*.

[71] Józef Rostafiński, *Średniowieczna Historya naturalna w Polsce/Symbola ad historiam medii aevi*, 2 vols. (Kraków: Uniwersytet Jagielloński, 1900), ii. 510; after a late 15th-cent. manuscript.

[72] Stanisław Urbańczyk *et al.* (eds.), *Słownik staropolski*, 10 vols. (Wrocław: Wydawnictwo PAN, 1952–2003); Michał Muszyński, 'Glosy, zapiski, i niektóre teksty polskie w starych drukach i rękopisach Biblioteki Kórnickiej do r. 1550 (part 2)', *Pamiętnik Biblioteki Kórnickiej*, 9–10 (1968), 213.

[73] Urbańczyk *et al.*, *Słownik Staropolski*; Aleksander Brückner, 'Średniowieczna poezja łacińska w Polsce, II', *Rozprawy i Sprawozdania posiedzeń Wydziału Filologii Akademii Umiejętności*, 22 (1893), 16.

[74] Jan Ursinus, *Grammaticae methodicae* (Zamość, 1619); quoted after Wiśniewska, *Świat płci żeńskiej*, 245; cf. Pliny the Elder, *The Natural History*, tr. John Bostock (London: Taylor & Francis, 1855), 8.22.

[75] Jakub Wujek, *Biblia w przekładzie księdza Jakuba Wujka z 1599 r.*, ed. Janusz Frankowski (Warsaw: Vocatio, 2000); the Vulgate uses *lamia*, the KJV *screech-owl*, the NRSV returns to *lilith*.

[76] Grzegorz Knapiusz, *Thesaurus*; quoted after Wiśniewska, *Świat płci żeńskiej*, 114.

[77] Waleryan Otwinowski, *Księgi Metamorphoseon, to iest Przemian* (Kraków: Andrzej Piotrkowczyk, 1638), bk. 4, v. 428.

These examples give us some notion of the range and ambiguity of the Polish night-witch, as its associations and connotations interconnected with local and classical demons, with prostitutes, with screech-owls. Similar questions of ambiguous categorization will be important in Chapters 9 and 10, below, when we examine the relationships of the devils in Polish witch-trials with Christian devils, pre-Christian demons, and fairy-folk. Turning now from the contemporary categorizations of the imagined witch to the actual categorization of actual witches—that is, real people successfully so labeled—one might hope to find a simpler or at least clearer picture. A vain hope: as we will see, contemporary stereotypes of the witch interacted with actual accused witches in complicated ways.

Polish literature of the sixteenth–eighteenth centuries, like its western counterparts, regularly depicts the witch as poor, ugly, and old. Ecclesiastical protests against secular witch-trials complained that a reputation for witchcraft attaches, illegitimately, to 'old women with ugly faces'.[78] At a more popular level, the ribald *Pilgrimage of the Hobos* presented witches as beggar-women using their pretended powers to dupe gullible matrons into generosity;[79] or as lame, delusional drunks sitting by the hearth at the alms-house and, consumed by envy, dreaming of the day they can take magical revenge on their betters.[80]

Despite a near consensus in literary sources, it is not at all clear from trial records themselves that accused witches would have fit the stereotype. They were very nearly all women—an important fact to which we shall return. But were they old, widowed, ugly, lame, and destitute? Historians of European witchcraft used to accept this image of the witch with little qualification, particularly as it fit so well with their explanatory models of the witch-hunts as attacks on eccentrics or deviants;[81] on surplus women or dangerously liberated widows;[82] on beggars asking for charity and inciting guilt in those who refuse it.[83] But recent scholarship has complicated the picture. Although Lyndal Roper has made a strong recent case that the accused witch in German-speaking lands was usually a postmenopausal 'crone', envious of and threatening to the fertility of young mothers,[84] elsewhere this pattern fits less comfortably with the trial records. In Scotland, for example, Lauren Martin argues that accusations occurred between

[78] *Instrukcya rzymska, abo postępek prawny, o sądach y processach, Iako maią bydź formowane, y wydawnane przeciw Czarownicom* (Kraków: Drukarnia Krzysztofa Domańskiego I.K.M. Typog, 1705 [1688]), fo. 15.
[79] Swizralus, *Peregrynacja*, 170–1; vv. 733–813.
[80] Ibid. 171–2; vv. 786–809.
[81] Richard Horsley, 'Who were the Witches? The Social Roles of the Accused in the European Witch Trials', *Journal of Interdisciplinary History*, 9 (1979).
[82] Sigrid Brauner, *Fearless Wives and Frightened Shrews* (Amherst, Mass.: University of Massachusetts Press, 1995).
[83] Alan MacFarlane, *Witchcraft in Tudor and Stuart England* (New York: Harper & Row, 1970); Keith Thomas, *Religion and the Decline of Magic* (Harmondsworth: Penguin Books, 1973).
[84] Lyndal Roper, *Witchcraze* (New Haven, Conn.: Yale University Press, 2004), 160–78.

'relative social equals', and that these were, for the most part, not beggars or the very poor but 'middling peasants' and the wives of craftspeople.[85] Marianne Hester notes that in England at least half the accused witches were married and most did not appear to be independent or rebellious or otherwise overtly threatening.[86] Speaking of Europe as a whole, P. G. Maxwell-Stuart reminds us that the image of the witch as 'old, lame, blear-eyed, pale, fowle, and full of wrinkles' is a literary trope with a complex relationship to demographic reality. 'Such descriptions formed an essential part of the propaganda; they were not intended to provide readers or listeners with a likeness drawn from life.'[87] Who, then, were the Polish accused witches, as presented in actual trials and as imagined in literary texts? And how did the literature match up with or affect the reality of trials?

Social estate, age, and marital status

It should come as no surprise that the great majority of witches were peasants. All those tried before village courts were peasants, but even before town courts, peasants comprised at least 52 percent of all accused.[88] This pattern is borne out by case-studies: in Wiślicz's analysis of the accused in Kleczew between 1682 and 1700: 60 percent were peasants and 40 percent were townsfolk.

The nobility never found themselves a primary target of witchcraft accusation anywhere in Europe.[89] In Poland it was functionally impossible for a noblewoman to be tried for witchcraft: among other things, she was immune from imprisonment without due process, and from interrogation under torture. Neither the town magistrates before whom witches were tried, nor the Magdeburg Law which guided those magistrates, had any jurisdiction over nobility. Although noblewomen made frequent use of witches' services (e.g. Lublin 1681, 1732) or even dabbled themselves, especially in love-magic (Praszka 1665, Kraków 1752),[90] they rarely paid the price for such activity. With the exception of a few women whose noble status was considered sufficiently doubtful by the courts to be ignored (the cunning-woman and procuress Anna Chociszewska, Poznań 1582b; the beggar-woman Regina

[85] Lauren Martin, 'The Devil and the Domestic: Witchcraft, Quarrels and Women's Work in Scotland', in Julian Goodare (ed.), *The Scottish Witch-Hunt in Context* (Manchester and New York: Manchester UP, 2002), 75. Cf. Christina Larner, *Enemies of God* (Baltimore: Johns Hopkins University Press, 1981), 94–102.

[86] Marianne Hester, 'Who were the Witches?', *Studies in Sexual Politics*, 26–7 (1988).

[87] Maxwell-Stuart, *Witchcraft in Europe*, 63; his characterization of the witch quotes Reginald Scot.

[88] Of the 19% of accused witches of unclear estate, most were probably peasants. This would accord well with Pilaszek's figure of 80% (Pilaszek, *Procesy*, 299).

[89] An exception to this rule might be the highly political trials against alleged preternatural assassins in 16th-cent. Muscovy: Ryan, 'Witchcraft Hysteria.'

[90] See also Anna Brzezińska, 'Accusations of Love Magic in the Renaissance Courtly Culture of the Polish-Lithuanian Commonwealth', *East Central Europe*, 20–3/1 (1996).

Wierbicka, Bochnia 1679), the only *szlachta* I know of to have been punished in any way for witchcraft were a married petty noble couple and their associate, jailed by the Crown Tribunal for the magical attack they attempted against the owner of the village leased to them (Lublin 1739). Accusers of noblewomen were apt to find themselves punished: a quite powerful nobleman attempted to punish a poor noble maiden of solid pedigree for the love-magic she had worked on his son; things went poorly for him, and he had to pay the wronged maiden an indemnity of 200 złoty (Kraków 1752).[91]

Of accused townswomen, most were the wives of petty craftspeople and traders (e.g. Dorota Pilecka, cobbler's wife, Słomniki 1674); house-servants (e.g. Maryna, Lublin 1627); or marginal women of the suburban slums (such as Zofia Baranowa, Lublin 1643). Higher-class women were accused less often, and received better treatment in the courts, including defense counsel and the option to appeal (e.g. Bydgoszcz 1638; Lublin 1661). Accusations against women of established family were unlikely to succeed, and indeed could act as a brake on witch-prosecutions. When in 1702 accusations of witchcraft in Płońsk began to affect the wives of city-councilmen on the one hand, and of petty nobility on the other, the enthusiasm of that court for prosecuting witches came to be dampened.[92] The court, which had executed eleven women in four trials in the period 1699–1701, did not see another case until 1708.

The Polish trial records say little about the age and marital status of accused witches. Witnesses or the accused only occasionally mention a husband; very rarely did the court describe an accused witch as a widow or maiden. One catches hints of the ages of some accused witches through epithets applied to them, such as 'old Dorota' (Kiszkowo 1761), or the *baba* Reina Bartoszowa (Kleczew 1693). In a very few cases, the court alludes explicitly to the witch's age, as in Kleczew (1682), where the two accused cousins were girls aged 10 and 12, or in Biecz (1655), where Gertruda Zagrodzka's defense counsel cited her advanced age— over 70—as grounds for dismissal.[93]

Table 1.1 summarizes what little is known about the age, marital status, and social estate of the accused witches in my database. Interpretation of the figures for age and marital status requires considerable caution, since in both cases the largest category by far is 'unknown'. One can form the impression that accused witches were much more likely to be young or old than in the prime of life;

---

[91] The near impossibility of accusing noblewoman can be illustrated by an abortive trial in Mazowsze, where an *ad hoc* court of local nobles heard a case against two noblewomen. Repeated resolutions of the Dobrzyń dietine attempted to advance this case at the Crown Tribunal but met with no success, and the women presumably remained unpunished (Lipno 1675).

[92] Lasocki, 'Szlachta płońska', 7–8.

[93] Explicitly elderly witches feature also in Łobżenica 1692, Lublin 1681, 1698. Prośka Kapłunka, lynched for her suspected role in causing an epidemic disease, was believed to have reached the ripe old age of 120 years (Krasiłów 1720).

Table 1.1. Age, marital status, and social estate of accused witches

Age	Young	Middle-Aged[a]	Old		Unknown	Total
	57 (6%)	41 (5%)	64 (7%)		730 (82%)	892
Marital status	Unmarried	Married	Widowed		Unknown	892
	57 (6%)	206 (23%)	37 (4%)		453 (51%)	
			Married or Widowed[b]			
			139 (16%)			
Estate	Peasants[c]	Townspeople[d]	Nobility	Clergy	Unknown	892
	489 (55%)	225 (25%)	9 (1%)	2 (<1%)	167 (19%)	
Estate (town trials only)	Peasants[c]	Townspeople[d]	Nobility	Clergy	Unknown	783
	409 (52%)	208 (27%)	5 (<1%)	1 (<1%)	160 (20%)	

[a] Roughly, adults with non-adult children.
[b] For example, mothers of legitimate children, with no explicit mention in trial record either of widowhood or of a living husband.
[c] Includes peasants *sensu strictu* and other village inhabitants, such as inn-keepers, smiths, prostitutes, vagabonds.
[d] Includes both plebeians and burghers.

however, this is likely an artifact of the records, which mention an accused witch's age only when it is a departure from the norm.

A few regional studies bear out the intuition that many or most accused witches were middle-aged and married. According to Wijaczka's study of the witch-trials in the Świętokrzyskie region, most were married, with few accused widows.[94] Tomasz Wiślicz's detailed study of the Kleczew trials reveals a few older witches, a few young witches (including a 10-year-old girl (Kleczew 1682), and the 15-year-old Marjanna discussed in Chapter 7); but most appear to be married adults.[95] According to Andrzej Karpiński, of the seventy-eight women accused of witchcraft in Poznań, Lwów, and Lublin, 80 percent were married.[96] Actual accused witches, as opposed to their literary or folkloric representation, appear to have quite usually been ordinary married women, in the prime of life.

Occupation

The great majority of accused witches were, as has been shown, peasant women; a smaller but significant number were commoner townswomen, most often from smaller towns. In neither of these categories does it usually make sense to speak of the women as having a specific occupation—which is not to deny that such women were constantly occupied. Although townswomen played an important role in

[94] Jacek Wijaczka, 'Procesy o czary w regionie świętokrzyskiego w XVII XVIII wieku', in J. Wijaczka (ed.), *Z przeszłości regionu świętokrzyskiego od XVI do XX wieku* (Kielce: Agencja Reklamowo-Wydawnicza 'JARD', 2003), 72.
[95] Wiślicz, 'Township of Kleczew', 73.
[96] Karpiński, *Kobieta*, 319–20.

the economy as small traders and distributors of their husband's craftwork,[97] little evidence for such economic activity appears in the trials. The economy of smaller towns, especially in the later seventeenth and eighteenth centuries, differed little from that of villages: like their village counterparts, most commoner townswomen will have been occupied with such tasks as bearing and raising children, agricultural work in the fields and gardens, tending and milking cattle, preparing and preserving foodstuffs, brewing beer, gathering herbs, berries, and mushrooms, weaving cloth from flax or wool, and selling any surpluses at the village market, thus bringing cash into the household.[98] Desperately difficult though such work must have been, it was approximately the same sort of work for the great majority of peasant women and small-townswomen, so that women were not differentiated from one another by occupation.

We know in scattered cases, usually from the accused's *maritonym*, that this or that peasant woman belonged to the household of a village craftsman—a wheelwright's widow or daughter (Kalisz 1613, Borek 1624); a carpenter's, or a mason's, or a weaver's wife (Kalisz 1616; Nowy Sącz 1670; Warta 1678a). Some few others were the daughters, wives, or widows of more important village personages such as the *sołtys* or village headman (Tuliszków 1684a; Klimkówka 1702a), smith (Nowy Koźmin 1690; Kleczew 1693; Szczerców 1716), innkeeper (Warta 1678a; Brześć Kujawski 1691), or miller (Kalisz 1613; Szczekociny 1706). One can detect no pattern in these affiliations, though they do add substance to the suggestion that accused witches were not always, nor even usually, from the margins of peasant society.

In fact, our findings point mostly in the other direction. Just four accused witches are known to have been milkmaids (Jędrzejów 1671; Płońsk 1699c); a further six were shepherdesses (Warta 1685; Kleczew 1688; Kiszkowo 1761). Considering their social marginalization as some of the poorest of the poor, their ample opportunity to perform malefice against milk and livestock, and the reputation for magic accorded shepherds in both Poland and elsewhere in Europe,[99] it is somewhat surprising there were not more.

Nor do beggars, vagabonds, and other marginal people figure in trials as often as one might suppose. A female vagabond, referred to as a *succubita*, was required to leave town before sundown at a village trial in the hills south of Kraków (Iwkowa 1602); a male 'hobo' figures among the accused in a large trial at Pyzdry

---

[97] Ibid.

[98] The economic activity of Polish women in small towns and villages remains understudied, but see Anetta Głowacka, 'Women in a Small Polish Town in the 16th–18th Centuries', *APH* 94 (2006); Maria Bogucka, *Białogłowa w społeczeństwie polskim XVI–XVIII wieku na tle porównawczym* (Warsaw: Wydawnictwo Trio, 1998); Pilaszek, *Procesy*, 297.

[99] E.g. Oskar Kolberg, *Dzieła wszystkie Oskara Kolberga*, ed. Julian Krzyżanowski, 68 vols. (Wrocław: Polskie Towarzystwo Ludoznawcze/Ludowa Spółdzielnia Wydawnicza, 1961–90 [1857–1907]), xix. 211–12; William Monter, 'Toads and Eucharists: The Male Witches of Normandy, 1564–1660', *French Historical Studies*, 20/4 (1997).

(1719); and there is an accused old woman 'from the poorhouse' in Łobżenica (1692). In Szadek, a self-styled witch-finder accused most of the beggar-women of that town of witchcraft; however, her accusations were rejected and the accuser sentenced to banishment for disturbing the peace (Szadek 1649b).[100]

The wandering thief and prostitute Barbara of Radom seems to have supplemented her income with milk-magic; she was arrested for theft and vagrancy, but burnt as a witch (Kalisz 1580). The beggar-women Maryna Mazurkowicowa and Regina Wierzbicka may or may not have engaged in petty malefice for pay; but they really did, apparently, steal an infant child in the hope that the child's presence would increase people's charity toward them (Bochnia 1679). Certainly beggars and vagabonds were not above resorting to the sorts of ruses celebrated and satirized in *The Pilgrimage of the Hobos*, which includes accounts of beggars pretending to heal, harm, sell love-charms, or even disguise themselves as werewolves.[101] Veiled threats of supernatural harm would increase a beggar's chances of receiving alms. For some beggars, however, such strategies proved fatal: an unnamed *baba* who claimed abilities to exorcize demons from a baker's wife was beaten in the street and died of her injuries in jail, a presumed witch (Bydgoszcz 1656). Other accused witches cannot be classified as beggars in the strict sense, but were instead poor village-folk who borrowed more often than they lent, and who sometimes underwrote this imbalanced reciprocity with veiled threats of preternatural harm (e.g. Katarzyna Mrowczyna, Słajszewo 1695). With their social vulnerability, their perhaps too-apparent envy, and with the exchange of food providing ample opportunity for bewitchment, such women were obvious candidates for witchcraft accusation.

Two other occupations providing both motive and opportunity for witchcraft appear often enough in the records to warrant comment. These are the position of *komornica* or lodger in a (relatively) well-off peasant household, and of *dziewka* or house-servant in the manor or in the home of a burgher in town. The two positions resemble each other. Both involve women extremely vulnerable to sexual exploitation from their masters (and thus also to the jealousy and suspicion of his wife, her mistress); both have constant access to the home, while not quite belonging to it; both were involved in the preparation of the food by which witchcraft was so often cast into its victims; both positions, though more secure than that of a beggar, involved constant occasions for envy. A *komornica* made a poor match indeed for the son of a land-holding peasant, while the peasant house-servants in the manor could not even dream of marrying into the family. We should expect, therefore, rampant envy on the one hand, and desperate attempts at love-magic on the other. To be more precise, we should expect, and do indeed find, what is functionally equivalent to such envy and love-magic: the suspicion of it on the part of accusers.

---

[100] The Kraków High Court reduced this sentence to a public apology and church penance (Kraków 1649b).

[101] Swizralus, *Peregrynacja*.

At least six accused witches were *komornice* in the homes of peasants at least marginally better off than themselves. For example, the lodger Zofia allegedly buried enchantments, including the entire carcass of a cow, in the garden of her landlord. She had previously threatened that if he threw her out of his house, he would be ruined (Warta 1678b). The landlord's accusation may be seen in terms of his resentment of a person he did not want about the house, or his guilt in attempting to drive her out of what was theoretically a position guaranteed for life.

Female house-servants in the manor or at the homes of the town patriciate, of which we have some seventeen examples, had both more cause for envy and a less secure position. As outsiders in the home, and as go-betweens between the village and the manor, they could become conduits for peasant enmity toward the village lord, or could be perceived by him as such. In one trial, the cook was accused of attempting to 'introduce deviltry' into her mistress's food; she confessed to doing this because her mistress refused to feed her pork (Warta 1691). Although it is not quite true that witchcraft constituted a 'quiet battle' of the peasants against their noble exploiters, it could certainly express peasant resentment; conversely, noblemen could come to perceive themselves as beleaguered by hostile, magically powerful serfs.[102]

Another risk, real or suspected, was that house-maids or cooks would attempt love-magic against their masters, especially after that master had sexually exploited the maid and then grown weary of the dalliance. This seems to be what happened to Zofia Filipowicowa, cook and head-servant to Sir Paweł Podłodowski: at her trial, she recounted in great detail her increasingly desperate attempts to recover the favor of her master and former lover—attempts that, in the estimation of Sir Paweł's heir and brother, eventually resulted in Paweł's death (Skrzynno 1639).[103]

A final 'occupation' must be mentioned: that of cunning-woman or folk-healer. Cunning had featured in the early trials before ecclesiastical courts, where the cooks and concubines of priests, among others, stood accused of folk-healing: the 'wieszcza baba' or 'knowledgeable old woman' accused in Poznań in 1476 is a clear example, as is the cunning-woman Małgorzata of Piasków, a *witness* in a church-court trial in 1532, who claimed to have helped medical doctors in difficult cases.[104] In secular court trials, a few early cases show a similar interest in rooting out folk-healers (Poznań 1544a, 1544b, 1549; Kalisz 1580, 1593, 1613). Beyond this handful of cases, none of the accused Polish witches can be unambiguously labeled as a cunning-woman. They were accused of witchcraft,

---

[102] Baranowski, *Procesy Czarownic*, 37; cf. Adamczewska, 'Magiczna broń'.

[103] Similarly, when young, female, impoverished noble lodgers fell in love with their patron's eligible son, the parents of the besotted or at any rate lusty heir preferred to suspect love magic, forestalling a socially disadvantageous marriage (Praszka 1665; Kraków 1752).

[104] Adamczyk, 'Czary i magia', 163–4.

not of cunning, and the spells and rituals they confessed to were, for the most part, of the sort that most peasant women could know, or could construct out of common materials (see Chapter 5). Accordingly, we must reject, in the Polish case, the influential thesis put forward by Horsley that a 'substantial number of the accused' in European witch-trials were cunning-women or folk-healers.[105]

However, we must also reject the counter-thesis advanced by Willem de Blécourt, that cunning-folk were rarely accused of witchcraft.[106] Blécourt problematically insists that cunning-folk formed a clear category of specialist healers, quite easily distinguished from witches by 'legislators, clergy, and even people without a formal education'.[107] Whether or not this is true of Western Europe, it does not fit the Polish material. 'Cunning' was neither a full-time job nor a clearly defined social role in early modern Poland. Barbara of Radom, for example, who admitted that she hired herself out to bless cattle against witchcraft and whose wide, detailed knowledge of several elaborate spells and rituals make her one of our best examples of a cunning-woman, was originally arrested neither for cunning nor witchcraft but for vagrancy, theft, and prostitution (Kalisz 1580). Like the beggar-healers of the *Pilgrimage of the Hobos*, Barbara evidently used her secret knowledge to eke out a living primarily earned otherwise. But even established cunning-women practiced their craft on a very part-time basis and for very little income: Apolonia Porwitka, a married townswoman who sold herbs to apothecaries, who was sought out for love-magic and especially for spells to fix witch-spoiled beer, and who had 'good luck in blessing cattle and other things, the Lord be praised'—and whose counter-magical spells are among the most elaborate recorded from the Polish witch-trials—received in return for her services such items as a bowl of flour, some cabbage, and a little meat, or some cloth to make a shirt for her child (Kalisz 1593).

Cunning-folk of wide reputation did exist. They often worked to cure witchcraft, or to find witches. Wojciech Koziełek travelled a considerable distance, for example, to visit the folk-exorcist Jakub Motai (Lublin 1698). Tomasz Browarczyk consulted a *planetarka* to learn who had bewitched and murdered his brother, and on the basis of her advice accused Katarzyna Mrowczyna of the crime (Słajszewo 1695; cf. Krzyżanowice 1772). Such cunning-folk were employed by members of every level of society: for example, the Lublin Jew Nech Abrahamów

---

[105] Horsley, 'Social Roles of the Accused', 712.

[106] Willem de Blécourt, 'Witch Doctors, Soothsayers and Priests: On Cunning Folk in European Historiography and Tradition', *Social History,* 19 (1994); cf. Robin Briggs, 'Women as Victims? Witches, Judges, and the Community', *French History,* 5 (1991); Jane P. Davidson, 'The Myth of the Persecuted Female Healer', in Darren Oldridge (ed.), *The Witchcraft Reader* (New York: Routledge, 2008).

[107] De Blécourt, 'Witch Doctors, Soothsayers, and Priests', 296–8, quotation at p. 296. But even Blécourt acknowledges the fuzzy boundary between cunning, ordinary peasant knowledge, and witchcraft.

requested that the cure of his insane daughter by an 'old woman-enchantress' be written into the Counsel court records.[108] However, the evidence from trials more often depicts not well-defined cunning-folk, but rather women or men with a magical reputation only marginally greater than that of their neighbors, recognized as wise-women or as witches depending on context. Witnesses complained of Dorota Łysakowa, for example, that she had done magic all her life, 'healing some, harming others, using all sorts of methods—splinters, herbs, and other things' (Chęciny 1665c). Others might be known for a limited range of spells, such as Katarzyna Wróblowa, whose bad advice on love-magic got her and her client burnt for witchcraft and sacrilege in Rzeszów (1718; see Chapter 6). Others had reputations, in a small way, for healing cattle (e.g. Lublin 1644), or children (e.g. Kalisz 1616; Nowy Wiśnicz 1662; Lublin 1678).

Polish cunning-women possessed no clear, defining characteristics to distinguish them from their neighbors. They lacked even a distinctive name. The polysemic term *baba* could mean anything from 'old woman' to 'peasant woman' to 'beggar-woman' to 'cunning-woman' to 'witch', and was usually, and usefully, ambiguous between these meanings (see Figure 1.3). In the early sixteenth century, medical doctors despairing of treatment sometimes suggested that their patients consult *mulieres antiquas*—probably a Latinization of *baba* or a variant on *vetula*, another term that might mean cunning-woman, old woman, or witch.[109] The *Witch Denounced* author speaks of *zabobonnice* or 'superstition-workers', apparently his own neologism by which to distinguish such women from *czarownice* or witches.[110] However, he applies the term not only to folk-healers and experts but to everybody who performs any sort of folk-magic or superstition; *all* peasant women would be *zabobonice* on this definition. Similarly, the terms *guślarka* and *guślarz* cannot be unambiguously distinguished either from witches on the one hand or from ordinary peasant 'superstition-practitioners' on the other. Although a few men and women were sufficiently specialized to merit some recognition by both their neighbors and by modern scholars—an issue to which we will return in Chapter 5—most did not; and a reputation for healing could easily imply its opposite.

Gender

The overwhelming majority of accused witches in Poland were women. In the cycle of intensive prosecutions before the Kleczew court between 1682 and 1700 that have been so closely analyzed by Tomasz Wiślicz, just three of the

---

[108] APLublin AMLublin sig. 172 fos. 58ᵛ–59. It is not clear why Abrahamów wanted this information written into the records—perhaps to guard the cunning-woman against later accusation as a witch; perhaps to register publicly that his daughter had been cured.
[109] Adamczyk, 'Czary i magia', 176.
[110] *Czarownica powołana*, 5.

Figure 1.3. The *baba*: witch, healer, or old woman? Detail from the title-page of *Baba abo stary inwentarz* [The *baba*, or the old inventory], Prokop Matłaszewski, *c*.1685. Courtesy of the Polish National Library.

accused were men; the remaining sixty-one (95 percent) were women and girls.[111] In Poland as a whole, 91 percent of the accused Polish witches (93 percent of those accused before town courts) were female—a percentage higher than anywhere else in Europe.[112] It was not impossible for a man to stand accused of witchcraft in early modern Poland, but such instances were

---

[111] Wiślicz, 'Township of Kleczew', 90–1.
[112] Pilaszek, drawing on a larger database, provides similar proportions: 89.4 percent of the accused were female (Pilaszek, *Procesy*, 297). Cf. Jacek Wijaczka, 'Men Standing Trial for Witchcraft at the Łobżenica Court in the Second Half of the 17th Century', *Acta Poloniae Historica*, 93 (2006): in this pioneering regional study of male witches, Wijaczka finds just 10 percent of accused witches before the Łobżenica court to be men; the proportion falls to just 1 in 18 of those executed. Eight-eight percent of the accused witches in Ukraina were women; a similar proportion obtained in Ducal Prussia. In contrast, despite its largely shared culture and political unity with Poland, a full 40 percent of accused witches in Lithuania were male (Dysa, 'Witchcraft Trials,' 40–7; Wijaczka, *Procesy w Prusach*, 297; Pilaszek, 'Litewskie procesy czarownic').

extremely rare.[113] This does not mean, however, that women were accused of witchcraft *because* they were women. Rather, the sorts of evil witches were imagined to do, the sorts of quarrels and conflicts lying behind witchcraft accusation, and the activities through which witchcraft was 'given' to its victims, were all associated with women. The strongly gendered imbalance of power in early modern Poland made women natural targets for accusation, but was not a directly causal factor in witch-trials. Just as the trials were not a sort of covert class warfare (although the accused were overwhelmingly peasants, and this correlation expresses class tensions), so too they expressed gendered conflict but should not be construed as a campaign against women. Witch-hunting was not woman-hunting, but women were, in Poland even more than in Western Europe, the overwhelming victims of witchcraft prosecution.[114]

On the question of gender, statistics correlate closely with discourse. The stereotype of the witch, at every level of discourse, was female. In humanist courtly poetry as in popular satire, in Protestant sermon and Catholic homily, in compendia of home remedies, in historical chronicles, in legal discourse, the witch was a woman. The female witches and cunning-women of the *Pilgrimage of the Hobos*—'Guza' the fortune-teller, 'Chroma' the drunken and hate-filled beggar, 'Zwoniczka' the seller of love-magic potions, 'Labajka' the ineffective cunning-woman, 'Latawica' the demonic, night-flying witch—are paired not with male sorcerers but with males who make their living otherwise: 'Wilkołek' frightens people into giving him food by pretending to be a werewolf, but the other male beggars use more standard methods such as simulating blindness or singing hymns at pilgrimage centers.[115] Those beggars represented as engaging in malefice, stealing milk, or interacting with demons, are exclusively women.

The stereotype of the female witch in Poland grows out of a general context of literary and homiletic misogyny, a context demonstrating the close conformity of male Polish educated attitudes with those of their western contemporaries.[116]

---

[113] Nearly all the witchcraft accusations against men are exceptional in some way. Men came to be involved in witch-trials by association, as collaborators or beneficiaries of witchcraft (e.g. Wschowa 1601; Kleczew 1646e; Turek 1652b; Chęciny 1665a; Pacanów 1741), or for having hired witches (e.g. Lublin 1681, Lublin 1732). In village trials men sometimes stood accused as a consequence of men's juridical responsibility for their wives (e.g. Klimkówka 1678, Jazowsko 1748). A peculiarity of larger trials is the accusation or denunciation of a single man, along with several women: the man, characteristically, stood accused of providing music for the dances at Bald Mountain, playing such instruments as the hoe, the fox's tail, a fish, or a rolling pin (see Ch. 5).

[114] It bears noting that, although witchcraft was never a common crime as compared to such capital crimes as banditry, murder, arson, it ranked among the most common capital crime committed by *women*: e.g. the Lwów court tried fifty-six female criminals between 1550 and 1699, mostly for prostitution and theft. But of twelve capital cases before that court with female defendants, four were infanticides, three were witches. See Karpiński, *Kobieta*, table 23.

[115] Swizralus, *Peregrynacja*.

[116] The literary misogyny of early modern Poland has been recently explored in the excellent work of Elżbieta Elena Wróbel and Halina Wiśniewska, from whom I draw much of the following material. Elżbieta Elena Wróbel, *Chrześcijańska rodzina w Polsce XVI XVII wieku* (Kraków: Wydawnictwo Naukowe Papieskiej Akademii Teologicznej, 2002); Wiśniewska, *Świat płci żeńskiej*.

Women were seen to be stupider, more passionate, less able to control themselves, above all more sharp-tongued than men. For the Catholic homilist Szymon Starowolski (d. 1656), the female of every animal is worse than the male: in some cases, as with the lioness, this means also that she is fiercer and more dangerous. 'So also, among humankind, the woman is always worse than the man.'[117]

Starowolski continues:

Usually women don't know how to maintain moderation in their lives and customs, but instead incline either to one side or to the other. If they love someone, they love without measure, If they hate someone, their hatred and wrath is measureless; when they begin to be good, they become saints.[118]

This trope of woman's inability to moderate her virtue and her vice originates with the Roman philosopher Seneca, enters Christian literature with John Chrysostom,[119] and is quoted in the *Malleus* (pt. 1 q. 6). The image finds its way also into Polish literary depictions of witches. Szymon Szymonowic, humanist poet and dean of the famous Akademia at Zamość, combined local with classical tropes to depict the Polish witch in his *Sielanki* (*Idylls*).[120] The wronged wife of *Sielanka* 15, driven to witchcraft out of jealousy and rage while her husband cavorts with his new young mistress, is modeled on Medea; while the lustful old widow of *Sielanka* 18, seducing a young peasant through enchantment, resembles Pamphile of Apuleus' *Golden Ass*. For Szymonowic, witchcraft arises from women's excessive and misdirected love; it is a crime of passion. Szymonowic pairs witchcraft ('czary') and a lack of moderation ('bez żadnej miary') in a series of rhymed couplets that form the refrain of *Sielanka* 15. The wronged wife repeats, with variations and with increasing hysteria, as she prepares to destroy her husband and his mistress:

> I know it's a great sin, I know all witchcraft
> Is harmful, but my resentment has no measure.[121]

Since female emotion, and its potential harmful effects, 'have no measure' and cannot be regulated by women themselves, male authors insisted that women must be controlled by their husbands. A constant theme in sermons depicted wives as weaker and more foolish than their husbands, as 'immature in understanding', in need of a male overlord for their own good and the good of society.[122] Preachers

---

[117] Szymon Starowolski, *Świątnica Pańska* (Kraków, 1682 [1645]); quoted after Wiśniewska, *Świat płci żeńskiej*, 13.

[118] Ibid.

[119] Ian Maclean, *The Renaissance Notion of Women* (New York: Cambridge University Press, 1987), 20–7.

[120] Szymon Szymonowic, *Sielanki i pozostałe wierze polskie Szymona Szymonowica*, ed. Janusz Pelc, (Wrocław: Zakład Narodowy im. Ossolińskich, 1964 [1614]).

[121] Szymonowic, *Sielanki*, 15 vv. 21–2; cf. vv. 29–30, 35–6, 41–2, 47–8, 53–4, 59–60, 65–6, 71–2.

[122] Wróbel, *Chrześcijańska rodzina*, 121–2; quoting a sermon of Piotr Skarga, *c.*1600.

reminded their flocks that Eve came from Adam's rib—not from his head, as if she should lead, nor from his foot, as if she should be totally abased or enslaved—rather to stand at his side, 'under his hand and protection'.[123] This strongly paternalistic conception of the husband's role could occasionally shield a woman from the full force of the law. When two sisters-in-law accused one another of witchcraft in 1709, the court of Szczekociny fined their husbands for 'not knowing how to shut their wives' mouths'.[124] More often, however, the husband's legal authority worked against an accused witch. The husband of Elżbieta Stepkowicowa declined her defense counsel's suggested appellate case—consigning his wife to torture and eventually to the stake (Nowy Sącz 1670).

If women were represented as unable to control their emotion, still less could they control its expression. Literary men saw cantankerous vituperation as the cardinal female sin. According to the letter of town law (though not in practice) women could not serve as witnesses in court, because their word was considered unreliable, 'various', and too easily swayed by spite.[125] Women were pictured as endlessly and irritably loquacious: a husband should act deaf to avoid quarrels in the home, while the good wife was defined as that rare woman who had overcome her 'natural tendency to gossip and obloquy'.[126] In an Easter Monday sermon, the Jesuit preacher Aleksander Lorencowic went so far as to claim that Jesus' first post-Resurrection appearance to Mary Magdalene could be explained by female weakness: as an incorrigible gossip, she would spread the Good News faster.[127] In another homily, with Salome's dance as his initial text, Lorencowic provides us with a rich panorama of biblical misogyny and its early modern Polish interpretation.[128] From Salome, that 'obscene female', he turns to the Whore of Babylon—a 'horrible witch' who drinks the blood of the saints—and thence launches into a breathtaking flight of rhetorical exegesis ranging through the biblical books of Esdra, Sirach, Jeremiah. A snippet will suffice to catch his tone:

With her wrath and fury, she subjugates kings, and turns wine into venom, and surpasses the lion in cruelty, more malicious than the dragon, worse than the bear; she can even triumph over devils. 'There is no anger worse than a woman's wrath. The greatest wickedness is the wickedness of woman'. (Sirach 25)

---

[123] Jakub Wujek, *Postylle Katholiczna* (Kraków, 1584); quoted after Wróbel, *Chrześcijańska rodzina*, 128.

[124] Władysław Siarkowski, *Materiały do etnografii ludu polskiego z okolic Kielc* (Kielce: Wydawnictwo Takt, 2000 [1878–9]), 93.

[125] Bartłomiej Groicki, *Porządek sądów i spraw miejskich prawda magdeburskiego w Koronie Polskiej*, ed. Karol Koranyi (Warsaw: Wydawnictwo Prawnicze, 1953 [1559]), 131–2, 35. In practice, women's testimony was quite frequent, in witch-trials and in other matters, and women could represent their own interests in court (Karpiński, *Kobieta*, 24–7, 66–7; Głowacka, 'Women in a Small Polish Town', 143–6).

[126] Wróbel, *Chrześcijańska rodzina*, 123–7; citing 17th-cent. sermons and satires.

[127] Aleksander Lorencowic, *Kazania na Niedziele Całego Roku*, 2 vols. (Kalisz: Drukarnia Kolegium Kaliskiego Soc: Jesu, 1671), ii. 7.

[128] Ibid. i. 7–12.

Lorencowic expresses a commonplace argument: what women lacked in physical and mental strength, they made up for in a verbal facility and a sharpness of tongue that could approximate the fury of God himself. Insofar as witchcraft was seen as a crime of cursing and malediction—or as a magistrate of Warta called it, 'an offence committed by unbridled tongues'—it was thereby also seen as a particularly female crime.[129]

Female vituperation, far from expressing and so relieving a woman's tendency to malice, was believed instead to exacerbate ill will. Jakub Kazimierz Haur, in a discussion of women's illnesses, drew on contemporary zoological theory to explain menstrual cramps as caused by the 'unbridled wrath, nagging, peevishness, and impatience' of some women; 'good, quiet, and modest' women, he claimed, experience menstrual pain less or not at all. Just as vipers and lizards contain no poison until they produce it when enraged, so women would not suffer painful menstruation if they had not been, themselves, its 'occasion and cause'.[130] Similarly, nagging and gossip were addictive behaviors which grew over time, increasing and encouraging a woman's natural propensities in this direction. Such practices, if not curbed and domesticated by a wise and forbearing husband, led to the further development of ill humors in the body—humors suggestively compared to poison.

Both secular and clerical discourse rendered the married woman as a quarrelsome gossip, held barely in check by the forbearance of her wiser, stronger, and more taciturn husband. This moderating influence ended with the husband's death, and Polish society looked on widows with deep suspicion. Outside the normative channels of male control, but with her sharp tongue and unbridled passion continuing unabated, the widow represented an intensification of all the worst qualities discursively ascribed to women more generally, with few compensatory positive qualities. Village widows came to be thought of as experts in those non-physical arts by which, having lost the feminine guile of youth, they now controlled or took vengeance on their neighbors. According to the Jesuit lexicographer Grzegorz Knapiusz, the word 'baba' had four distinct but closely inter-related meanings: old woman, grandmother, midwife, and 'superstitious old woman, who heals not by witchcraft, but by invented ceremonies'.[131] Although Knapiusz scrupulously discriminates between the superstitious 'baba' and the witch proper, others perceived no such difference.

Daniel Naborowski (1573–1640), court poet to the aristocratic Calvinist Radziwiłł family, listed the features of the 'baba' in a poem that loses none of its cultural significance for being an exercise in humanist hyperbole:

---

[129] Pilaszek, 'Procesy czarownic w Polsce', 83.
[130] Jakub Kazimierz Haur, *Skład Abo Skarbiec Znakomitych Sekretow Oekonomiey Ziemianskiey* (Kraków: Drukarnia Mikołaia Alexandra Schedla, 1693), tr. 25 p. 434; cf. p. 387.
[131] Knapiusz, *Thesaurus*; after Wiśniewska, *Świat płci żeńskiej*, 136; cf. Renata Dźwigol, *Polskie ludowe słownictwo mitologiczne* (Kraków: Wydawnictwo Naukowe Akademii Pedagogicznej, 2004), 78–9, on the semantic range of *baba* in modern times.

Toothless old woman, ugly and unhappy,
Displeasing old woman, a stranger to virtue
Old woman full of treachery, indecent old woman
Ancient seducer, old woman full of wrath
Old woman, procuress of virtuous maidens,
Old woman, who induces modest wives to sin,
Old woman without mercy, exuding venom,
Old woman, with rough froglike skin,
Stinking old woman, packed full of every filth
Who never has a good word for anyone at all,
Accursed old woman, yourself cursing others,
Old woman, whom the devil arouses against the virtuous
Rank drunkard, worn-out wanton,
Nursing young devils at your drooping tits,
Quarrelsome old woman, who with your witchcraft
Outdoes Medea and Circe, in my opinion
Old woman, unworthy to walk the earth,
Carried instead, by an indisposed devil,
Old woman, who has never confessed her sins
Nor cried contritely, your eyes dry of tears
Old woman, farting from her foul behind
Barking like a cannon loaded with manure
   . . .
Hide yourself, obscene old hag, infectious vapor!
Hide yourself, ignoble blemish of our age!
Who, known to the world only for your nasty deeds,
Outdoes Taida with your obscenities.[132]

The poem hardly requires comment. The *baba* embodies every evil: she is ugly, dried up, useless, aggressive, quarrelsome, smelly, obscene. She practices magic and nurses devil familiars. We have returned to the stereotype with which we started—the witch as old, wrinkled, ugly, and female—but we are not, perhaps, very much closer to an understanding of the relationship between such imaginary representations and the actual practice of witch accusation and trial.

What connection can be made between the pervasive misogyny of early modern Polish culture, on the one hand, and the overwhelming disproportion of female accused witches to males? Is witch-hunting women-hunting after all?

In this simplistic formulation, such a question is ill posed. Sigrid Brauner has argued that any attempt to derive the witch-trials from the generalized misogyny of western civilization must fail: while Christian misogyny goes back at least to Paul, and has earlier roots in Greek and Jewish culture, the emergence of the

---

[132] Daniel Naborowski (1573–1640), 'Do złej baby'; quoted after Wiśniewska, *Świat płci żeńskiej*, 137–8.

gendered witch occurs in a specific time and place.[133] Stuart Clark, in an
influential argument, has insisted that to interpret witchcraft accusation as an
expression of misogyny is to misread them: through such a method one learns
'how certain women become marginalized and thus susceptible to being accused
of crimes, but not what this meant, and not why *this* crime: why accusations
should have concerned *witchcraft*, rather than some other crime'.[134] The representation of women as quarrelsome, shrewish, obstinate, and wrathful, as unable
to control their loves and their hatreds, their jealousy, and envy, and lust, made
them particularly susceptible to witchcraft accusation. But not all women were
thought of as witches, even if nearly all accused witches were women. Accused
witches were so accused not because they were women, but because they were
witches—the distinction must be maintained even though witchcraft, to some
degree, may be understood as the quintessence of all that was thought to be worst
about the female gender. As Christina Larner argues, 'the pursuit of witches was
an end in itself', not a cover for attacks on women as a group.[135]

   Indeed, as Clark shows, demonological literature was not particularly interested in gender; in contrast, the defenders of witches dwelt on female inadequacy.
For authors such as Johann Weyer and Friedrich Spee, precisely *because* women
were foolish, gullible, and indeed given to delusion, they should be pitied
rather than feared.[136] This European pattern holds true in Poland, where *The
Witch Denounced*, an anonymous pamphlet against witch-trials, explains that
female superstition derives from the 'small and frivolous understanding' of
that gender.[137] Serafin Gamalski's later *Spiritual Warning* enjoins magistrates
to weigh carefully whether an alleged act of witchcraft really occurred, or came
rather 'from frivolous thinking, from curiosity, from a mixture of fantasy,
melancholy, and hypochondria'.[138]

   Clark's problematization of the gendering of witchcraft, though a welcome
corrective to simplistic theories of misogynistic persecution, is incomplete. Two
recent lines of argument have tended to reintroduce gender into our understanding of witch-trials and the imagination of witchcraft. First, as several scholars
have argued, the gender of accused witches was overdetermined by social conditions. Quite apart from their representation in literature and folklore, witches
were women because women had both motive and opportunity to practice
witchcraft and to engage in the invidious exchanges that gave rise to witchcraft
accusation. Witchcraft accusation developed out of the networks of interdepen-
dence and neighborly conflict endemic to village life, and these were primarily
female spheres: child-rearing, food-preparation and borrowing, illness and

---

[133] Brauner, *Fearless Wives*, 13–14.
[134] Stuart Clark, *Thinking with Demons* (New York: OUP, 1997), 107–8.
[135] Larner, *Enemies of God*, 102.
[136] Clark, *Thinking with Demons*, 116 ff.
[137] *Czarownica powołana*, 5; cf. 35–7.
[138] Gamalski, *Przestrogi Duchowne*, 11; *Instrukcya rzymska*, fo. 15ᵛ.

healing with the accompanying small-scale magic; haggling with its potential for quarrels and intimidation. They were also spheres in which married, non-marginalized women took the active part.[139] Éva Pócs suggests that the great majority of witchcraft accusations followed currents of village rivalry and tension among working, house-holding women. It was women who visited their neighbors to borrow or lend the foodstuffs through which witchcraft was so often passed, women who milked the cows and made the cheese and butter so intimately associated with the milk-thieving activities of witches, and women who took steps to protect the cattle from such attack. It was women who helped each other out and sought each other's advice over the healing of their children, and thus women who were blamed when things went wrong. Moreover, where men could resort to physical violence to resolve quarrels, women were more likely to fight with words—especially with the curses which could retrospectively be reinterpreted as the casting of a spell. I explore this context of suspicion and its disproportionately female character in Chapter 3.

Secondly, the imagined female witch, and the reality of witchcraft accusation, worked together as a mechanism enforcing oppressive gender norms. Though the prosecution of female cursing as witchcraft was, in a sense, no more a gendered persecution than the prosecution of male brawling or dueling was an attack on men, in effect it demonized women's only available means of aggression and defense.[140] The image of the witch held up a warning mirror for women, providing them with an anti-model against which to measure good female behavior: the witch was an anti-mother who eats fat, juicy babies instead of bearing children, an anti-wife cavorting sexually with demons rather than staying at home with her husband, an anti-housewife spoiling or consuming the profit of field and dairy, rather than producing that profit for her husband and children. Though the vast majority of women were never accused of witchcraft, the image of the witch kept women in their place, and admonished them about the consequences of leaving it.[141] Finally, as Roper has cogently argued, demonology and witch-trials both celebrated fertility, pregnancy, and motherhood, and constructed the witch as their opposite. Witchcraft and the accusation of witch-craft formed a drama of fertility and sterility, pregnancy and stillbirth, moisture and dryness, milk and its spoiling—in general, a drama of fecund prosperity and envy of that prosperity: witch-trials 'mobilized anxieties about fertility and motherhood' and projected that anxiety onto older, post-menopausal women, who acted as 'lightning conductors' for these fears. Despite the formal gender-neutrality of most demonological theory, in practice witchcraft fears focused on

---

[139] Éva Pócs, 'Why Witches are Women', *Acta Ethnographica Hungarica*, 48/3–4 (2003), 374–6; Martin, 'Devil and the Domestic', 84–7; cf. Briggs, *Witches and Neighbours*, 265–71, 76.

[140] Christina Larner, 'Was Witch-Hunting Woman Hunting?', in *Witchcraft and Religion* (London: Blackwell, 1984).

[141] Louise Jackson, 'Witches, Wives, and Mothers', in Darren Oldridge (ed.), *The Witchcraft Reader* (New York: Routledge, 2008).

the infertile or post-fertile woman as a source of danger in a society dependent on human, animal, and agricultural reproduction.[142] Although the Polish witches seem not to have usually been the elderly 'crones' expected under Roper's theory, her focus on milk and fertility as arenas of female anxiety and power otherwise fit the Polish material very well. I return to a reading of witchcraft as the overconsumption or destruction of moisture, symbolized by human and bovine milk, in Chapter 5.

---

[142] Roper, *Witchcraze*, 138ff., 74.

2

Imagining Witchcraft in Literature and Law

SECULARIZATION OF WITCHCRAFT

Before the sixteenth century, only ecclesiastical courts tried *sortilegae* in Poland; and these courts continued to inquire into magic well into the 1500s.[1] A synod in Poznań in 1420 expressed the Polish church's growing worry over magic, 'excommunicating and anathematizing all sorcerers, who, by the invocation of demons or use of sacred things, practice sorcery'.[2] However, church courts exerted themselves very little in the search for practitioners of illicit magic. Although Joanna Adamczyk's thorough study of ecclesiastical court records has found sixty church-court trials that have *something* to do with magic between 1404 and 1551; just twenty-three of these cases feature magic as a central concern. The church expressed most disquiet with what it regarded as the superstitious misuse of ecclesiastical objects such as holy water and blessed candles: records speak of *incantrices* and *vetulae* who pick herbs and roots, prepare amulets, divine with wax and lead. The accused, called *sortilegae, vetulae,* or *mulieres antiquas,* were usually freed through oaths of expurgation, oaths of renunciation (something like a no-contest plea, in which the accused accepted the charges and promised to give up magic in the future), or church penance. Summing up this material, Adamczyk finds a 'relatively minimal interest in the problem of magical practices' in church courts of the fifteenth and early sixteenth centuries; Pilaszek concurs, noting that trials involving magic in any way make up about 0.5 percent of the trials before church courts in this period.[3]

However, the church-court trials provide evidence that at least two fifteenth-century Polish witches were threatened with capital punishment before secular courts—including our earliest record: the wife of Piotr Zawarty, who in 1430 sought annulment of his marriage before the Poznań consistory court on the grounds that his wife was a witch.[4] The anonymous witch burnt in Chwaliszewo

---

[1] For church-court sorcery trials in the 15th and early 16th cents. in Poland, see Koranyi, 'Czary i gusła'; Bylina, 'Magia'; and esp. Adamczyk, 'Czary i magia'.

[2] Władysław Rubin, 'Lud w polskim ustawodawstwie synodalnym do rozbiorów Polski', *Sacrum Poloniae Millenium,* 2 (1955), 140; cf. Adamczyk, 'Czary i magia', 125–8.

[3] Adamczyk, 'Czary i magia', 249; Pilaszek, *Procesy,* 146.

[4] Adamczyk, 'Czary i magia', 198–209.

in 1511 was not, then, the first to be sentenced to death; rather, she is the first for whom we have a record that this death sentence was carried out. Nor does that case seem to have been particularly exceptional: the Poznań canon who insulted the people of Chwaliszewo, saying they should all be burnt just as they had recently burnt a witch, was joking. The insult intended, most likely, was that the people of Chwaliszewo were as superstitious as their burnt witch—not that they were cruel or unusual for having burnt her.

In fact, Polish town law demanded death by the stake for the crime of witchcraft from its very inception. Polish towns, and some villages, were founded on the model of medieval German (Saxon) Law, most often in the variants called Magdeburg law and Chełmno law. This legal tradition was quite separate and autonomous from the tradition of Polish Law practiced in the noble *gród* and *starościnskie* courts, and of the canon law practiced in episcopal and consistory courts. The *Sachsenspiegel*—the thirteenth-century law-book that (much modified, revised, and variously interpreted) formed the basis for Polish town law—stipulated death at the stake for sorcery.[5] However, this stark ruling, which Polish courts certainly did not follow with any consistency in the late medieval period, is best read as a formula describing methods of execution. The influential Kraków jurist Bartłomiej Groicki glosses the *Speculum* thus: 'schismatics from the Christian faith are to be burnt. Magicians or poisoners should meet the same death.'[6] In other words, *if* an accused witch is sentenced to death, that death should be by fire.

The understanding of witchcraft as a capital offence came to be strengthened but also qualified in the *Carolina*, the early modern law-code of the Holy Roman Empire promulgated in 1532. The *Carolina* distinguished between malefice and harmless magic: practitioners of the former deserved capital punishment, of the latter, lesser sanctions. Groicki's influential translation of selected articles from the *Carolina* lays down the conditions under which a suspected practitioner of harmful magic may be sent to torture:

If it should be shown that someone wishes to teach another these things or that someone should threaten another with them, and that because of this something should befall the person thus threatened, or if the suspect should demonstrate by word, practices, or other things, which are found among such people, and which such people make use of, and if they be known for this, such a person ought to be accused and may be sent to torture on the basis of these signs, because all such abilities, which are opposed to the Lord God (nor is it decent for Christian people to have doings with them) are to be answered by the law, and sternly punished.[7]

---

[5] Mikołaj Jaskier, *Juris Provincialis quod Speculum Saxonum vulgo nucupatur libri tres...* (1535), bk. 2, art. 13. Polish 16th–18th-cent. town courts used Mikołaj Jaskier's Latin translation (1602 [1535]), Paweł Szczerbic's Polish translation (1610 [1581]) and, probably most often, Bartłomiej Groicki's selection of the more important parts of the *Speculum*, his *Artykuły prawa magdeburskiego*, ed. Karol Koranyi (Warsaw: Wydawnictwo Prawnicze, 1954 [1558]).

[6] Groicki, *Porządek sądów*, 199.

[7] *Artykuły prawa magdeburskiego*, 117 (art. 24).

Groicki's translation of this section of the *Carolina* constitutes an important development in Polish jurisprudence concerning witchcraft. Although witchcraft had always, technically, been a capital crime, it is here for the first time defined as a secular crime of magical harm. Despite his mention of witchcraft as 'opposed to the Lord God', Groicki emphasizes malefice and the proofs sufficient to send an accused witch to torture. Witchcraft is the crime of harming others magically, and the signs of such harm are, above all, that someone should first threaten magical harm and that such harm indeed later befalls the person threatened. We do not yet find mention of a pact with the devil, or of the anti-society of witches, or even of renunciation of God: witchcraft is a secular crime because it causes harm to people and property through specific magical acts.

Throughout the sixteenth century, many European states promulgated laws to increase the penalties for witchcraft and to define it more securely as a secular crime. A law of Electoral Saxony in 1572 asserted that anyone who has anything to do with the devil is to be 'condemned to death by fire'.[8] The Elizabethan witchcraft statute of 1563, and the statute of the Scottish Parliament in the same year, set the stage for intensified witch-trials. Characteristically, these edicts emphasized the changing perspective on witchcraft as *crimen laesae maiestatis*, a sort of treachery against God and the State, while remaining a crime of magical harm—on both counts, witchcraft belonged in the secular courts.

There is no equivalent edict or decree in Poland. In contrast, and against the grain of sixteenth-century jurisprudence, a *Constitutio* of the Polish Sejm in 1543 explicitly reserved jurisdiction over witchcraft to the ecclesiastical courts.[9] Until recently scholars have found the origin of secular-court witch-trials in a subclause to the *Consitutio*, stating that 'in cases where the witchcraft caused harm to anybody, the secular courts have the right to intervene and to inquire into the crime'. In fact nothing like this subclause can be found in the *Constitutio*. As I have detailed elsewhere, the mistaken belief that the *Constitutio* of 1543 gives secular courts jurisdiction over malefice seems to have arisen from a late-nineteenth-century misreading of Herburt's legal digest *Statuta Regni Poloniae*,[10] whereby portions of the *Constitutio* were conflated with an entirely unrelated law of 1505.[11] Moreover, as a document of the mid-sixteenth-century struggle between the *szlachta* and the church over the extent of noble freedoms, the

---

[8] H. C. Erik Midelfort, 'Heartland of the Witchcraze', in Darren Oldridge (ed.), *The Witchcraft Reader* (New York: Routledge, 2002 [1981]), 117.

[9] Wacław Uruszczak, Stanisław Grodziski, and Irena Dwornicka (eds.), *Volumina constitutionum* part 1 (Warsaw: Wydawnictwo Sejmowe, 1996–2000), ii. 252. On the complex translation history of this *Constitutio*, see Jakub Sawicki, 'Z ksiąg Metryki Koronnej: Tekst pierwszych konstytucji sejmowych w języku polskim z r. 1543 w sprawie sądownictwa świeckiego i duchownego', *Teki Archiwalne*, 2 (1954), 54–82.

[10] Jan Herburt, *Statuta Regni Poloniae in ordinem alphabeti digesta* (Cracow: Łazarz Andrysowic, 1563), 253.

[11] Ostling, 'Konstytucja 1543'. Zygmunt Gloger's widely read *Encyclopedia staropolska* disseminated this misreading (Warsaw: Wiedza Poweszechna, 1972 [1900–3]), ii. 267, the source

Constitutio entirely neglected the autonomous, independent structures of the Saxon-Law town courts that tried cases of witchcraft;[12] nor was it ever ratified by the Sejm.[13]

There exists, then, no decisive moment or decree whereby witchcraft became a secular crime in Poland, punishable in the secular courts. Rather, we have a slow but accelerating inclination by secular courts to hear witch-trials and to apply severe punishment to convicted witches; an inclination guided by the adoption of concepts and attitudes developed in the West rather than by decrees or edicts originating from any of the multifarious organs of Polish Law. I turn now to this question of western sources and their adoption, with modification, in Poland.

WESTERN AND LOCAL CONCEPTIONS

In 1614, the otherwise little-known Stanisław Ząbkowic published his Polish translation of Heinrich Institoris's infamous *Malleus Maleficarum* in Kraków.[14] Under the title *Młot na Czarownice* (Hammer against Witches), Ząbkowic published a work that established most of the main points of the western witch-stereotype: the overwhelmingly feminine character of witchcraft and its root in unbridled lust; the particular hatred of witches for children; and the essence of witchcraft in the devil-pact and in the renunciation of God (see Figure 2.1). Ząbkowic presented his translation as a necessary intervention in a society which mistakenly supposed that 'witchcraft is nothing, and can bring no harm to anyone', and as a protest against a judiciary which had 'become lukewarm in the punishment of witch's ungodliness, so that witchcraft, unpunished, becoming habitual among evil people, from day to day multiplies and grows more'.[15]

This is standard demonological hyperbole, but Ząbkowic exaggerates judicial indifference less than might be supposed. Although Poland saw very few

---

of the quotation above), which influenced most scholars of witchcraft in the 20th cent., including Baranowski, Tazbir, and Zdrojkowski.

[12] A brief, solid discussion of the battle between church and *szlachta* over jurisdiction may be found in Henryk Wisner's, 'Jurysdykcja duchowna skażona', in *Rozróżnieni w wierze: Szkice z dziejów Rzeczypospolitej schyłku XVI i połowy XVII wieku* (Warsaw: Książka i Wiedza, 1982).

[13] Sawicki, 'Z ksiąg Metryki Koronnej'.

[14] On the authorship and reception of the *Malleus*, see Tamar Herzig, 'The Bestselling Demonologist: Heinrich Institoris's *Malleus Maleficarum*', in J. Machielsen (ed.), *The Science of Demons: Early Modern Authors Facing Witchcraft and the Devil* (London: Routledge, 2020). Ząbkowic's translation omitted most of the first book of the *Malleus*; but, like many Latin edns., bundled it together with Johannes Nider's *Formicarius* and Ulrich Molitor's *De lamiis et phitonicis mulieribus*. A recent popular edn. of Ząbkowic omits these, as well as Ząbkowic's preface and dedication: Stanisław Ząbkowic, *Młot na czarownice*, ed. W. Lewandowski (Wrocław: Wyspa, 1992).

[15] Stanisław Ząbkowic, *Młot na czarownice: Postępek zwierzchowny w czarach, także sposob uchronienia sie ich, y lekarstwo na nie w dwoch częściach zamykaiący* (Cracow: Szymon Kempini, 1614), fo. 2.

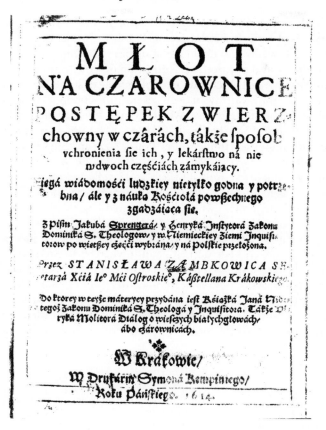

Figure 2.1. Western demonology comes to Poland. Title-page of the *Młot na czarownice* (Hammer for Witches), Stanisław Ząbkowic's translation of the *Malleus Maleficarum,* Kraków 1614. Courtesy of the Polish National Library.

witch-trials in the sixteenth century, elite attitudes toward the witch-crime had begun to shift by the beginning of the seventeenth. An early notation in the village-court records of Klimkówka, before any witches had been tried at that court, traces this shift in attitude: in 1611 the noble owner of Klimkówka reminded the court that 'concerning witch-craft, . . . the law commands that if such a one [a witch] should threaten, she must be punished with death'.[16]

The importation of demonology into elite attitudes and into Polish town law owes little to Ząbkowic's little-read translation of the *Malleus.*[17] Purely legal

[16] Ludwik Łysiak (ed.), *Księga sądowa kresu klimkowskiego, 1600–1762* (Wrocław: Zakład Narodowy im. Ossolińskich,1965), item 72.

[17] Despite its emblematic status in the Polish historiography of witchcraft, Ząbkowic's translation of the *Malleus* was not a publishing success. It does appear in a few bookbinders'

treatises, such as the *Praxis rerum criminalium* of the Flemish jurist Joos Dam-houder, exercised far wider influence on Polish jurisprudence. Introduced into Polish jurisprudence by Groicki in the mid-sixteenth century, Damhouder's text nudged Polish judicial practice in the direction of western inquisitorial norms.[18] Damhouder categorized witchcraft as an offense against the Divine Majesty, and considered it a crime worthy of very severe punishment. He also provides a detailed description of the *sabbat.* Witold Maisel has suggested, quite plausibly, that this is the source for the developed *sabbat* concept as it appears in Polish trials.[19] A later important influence on Polish legal attitudes toward witchcraft, Benedict Carpzov's *Practicae novae rerum criminalium* of 1635 largely replaced the *Carolina* as a guide to criminal justice, and it reflected the developed attitudes of the western demonological tradition. Witches were 'tools of the devil' and 'enemies of the human race', who, having entered into the devil pact, desire only the destruction of others.[20]

Popular literature, mixing local concerns with anecdotes and notions from throughout Europe, created another conduit whereby Western attitudes toward the witch could spread in Poland. Well before trials had become at all regular in Poland, Wit Korczewski's mid-sixteenth-century *Polish Conversations, intermixed with Latin* presciently foreshadowed the contrasting approaches secular and ecclesiastical authorities were to take in the following centuries. One conversation depicts a noble manor-lord in conversation with a *baba* (that is, an old

inventories, and, intriguingly, as an item in the will of a Lublin juryman in 1633: Elżbieta Toruj, *Inwentarze księgozbiorów mieszczan lubelskich 1591 1678* (Lublin: Wydawnictwo UMCS, 1997), 135 ff.; *Inwentarze książek lubelskich introligatorów z pierwszej połowy XVII wieku* (Lublin: Wydawnictwo UMCS, 2000), 88; Jan Riabinin, *Lublin w księgach wójtowsko ławniczych XVII—XVIII w.* (Lublin: Wydawnictwo Magistratu m. Lublina, 1928), 48–61. Educated magistrates may have preferred the Latin original: at least one 16th-cent. Poznań court scribe owned a copy, as did the Poznań cathedral chapter as early as 1526: Witold Maisel, *Poznańskie prawo karne do końca XVI wieku* (Poznań: Uniwersytet im. Adama Mickiewicza w Poznaniu, 1963), 212.

[18] Jodocus Damhouderius, *Praxis rerum criminalium . . .* (Antwerp: Ioan. Belleri, 1601 [1554]); Karol Koranyi, 'Wpływ prawa flandryjskiego na polskie w XVI wieku (Damhouder-Groicki)', *Pamiętnik historyczno-prawny*, 4/4 (1927); Zbigniew Zdrójkowski, '*Praktyka kryminalna*' Jakuba Czechowicza: *Jej źródła i system na tle rozwoju współczesnego prawa karnego zachodniej Europy* (Toruń: Towarzystwo Naukowe w Toruniu, 1949), 116–17.

[19] Damhouderius, *Praxis rerum*, cap. 61, 'de crimine laesae Maiestatis divinae', §§ 90–143; Maisel, *Poznańskie*, 211.

[20] Benedict Carpzov, *Practicae novae imperialis Saxonicae rerum criminalium* (Frankfurt, 1635), part 1a qu. 48, 'de crimine sortilegii'; cited after Uruszczak, 'Proces czarownicy', 193. Pilaszek has shown that esp. in Wielkopolska and Royal Prussia, town court magistrates sometimes explicitly cited Carpzov, along with Matthias Berlich and Peter Binsfeld, in their verdicts (Pilaszek, *Procesy*, 194). The Chełmno jurist Jakub Czechowicz based the long discussion of witchcraft of his posthumous *Praktyka kryminalna* (1769) largely on Carpzov's work. Although the *Praktyka kryminalna* has sometimes been mentioned as an example of the late flowering of Polish demonology, Zdrójkowski has demonstrated that it was entirely derivative and was entirely ignored: '*Praktyka kryminalna*', 117–21.

woman, a village-woman, a cunning-woman, a witch). She complains that the parish priest has placed her under ecclesiastical censure 'because I did a little witchcraft, when I gave my daughter in marriage'. She cast a spell to keep her daughter's husband from beating his new wife. Under subsequent questioning, she admits to having blinded a vagabond and drawing milk from a church-bell on St John's Eve. When the *baba* refuses to say more in front of the priest, for fear of receiving further censure or penance, her noble master responds angrily:

> You don't deserve censure, old hag
> But a pyre of wood, and fire!
> . . .
> You've given yourself to the devil!
> Go to your place in hell,
> I don't want to listen to you any more.[21]

The poem demonstrates that secular fear of witchcraft was well established by the mid-sixteenth century. Whereas her parish priest treats the *baba*'s actions as superstitious, and wishes to reform her behavior using the tools of church discipline, her secular lord understands her to be a witch, guilty of love-magic, malefice, and milk-theft, drawing her powers from a pact with the devil. She is a danger to human society, deserving nothing less than the stake.

Both 'popular' and 'elite' ideas about witches and devils were reflected, disseminated, and constructed by the ribald verse dramas, moralizing satires, and picaresque adventures known to Polish literary historians by the untranslatable term 'literatura sowizdrzalska'.[22] Published primarily in the first few decades of the seventeenth century, the genre enjoyed tremendous popularity throughout the seventeenth and eighteenth centuries. Sold in cheap editions at fairs and markets, and especially at the parish church-fairs where local townspeople and peasantry might also have been able to enjoy a dramatic performance of a *sowizdrzał* play, these works were especially well suited to work as conduits of cultural materials between 'elite' and 'popular' levels, blurring the distinction between them. As Urszula Augustiniak argues, it was a truly popular form reflecting and shaping the attitudes and expectations of its wide readership.[23] Its authors ranged from noble-men, priests, and well-educated burghers to a class of *klechy* or 'under-clerks': church

---

[21] Wit Korczewski, 'Rozmowy polskie łacińskim językiem przeplatane', ed. J. Karłowicz (Cracow: Akademia Umiejętności, 1889 [1553]), 70–1.

[22] The term derives from *Sowizdrzał* (or *Sowiźrzał* or *Sowirzalius*), a popular pseudonym for the usually anonymous authors of the genre. This is a corruption from *Sownociardłko*, which translates *Eulenspiegel* or Owl-Glass, the traditional hero of a cognate genre in German literature.

[23] Urszula Augustyniak, *Koncepcje narodu i społeczeństwa w literaturze plebejskiej od końca XVI do końca XVII wieku* (Warsaw: Wydawnictwo Uniwersytetu, 1989), 7–16. Augustyniak effectively contests the Bakhtinian perspective popular among literary scholars of the last several decades who read the *sowizdrzał* literature as an anti-feudal response to noble and ecclesiastical hegemony. See esp. Stanisław Grzeszczuk, *Błazeńskie zwierciadło: Rzecz o humorystyce sowizdrzalskiej XVI i XVII wieku* (Cracow: Wydawnictwo Literackie, 1970).

organists, choir-masters, and parish school-teachers, often of peasant or plebeian origin. These latter often boarded in the village tavern or the parish alms-house, cheek-by-jowl with the vagabonds, cunning-woman, beggars, and prostitutes they describe.[24] The *sowizdrzał* literature functioned, in part, as a kind of ethnography, displaying both a good folkloristic knowledge of popular practices and a critique of those practices, intermixed seamlessly with notions and models drawn from elite, western, or classical literature.

Many of the most popular *sowizdrzał* works featured demons, devils, and witches as central characters. The *Infernal Parliament*, which depicts an assembly of devils reporting to Lucifer concerning their work against the human race, must be considered one of the best-sellers of the seventeenth and eighteenth centuries in Poland; it went through at least twelve editions between *c.*1615 and 1807.[25] Other works in the genre with strong themes of witchcraft and demonology include the *Devil's Lawsuit*, depicting a lawsuit brought by Lucifer against Christ to win back his promised sovereignty over sinning human souls;[26] the already mentioned *Pilgrimage of the Hobos*, which recounts the adventures of several beggars, including some who self-identify as witches;[27] and the *Synod of the Under-clerks of the Podgórski Region*, depicting a gathering of church-organists, parish school-teachers, and other minor church functionaries who air their grievances against the superstitious practices of their parishioners.[28] Many of these works remained popular into the eighteenth century, by which time other forms of mass literature had arisen to supplement their depiction of the witch. As late as the 1750s, the Jesuit Benedykt Chmielowski in his popular encyclopaedia *The New Athens*, and the rector of the Zamoyski Academy Stanisław Duńczewski in his even more popular almanac *The Half-Century Calandar*, continued to disseminate by-then thoroughly outdated elite views of the witch-crime.[29]

---

[24] Augustyniak, *Koncepcje narodu*, 17, 23–4; Marian Surdocki, 'Pensjonariusze szpitali wielkopolskich w XVII i XVIII wieku', *Roczniki Humanistyczne KUL*, 37/2 (1990).

[25] *Seym Piekielny straszliwy, y Examen Xiążęcia piekielnego . . .* (Cracow: 1622). On its publication history, see Badecki, *Literatura mieszczańska w Polsce XVII w* (Lwów: Zakład Narodowy im. Ossolińskich, 1925). The *Sejm piekielny* was partly modeled on the moralizing 'devil-books' popular in Germany in the same period, but was more directly indebted to the *Postępek prawa czartowskiego* (*The Devil's Lawsuit*: see next note).

[26] *Postępek prawa czartowskiego przeciw narodowi ludzkiemu*, ed. Arthur Benis (Cracow: Wydawnictwo Akademii Umiejętności 1891 [1570]). First publ. at the press of the Calvinist humanist Cyprian Bazylik, who may also have been the author: unlike the other works discussed here, the *Lawsuit* was a sophisticated work of prose.

[27] *Peregrynacja dziadowska*. First publ. in 1614, authored by 'Januariusz Sowizrzalius'.

[28] *Synod Klechów Podgórskich*, in *Antologia literatury sowiźrzalskiej*, ed. Stanisław Grzeszczuk (Wrocław: Zakład Narodowy im. Ossolińskich, 1985 [1607]). As a rough measure of the popularity and availability of these works, one might note that the Lublin bookbinder Wawrzyniec Latowicki, at his death in the 1630s, left seventeen copies of the *Devil's Lawsuit*, eight of the *Synod of the Under-clerks*, six of the *Pilgrimage of the Hobos*, and one of the *Parliament of Hell* (Toruj, *Inwentarze ksiązek*, 47–60).

[29] Benedykt Chmielowski, *Nowe Ateny, albo Akademia Wszelkiej Sciencyi pełna*, 4 vols. (Lwów: Drukarnia JKMci Collegii Societatis Jesu, 1754–6); Stanisław Józef Duńczewski, *Kalendarz polski i*

The source of Polish attitudes toward witchcraft cannot be ascribed to any single book or author. Intellectual currents from the West certainly affected Polish elite attitudes, as shown in the work of Korczewski, by the mid-sixteenth century at the latest. For at least some among the learned, the witch had become in the sixteenth century something more than a cunning-woman or enchantress. The *sowizdrzalski* texts of the early seventeenth century depict a wide variety of witches, cunning-women, devils, and demons; moreover the popularity of this literature and its wide dissemination in oral form—in dramas at church feasts, for example—help explain the wide currency of such notions as the devil-pact in seventeenth-century Poland. At the same time, this literature often depicts peasant and plebeian practices for the purpose of satire or censure, and the depictions are accurate enough from what we know otherwise to suggest that *sowizdrzalski* texts both produced and reflected popular notions. In the long run, probably more important for the prosecution of trials were the legal theories of Carpzov and Damhouder, describing witchcraft as a *crimen exceptum*, a form of treason, and a crime that could be prosecuted under relaxed rules of judicial procedure because of its horrendous nature. Such judicial attitudes met, starting in the seventeenth century, with increasing popular fear of witches, and with an over-all increasing tendency of town courts to mete out harsh and exemplary justice for all crimes. By the early seventeenth century, witchcraft had become well established as a secular crime, tried in secular town courts, and punishable by the stake.

REFORM AND ABOLITION

Such an understanding of the crime of witchcraft did not, however, go uncontested. From the 1630s, Polish ecclesiastical writers began a campaign against secular witch-trials that was to continue through the eighteenth century. From around 1670, as witch-trials were approaching their peak, this clerical opposition to the abuses of witch-trials gained strength from a parallel effort, on the part of the Royal Assessory Court, to reform and rationalize the practice of small-town courts; however, neither attempt at reform made any difference to the practice of those courts before the late eighteenth century.

The Polish ecclesiastical opposition to witch-trials was part of the Europe-wide clerical worry that people were suffering in the courts; the sort of worry that led to works such as Spee's *Cautio criminalis*.[30] However, despite the sharp bite of its often wonderfully acerbic rhetoric, this opposition represented something more

---

ruski na rok pański 1759 (Zamość, 1759); see Bronislaw Baczko and Henryk Hinz (eds.), *Kalendarz półstuletni 1750 1800* (Warsaw: Państwowy Instytut Wydawniczy,1975), esp. pp. 55–6. Both authors combine local folklore with entirely derivative demonology borrowed largely from Del Rio.

[30] Clark, *Thinking with Demons*, 518; Friedrich von Spee, *Cautio criminalis, seu De processibus contra sagas liber* (Poznań: Albertus Regulus, 1647 [1632]).

than a disinterested protest against cruelty or ignorance. Church authors attacked secular cases against witchcraft, above all, because such cases ought to be tried in ecclesiastical courts—the primary conflict was over jurisdiction. Moreover, the arguments *against* secular witch-trials were also arguments *for* the ecclesiastical courts' right to try heretics—that is, Protestants—a right that had been weakened by the Sejm in a series of decisions through the mid-sixteenth century, and abrogated by the famous Confederation of Warsaw of 1573. The Catholic attack on witch-trials was, thus, also a Counter-Reformation attack on the religious freedoms that Protestant nobility (and, in practice, Protestant burghers) had enjoyed in the sixteenth and early seventeenth centuries.[31]

The first and fiercest condemnation of secular witch-trials was the anonymous *Witch Denounced* or *Czarownica powołana*, published in 1639 in Poznań (see Figure 2.2). Although the authorship of the *Witch Denounced* remains in dispute,[32] several of its motifs and some of its style point to a Jesuit author.[33] It is difficult to determine how widely the text was read; however it was reissued in 1680 and again in 1714, and was clearly read, at least, by other opponents of witch-trials, who repeat its themes well into the eighteenth century.

The jurisdictional focus of the *Witch Denounced* is apparent already in its preface, where the author draws on the *Constitutio* of 1543 to show argue that witchcraft falls under ecclesiastical court jurisdiction. The author of the *Witch* then draws his conclusion, depicting town-court magistrates as ignorant and lawless:

Therefore do not say, painted *Jurist*, that there is nothing in the Polish Law concerning Witches, how to judge them or proceed in their cases. There is nothing! because Secular Courts were excluded from such judgements . . . Read Herburt's entry under *Spiritualis*, or Januszewski on the Witch. And do not say, that customarily the Secular Office judges Witches, caring little for the Constitution of the plenary Sejm. *By what law?*[34]

---

[31] Tazbir, *State without Stakes*, remains the classic discussion of this development.

[32] Publ. in 1639 by Albertus Regulus, who also publ. an edn. of Spee's *Cautio criminalis* in 1647. Regulus had been a teacher at the Lubrański Academy in Poznań, where among his other pupils he taught Krzysztof Opaliński, whose *Satyry* (1650) later lampooned witchcraft beliefs in Poland. Koranyi has compared the *Czarownica* with Daniel Wisner's *Tractatus brevis de extramagis lamiis, veneficis* (also publ. by Regulus in 1639), arguing that, despite many similar concerns, the two works probably did not share authorship. Jan Sójka, 'Regulus Wojciech', in A. Kawecka-Gryczowa, K. Korotajowa, and J. Sójka (eds.), *Drukarze dawnej Polski od XV do XVIII wieku* (Wrocław: Zakład Narodowy im. Ossolińskich, 1977), 212–13; Karol Koranyi, 'Danielis Wisneri *Tractatus brevis de extramagis lamiis, veneficis* a *Czarownica powołana*: Szkic z dziejów polskiej literatury prawniczej', in K. Koranyi (ed.), *Pamiętnik 30-lecia pracy naukowej Przemysława Dąbkowskiego* (Lwów: Kółko Historyczno = Prawne Słuchaczów Uniwersytetu Jana Kazimierza, 1927).

[33] An anecdote in the *Czarownica* concerning a woman deceived by the devil into distrusting the Jesuits (qu. 13, p. 79), along with other references to the good works of the Jesuits, are so characteristic of contemporary Jesuit propaganda as to strongly suggest an author from that order see further Ostling, 'Accuser of Brothers'. On Polish Jesuit propagandistic anecdote, see the materials collected in Mariusz Kazańczuk, *Historie dziwne i straszliwe* (Chotomów: Verba, 1991).

[34] *Czarownica powołana*, 9–10.

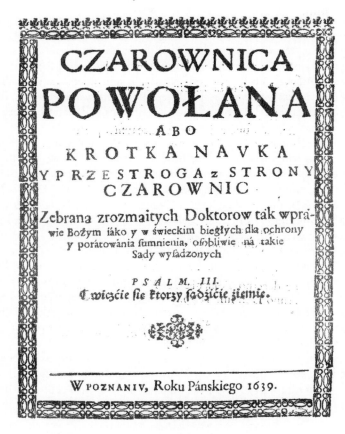

Figure 2.2. Opposition to secular witch-trials. Title-page of the anonymous *Czarownica powołana* (The Witch Denounced), Poznań 1639. Courtesy of the Polish National Library.

The argument is itself legally ignorant, or at best tendentious: the *Constitutio* was never ratified, was superseded by later Sejm decrees and by the Confederation of Warsaw, and in any case was never intended to regulate the legal jurisdiction of town courts. Nevertheless, following the *Witch Denounced*, a litany of ecclesiastical authors cited the *Constitutio* of 1543 to protest the lawless secular courts. In a widely reprinted pastoral letter of 1669, the bishop of Włocławek Kazimierz Florian Czartoryski explicitly recommended the *Witch Denounced*, along with Spee's *Cautio criminalis*, and reminded the secular courts that 'in the Statute of the Crown, A. D. 1543 the Law was established, that trials concerning Witches, and enchantments, belong to the Clerical office and to its judgements'.[35] The Franciscan provincial Serafin Gamalski, as well, cited the Constitution of 1543 to the effect that all trials concerning *noxias artes daemonorum* belong to the ecclesiastical court.[36]

Czartoryski's pastoral letter was reissued several times over the next several decades, was translated into Polish, and was usually appended to a text called the *Instructio circa judicia sagarum* (in Polish editions, *Instrukcya rzymska*, Roman Instruction)[37] which text enjoyed at least nine editions in Poland between 1670 and 1739.[38] Polish editions of this work did not advertise its origin—as an internal document of the Roman Inquisition setting forth that institution's 'cautious and mild approach to witch-trials'.[39] These textual salvos were followed, in the eighteenth century, by a series of pastoral letters and synodal decrees in nearly every diocese of the Commonwealth: Kraków (1711); Wilno (1717, 1744); Poznań (1720, 1738, 1739); Łuck (1722, 1726); Kamieniec (1724); Włocławek (1727); Płock (1733), Gniezno (1743), and Chełmno (1745).[40] In the north and northwest, where trials were especially numerous, the church hierarchy was correspondingly active in its resistance to these trials. In 1699, a successor to Czartoryski as bishop of Włocławek (a diocese encompassing Kujawy and part of Royal Prussia, both areas with numerous trials) Stanisław Dąbski promulgated an edict forbidding the torture of witches accused on the basis of gossip or denunciation. Dąbski's successor, Krzysztof Antoni Szembek, was particularly active combating witch-trials in his diocese: he threatened all accusers and magistrates who failed to bring accused witches to ecclesiastical courts with church censure.[41]

Due to Szembek's lobbying efforts, King August II promulgated a rescript in 1703 forbidding town and village courts in the Włocławek diocese from trying witchcraft cases without prior examination in an ecclesiastical court; the dioceses

---

[35] Kazimierz Florian Czartoryski, *Mandatum pastorale ad universum Clerum et populum Diocesis suae de cautelis in processu contra sagas adhibendis* (1705 [1669]), fos. 12, 22–22ᵛ.

[36] Gamalski, *Przestrogi Duchowne*, 10.

[37] *Instrukcya rzymska, abo postępek prawny, o sądach y processach, Iako maią bydź formowane, y wydawane przeciw Czarownicom.*

[38] The publishing history of this text is complex. The Latin text was published in Cracow in 1657 and again in 1670 and 1705; Poznań 1680; Gdańsk 1682, 1696; Wilno 1731; Lwów 1732. The Polish translation was published in 1688; twice again before 1705; in 1705 (Cracow); and 1739 (Poznań). It was often bundled with other works, as in the Cracow edn. of 1705, which includes the *Instructio* in Latin and Polish, Czartoryski's *Mandatum* in both languages, and a Latin 'Notandum' recommending Spee's *Cautio criminalis* and the *Czarownica powołana*.

[39] John Tedeschi, 'The Roman Inquisition and Witchcraft: An Early 17th-Century "Instruction" on Correct Trial Procedure', *Revue de l'Historie des Religions*, 200/2 (1983): quotation at 188.

[40] Henryk Karbownik, 'Management of Witchcraft Trials in the Light of Synod Resolutions and Bishops' Regulations in Pre-Partition Poland', *Review of Comparative Law*, 2 (1988), 68–71; M. Aleksandrowicz, 'Z badań nad dziejami religijności wiernych na przykładzie archidiakonatu gnieźnieńskiego w początku XVII wieku', *Roczniki Humanistyczne*, 24/2 (1976), 9; Wijaczka, 'Procesy o czary w Polsce', 41–2; *Kościół wobec czarów w Rzeczypospolitej w XVI–XVIII wieku* (Warsaw: Neriton, 2016).

[41] Wijaczka, 'Procesy o czary przed sądami miejskim', 82–4. Several of Szembek's personal interventions in specific trials are preserved in *Monumenta Historica Dioceseos Wladislaviensis*, 25 vols. (Włoclawek: Seminarii Dioecesani, 1881–1910), v (1885), 10–15, 59–68.

of Płock and Chełmno received similar rulings from King August III in 1727 and 1740, respectively.[42] These rescripts established extremely harsh penalties: a fine of 1,000 *złotych* for town magistrates who dared hear witch-trials, the death penalty for village judges.[43] And yet these rescripts applied only in the dioceses to which they had been granted; even within these dioceses, they were little enforced, and were almost entirely ignored.[44] And in the rare instances when ecclesiastical courts succeeded in disciplining town courts for witch-trials, the secular court did not always learn its lesson. The Gniezno consistory court levied heavy punishments against the tiny town of Kiszkowo for a witch-trial in 1716 marked by exceptional brutality—one of the accused died under torture. The executioner was publically flogged, while the town magistrates and noble plaintiffs endured public penance in the church over several successive Sundays.[45] Although this put an end to witch-trials in Kiszkowo for a generation or more, this very same court willingly took on the trial of the Gorzuchów witches four decades later—one of the largest witch-trials in Polish history (Kiszkowo 1761).

Beginning around 1670, the vestigial and ineffective Polish central judiciary began its own attempt to reform small-town courts, and in particular small-town witch-trials. The Royal Assessory Court, ostensibly an arbiter of conflicts between royal-town city councils and the local representative of the Crown, had by the mid-seventeenth century become, by default, the most usual court of appeal from the decisions of royal-town courts.[46] The Assessory Court was something of a jurisprudential curiosity. Its magistrates were drawn from the highly educated noble personnel of the Royal Chancellery, well-trained in the Polish Law which regulated civil and criminal order among the *szlachta*; but they were called upon to hear appellate cases from the town courts, which used Saxon Law intermixed with contemporary western legal theory. It was thus the only legal forum in which principles such as those enshrined in the *Constitutio* of 1543 could be applied to the separate tradition of town law.

---

[42] Karbownik, 'Management of Witchcraft Trials', 74; Zdrójkowski, '*Praktyka kryminalna*', 56; Wijaczka, 'Procesy o czary w Polsce', 22–3. Scholars often mistakenly date the Chełmno decree to 1745, but Józef Rafacz demonstrates that it was issued in 1740: 'Sprawy karne w sądach miejskich w epoce nowożytnej', *Kwartalnik Historyczny*, 47 (1933), 563.

[43] Jakub Sawicki (ed.), *Wybor tekstów źródłowych z historii państwa i prawa polskiego* (Warsaw: Polskie Wydawnictwo Naukowe, 1951–2), i/2. 243–4.

[44] I know of just two cases where secular court magistrates did request ecclesiastical expertise as required by the rescripts: the first case was dismissed, while in the second all four accused witches were nevertheless burned at the stake (Gdańsk 1731; Nowe 1747). When the ecclesiastical consistory court of Wocławek collaborated with a town court in a witch trial, this seems not to have mitigated the brutality of the proceedings: one of the accused died in prison, probably from the effects of torture (Inowrocław 1731).

[45] Wijaczka, 'Procesy o czary w Polsce', 34; Aleksandrowicz, 'Z badań', 10.

[46] Maria Woźniakowa, *Sąd Asesorski Koronny 1537–1795* (Warsaw: Naczelna Dyrekcja Archiwów Państwowych, 1990), 28; Pilaszek, 'Apelacje', 114. All of its archival records, some 546 vols. covering the period 1537–1794, were destroyed by the Nazis in 1944 (Woźniakowa, *Sąd Asesorski Koronny*, 1–15). Accordingly, all recent studies are based on scattered documents of various kinds, or on pre-war studies such as Rafacz, 'Sprawy karne'.

In 1668, the accused witch Anna Ofiarzyna appealed to the Assessory Court, which in its decision required the city court of Łęczyca to consult the higher court in all future witch-trials (Łęczyca 1668). Two more appellate decisions (Krzywin 1672; Kłodawa 1673) attempted to generalize this ruling; small-town courts were forbidden to judge cases concerning *crimen tam ratione sacrilegii, quam veneficiorum sive maleficiorum.*[47] Small-town courts could not hand down capital sentences in such cases, but must refer them to the more expert magistrates of larger towns. In the Kłodawa decision, which came too late to save five accused witches from the stake, the court scolded small-town magistrates for sloppy procedure: they should make their judgements 'not on the mere basis of accusation or denunciation, but rather by proof and sufficient evidence concerning the commission of the crime'.[48]

These appellate decisions, like the rescripts granted to the northern Polish dioceses, had almost no effect on small-town witch-trials. Almost eighty years after it had forbidden all small-town courts from trying witches, the Assessory Court had to reiterate its 1673 ruling in appellate decisions against Kowalewo (1749) and Przemyśl (1750).[49] Finally in 1768, the Assessory Court categorically forbade the deputation of town-court magistrates to villages, and required village-owners to bring *all* witch-cases before noble *gród* courts or to the Saxon Law courts of larger towns.[50] If enforced, this edict would have effectively ended village witch-trials—by the later eighteenth century, the magistrates of large towns were skeptical of witchcraft. But it was not enforced. In the absence of any mechanism for the oversight of small-town courts, and with no method for the enforcement of its ordinances, the Assessory Court could effectively intervene only in response to specific appeals. Moreover, as Pilaszek has argued, its authority over the courts of private towns—the majority of medium and small towns in Poland—was essentially non-existent.[51]

The Assessory Court could not prevent, for example, a mass witch-trial before the court of tiny Grabów—the famous trial fictionalized by an anonymous 'eyewitness' in the early nineteenth century (see the Introduction). However, as Tazbir and others have noted, what little we know about this trial derives from records of a quarrel between the townspeople of Grabów and one *pan* Przybyłowski, agent to the town's aristocratic leaseholder—a quarrel in which

---

[47] Rafacz, 'Sprawy karne', 562–4; Woźniakowa, *Sąd Asesorski Koronny,* 338–40. Karbownik and others have suggested that the Assessory Court decision of 1672 asserted ecclesiastical-court jurisdiction over witch-trials (Karbownik, 'Management of Witchcraft Trials', 72; Woźniakowa, *Sąd Asesorski Koronny,* 129; Zdrójkowski, '*Praktyka kryminalna',* 56). This seems unlikely, as the ordinance of the same court in 1673 made no mention of ecclesiastical courts.

[48] Woźniakowa, *Sąd Asesorski Koronny,* 338–40.

[49] Rafacz, 'Sprawy karne', 565. Cf. the similar ruling in Kowalewo 1749.

[50] *Volumina legum,* 10 vols. (Petersburg: Jozafat Ohryzko, 1859–60 [1732–82]), vii. 280.

[51] 'Apelacje', 122.

Przybyłowski took the witches' side. Disregarding the autonomy of Saxon-Law town courts, he had removed the Grabów *wójt* and jurymen from office, 'for the good of the town, since they, unskilled and having no education . . . ordered six women, alleged witches, to be burnt without sufficient proof'.[52] Assessory Court rulings could not prevent witch-trials; local noble officials could, and their attitudes were beginning to change.

By the mid-eighteenth century educated opinion had begun to sour on witch-trials. Appeals, protests, and interventions became more common. When *pan* Franciszek Łodziński accused an impoverished young noblewoman of gaining his son's affections through witchcraft, her case was appealed to the episcopal court in Kraków: this court not only dismissed all charges, but also required Łodziński to pay the accused witch an indemnity of 200 złotych. Similarly, when in 1768 the Lublin *wójt* Józef Kurowski slandered his would-be successor, spreading the rumor that 'His honor Mr. Kreps killed someone in the Krępiecki forest, and His Wife is involved in Witchcraft', the strategy backfired. Kurowski was compelled to retract his assertions, and to apologize for 'frivolously and inconsiderately' accusing his colleague.[53] In small towns too, accusations no longer stuck as they once had. A plaintiff in tiny Krzyżanowice found himself sentenced to church penance, public apology at the church door, and a fee of beeswax candles for the church, while the accused witch went free (Kryżanowice 1772).

By the latter part of the eighteenth century, all Polish elites—ecclesiastical, jurisprudential, intellectual, and noble, as well as the emerging bourgeoisie of the larger towns—were opposed to witch-trials. Participants in the late blooming Polish Enlightenment expressed their embarrassment that 'en Pologne on brûle les sorciers souvent sans aucune inquisition'.[54] And such Enlightenment voices were beginning to be heard in the halls of power—in the reforming Sejm and the new, centralized Permanent Council which, unlike the toothless Assessory Court, did have some chance of enforcing a ban on witch-trials. At the Sejm of 1776, King Stanisław August proposed a *constitutio* abolishing the judicial torture. Apparently quite spontaneously, the Castellan of Biecz Wojciech Kluszewski proposed an amendment, abolishing death sentences 'in cases of malefice and witchcraft'. The *constitutio* passed unanimously, without deliberation. It stated in part:

[52] Michalski, 'Jeszcze o konstytucji', 94. The ongoing debate over the Grabów trial can be traced through the following: Baranowski, *Procesy Czarownic*, 68; Tazbir, 'Z dziejów'; Baranowski, 'Posłowie', 429; Michalski, 'Jeszcze o konstytucji', 93–4; Joanna Tokarska-Bakir, '*Gans Andere*? Żyd jako czarownica i czarownica jako Żyd w Polskich i obcych źródłach etnograficznych, czyli jak czytać protokoły przesłuchań', *Res Publica Nowa*, 8 (2001); Tazbir, 'Liczenie'; *Cudzym piórem*. Tazbir notes, correctly to my mind, a marked unwillingness among some scholars to forego the sensationalism of the original 'eyewitness report'.

[53] APLublin, AMLublin sig. 184 (Consularia), fos. 34–6.

[54] M. A. Trotz, *Nouveau Dictionnaire François, Allemand et Polonais*, 1749; quoted after Pilaszek, *Procesy*, 68.

All Courts and magistrates are to conform themselves according to this same regulation in cases of malefice and witchcraft, in the verdicts for which, we forever abolish the penalty of death. And this whole decree applies as well to the Grand Duchy of Lithuania.[55]

This decree put an end to legal witch-trials in Poland. Andrzej Młodziejowski, Royal Chancellor of the Korona, ended the Sejm session with a speech expressing the Enlightenment condemnation of witch-*trials*, rather than witchcraft, as a scandal to educated society: 'At last these trials for witchcraft, with their horrible consequences disgraceful to the human race, will have no place in our nation.'[56]

Although witchcraft was no longer a capital crime in Poland, Poland had not much longer to be a country: the Sejm of 1776 already presided over a much-reduced Commonwealth as the encroaching Russian, Prussian, and Habsburg empires began to carve up the country. Soldan reports a trial near Poznań in 1793, during the legally confused and socially contentious period immediately following the Second Partition; the evidence for this trial is, however, scanty.[57] The 'enlightened despots' of the partitioning powers all had abolished the crime of witchcraft during the eighteenth century; and all favored far more centralized and rationalized judicial systems than had the loosely structured Noble Republic. Within these new and stricter legal contexts, witch-trials were no longer possible.

Nevertheless, courts continued to hear civil trials related to witchcraft— defamation suits, protestations, quarrels over the alleged ownership of milk-stealing demons, inquiries into attempts at forced dunking of alleged witches.[58] Belief in the witch and her powers remained largely undiminished through at least the nineteenth century. As recently as March 9, 2004, the Kraków district court required one Anna B. to apologize to Jerzy M., for having 'publicly attributed to him paranormal influence over the milk-production of cows'. That is to say, she accused him of bewitching her cattle to steal their milk.[59] The next chapter begins with such accusations and the suspicions from which they originate, and traces the steps leading, in the early modern period, from suspicion to the stake.

---

[55] *Volumina Legum*, viii. 882–3. For a detailed analysis of the statute and its historiography, see Jerzy Michalski, 'Problem *ius agratiandi* i kary śmierci w Polsce w latach siedemdziesiątych XVIII w', *Czasopismo Prawno Historyczne*, 10/2 (1958); cf. Michalski, 'Jeszcze o konstytucji'; Pilaszek, *Procesy*, 220–4.

[56] Quoted after Michalski, 'Jeszcze o konstytucji', 90.

[57] Wilhelm Gottlieb Soldan, *Gesschichte der Hexenprozesse*, ed. Max Bauer, 2nd edn. (Munich: Georg Müller, 1911 [1843]), 332; see also Wijaczka, 'Procesy o czary w Polsce', 56; for critique, see Pilaszek, *Procesy*, 296.

[58] Karol Koranyi, 'Czary w Polsce', in L. Sawicki (ed.), *Pamiętnik II zjazdu Słowiańskich Geografów i Etnografów odbytego w Polsce w roku 1927* (Cracow: Komitet organizacyjny II. Z.S.G. E, 1930); Jósef Rosenblatt, *Czarownica powołana* (Warsaw: Wydawnictwo S. Orgelbranda Synów, 1883), 63–4; Wijaczka, 'Procesy o czary w Polsce', 51–7; Pilaszek, *Procesy*, 326–30.

[59] 'Pierwszy od 300 lat w Polsce proces o czary', *Gazeta Wyborcza* (Mar. 10, 2004), 2.

3

A Winding Road to the Stake

Early western scholars of witchcraft envisioned a short and direct road from suspicion of witchcraft to death at the stake. A woman who fell under the slightest suspicion of dealings with the devil—anyone who was strange, or non-conformist, or who had been seen doing or saying something peculiar, or who had been in the wrong place at the wrong time, or associated with the wrong people, or who was unlucky enough to have been denounced by an accused witch under torture, or who had acquired, deservedly or not, the wrath or jealousy or spite of neighbors—would be accused as a witch. Such accused women were dunked; having floated they were sent to torture, where, broken at the rack, they confessed what the court expected to hear, perpetuating the witchcraze by denouncing a wide circle of neighbors, and went to the stake.

Such a narrative is misleading. It is part of a discourse tracing, in Poland, to ecclesiastical denunciations of the ignorance and excesses of secular courts; a discourse later taken up, ironically, by successive waves of Enlightenment, positivist, and Marxist critics of the fanatical Catholic Church. The depiction achieves literary eloquence, at the cost of historical nuance, by reversing the signs: magistrates, who ought to be wise, impartial, guardians of justice and order, become ignorant, venal, cruel, disseminators and executors of a bloodthirsty ideology. Witches, symbols of evil and disorder, perpetrators of the most ghastly crimes, heartless tormentors of innocent children, become themselves emblems of innocence. Feared for their supernatural power to harm, they are in fact helpless victims of the courts' very real power to torture and kill.

Despite the simplicity of this schema, and despite the various agendas to which it has been put, it bears saying that in some places, at some times, it approaches the truth. In the villages and small towns of northern and western Poland in the last decades of the seventeenth century, it did not take much to become suspected as a witch. Courts applied torture routinely, and the resulting death sentence was very nearly a foregone conclusion. In a place like Kleczew and its hinterland, where sixty-four persons were accused of witchcraft, fifty-nine sent to torture, and at least forty sent to the stake between 1682 and 1700, one really does find something approaching runaway witch-panic and an out-of-control, persecuting town court.[1] Yet even

---

[1] Wiślicz, 'Township of Kleczew'.

in the jurisdiction of the bloody Kleczew court, a woman such as Anastazja Kaczmarka could be denounced numerous times over two decades, before finally coming to trial and to the stake in 1700.[2] This example of a widely reputed witch surviving so long near the epicenter of the largest documented witch-hunt in Poland illustrates an important point: the road to the stake was neither straight, nor short, nor predetermined. It might be more accurately imagined as a twisting path with numerous forks—some leading away from execution. In this chapter we walk down that road, noting the various off-turns, and reviewing the process by which, despite these forks in the road, so many Polish women were judicially transformed from suspects to defendants to condemned and executed witches.

SUSPICION

Ever since Jadwiga Macowa came to Zofia Skrzyneczka's house asking for onions, Zofia's cows stopped giving milk, and her calves dried up and died. Accordingly, Zofia accused Jadwiga, ascribing 'guilt to nobody except to that same Jadwiga Macowa, and I ask for justice from her' (Nowy Wiśnicz 1688a; cf. Poznań 1610; Słajszewo 1695). This resembles the mechanism of 'charity refused' developed by Alan McFarlane and Keith Thomas to explain witchcraft in England, whereby witchcraft accusations resulted from an outward projection of the guilt engendered by refusing traditional demands for neighborly generosity.[3] However, no unconscious psychological mechanism need be proposed in the Polish case: the accuser herself, quite explicitly, located the occasion and motivation for bewitchment in these exchanges. Zofia was perfectly cognizant of having trespassed on neighborliness; the ensuing misfortune therefore had a clear and obvious source. In accusing Jadwiga as a witch, she recognized her own unsocial behavior, but asserted that the revenge taken had been radically disproportionate—an example, perhaps, of the 'unchecked passion' thought to be women's greatest fault.

In these and many other cases, a woman came under suspicion for having publicly cursed or threatened her accuser, who subsequently suffered misfortune, sickness, or the death of a family member. A trial before the Lublin court expresses this dynamic very clearly. During an argument over a right of way through a field, the young peasant Wojciech Koziełek told Regina Lewczykowa to 'go eat a devil'. She responded: 'eat him yourself, since you're younger'. A year later, when Wojciech suffered sudden pain and paralysis in his leg and fainting spells, he knew whom to blame (Lublin 1698; cf. Kalisz 1613; Warta 1678b). Early modern Poles recognized that malediction and curse were properly female modes of attack, and could even admire an eloquent curse: in the appropriate context, a woman's curse could be recognized as a legitimate form of violent

---

[2] Wiślicz, 'Township of Kleczew', 90.
[3] MacFarlane, *Witchcraft*, 174, 205–6; Thomas, *Decline of Magic*, 560–7.

expression.[4] Małgorzata Pilaszek has noted the structural parallelism between curses—verbal attacks with real consequences—and the similarly verbal, consequential accusations of witchcraft: both make use of violent words.[5]

Such cursing must have been very common. According to Jan Kazimierz Haur, Poland suffered from more cases of demon possession than any other Christian nation due to the 'constant cursing and unbridled malediction' of his countrymen.[6] Haur cannot have meant that every curse causes demon possession or bewitchment; nevertheless, he reflected contemporary sentiment in finding curses rather stronger than mere figures of speech. The target of a curse judged its power retrospectively, according to subsequent experiences. This is clear in the quarrel between Regina Lewczykowa and Wojciech Koziełek. As the court noted, the accuser had himself been 'the author of a threat and of improper words' when he told Regina to eat a devil. But she had suffered no misfortune from his words, while he had suffered from hers. The central question of the trial became, then, when is a curse just a curse, and when is it an act of witchcraft? Regina's sharp retort, telling him to 'eat a devil', became, for Wojciech, a real and effective curse and so an act of witchcraft retroactively, when he later experienced symptoms of witchcraft (Lublin 1698).

Cursing could take many forms, but the most common—telling a person to 'eat a devil'—suggests a connection between bewitchment and the ingestion of dangerous food.[7] Indeed, suspicion arose most frequently where victims correlated illness or misfortune to prior exchanges of foodstuffs. Agnieszka Draganka sent 'deviltry' into her victims in bread (Wyszogród 1701); Zofia Marchewka sent a devil hidden in a batch of cooked groats (Brześć Kujawski 1717); others bewitched through apples, cheese, chicken, parsnips, even crayfish (Warta 1685; Kleczew 1693; Wyszogród 1705; Nieszawa 1721a; Pyzdry 1740). One unfortunate victim of witchcraft believed himself to have imbibed 'forty infernal beings (*piekielnicy*) in a mug of beer' (Płońsk 1708c).[8] As with cursing, so with

---

[4] e.g. the 17th-cent. memoirist Jan Pasek put into the mouth of an elderly noblewoman sentiments he could not safely present as his own: 'Oh just God...show your justice today over our king, Jan Kazimierz. Let thunderbolts smite him from a clear sky, let the earth eat him up alive, let not the first bullet miss him!' At a lower social register, the anonymous author of the early 17th-cent. *Poverty and Dearth Leave Poland* depicts an old woman chasing away the titular personifications of misfortune with her sharp tongue: 'To the demons with you, infernal old hag.... Eat a devil, you whore!' Jan Chryzostom Pasek, *Tales of the Polish Baroque*, tr. Catherine S. Leach (Berkeley, Calif.: University of California Press, 1976), 180; *Nędza z Biedą z Polski idą*, in S. Grzeszczuk (ed.), *Antologia literatury sowiźrzalskiej* (Wrocław: Zakład Narodowy im. Ossolińskich, 1966 [*c*.1624]), 622–3.

[5] Pilaszek, *Procesy*, 57–61.

[6] Haur, *Skład Abo Skarbiec*, 456.

[7] e.g. a quarrel in the Lublin street *c*.1650, in which one woman told another to 'eat a hundred devils' (APLublin, AMLublin sig. 61 fo . 121); or a village tavern brawl where a customer 'fed the innkeeper devils, as many as four-hundred': Stanisław Grodziski (ed.), *Księgi sądowe wiejskie klucza jazowskiego 1663–1808* (Wrocław: Zakład Narodowy im. Ossolińskich,1967), item 281).

[8] Eating devils or demons could also turn victims into witches themselves (e.g. Kleczew 1688, 1691a; 1738; Łobżenica 1692; Skarszewy 1699a, 1699b; Nieszawa 1721a; cf. Wijaczka, 'Witch and Sorcerer-Hunts', 111–12). This motif seems particularly common in northern Poland.

gifts of food: they became means of bewitchment only if followed by misfortune. Thus Krystyna Danieleczka denounced a neighbor who had given her peas and turnips in exchange for some butter. Ever since, her work had gone to rack and ruin: her butter spoiled, and there were worms in her cottage cheese (Słomniki 1674a). Such food exchanges characterized village sociability, and especially the interactions between women, who would be seen as anti-social if they refused to share or turned down food given, but who opened themselves to charges of witchcraft if giving food to neighbors with whom they had quarreled. We see again how the gender of witch-accusation could be overdetermined: women exchanged gifts of food; women put themselves at constant risk of witchcraft accusation simply by being social.[9]

In cases such as those described above, the suspected witch need not have evinced any particularly 'witchlike' features: she need not have a reputation for cunning or knowledge of spells or anti-social tendencies. In other cases, however, witnesses and accusers based their suspicions on more concrete evidence, often gathered over many years but only crystallized into accusation after a misfortune befell the accuser.

One can find only loose hints of a pattern in the sorts of activity that could bring suspicion of witchcraft onto a woman. Some activities, such as gathering dew before dawn, were well-known techniques of witchcraft: the gathered dew brought prosperity to the witch, while removing fertility from the fields and cattle of the neighbor whose dew was stolen (e.g. Słomniki 1674a). Similarly, gathering herbs before dawn, especially on the symbolically significant borders between neighboring fields, could be part of milk-stealing magic (e.g. Chęciny 1665d). However, all women gathered herbs for folk medicine, often before dawn, so that such activity could often be legitimate (see Chapter 5). Less easily explainable activities included the collection manure from a neighbor's cow, or earth from a cow's hoof-prints, also as a means of milk-theft (e.g. Dobczyce 1687; Nowy Wiśnicz 1689a; Słomniki 1700).

Other suspected witches were found in the possession of suspicious magical objects, such as an Easter cake filled with manure (Chęciny 1665d) or dried snakes (Lublin 1643); or they were caught in the act of stealing such objects, including a live human baby (Bochnia 1679). Human remains stolen from the gallows had no possible legitimate purpose; their possession provided clear evidence of witchcraft (Poznań 1559; Kielce 1605; Lublin 1627; Kraków 1737). Stolen Eucharist hosts could be used for healing, but their theft was itself a blasphemous crime against God (see Chapters 6–7). But ownership of suspicious objects—herbs, candle-wax from the church, pots of strange ointment— usually emerged late in the process, sometimes as a result of a formal search of the accused witch's lodgings. Similarly, witnesses and accusers often alleged that an

---

[9] On food-sharing as ambivalent symbol, signifying both community and treachery, see D. W. Sabean, *Power in the Blood* (New York: CUP, 1985), 110.

accused witch had buried bones or other enchantments on their property to cause magical harm; however, although accusers did often find such buried objects, they rarely caught the witch burying them. Accusers and witnesses ascribed such material evidence to a particular accused witch *ex post facto*—material evidence rarely formed the basis for initial suspicion.

Women could also come under suspicion if they were witnessed at inappropriate times or in inappropriate states of undress. The maid Regina of Młotkowo aroused her peasant master's suspicion when he found her awake and fully dressed well after midnight (Łobżenica 1692). Regina Frąkowa confirmed the suspicions against her when she was seen running 'naked', in a nightshirt only, through her garden (Słomniki 1700). Regina Frąkowa admitted under torture that her naked ritual had been part of a magical procedure to get rid of fleas, but the motif also shows how reputation for witchcraft related to reputation more generally: a woman out at night, semi-clothed, was up to no good by definition.

Finally, activities of clearly malicious intent incited accusation. Another Lublin trial illustrates the aggression that could be expressed through seemingly mundane activities, the suspicion such aggression aroused, and strategies by which such suspicion could be allayed or deflected. In 1631 the Lublin townswoman *pani* Michałowa attempted a ritual bath in herb-infused water to heal her child of consumption. She sent a servant girl to pour the wash water out at the crossroads (thus sending the sickness into the wide world and away from the community) but the servant seems to have poured it out instead in a nearby street, transferring the purged disease onto others. When a neighbor complained that Michałowa's servant 'poured some sort of Witchcraft out in front of me', Michałowa 'grabbed the girl herself and began to punish her, saying "I didn't tell her to pour it out there, but out past the suburbs."' Michałowa explained herself before the court: 'By the will of *pan* Michał I went to *pani* Deczowska, who advised me to buy a shilling's worth of beef from a yearling cow, and to boil it with herbs in a new vessel, and wash the child in the water three times, and then pour out the water at the crossroads; she said she'd done the same for her own daughter. . . . I didn't do it for witchcraft, but out of need' (Lublin 1631).[10]

Pani Michałowa deflected what could have become a serious accusation in several ways: she ostentatiously punished her servant, in front of the accuser; she explained what her intentions had been and how they had gone awry; she admitted everything before the town council, noted that her own husband had approved of the action, and explained that she had learned of this procedure from another respected woman of the town, who had tried it herself with good results. She was at pains to make clear that she had no special knowledge, and that the key act of potential witchcraft—pouring out the sickness-bearing water in the city rather than outside the community—was unintended. Nevertheless,

---

[10] I would like to thank Magdalena Kowalska-Cichy for helping me understand aspects of this trial.

had the victim wished to lodge a formal complaint, or had *pani* Michałowa's reputation been worse than it seems to have been, or had she been less astute in justifying herself to the court, things could have ended very badly. Elżbieta Stepkowicowa of Nowy Sącz, similarly accused of pouring wash-water out near a neighbor's house, reacted with a defamation case against the accuser, demanding proof or an apology. The accuser did provide proof (or at least witnesses): despite the help of legal counsel, Stepkowicowa's defamation case quickly turned against her, and she was burnt at the stake (Nowy Sącz 1670).

Nearly any activity at all could lead to an accusation of witchcraft. However, even the most unusual or aggressive activities remained merely suspicious unless combined with inexplicable misfortune visited upon the accuser or his or her household. Women begged and borrowed every day; they picked herbs, performed rituals to protect their cattle from milk-magic, came home from the tavern late at night; they poured wash-water out at the crossroads or into running water; they threatened, and cajoled, and cursed their neighbors to the devil. For any such activity to become the proximate cause of an accusation of witchcraft, it had to co-occur with a number of other factors: sudden or inexplicable misfortune, a prior animosity between the accuser and accused, a long ambivalent reputation. Bringing formal accusations against a neighbor was a serious, expensive, and uncertain business, and such steps were not taken lightly. Even the most blatantly malevolent activity could be overlooked or discounted, perhaps warded off with a prayer or counter-magic, unless confirmed by subsequent misfortune. When Regina Skotarka approached a neighbor, plucked a leaf from a tree and chewed it, circled him once and went away quickly, declaring as she went 'you weren't a cripple, but now you will be', one can hardly ask for clearer evidence of intentional malefice. Yet even such an incident would probably have been deflected with a prayer or counter-curse, had not Regina's victim indeed gone lame and lost twenty goats to sudden illness within the space of a week (Kleczew 1690a).

Thus witchcraft accusation depended less on suspicious acts or reputation than on confirming subsequent misfortune. A person experiencing sudden misfortune looked around for likely agents, and if they had recently exchanged curses with a neighbor, or taken food, or seen the neighbor doing something strange, and if that neighbor already fulfilled some of the stereotyped attributes of a witch (most saliently by being of the appropriate gender), then an accusation was likely to follow. Most of the evidence against accused witches, including their various suspicious activities, appears not as part of the initial statement of accusation but as witness testimony. Accusation itself consisted primarily of a long, detailed list of misfortunes suffered by the accuser or their kin, while the rest of the evidence consisted of circumstantial indications that this or that specific woman, rather than some other, had caused the misfortune.

RITUALS OF ACCUSATION AND ATONEMENT

Suspicion of witchcraft could remain suspicion for many years. In towns, it could become the subject of public slanders and the resulting protestations of innocence which pepper town-court books throughout the early modern period, and which very rarely led to formal witch-trials. The informal accusations motivating such protestations of innocence were extremely common. They could range from simple insult to a more pointed admonition or accusation; it would not always be clear to the insulted person, or to the audience, to which purpose the insult was being used: and this ambiguity of insults, their deniability, is an important feature of such allegations. When a certain Łopatkowicowa exclaimed before the Nieszawa court in 1716, 'in this Town there's nobody honorable, only Whores and Witches' the court seems to have understood the rhetorical nature of her exclamation.[11] But elsewhere the insult could be more pointed, and demanded a response. When a woman yelled to her neighbor on a Lublin street 'you old hag, you witch!' the insulted woman 'took off her wooden shoe and punched her in the gob' (Lublin 1640).[12] Małgorzata Pilaszek has analyzed such insults and the resulting defamation suits or protestations as strategies by which early modern Poles attacked, defended, and preserved their most valuable social capital, public honor.[13] This is indubitably correct, but it is also true that public, informal accusation could function to nip witchcraft in the bud. When *pani* Michałowa's neighbor publically accused her of 'pouring out witchcraft before me', she elicited the series of denials, explanations, and apologies by which Michałowa restored good relations, and thus removed the possibility of witchcraft. Informal accusation could work ritually, as a kind of counter-magic.

Such a ritual, counter-magical, and restorative function of accusation can be seen more clearly in village-court trials, which make no distinction between defamation cases and witch-trials proper. Since village courts functioned on a model of restorative justice, the court tended to focus not on who was wrong but on how to set things right. Sentences often consisted in fines against *both* parties and a warning of much more dire consequences should either side renew the conflict. Thus when one Kaśka and her mother-in-law Oryna accused each other of witchcraft, the Klimkówka village court fined Oryna for her suspected enchantments, but also fined Kaśka for having attacked her mother-in-law, and required her to apologize. If either were to raise the issue again, they would be fined heavily, and whipped: the court thus ritually removed the power of

---

[11] Pilaszek, 'Procesy czarownic w Polsce', 85.
[12] APLublin, AMLublin sig. 109 fo. 139ᵛ; quoted after Wiśniewska, *Świat płci żeńskiej*, 114, 284, 88.
[13] Pilaszek, 'Procesy czarownic w Polsce', 83–7.

witchcraft, enforced amity, and put both women on notice (Klimkówka 1697; cf. Klimkówka 1677a).[14]

Whereas town courts emphasized exemplary punitive justice, traditional village law nearly always attempted restoration of order, and restitution for harm done.[15] Thus when the *sołtys* of the village of Łoś complained to the Klimkówka village court concerning the witchcraft practiced by the wife of Łukacz Grylas, the court decreed that 'Łukaczka Grelaczka is to give her oath, that she has done no harm to anyone, and will do no harm' (Klimkówka 1618). The expurgatory oath cleared Łukaczka of guilt, but it also undid any witchcraft she may have actually practiced. Even more impressive is the collective ritual of accusation and expurgation that the Klimkówka village court facilitated for itself and nearby Kunkowa, during a season of dearth. In both villages, the entire community was accusing one another of 'great harm in the village, partly from witchcraft, partly from thievery, so that there is no profit from the cattle'. To restore order and goodwill, all male heads of household were to gather publicly, and publicly swear for themselves, their families, and their servants, that they engaged in no witchcraft and had no evidence that anyone else did (Klimkówka 1668). Here quite explicitly, the trial functioned as a communal rite of expurgation and atonement. Less spectacularly, most other village-court trials attempted reconciliation and restoration of good relations through oaths of expurgation, public apology, and small fines of money or beeswax to the church. Of fifty-three village-court witch-trials between 1529 and 1766, just nine involved corporal punishment (whipping), and three carried sentences of banishment from the village.[16] The overwhelming focus of village witch-trials remained consistently to restore order and amity; oaths and apologies before the court functioned as rituals of social atonement.

One village case provides us, however, with an indication of how village courts may have dealt with recidivism, and how a persistent reputation for witchcraft might eventually have led village leaders to seek more permanent redress against suspected witches. Kaśka, widow to Danko, accused Olena Baniaska of witchcraft. At some previous time, Danko had stood warrant for Olena, taking his oath that she was not a witch. He died the next week. Moreover, the accused 'walked

---

[14] Łysiak, *Księga sądowa*, item 1092. Concerning defamation proceedings in village law, including public accusations of witchcraft, see Michał Staszków, 'Sprawy o "zabranie sławy" w sądownictwie wiejskim Małopolski XV XVIII wieku', *Lud*, 46 (1960); and Ryszard Łaszewski, 'Przestępstwo preciwko religii i dobrym obyczajom w prawie wiejskim Rzeczypospolitej szlacheckiej', in E. Borkowska-Bagieńska and H. Olszewski (eds.), *Historia prawa, historia pultury* (Poznań: Printer, 1994).

[15] My analysis of witch-trials in village courts is based primarily on the records of several villages in the area to the south and east of Kraków (Iwkowa, Jadowniki, Klimkówka, Łącko, Wara, and Zawada), all publ. in the series *Starodawne Prawa Polskiego Pomniki*. I have also treated as "village courts" some other rural courts (e.g. Ekonomia samborska, in Ruthenia, and Starogród, in Royal Prussia); despite some peculiarities of legal tradition, these court operated very much like village courts *sensu strictu*. On village-court witch-trials, see esp. Wiślicz, 'Czary przed sądami wiejskimi w Polsce XVI XVIII wieku', *Czasopismo Prawno Historyczne*, 49/1–2 (1997).

[16] Wiślicz, 'Czary przed sądami wiejskimi', 62.

among other peoples' fields during the holiday, at dawn, providing the credible impression of witchcraft'. The court assessed a heavy fine, but also warned that, should Olena provide any future occasion for suspicion, 'she will be sentenced to death as a manifest witch' (Klimkówka 1702c). Such a threat of execution in case of renewed suspicion was typical of town-court acquittals. In the village-court context, where capital sentences could not be imposed, this sentence carried a different meaning: should Olena reoffend, the village court would request of their manor-lord that her case be sent on to a town court for fuller investigation. Ominously, the court assumes that the result of such an investigation will be death.

With some exceptions, peasant and noble accusers seem to have collaborated closely in the effort to rid the community of a threat to its social harmony and economic productivity. Considering that a majority of accused witches were peasants, while a majority of trials took place before town courts which held no jurisdiction over peasants, such cooperation was necessary for capital witch-trials to occur at all. When the semi-ritualistic village-court sanctions failed to deal with a suspected witch, her master permitted, facilitated, and usually paid for her trial before a town court.

However, before this final formal step, the accused was likely to undergo the ordeal by water—the infamous 'swimming' or 'dunking' of witches (in Polish, *pławienie*). The basic procedure of dunking can be described briefly, from a fascinating trial brought to light by Jacek Wijaczka. Five accused witches were dunked at their own request. They all floated, but complained that this was the executioner's fault: in the words of one of the accused, he had 'pulled on the rope'.[17] The owner of Łobżenica devised a test to counter such complaints: he ordered the executioner to tie the hands and feet of an innocent boy and girl, to see if they would float as well. If they sank, they were to be dragged out quickly, and given vodka against the chills. They did float, as did several other children tested in the same way: nevertheless, the Łobżenica witches were brought to torture, confessed, and four were sent to the stake Łobżenica 1692; cf. Dobczyce 1689). Despite this bloody outcome, both accused witches and their accusers continued to see in the water ordeal a means by which witchcraft or innocence could be proved, avoiding the expense of a trial. Sometimes, as in Łobżenica, suspected witches themselves requested to be dunked as a means of clearing their names and restoring honor (Łobżenica 1692; cf. Kowalewo 1647; Zbąszyń 1681 Wągrowiec 1717, 1738, 1741).[18] More often, dunking belonged to the pre-trial and semi-formal procedures of witchcraft accusation. It was not part of accepted legal procedure, and indeed was repeatedly and emphatically condemned by the

---

[17] In an earlier trial in the same town, the accused complained that the executioner 'didn't let loose the rope, and held them up, and kept them up in the water with his staff' (Łobżenica 1690b). For similar complaints, cf. Chęciny 1665a; Lublin 1700.

[18] This strategy sometimes worked, as in an early trial in Kleczew (1625b), where the court dismissed Anna Buszkowska after she sunk during the water ordeal. Nevertheless, suspected witches would not undergo this procedure lightly: a suspected witch died immediately after dunking, suggesting that the experience could be quite violent (Wągrowiec 1738).

higher courts as a practice derived not from law but *'diabolica suggestione'* (Pilica (appeal: Kraków 1645)).[19] Nevertheless, it should be noted that small-town courts accepted the evidence of dunking as grounds for bringing an accused witch to torture or the stake (e.g. Słomniki 1674a).[20]

Informal gossip, public slander with its attendant denials or apologies, village-court oaths of expurgation, or the water ordeal all offered alternatives to the formal witch-trial before a town court. In villages, if suspicion of witchcraft became serious enough to bring to the attention of the manor-lord, he could, without involving town courts or a formal trial of any kind, banish his subject or impose minor punishments such as whipping. He could also refrain from pursuing the case, leaving the peasantry to make do with counter-magic and informal sanctions. However, insofar as we now have any record of the matter at all, this is nearly always because the manor-lord took the problem sufficiently seriously to bring the suspected witch to trial with a formal accusation before a Saxon-Law town court.

BEFORE THE COURT

Throughout the period of the witch-trials, Polish Saxon-Law town courts displayed a curious mixture of accusatory and inquisitorial law. Despite the considerable influence of the Roman-Law inquisitorial model, as disseminated in the works of Groicki, Damhouder, and Carpzov, witchcraft cases continued to be treated as private or civil suits. Once initiated, criminal cases were often investigated and prosecuted by the magistrates of the court or by the court-appointed *instigator*; but with few exceptions they required a private accusation by a private citizen in order to commence.

Such private accusation began when a person appeared before the court and made a formal, accusatory oath, outlining the suspect's crimes. The oath of the peasant Stanisław Gałek, acting in the name of his manor-lord *pan* Tomasz Milewski, may be taken as a model:

I Stanisław swear to the Omnipotent God, one in Holy Trinity, that, not out of hatred, or rancor, or spite, or wrath, and not having been persuaded, nor paid nor hired [to make

---

[19] Ecclesiastical polemics against secular witch-trials also consistently condemned dunking: *Czarownica powołana*, 51–7; Czartoryski, *Mandatum*, fo. 22; and at greatest length Józef Jędrzej Załuski, *Objaśnienie błędami zabobonów zarażonych, oraz opisanie niegodziwości, która pochodzi z sądzenia przez próbę pławienia w wodzie mniejmanych czarownic* (Berdychów: Drukarnia WW. OO. Karmelitów Bosych, 1766). Despite these repeated and emphatic condemnations, dunking continued to be practiced well into the 18th cent., esp., as in the Middle Ages, as a communal ritual to end drought or disease. See Russell Zguta, 'The Ordeal by Water (Swimming of Witches) in the East Slavic World', *Slavic Review*, 36/2 (1977), 222–9; Baczko and Hinz, *Kalendarz półstuletni 1750 1800*, 55–6; Karłowicz, 'Czary i czarownice', 219; Rosenblatt, *Czarownica powołana*, 63–4; cf. Jadowniki 1698b). Such collective dunkings illustrate the deep and persistent Slavic notion that women are responsible for the proper circulation of the moisture upon which the fertility of fields, cattle, and humans all depend.

[20] In at least one trial, dunking formed the *only* evidence against an executed witch (Kleczew 1670b).

this accusation], but because of the facts and the truth, I [accuse] the accused Anna and Zofia, and swear that they are true witches. They attacked the health of our manor Lord and Lady, they wounded them, poisoned them and caused them so much harm, spoiling their cattle with witchcraft, for which there is evidence. If I have sworn falsely, I call God's vengeance and terrible Judgment upon myself, that the Lord God might punish my soul, and my body, and my property, and damn me forever. (Nieszawa 1721a; cf. the nearly identical oath in Pyzdry 1699)

Such an oath is at once an accusation, a presentation of evidence or testimony, and a form of evidence itself. For a judicial system in which oaths of expurgation could take the place of sentencing, and where oaths of warranty could, albeit rarely in witchcraft cases, suffice to free an accused criminal, the accusatory oath must be counted as, already in itself, initial evidence that honorable community members suspected the accused of witchcraft.

However, many accusers and witnesses seem to have gone out of their way to weaken the evidentiary force of such oaths. Satirists such as Krzysztof Opaliński could depict the Polish peasantry as bloody-minded and credulous, only too willing to make witchcraft accusations:

> When Spring comes, but there's no rain in May,
> The witches did it. A steer dies, and a second
> Or some calves: blame the witches.[21]

In reality, Polish peasants and townspeople could be extremely reticent in their witchcraft accusations. Whatever they may have thought privately, or grumbled among friends or even shouted at the tavern, peasants faced with a formal oath of accusation, kneeling before a crucifix, tended to become extraordinarily circumspect in their accusations. At this formal stage, peasant accusers tended to hedge their assertions with endless qualifications, clarifications, and demurrals. When, for example, the Łobżenica court asked the village commune of Młotkowo for its collective opinion of the witches accused in that village (witches who, as we have seen, also floated when dunked), the village headman provided an answer that is a masterpiece of circumlocution:

We have nothing but nothing against these women, although indeed we have good reasons to accuse someone, but we don't know why such catastrophes have befallen us, whether from God or from evil people—what can we have to say against anybody, since we don't know ourselves, although we do wonder why cattle don't die anywhere nearby, only among us: we've been ruined by this. These women have never quarreled with us or threatened us, and we've never heard anything bad about them, or that they've been denounced for witchcraft. You won't find any accuser against them among us, we don't have any evidence against them either, except what Kotarski said about Regina. (Łobżenica 1692)

---

[21] Krzysztof Opaliński, *Satyry Albo Przestrogi do Naprawy Rządu Y Obyczajów w Polszcze należące* (Wrocław: Zakład Narodowy im. Ossolińskich, 1953 [1650]), 25; Satyra 3 vv. 62–4.

Individual witnesses could be just as reticent. Very nearly every witness in the trial of Regina Lewczykowa—both the witnesses for the plaintiff and for the defense—refused to say anything specific about her potential witchcraft, restricting themselves to such evasions as

I don't know about that, whether the accused Lewczykowa is supposed to have practiced witchcraft, although this year Jakub Gloch, who is here with us as a witness, complained to me that the servant girl of that same Lewczykowa milked his cow in the field, from which time that cow didn't want to give any more milk, so that he had to sell it; and I don't know about that, whether she is supposed to have bewitched this here Koziełek.

In the end, even her accuser confined himself to reporting the bare co-occurrence of her curse and his illness (Lublin 1698).

Such qualifications on the part of accusers and witnesses demonstrate how seriously they could take the act of swearing, and the sin of swearing falsely. Nuanced and qualified accusations also indicate the serious reservations accusers and witnesses could have concerning the guilt of a suspected witch, reservations which contributed to a general unwillingness to bring witchcraft accusations to court. However, they also indicate the degree, after formal accusations were lodged in court, to which accusers and their community depended on the magistrate not only to mete out justice but, perhaps more importantly, to determine the truth of the accusations through the witch's extracted confession. Witnesses could testify equivocally in part because they shared with magistrates a conviction that the true determination of guilt lay in torture, and in the accused witch's reaction to it. The truly innocent would withstand torture, while the guilty would confess. The first and most decisive fork in the road to the stake, therefore, lies here, in the decision of self-identified victims of witchcraft to bring their accusations to the court of law rather than to seek the many other possible forms of redress, such as asking the accused to heal the illnesses she had caused. After this decision had been made, accusers committed themselves to the witch's guilt, while also maintaining reservations in expectation that the court would succeed in confirming accusation through confession—as, so often, it did.

he majority of Polish witch-trials took place before the courts of small or medium-sized towns, presided over by a *wójt* (magistrate) who was expected to have some knowledge of the Saxon Law, and two or more jurymen chosen from among the respectable citizenry of the town. What were such courts like, and what sort of justice might be expected from them? The literature of legal reform, from Groicki through the *Witch Denounced* to the *Constitutio* of 1776, consistently depicted the magistrates of such courts as drunkards,[22] 'legal ignoramuses,'

---

[22] An 18th-cent. pamphlet asks 'What is witchcraft? Even sober judges can't guess/Who is a witch? Can vodka make that test?' *Wodka Zelixierem proprietatis Powtornie na poczesne dana…* (1729); cf. Groicki, *Porządek sądów*, 190. Both borrow the drunken-judge motif from Isa. 5: 20–3.

'analphabetic hillbillies', venal oafs.[23] This tradition of rhetorical disdain obscures the imperfect but functional reality; though small-town magistrates were poorly educated, they probably could make their way through Groicki's popular guides to the Saxon Law and to the *Carolina*. Recently, Marian Mikołajczyk has written positively of small-town judges' ability to take into account numerous factors and circumstances, and to shape their verdicts and sentences accordingly; and Pilaszek has shown that they did work hard to interpret the law faithfully and seek out the truth in criminal matters.[24] On the other hand, in the very numerous private towns but even in smaller royal towns, magistrates depended for their position on the goodwill of the town patriciate and local nobility, whose wishes could count for a great deal in witch-trials. When a local nobleman brought a suspected witch to a town court, or invited the court to his village to hear the case *in situ*, he had already decided that she was a witch. Rather often, town magistrates eagerly concurred.[25]

Despite a considerable literature on the history of Polish criminal law,[26] the judicial *practice* of Polish towns continues to be poorly understood. Zdrójkowski notes that towns lacked an established procedure of criminal law, and despite the standardizing influences of works such as Groicki's *Porządek* or Damhouder's *Praxis*, courts were free to develop their own local versions of the Saxon Law.[27] In addition, the relatively short terms of service for most *wójtowie* [magistrates] and *ławnicy* [jurymen], and the part-time, somewhat amateur nature of the work, ensured that even within a given town no strong tradition of practice could usually establish itself. In most courts the only really permanent employees were the scribe and, where such a functionary could be afforded, the executioner.

Under the accusatory model of jurisprudence, courts could not initiate trials on their own: a case had to be brought before the court by a private accuser or plaintiff. Only very rarely did courts initiate a trial themselves on the basis of *fama publica* (e.g. Chęciny 1665c; Rzeszów 1718; Kraków 1737). If a witch were caught *in flagrante delicto*, magistrates could bring charges against her without

---

[23] *Czarownica powołana*, qu. 7, p. 52; Gamalski, *Przestrogi Duchowne*, 12–12ᵛ; Krzysztof Antoni Szembek, 'Edictum ne judices saeculares audeant judicare sagas absque cognitione fori spiritualis', *Monumenta Historica Dioceseos Wladislaviensis*, 5(1885 [1727]); *Volumina Legum*, viii. 567; Sawicki, *Wybor tekstów źródłowych*, i/2. 244–5.

[24] Mikołajczyk, *Przestępstwo i kara*, 169; Malgorzata Pilaszek, 'W poszukiwaniu prawdy: O działalności sądów kryminalnych w Koronie XVI–XVIII w', *Pregląd Historyczyny*, 89/3 (1998).

[25] I discuss this issue in greater detail in Ch. 4.

[26] See e.g. Krystyna Bukowska, 'Proces w prawie miejskim', in J. Bardach, Z. Kaczmarczyk, and B. Leśnodorski (eds.), *Historia państwa i prawa Polski* (Warsaw: Polskie Wydawnictwo Naukowe, 1971 [1968]); Stanisław Płaza, *Historia prawa w Polsce na tle porównawczym*, 3 vols. (Kraków: Wydawnictwo Naukowe 'Księgarnia Akadamicka', 1997).

[27] Zdrójkowski, '*Praktyka kryminalna*', 14. Mikołajczyk's recent archival studies have underlined Zdrójkowski's point: on fundamental issues such as execution rates or the use of defense counsel, practices varied extremely between towns and over time within single towns. See Mikołajczyk, *Przestępstwo i kara*; 'Prawo oskarżonego do obrony w praktyce sądów miejskich w Polsce XVI–XVIII wieku', in Jerzy Malec and Wacław Uruszczak (eds.), *Ustrój i prawo w przeszłości dalszej i bliższej* (Kraków: Wydawnictwo Uniwersytetu Jagiellońskiego, 2001).

waiting for a private accusation; however, because of the occult nature of most witchcraft, such court-initiated trials occurred only where the accused did something rather obviously bad (e.g. Szadek in 1649a, where the accused publicly boiled a cheesecloth outside the church during Easter Mass; or Bochnia 1679, where the accused, two beggar-women, kidnapped an infant child). However, once initiated by a private accuser, witch-trials were usually taken over by the court, which appointed an instigator or, more commonly, prosecuted the trial itself. On her side, the accused witch could only rarely rely on the assistance of a defense attorney. Although those courts which assigned defense counsel routinely also provided counsel to accused witches (e.g. Biecz 1655; Nowy Sącz 1670; Kraków 1713, 1717a, 1737), in most smaller towns defense advocates were unknown, for those accused of any crime.[28] Inquisitorial practice, with its investigative magistrate, its court-initiated trials, and its rejection of the old model of private accusation, never took full hold in Polish town law, where an uneasy admixture of the old Magdeburg practice and the reforming tendencies coming from the West continued throughout the witch-trial period.[29]

SIDE-TRACKS: INTERCESSION AND APPEAL

After the formal accusation against an alleged witch, she was allowed to respond to the accusations in a *responsio*. Alternatively, the court first heard from witnesses, after which the accused responded to their allegations face to face, in a *confrontatio*. Although witness testimony and the accused's *responsio* or *confrontatio* were both, in theory, discrete episodes of the trial procedure, in practice they tended to blur into other episodes: witness testimony following immediately after the accusation could be, in effect, an extension of the accusation, while the defendant's response could segue unceremoniously into the initial *benevole* (that is, without torture) round of interrogation. Moreover, both could be skipped: some trials proceeded more or less directly to interrogation.

Very rarely, the testimony of witnesses sufficed for the dismissal of the accused. On the strength of two witnesses stating under oath that Katarzyna Stokowcowa knew nothing about witchcraft, the Chęciny court paroled her into the care of her husband, who staked his entire property as warranty of her innocence (Chęciny 1665c; cf. Wągrowiec 1578; Kleczew 1678a). The presence of eight witnesses testifying to Regina Lewczykowa's innocence contributed to the Lublin court's decision to free her on the strength of an expurgatory oath, without torture. One somewhat hostile witness's counterfactual argument may have seemed as

---

[28] Mikołajczyk, 'Prawo do obrony', 397–401.
[29] Uruszczak, 'Proces czarownicy'; Pilaszek, *Procesy*, 123; Mikołajczyk, 'Jak obronić'. Polish historians continue to dispute the degree to which criminal trials followed accusatory or inquisitorial models; what seems clear is that judicial practice was at least as various as are recent scholarly opinions about it.

compelling to the Lublin magistrates as it does to modern readers: Jan Wiącek testified that 'nobody complains of her concerning [witchcraft]; of course it happens that along with a neighbor I beat up her husband, and after all she didn't do anything to me!' (Lublin 1698). Courts could also dismiss the case where witness testimony was exceptionally weak or vague (Chęciny 1666).

However, by this stage torture was nearly inevitable for most accused witches who did not make a *benevole* confession (and they, too, were usually tortured). The example of Katarzyna Mrowczyna may stand for many others. Confronted with the testimony of the principal witnesses against her, Katarzyna denied all. Threatened with torture, she again denied all and 'in no manner nor in any thing wished to admit her wrath'. Warned that if she did not cooperate she would 'suffer, according to the law, what the law demands' she responded that 'she is innocent, and has no evil spirit with her'. Warned a third time of torture, she again declared her innocence, but added, 'however if the court knows that she is a witch, then the court is to do with her as they understand necessary and as they wish themselves' (Słajszewo 1695). The *confrontatio* moved smoothly from denial through initial interrogation, to the repeated threat of torture, and finally to its application.

Formally, and often in practice, the decision to send the accused to the torture chamber required an official ruling of the court.[30] At this point we find another juncture in the road to the stake: very rarely, and only in large towns, magistrates could deny the instigator's request for torture (Kraków 1713). Outsiders could also intercede, asking the court for clemency: in Kraków in the early eighteenth century, the Arch-Confraternity of the Lord's Passion interceded for, and gained the freedom of, two women accused of witchcraft (Kraków 1715, 1717b). In smaller towns, local dignitaries could intercede on the behalf of the accused. Just before three accused witches were handed over to the executioner at Skrzynno, for example, 'respectable people came forward to intercede strongly, particularly persons of the clergy and of the noble estate, requesting that this horrendous sentence might, out of the kindness of the court, be changed over into a milder sentence'. With the permission of the accuser, the court spared torture and probable death at the stake, but 'lest similar crimes should become widespread, in order to frighten others', the accused were publically flogged and then banished from a ten-mile radius of their former home (Skrzynno 1639).

It was also at this stage, after the initial interrogation but before the commencement of torture, that appeals could be sought and more rarely granted.[31] Where appeal was granted, this was almost always to the advantage of the accused. Not every appeal succeeded: Anna Markowa's complex case, involving

---

[30] Uruszczak, *Acta Maleficorum*, 10.

[31] Pilaszek, 'Apelacje', 114, 24–7. Without a standard enforced appellate procedure, appeals could go to any number of courts: to the Superior Court of the German Law in Kraków, to the Crown Assessory Court; to the Royal Tribunal at Lublin and thence through relegation to the Lublin town court; to the court of the nearest larger town; even to the noble *gród*-courts (e.g. Bydgoszcz 1638).

the spectral testimony of demons, was appealed from Biecz to the Kraków Castle Superior Court, which turned it over to the episcopal court. That court returned the case to the Biecz magistracy after review, ending in a death sentence for Markowa (Biecz (appeal: Kraków 1644)). But generally, unless accused witches spoiled their appellate case by running away (e.g. Radoszycze (appeal: Kraków 1638); Lublin 1660 (appeal: Lublin 1661)), higher courts handed down verdicts of acquittal, dismissal, or the weakest form of bet-hedging possible guilt: the oath of expurgation (e.g. Wschowa (appeal: Kraków 1601); Szadek (appeal: Kraków 1632); Pilica (appeal: Kraków 1645); Łęczyca 1668 (appeal to Assessory Court)). Appeal was a rare but important turn-off from the road to the stake; those who managed to take this fork in the road usually escaped serious punishment.

TORTURE

The great Renaissance legal reformer Bartłomiej Groicki, echoing the ancient Roman jurist Ulpian, cautioned that too much faith should not be put into confessions under torture: some hardened criminals will withstand any amount of pain without confessing, while others, including the innocent, will confess the most horrific crimes to avoid torture.[32] Despite this scruple, Groicki shared the opinion of nearly all early modern jurists that torture remained an essential procedure for the investigation of crime. As Edward Peters has shown, the judicial revolution of the early modern period set standards of evidence so extraordinarily high that, ironically, torture became the primary investigative tool for the rationalized magistracy. Raising the status of confession to 'the queen of proofs', while rejecting many other types of evidence as insufficient, untrustworthy, or circumstantial, the new theories of inquisitorial judicial procedure associated with the rediscovery of Roman Law made torture one of the main instruments of law.[33] In Poland, though inquisitorial procedure never fully replaced older models of accusatory justice, courts applied torture routinely in the investigation of capital offenses. The Nowy Wiśnicz court, for example, applied torture to *every* offender investigated for serious offenses between 1629 and 1665.[34] Larger towns tended to use torture more sparingly, though Kamler's estimate of 19 percent brought to torture in larger towns is probably too low.[35]

---

[32] Groicki, *Porządek sądów*, 191; cf. Ulpian, *Digest* 48.18.1.23; after Edward Peters, *Torture* (Philadelphia: University of Pennsylvania Press, 1996), 58. Compare the opinion of the Kraków appellate court, that 'under torture people sometimes confess to things they had never even thought of' (Kraków 1645; appeal of Pilica 1645).

[33] Peters, *Torture*.

[34] Uruszczak, *Acta Maleficorum*.

[35] Marcin Kamler, 'Rola tortur w polskim sądownictwie miejskim w drugiej połowie XVI i pierwszej połowie XVII w', *Kwartalnik Historyczny*, 95/3 (1988). Kamler's database of 2,462 accused criminals (excluding witches) from Kraków, Poznań, and Lublin includes a large number of trials for minor theft, skewing his results in the direction of leniency.

Witchcraft was a capital offense requiring the solid evidence of confession to reach a verdict. Accused witches were therefore usually tortured: of 361 accused for whom I have good data, 268 (74 percent) were sent to torture.

Large towns had a dedicated torture chamber, usually in the basement of the town hall. Smaller towns had no such separate chamber—indeed, they often enough had no town hall—and improvised a space in some other cellar or barn; as did those courts which traveled to villages to hear witchcraft cases on site. The town scribe, the *wójt* or magistrate, and at least one juryman had to be present during torture to ensure that it proceeded according to law. This law envisioned three sessions of 'pulling', and, if necessary, an additional three sessions exacerbated by fire—either red-hot iron or the flame of a candle, usually applied to the victim's side or behind the knees. Records are vague concerning the torture instrument, usually mentioning only a *palus torturarum*: this seems most usually to have meant the strappado, though a ladder or rack could also be used. Torture was administered *primo, secundo intensius, tertio intensime*; burning with fire followed the same order. The victim of torture testified both during the torture itself and immediately afterwards; formally though not always in practice, such testimony had to be confirmed *benevole* outside the torture chamber, before the full court, to be counted as valid.

I have found little evidence to support the claims of Baranowski and others that the torture and other humiliating practices visited upon accused witches were different in kind to what was standard practice in other criminal trials. Witches were not regularly shaven 'above and below'; nor were they stripped naked;[36] examination of the witch's body to search for the 'devil's mark' was almost unknown in Poland.[37] Accused witches do not seem usually to have been kept in barrels or stocks while in prison, still less during interrogation—although there is some scattered evidence for such a practice.[38] Despite demonological polemic,

---

[36] The oft-repeated claim that witches were stripped and shaven derives from the nobleman-priest Kitowicz's famous *Description of customs in the reign of August III*; he seems to have derived this assertion from the normative legal and demonological literature: *Opis obyczajów za panowania Augusta III*, ed. Maria Dernałowicz (Warsaw: Państwowy Instytut Wydawniczy, 1985 [1840–1]), 136. On Kitowicz's reliability as a source for torture, see Kamler, 'Rola tortur', 107. Demonological texts sometimes recommend the shaving of witches; although the practice was opposed by the *Instructio* of the Roman Inquisition (*Institoris, Malleus*, bk. 3, qu. 15; Del Rio, *Disquisitiones*, bk. 5, sect. 9; *Instrukcya rzymska*, 1705 fos. 6, 17ᵛ; Spee, *Cautio criminalis*, qu. 31; Groicki mentions the shaving of criminals (not witches) who resist torture (*Porządek sądów*, 196; after Damhouderius, *Praxis rerum*, cap. 37, sect. 22, p. 76). The accused witch Elżbieta Stepkowicowa, searched for a *signum diabolicum*, was found to have no pubic hair (Nowy Sącz 1670). Certainly this would have been noticed earlier in her trial had she been previously stripped bare, let alone shaven above and below!

[37] But see Nowy Sącz 1670; Nieszawa 1721a–b; Kleczew 1730.

[38] Baranowski has claimed that accused witches were usually kept in barrels to prevent their touching the ground or otherwise making use of their powers (Baranowski, *Procesy Czarownic*, 98–101). Several synodal decrees and pastoral letters from 1720 onwards decried throwing witches into stocks or barrels between sessions of questioning; the text of the Płock Synod suggested that this practice was standard: Karol Koranyi, 'Beczka czarownic', *Lud*, 27 (1928); Sawicki, *Wybor tekstów źródłowych*, i/1. 244. However, I know of just five cases, all quite late, and all but one in northern Poland: Konin 1674

and despite courts' self-understanding as semi-sacramental arenas where God's will became manifest, there is no evidence to suggest that witches were placed on a table anointed at its four corners with holy oil, their feet not allowed to touch the ground.[39] This is not to say, however, that the formal procedures of torture were always observed. The court of Łobżenica seems to have been particularly brutal: during her first round of torture, the accused witch Anna was hung for fifteen minutes, and burnt, in disregard for the process of the law. In the same trial, the destitute widow Barwa was first tortured 'lightly' on account of her age; but during her second session she was burnt with sulphur on her elbows, shoulders, breasts, and knees (Łobżenica 1692). Other courts may have been equally brutal but less meticulous in their record-keeping: at least five accused witches died during or immediately after torture ((Poznań 1567; Grudziądz 1568; Kłodawa 1673, Kleczew 1693; Czerniewo 1727; possibly Inowrocław 1731). One accused witch died from rough treatment during the water ordeal (Wągrowiec 1738), and at least two seem to have committed suicide in prison (Łódź 1652; Kłodawa 1673).

Accused witches could display extraordinary fortitude under torture. Anna, whose brutal first round of torture I have just described, declared: 'kill me, shoot me, I have nothing on my conscience'. She maintained her innocence for three more sessions of torture, and was eventually acquitted by the court, whereas all her co-accused were sent to the stake (Łobżenica 1692).[40] Paraszka Hłacholicha maintained her innocence through six sessions of torture, saying after the third: 'You can pull me apart into pieces; I don't know and won't say any more; I don't have any more to tell' (Lublin 1681).

Such declarations are something more than the anguished cries of the innocent. Paraszka Hłacholicha, declaring her intention and ability to withstand torture, was drawing on cultural assumptions about torture as ordeal, the pain of which 'God either gave or withheld the resolution to withstand according to the truth of the matter.'[41] Like dunking, which as we have seen was sometimes requested by the accused witches themselves, torture provided an opportunity to decisively prove one's innocence. When the Nowy Wiśnicz court sent Regina Smalcowa to torture despite her denial of any wrong-doing and the paucity of evidence against her, it remarked that this was 'so that the [torture] might make clear the evidence for the court, and also so that Smalcowa, if she is innocent, can clear herself'. In fact she withstood all six rounds of torture without confession, and was acquitted (Nowy Wiśnicz 1688c). In courts where the accused had some faith in the system, sharing

(an extra-judicial imprisonment); Nowe 1689, 1701f; Inowrocław 1731; Barcin 1735. One is left to wonder whether we are dealing with a standard practice passed over in silence in most court records or with an occasional practice, possibly restricted to the small towns of northern Poland.

[39] Baranowski, *Procesy Czarownic*, 101; after the *Malleus*, pt. 3, qu. 8; cf. a critique of such procedures in the *Czarownica powołana*, qu. 7, p. 53, here following Gratian's 12th-cent. *Decretum*. I have found no reference to such a practice in trial records.

[40] Despite her acquittal, her manor-lord banished her from the village.

[41] Clark, *Thinking with Demons*, 592; cf. Norman Cohn, *Europe's Inner Demons*, rev. edn. (Chicago: University of Chicago Press, 2000 [1993]), 233.

with their judges and tormentors a belief that the truly innocent would be able to withstand the pains of torture, some accused witches did withstand that pain and were acquitted (in addition to trials cited above, see Lublin 1644; Warta 1685; Nowe 1701d). Such a faith would have been misplaced before the bloody Kleczew court, which sent at least one accused witch to the stake despite her endurance of torture without confession (1672). Characteristically, accused witches in Kleczew tended to confess almost immediately.

Indeed, demonological theory provided a loophole through which the fortitude of innocence could appear as diabolical obstinacy. Witches were said to be unable to cry[42] or they made use of herbs and powders to dull the pain of torture.[43] Although the church strongly opposed such *indicia* from the early seventeenth century onward,[44] some Polish courts did treat a witch's apparent insensibility to torment as evidence against her (Grudziądz 1568; Nowy Wiśnicz 1688c; Muszyna 1678; Bochnia 1679; Szczerców 1716). Courts could attribute such insensibility to diabolical assistance, and when an accused witch finally broke, she confirmed this assumption. Agnieszka Rośmika had several devils hidden about her person, preventing her confession (Zbąszyń 1708); Dorota of Mruczyna had a devil hidden in her shirt (Fordon 1700); while Barbara Karczmarka's torture-resisting devil hid behind her left knee (Pyzdry 1732). However, when the Łobżenica court asked the accused witch Barwa how she withstood the pain of torture without crying, she answered against the court's demonological expectations: her resistance came from Jesus Christ, 'to whom she recommends her soul and to whom she prays, day and night in the prison' (Łobżenica 1692).

The centrality of torture to witch-trials cannot be overstated: in important respects, torture created the witch-trial era in Poland as elsewhere in Europe. Without torture there would still have been accusations of harmful magic, of milk-theft, of children and cattle stricken with illness, of healing magic gone wrong. There would also, most likely, have been judicial or popular execution of accused witches: as the English, colonial American, and many African examples show, there can be witch-trials without torture. But without torture, the primary accusations of malefice could not have been transformed, as they so often were, into the more nefarious confessions of diabolism and radical evil. Sigrid Brauner sums up the effect of torture on the creation and maintenance of the imagined witch: 'witches with the diabolical powers described in the trial records did not exist. Instead, they were created in a complex social process as those on trial were forced

---

[42] *Institoris*, pt. 3, qu. 15; Jean Bodin, *On the Demon Mania of Witches* (Toronto: Centre for Renaissance and Reformation Studies, 1995 [1580]), bk. 4, ch. 1.

[43] Carpzov, *Practicae novae*, pt. 3, qu. 125, no. 67. The Lithuanian Statutes of 1468, 1529, 1566, and 1588 bear witness to the conviction that criminals could withstand torture by means of special herbs; the earliest of these laws calls for the death penalty against such a 'zeljenin' or 'herbalist': Karol Koranyi, 'Czary w postępowaniu sądowym: Szkic prawno etnograficzny', *Lud*, 25 (1926), 16. Polish and Saxon law lacked these specific provisos of the Lithuanian statutes, although similar beliefs prevailed in the Crown lands: see e.g. APLublin, AMLublin sig. 48 fo. 816.

[44] *Instrukcya rzymska*, fo. [17v]; Gamalski, *Przestrogi Duchowne*, 13[v]; Koranyi, 'Danielis Wisneri', 138.

under interrogation and torture to assume the very identities of which they were accused.'[45] Witchcraft and witches were produced in the torture chamber. Through the mechanism of denunciation, they could also be multiplied.

DENUNCIATION

In accusation, free persons freely bring a complaint to the court, and may obligate themselves thereby to pay expenses or face fines should the complaint prove false or frivolous. In denunciation, an accused witch, bound to the implement of torture and under extreme duress, provides the names of other witches in the neighborhood. These differences in circumstance account largely for the difference in character. As we have seen, accusation tended to be cautious, circumspect, focused on specific allegations. By contrast, denunciations, in those trials where they occur, could be profligate and wild, radiating out along lines of resentment or envy to entangle ever greater numbers into the web of suspicion. This multiplicatory tendency made denunciation a central focus of critique in the anti-witch-trial polemics of the seventeenth and eighteenth centuries, starting with the *Witch Denounced* in 1639. While affirming the reality of witchcraft and the devil's ability to transport people through the air, the *Witch Denounced* author asserted that nevertheless the 'banquets, dances, obeisances to the devil, and other disgusting things unworthy of mention' reported by witches were usually dreams or fantasies created by the devil during sleep. On waking, such women told others about their fantastic flight and festivities:

For which reason, they cannot deny their mistaken fantasy, and indeed they testify together freely before the court, and denounce certain other acquaintences, whose [presence at the banquet] their mistaken fantasy, and the devil, that great enemy of humankind, impressed on them strongly as they slept. For which reason judges do not proceed very safely, when, on the basis of such bare testimony of witches, either given freely or tormented out of them during interrogation . . . they condemn them to death without any better evidence.[46]

Variations of this assertion entered the standard repertoire of those who opposed witch-trials. The anonymous author of *Wodka with Elixer* (an eighteenth-century temperance tract with asides on witchcraft and superstition) put the matter succinctly:

> One is put to torture, she denounces ten,
> And each of these denounces ten more yet again.[47]

Serafin Gamalski, giving a spin to the still-current Polish proverb 'where the devil fails, he sends a woman', suggested that Satan uses one real witch to multiply the

---

[45] Brauner, *Fearless Wives*, 10.

[46] *Czarownica powołana*, qu. 2, p. 31. This argument has, of course, an illustrious history, from the 10th-cent. *Canon episcopi* through Weyer's *De praestigiis daemonum*.

[47] *Wodka zelixierem*, quoted after Baranowski, *Procesy Czarownic*, 63; cf. Opaliński, *Satyry*, 25.

number of innocent women sent to the stake.[48] 'However, one should not so quickly put one's trust in the yapping of an old woman; and indeed one must believe, that such a one who has renounced the true God and the very essence of truth, and who has become a daughter of the father of lies, or a wife to the father of tricksters, will never tell the truth.'[49]

Modern scholars of Polish witchcraft have themselves put rather too much trust in the rhetoric of Gamalski and the *Witch Denounced*. Edward Potkowski has suggested that every accusation led to new accusations and that through the mechanism of denunciation 'a few to a dozen or more' came to be interrogated in each trial.[50] Such a statement is wildly inflationary. In fact, nearly two thirds of town-court witch-trials in Poland featured a single defendant, while slightly less than one third included from two to five accused witches. Large trials were extremely rare, and the largest known are also among the least bloody.[51]

This is not to say, however, that denunciation had no effect. Figure 3.1 charts the size of trials (number of accused per trial) over time, and shows that, although single-defendant trials remained the norm, larger trials became increasingly popular. This tendency toward larger trials is extremely modest: trials of six or more accused remained rare. But we see an important increase of trials involving two to five witches, and this is at least in part a result of denunciation under torture. (More speculatively, the sharp drop in trials with two or more accused after 1700 may point toward increased judicial skepticism concerning denunciation.)

Although legal and demonological texts looked on denunciation as a sufficient *indicium* for the initiation of legal proceeding,[52] the magistrates of many Polish town courts distrusted denunciation. I have found no instance, for example, of the Lublin court acting on the denunciations extracted by its own executioner. The Superior Court of the Kraków Castle, in several decisions, dismissed evidence from denunciation as deriving either from hatred or from the pains of torture (Wschowa (appeal: Kraków 1601); Sambor (appeal: Kraków 1638); Pilica (appeal: Kraków 1645))[53] Even smaller courts often declined to bring in women denounced under torture, though their reasons for so refraining might

---

[48] 'Gdźie sam diabeł niemoże, tam babę posyła.' On the history and variations of this proverb, see Julian Krzyżanowski, *Mądrej głowie dość dwie słowie. trzy centurie przysłów polskich*, 2 vols. (Warsaw: Państwowy Instytut Wydawniczy, 1958). The same proverb was familiar in the West, found in the works of Geiler von Kaysersberg, Erasmus, and Melanchton, among others: Brauner, *Fearless Wives*, 74–5.

[49] Gamalski, *Przestrogi Duchowne*, 15ᵛ–16.

[50] Edward Potkowski, *Czary i czarownice* (Warsaw: Książka i Wiedza, 1970), 250–2; cf. Baranowski, *Procesy Czarownic*, 88, 114.

[51] Seventeen women underwent the water ordeal in Jadowniki in 1698, but they all went free (in some cases paying a small fine) thanks to the intervention of the noble landlady of that village (Jadowniki 1698a, 1698b). Jan Tarło, palatine of Lublin, invited the Chęciny town court to a village that he owned to interrogate nineteen women; again, most were acquitted (Chęciny 1665d, and see Chapter 3 below). A trial in Szadek names twenty-two witches, but the defendant in this trial was their accuser, a cunningwoman who had identified the alleged witches using a magical divinatory belt (Szadek ca. 1649b).

[52] *Carolina*, art. 31; Carpzov, *Practicae novae*, pars IIIa, qu. 122, nos. 60–9; both after Uruszczak, 'Proces czarownicy', 200. Cf. Del Rio, *Disquisitiones*, bk. 5, sect. 3.

[53] See also Pilaszek's discussion of these same materials ('Apelacje', 115).

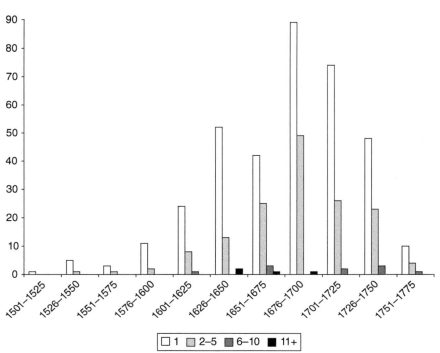

Figure 3.1. Trial size (number accused per trial).

often have been more practical than jurisprudential. If the denounced woman was enserfed to a neighboring nobleman, she could not be turned over to the court without his permission. More often than not, in such cases, the denounced woman's lord preferred to withhold his permission unless he or his own villagers already had strong reason to suspect her (I return to this issue in Chapter 4).

Although the denunciation of a single accomplice often resulted in her interrogation, large-scale denunciation very rarely resulted in large-scale arrests. Under torture before the court of Pyzdry, Anna Ratajka methodically listed at least twenty people from surrounding villages, remarking, perhaps sarcastically 'that these Witches are nearly everywhere' (Pyzdry 1699). The court brought to trial only three of the twenty denounced. This pattern holds in many other courts as well: if large-scale denunciation inflated the lists of suspected witches, it could also devalue any particular condemnation, as magistrates became skeptical of ever-expanding lists of witches.[54] This is true even in Kleczew, our only strong

---

[54] E.g. Poznań 1544a: seven denounced, none interrogated; Warta 1679b: twenty-five denounced, none interrogated; Nowy Sącz 1670: ten denounced, none interrogated; Lublin 1678: eleven denounced, none interrogated; Nieszawa 1721a: eight denounced, one interrogated; Pyzdry 1731: eighteen denounced, none interrogated either immediately or in the large trial before the same court the following year (Pyzdry 1732).

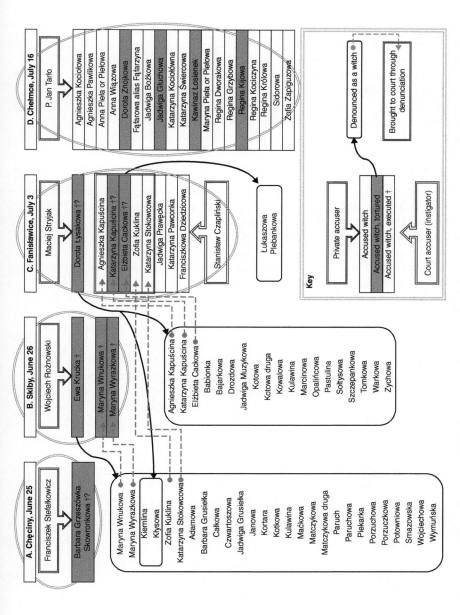

Figure 3.2. Accusations, denunciations, and executions, Chęciny 1665.

example of a witch-panic in Poland—a place where confessions under torture often devolved into a mere list of the names of accomplices seen at the Bald Mountain feast, and where denounced witches were quite likely to be brought immediately into trial or to be tried soon after (e.g. Kleczew 1680c, 1698, 1701). Nevertheless, at least three people were denounced for every one who stood trial before the Kleczew court, which tried sixty-two accused witches but recorded the denunciation of 224 suspects between 1682 and 1700.[55]

Figure 3.2 details an intensive cycle of trials before the court of Chęciny in central Małopolska over a period of three weeks, from June 25 to July 16, 1665. In this brief period, largely through the mechanism of denunciation, the Chęciny court-books came to include the names of some seventy-three women as possible witches. However, a close analysis of the trials shows that few of these women were ever formally accused or brought before the court; fewer still were tortured or sentenced as witches.

A. The first Chęciny trial is typical: a single private accuser accused a single woman of witchcraft. Barbara Grzeszówka was brought to court; was dunked; floated and was sent to torture. Her husband was also dunked (and also floated), and testified on her behalf. The records provide no verdict; in all probability the case was dismissed.

B. The next day, the Chęciny court visited the village of Skiby at the invitation of it leaseholder, *pan* Wojciech Gorzechowski. With his manor-lord's permission, the peasant Wojciech Rożnowski accused Ewa Krucka of maleficent milk-theft. During torture, Ewa denounced a total of twenty-six women and one man, from seven nearby villages and towns. Of these, the court immediately brought in just two for interrogation. Maryna Wyrazkowa and Maryna Wnukowa were tortured but denounced nobody; together with Ewa Krucka, they were burnt at the stake.

C. The next week, the Chęciny court visited the village of Fanisławice, where the peasant Maciej Stryjak accused Dorota Łysakowa, on the basis of her long reputation as a witch (despite this long reputation, she had not been denounced by Ewa Krucka). Dorota, before torture, denounced twenty-one women who had flown to Bald Mountain. Only two of these women (Kiemlina and Kłysowa, both of Małogoszcz) overlapped with the list of women denounced by Ewa Krucka, but despite this double denunciation, neither of the two were brought to trial. However, two others denounced by Dorota were brought to trial; one of these (Elżbieta Cackowa) herself denounces three women, of whom one (Agnieszka Kapuścina) had also been denounced by Dorota. Furthermore, the Chęciny instigator, apparently wishing to tie up some loose ends, brought in a further seven women for questioning: of these, two had been previously denounced by Ewa Krucka, two by Dorota Łysakowa, one (the aforementioned Agnieszka Kapuścina) by Dorota and by Elżbieta Cackowa; the other three had not previously been mentioned by anyone. No verdict is recorded, but Dorota,

---

[55] Wiślicz, 'Township of Kleczew', 78.

Elżbieta, and Katarzyna Kapuścina were all subjected to torture: it seems likely that all three were executed.

D. Possibly motivated by the large number of denunciations emerging from the previous two trials, the palatine of Lublin Jan Tarło seems to have decided to have all the women in the collection of villages he owned in the area, or at least all those in any way suspected of witchcraft, to be tried at once. However, none of these women had been denounced in the immediately previous trials. The Chęciny court moved to Chełmce, the central village of *pan* Tarło's local properties, and interrogated a total of nineteen women. Four of them were tortured, and a further two taken with the executioner to Chęciny for further questioning (there is however no further record of this questioning or of their eventual fate). However, quite obviously in deference to the will of *pan* Tarło, most were questioned without torture. In this quite extraordinary trial, which provides a great deal of insight concerning folk-healing and milk-protection practices, twelve accused witches were acquitted, four assessed fines in the range of 8–20 grzywne (364–960 grosze: these are heavy but not insuperable penalties); one was sentenced to thirty lashes. The fate of the two who went to Chęciny remains unknown, but it seems unlikely they were executed. Nobody was denounced.

In Chęciny, over the course of just two weeks if we exclude the anomalous trial in *pan* Tarło's properties, a total of some fifty-four women were accused or denounced. Of these, thirteen came to trial, six were interrogated under torture, and only three were definitely executed (although probably all six of those tortured were executed). Only seven women come before the court as a result of denunciation, and of these, at least two (but probably four) were sent to the stake. What appears at first sight to be a true witch-panic devolves, on inspection, into an intensive but ultimately quite small series of trials.[56]

The Chęciny case analyzed above should not suggest, however, that denunciation carried no consequences for the person denounced. Women denounced could find themselves 'admonished' without formally coming to trial: three girls denounced before the Płońsk court, for example, were made to witness the execution by burning of their denouncers; they were also given fifty lashes each, and swore oaths of expurgation (Płońsk 1701b). Moreover, a denounced woman could rarely free herself entirely of suspicion, and denunciations from years past could count as strong evidence in new trials (Kalisz 1616; Bydgoszcz 1638; Tuliszków 1684a; Słajszewo 1695). Conversely, accused witches could point to their never having been denounced as implicit evidence of their innocence, as did two accused witches during torture before the Łobżenica court (Łobżenica 1692).

---

[56] A similar pattern obtains in the series of four trials before the Nowy Wiśnicz court in Aug. and Sept. 1688. An initial private accusation against three women (a mother and her two daughters) resulted, over the next month, in the denunciation of thirty-three other women and three additional trials. However, just four of the denounced came to trial, and just two of these were sent to the stake (Nowy Wiśnicz 1688a–d). Again, denunciation simply did not result, usually or even often, in domino-trials or large-scale witch-hunts.

SENTENCE AND PUNISHMENT

We are nearing the end of the winding road to the stake; a very few potential forks in that road remain. After she had endured torture, after confessing, as she usually did, and, in formal law though not always in practice, after she had confirmed her confession 'freely' outside the torture chamber, an accused witch awaited the court's verdict and sentence. Although formally distinct, these two stages tend to blur together in court documents and, one suspects, in practice.

The distinction between verdict and sentence, always blurry, is least sharp in matters of acquittal. For the court to set an accused witch free did not necessarily imply that it had found her innocent of the charges. In his study of town-court punishments, Marian Mikołajczyk distinguishes between acquittal proper and the much more frequently encountered dismissal from the court or disinclination to levy a punishment because of unclear evidence, a good reputation, or the willingness of third parties to stand warrant for the accused.[57] There are few clear examples of a full acquittal in the records of Polish witch-trials. For example, though the Lublin court officially found Katarzyna Hutkowa and Anna Woytaszkowa innocent of magical use of the Eucharist, it still required them to witness the beheading of their co-accused, Maryna Białkowa (Lublin 1664). Courts could banish women acquitted of witchcraft (Łobżenica 1692; Kleczew 1729), or have them flogged, as a warning (Klimkówka 1682). Dismissal thus did not imply exoneration, but rather the inability of the court to find sufficient evidence for a verdict. Dismissed or acquitted witches did not cease to be suspect, and the fact of previous involvement in witch-trials could be used against them at a later time.

Although an accused witch could never fully remove the suspicions against her, she could mitigate them to a very large degree by making an oath of expurgation. Such oaths had featured prominently in the witch-trials before episcopal courts of the fifteenth and early sixteenth centuries,[58] and were standard in village-court trials right into the eighteenth century. Though much rarer in the capital cases before town courts, they were often prerequisite to dismissal from those courts: at least thirty-seven of the 132 accused witches dismissed or acquitted in town trials were required to make an expurgatory oath, as were many of those sentenced to penalties of flogging or banishment.

Such an oath served several functions simultaneously. Where, as was often the case, the accused had to find a number of respectable compurgators, these stood warranty for her and demonstrated that her community had not reached consensus concerning her guilt. Thus, for example, Barbara Drozdakiewiczowa cleared her name by finding six witnesses to swear that 'she is unable to harm anyone:

---

[57] Mikołajczyk, *Przestępstwo i kara*, 170–1.
[58] Adamczyk, 'Czary i magia', 198–209.

their health, their children, their profit, or anything else' (Płońsk 1708a; cf. Nowy Wiśnicz 1688c). Warranty of this kind, where it could be achieved, demonstrated that the community accepted the innocence of the accused, and that she could be reintegrated into society. Secondly, the oath of innocence restored right relations between the accuser and the accused or between the alleged witch and her supposed victim, assuring that the former would not perform any more malefice against the latter, and that he in turn would seek no further redress from her. As in village trials, the court sometimes required the accuser to listen to the oath publicly and thus publicly accept the alleged witch's declaration of innocence; accuser and accused must thereafter live in amity, leaving their formal quarrel in 'perpetual silence' (Sambor (appeal: Kraków 1638); cf. Bełżyce 1598b). Such a public avowal of innocence, proclaimed in church or before a crucifix, and accepted as legitimate by the court, had the character of a performative utterance. By the properly constituted declaration of innocence, the accused became innocent, legally and socially; while the accuser, in publicly hearing and accepting the oath, bound himself to accepting its contents.

A strong savor of the medieval ordeal remains in the expurgatory oaths of the witch-trials: they were not taken lightly, nor demanded frivolously. Some sense that such oaths were felt as an imposition can be gleaned from the Kraków court's appellate reversal of a lower court's verdict: they were to be set free, without even an oath required of them (Pilica (appeal: Kraków 1645)). Although an oath of expurgation could sometimes suffice to clear an accused witch's name (e.g. Kleczew 1662a), it was recognized that such oaths could be falsified by future acts of witchcraft. Paradoxically then, oaths of expurgation cleansed the accused of suspicion and imposed amnesty, but also set the conditions for future suspicion. A woman who committed witchcraft after having sworn denial proved herself utterly shameless and lacking fear of God. Indeed she proved herself to be a witch, and could expect no mercy from the courts. This is made explicit in the oath of Zofia Filipowicowa: 'And if I ever give voice to any word of threat, or if some harm should befall them, then I am without any mercy whatsoever to be punished by death, so help me Lord God and his Holy Passion' (Skrzynno 1639; cf. Bełżyce 1598b; Nowy Wiśnicz 1688c). Such oaths preemptively cleared the court of any procedural wrongdoing; should the accused prove recidivist, she could be punished immediately and without legal niceties.

About a quarter of accused witches escaped punishment through acquittal, dismissal, or expurgation.[59] Just 12 percent of those standing trial before town courts received non-capital sentences: the rest were executed, nearly always by burning at the stake (see Figure 3.3). Of non-capital sentences, the most frequent

---

[59] This and the following proportion are based on known sentences only, and may be too high.

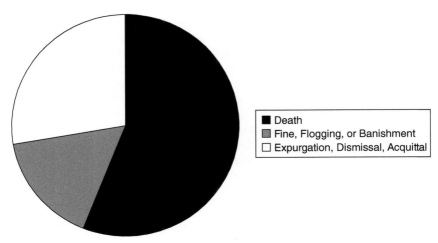

Figure 3.3. Penalties for the crime of witchcraft.

were flogging; banishment from the town or village; or, most usually, both of these together. The number of lashes is rarely recorded, but Regina Kociczana's punishment of thirty lashes may have been typical (Chęciny 1665d).[60] Out of clemency, flogging could be administered in private in the torture chamber (e.g. Lublin 1643), but more usually it was a public, shaming spectacle. Similarly, banishment usually included a shaming, ritual character.[61] Such a humiliating *wyświecenie*, in which the convict was paraded out of the town in a torchlight procession, was the most severe punishment a village court could mete out on its own authority. Haur recommends it, as an alternative to the death penalty, for infanticides,[62] and we find it applied also as an alternative or lightening of the death penalty in a very few witch-trials (e.g. Skrzynno 1639). Something of the force of this shaming punishment may be garnered from an insult recorded in the account of a public disturbance in Lublin in the 1650s: 'Shit-head, banished woman, they banished you from the city, whore, ass-wiggler, you were paraded from Kraków by torchlight, and you'll soon be kicked out of Lublin in the same way.'[63] Łaszkiewicz suggests that banished criminals often returned undetected to larger towns,[64] but this could only have been true of thieves or prostitutes

---

[60] According to Kamler, typical floggings for crimes such as minor theft ranged from ten to sixty lashes: 'Kary za przestępstwa pospolite w dużych miastach Polski w drugiej połowie XVI i pierwszej połowie XVII wieku', *Kwartalnik Historyczny*, 101/3 (1994), 27. Thus sentences of 150 or 200 lashes (Nowy Wiśnicz 1703; Wyszogród 1703) seem exceptionally severe: but such sentences may have been recorded precisely because they *were* exceptional.

[61] Hubert Łaszkiewicz, 'Kary wymierzone przez sąd miejski w Lublinie w drugiej połowie XVII wieku', *Czasopismo Prawno Historyczne*, 41/2 (1989), 141.

[62] Haur, *Skład Abo Skarbiec*, 238.

[63] APLublin, AMLublin sig. 107 fo. 445; cf. a similar insult from the 1730s, sig. 49 fo. 338.

[64] Łaszkiewicz, 'Kary wymierzone', 142.

enjoying a network of support in the criminal underworld; convicted witches would not likely be welcomed back by anyone. The future of a woman so banished must have been bleak indeed; with her reputation ruined, a stranger wherever she went, her options would in effect be restricted to prostitution or begging.

And so we come to the end of the line: death at the stake. In this chapter I have emphasized the many paths leading away from such a death in order to counteract outdated stereotypes of the fanatical, bloody witch-trial. And yet it can hardly be denied that, of those suspected women (and a few men) who were accused before town courts in Poland, the majority were executed, nearly always by burning at the stake.

Of the 783 accused witches before town courts upon which this study is based, 360, or about 48 percent were sentenced to death.[65] However, if one removes cases where the sentence is uncertain or unknown from these calculations, the rate of execution rises to 65 percent.[66] These can be treated as lower and upper limits to the execution rate in Poland. This is higher than the average of some 47 percent that Levack has proposed for Europe as a whole, excluding the Holy Roman Empire; and higher even than the rate of 50 percent or so proposed for the Empire itself.[67]

This rate of execution, shockingly high though it may seem to us, must be compared to the general rate of execution in early modern Poland, for other crimes. Mikołajczyk's recent work has shown that these rates varied quite strongly from town to town, but were high everywhere: from 65 percent in Miechów to over 90 percent in Żywiec (where, however, a majority of criminals tried were mountain bandits).[68] Moreover, even my higher calculated execution rate for witches remains lower than typical rates for other serious crimes in large towns: Kamler's major study of sentencing in Lublin, Kraków, and Poznań between 1550 and 1650 shows that witchcraft was punished more leniently than arson, banditry, bigamy, counterfeiting, church-robbery, infanticide, murder, and rape.[69] Though a very serious crime indeed in early modern Poland, witchcraft was not the worst thing a person could do.

A capital sentence for witchcraft nearly always meant burning at the stake, in conformance to the Saxon Law and pan-European norms. Out of 246 known capital sentences, just nine accused witches were beheaded out of clemency or

---

[65] I have included the few known cases of death during torture as executions.

[66] Pilaszek has calculated a considerably lower rate of execution: 558 executed out of 1,316 accused (42 percent). However, Pilaszek counts as 'witch-trials' various sorts of protestation of innocence or defamation suit that I have excluded from my calculation; this partially explains her lower calculated rate of execution.

[67] Brian Levack, *The Witch Hunt in Early Modern Europe*, 3rd edn. (London: Longman, 2006), 22.

[68] Mikołajczyk, *Przestępstwo i kara*, 186–8.

[69] Kamler, 'Kary za przestepstwa'. Kamler's study excluded witch-trials.

because they had cooperated fully with the court (see e.g. Nowy Wiśnicz 1659; Tylicz 1763; Bełżyce 1774), while eight died under torture, in prison, or as an effect of the water ordeal (e.g. Łódź 1652; Kłodawa 1673; Kleczew 1693; Wągrowiec 1738). Of those burnt at the stake, a few also had their punishment exacerbated, if that is possible, by additional punishments: in Rzeszów, Zofia Janowska's hand was cut off and nailed to the city gates, for having dared to touch the Body of Christ in the Eucharist; her accomplice Katarzyna Wróblowa who had encouraged the host theft, had her hands burnt with sulphur (Rzeszów 1718; cf. Nowy Wiśnicz 1643; Pyzdry 1699; Wyszogród 1705).

Court records go into no detail about this punishment, and the best efforts of later scholars are based on speculation.[70] Nevertheless, it is clear that burning at the stake had a more ritual function even than is usual of early modern punishments. The stake was reserved for certain types of criminal: sorcerers, poisoners, apostates, 'sodomites', counterfeiters, church-robbers, and arsonists.[71] With the exception of arson, these crimes are united by a motif of treachery or treason. Sodomites, according to conceptions of the time, betrayed the natural law; counterfeiters committed treachery against the very idea of a law-governed state; apostates and church-robbers betrayed the one true faith. This was also true of witches, but their association with poisoners reveals a different understanding: like poisoners, and unlike murderers or bandits, witches killed in secret and by stealth; they killed dishonorably, denying their victims even the right to a fair fight. Death at the stake was the worst and most shaming of capital sentences; it promised a foretaste of hell and seemed to imply, since the body was utterly destroyed and the ashes scattered, that the victim would not take part in the general resurrection of the flesh. Burning at the stake was usually specified to take place *na granice*—at the border of the village or town, a liminal space and significantly, the typical site of Bald Mountain or the witches' orgy. A woman could take her first steps down the road to the stake, as in some of our examples from the beginning of this chapter, by failing to pour out water imbued with illness or misfortune at the crossroads or beyond the suburbs or into running water. At the end of that road, she was herself burnt and scattered to the winds, evicted from a human society which had labeled her its enemy and the enemy of God. As the Nowy Wiśnicz court declared in its sentencing of Jadwiga Talarzyna: 'since she opposed God, and wishing to liken herself to Him, dared to fly through the air, and also caused harm to the property of poor people, therefore she is to be burnt alive at the border' (Nowy Wiśnicz 1688b).

---

[70] E.g. Marjan Wawrzeniecki, 'Przyczynek do procesów o czary', *Lud,* 24 (1926).
[71] Groicki, *Porządek sądów*, 199; Kamler, 'Kary za przestepstwa', 27.

4

Mechanisms of Justice

Our tour of the road from suspicion to the stake has demonstrated that this road was not always short or straight. A suspected witch was not always accused; an accused witch not always brought to trial; a defendant in a trial for witchcraft not always tortured. Nor did the tortured always confess, nor were those who confessed always convicted; finally, sentences were sometimes lessened or miti-gated or simply not carried out. None of these many exceptions should detract from our understanding of what was nevertheless the rule—after a trial for witchcraft was successfully initiated, it usually ended in death at the stake for the accused witch. However, these exceptions or side-roads do complicate that rule to a very considerable degree, and they require from us an appreciation for the particularities of individual trials. It remains to briefly set out some general conclusions. In this chapter, I will explore the following question: to what degree, and in what ways, did social and jurisprudential factors ameliorate or exacerbate the numbers of witch-trials in Poland? What factors tended to limit witch-trials, and what factors tended to increase them?

ACCUSATORY JURISPRUDENCE

Baranowski has suggested that the accusatory, private model of Polish Saxon Law would have strongly limited the number of trials in Poland.[1] Mindful that they could themselves be punished should the court find the accusations groundless, victims of witchcraft would refrain from bringing accusations to court unless they were convinced of the justice of their case. Norman Cohn has made a similar argument, suggesting that the medieval *lex talionis* effectively ruled out witch-trials, which do not appear until this system was replaced with the inquisitorial model.[2]

Both Cohn and Baranowski overstate the case. In Poland (as in the West) the inquisitorial model of jurisprudence never fully replaced older accusatory proce-dure. Most trials were initiated by a private accuser, and this did set important limits on the spread of trials. However, fear of reprisal or court fines could not have been a very important limiting factor, although it may have prevented

[1] Baranowski, *Procesy Czarownic*, 84.
[2] Cohn, *Europe's Inner Demons*, 215–17.

frivolous cases. With the exception of village trials, with their emphasis on restorative justice and on the reparation of good neighborly relations, such retaliative punishments were extremely rare. Some town cases at the hazy border between witch-trial and defamation suit could result in a fine levied against the accuser (e.g. Sambor (appeal: Kraków 1638)). More rarely still, a case deemed frivolous by the court could result in sanctions against the accuser. For having accused Anna Mizerka on the flimsy basis of another witch's denunciation, the Tuliszków court sentenced Stanisław Tyczka to pay a money fine and church penance (Tuliszków 1684b; cf. Kleczew 1689c); while the accusers of Regina Kuklikowa, failing to provide 'any lawful evidence' against her, were fined, sentenced to two weeks' imprisonment, and obligated to 'restore her good name among the community' (Łobżenica 1680 cf. Czwartek Lubelski 1637). However, by the seventeenth century, town law had moved so far in the direction of the inquisitorial model that the role and responsibility of the original plaintiff was everywhere substantially reduced. Right through to the end of the witch-trial period, town law remained 'private' at least in the important sense that law cases had to be initiated by a plaintiff; only very rarely, as in some of the later trials in the Nowy Wiśnicz cycle of 1688–9, do we find the court instigator accusing witches at his own initiative. As we have seen, this plaintiff-driven model of jurisprudence will have severely limited the number of trials; in particular, it meant that village witches had to attract the suspicion of their manor-lord or his representative before peasant accusations against them could receive an airing in town courts. Considering that the majority of accused witches were peasant women, while all capital witch-trials took place before town courts, this imposes a very strong limiting factor on witch-trials. However, as Uruszczak has suggested, by the seventeenth century Polish Saxon-Law jurisprudence had become 'mixed' to the extent that, once the trial commenced, the instigator or the magistrate largely took over responsibility for the investigation of the crime. Plaintiffs had little role to play after his or her initiating *propositio* or accusation; and their responsibility should the accused be found innocent was reduced correspondingly. Town courts would not be very eager, nor able, to levy punishment against the *szlachta* accusers of witches who had come under the court's jurisdiction only by the sufferance of those very accusers. A general distrust of the courts, as well as structural inaccessibility to them, must have limited accusations from peasants and the poorest of townsfolk, but the nobility and upstanding townsfolk who so often brought accusations against witches do not seem to have feared penalties if their accusations proved unjustified.

EXPENSE

Bringing in a trained and licenced executioner (without whom there could be no legal judicial torture, let alone the execution that so often followed) cost a great deal—perhaps as much as 40 *złotych*, or about the price of two steers, by the early eighteenth century.[3] Although in towns the executioner was a civil servant, paid out of city funds, accusers from outside the city had to bear his costs.[4] Maria Bogucka has suggested that consideration of this expense might have acted to discourage witch-trials in villages and in small towns, which usually did not maintain their own executioner.[5] Although small towns often made arrangements to borrow the executioner from larger municipalities when needed, they had to pay the costs of travel, at the very least (see e.g. Tuliszków 1684a–b).[6] Other small or medium-sized towns with torturers of their own had a tendency to become centers to which neighboring towns were in the habit of sending their capital cases, including witchcraft cases. The court of Nowy Wiśnicz heard cases from the towns of Bochnia, Lipnica, and Wojnicz, as well as the surrounding villages,[7] while at least part of the explanation for the large number of witch-trials in Kleczew has to do with the tendency of neighboring towns such as Kazimierz, Ślesin, and Wilczyn to send their witchcraft cases to the Kleczew court.[8] But in such cases as well, the referring town would be expected to bear the costs. Village and manor courts, of course, could not hear capital cases at all, and had to either send the accused to a town, paying for the trial and also for the accused's upkeep in prison, or bring the executioner and representatives of the court to their own village. Both options cost, and this must have provided a motivation for village or small-town courts to content themselves with the lesser punishments available to them without torture or an executioner—notably whipping and banishment. In all likelihood, a great many village suspects were dealt with in this way, without a formal trial even in the village court, and thus with no record.

Jakub Kazimierz Haur, for example, insists that manor-lords should bring serious criminals to town courts, where their crimes can be punished properly. For Haur such criminals include murderers, arsonists, bandits, thieves on a large scale, practitioners of incest, 'blatant adulterers', church robbers, counterfeiters, kidnappers, 'godless women who do away with their babies, [and] harmful and evident Witches'.[9] However, albeit such criminals should in principle be executed 'as an example for others', Haur acknowledged that this route might not always be in keeping either with the Christian virtue of mercy or with manorial interests in keeping costs down. Women guilty of infanticide, in particular, ought to be treated with mercy, and therefore only whipped out of the village by the entire village commune, and banished for life. In similar vein, adulterers

---

[3] Pilaszek, *Procesy*, 323.

[4] A well-worn anecdote relates that the Sandomierz city council refused the services of its executioner to a neighboring town, on the grounds that 'we maintain an executioner and gallows for the convenience of our own citizenry only': Ksawery Bronikowski, *Pamiętniki polskie* (Przemyśl: Adam Kaczuba, 1883), ii. 62.

[5] Bogucka, 'Law and Crime', 178.

[6] Hanna Zaremska, *Niezgodne rzemiosło* (1986), 24, 29–30.

[7] Uruszczak, *Acta Maleficorum*.

[8] Wiślicz, 'Township of Kleczew', 68.

[9] Haur, *Skład Abo Skarbiec*, 225; paraphrasing Groicki, *Artykuły prawa magdeburskiego*, 117.

may be handed over to town courts if the manor-lord wishes 'to pay for the Law', but whoever 'does not thirst for blood' ought to administer a milder punishment at the manor or village-court level.[10]

We have some fragmentary evidence that Haur's normative suggestions reflect actual practice. A small-town court in Ruś sentenced a young infanticidal mother to whipping and banishment, despite the town administrator's wish for a harsher sentence. As he explained in a letter to the town's owner, 'the townspeople here absolutely did not want to send for the executioner, or to pay for him'.[11] Similarly, in Nowy Wiśnicz the court chose not to execute a young townswoman accused of witchcraft and magical healing:

Considering the great evidence and testimony [against her], the accused Małgorzata deserves the punishment to fit her deeds. However the court has respect for her mother and kin, and for the cost to the town, as an executioner would have to be sent for, [therefore] the court puts off [such punishment] in this case; however she should sit in prison behind bars until Friday, and then should receive 150 strokes of the lash in the town-hall. And if later she is found to harm people's health . . . she will be punished not by the lash, but as those who do witchcraft are punished, by fire. (Nowy Wiśnicz 1703)

In this case, concern for the cost of execution forms just one of a complex group of motivations, including the reputation of the girl's mother and consideration of her age. It does not seem likely that cost considerations would usually have formed a significant factor in town trials once these were under way; however, in village cases, such considerations must have played an important and negative role in the decision to bring a case to town at all.

JUDICIAL DEPENDENCE

If considerations of cost probably reduced the total number of capital witch-trials in Poland, the same considerations will have tended to increase the execution rate for those cases that were brought to trial. Small towns, having paid to bring an executioner, will have expected him to produce results. This is even more the case for the common scenario of noblemen paying both the executioner and the *wójt* and jurymen from a nearby town to come to his village, stay as his guests, and try a women he had accused, or who had been accused by one of his serfs with his permission. Moreover, noblemen could, to a certain extent, choose which town court they preferred to hear their case, and would presumably attempt to bring in a magistrate and executioner whom they could count on to provide the preferred verdict.[12] Such pre-selection of a compliant court, together with the magistrate's

---

[10] Haur, *Skład Abo Skarbiec*, 237–8.

[11] Irena Grochowska, *Stanisław Antoni Szczuka* (Warsaw: Polskie Wydawnictwo Naukowe, 1989), 72.

[12] Baranowski, *Procesy Czarownic*, 78.

strong tendency, in a society structured by networks of patronage, to favor the manor-lord's side, had predictable effects on the course of justice.

Figure 4.1 contrasts those town trials that took place in the town court-house itself, with those trials which were thus 'deputed'—that is, wherein at the request and expense of a local nobleman, the court sent a few members, together with the executioner, out to a village for the trial. The Assessory Court decisions of 1673, and the belated decree of 1768 forbidding deputation to villages, were largely aimed against this system, for obvious reasons: a nobleman who paid for a local small-town court to come to his property expected, and often got, the verdicts and sentences he was looking for.

Analyzing only those trials for which the deputation status is clear, we get the following interesting results. Although there were fewer deputed trials (about 45 percent), they account for slightly more than half of the accused, and 61 percent of the executions. Confining our analysis to those trials for which the sentence is known, the execution rate for deputed trials was 70 percent, as compared with 59 percent in non-deputed trials. Clearly, magistrates and jurymen who stayed at the manor as a guest felt beholden to provide the verdicts desired by their hosts.

Wiślicz describes a particularly egregious example of the abuses to which deputation could lead. In 1691 the noble Zbierzchowski brothers invited the *wójt* and jurymen of the notorious Kleczew court to their village of Szyszynko, to

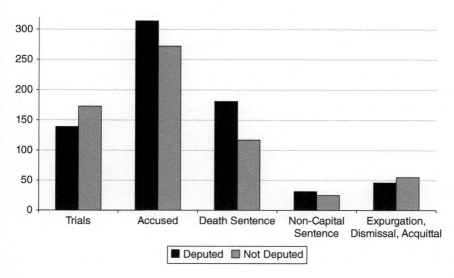

Figure 4.1. Effects of deputation on sentencing.

try Jadwiga Wieczorkowa and another woman who had bewitched the accusers'
mother. After the initial interrogation, the court dismissed the case for want of
evidence. However, the brothers 'demanded from the court that [the accused] be
put to torture, taking all responsibility for the sentence on Jadwiga Wieczorkowa'. Although Jadwiga confessed to nothing during torture, the court decreed
that 'the above-mentioned gentlemen takes all responsibility for [Wieczorkowa's]
fate before Our Lord Crucified and relieve the court of any responsibility'. She
was burnt at the stake in what Wiślicz rightly describes as a thinly disguised
legitimization of murder (Kleczew 1691a; cf. Kleczew 1670b, 1680b, 1690b,
1699; Wągrowiec 1725).[13]

Furthermore, small-town courts enjoyed far less independence from their
noble neighbors than did the courts of larger towns. Many small towns were
the private property of the *szlachta,* while even small royal towns could be treated
very nearly as the property of the local *starosta.*[14] In either case, local nobility
could bring strong pressure to bear on magistrates; insofar as such local nobles
were also the accusing parties in witch-trials, the magistrates would be inclined to
find the accused guilty. Despite the *de jure* independence of the magistracy,
which allowed, for example, the court of tiny Krościenko to dismiss a case against
a townswoman accused of witchcraft brought by the *starosta* of Czorsztyń
(Krościenko 1622), smaller town courts often acceded to local wishes. Unsurprisingly, and quite apart from the growing skepticism concerning witchcraft in
larger towns in the eighteenth century, Polish witch-trials tended to be a small-
town phenomenon.

Taken together, the data presented above suggest a similar situation, in
Poland, to the pattern recently outlined by Brian Levack for the witch-trials in
Scotland.[15] In contrast to Christina Larner's influential interpretation of witch-
trials as a tool of the centralizing state,[16] recent work has made plain that most
Scottish trials were run by local elites. Whereas the execution rate in the centrally
managed trials was something like 50 percent, it ran as high as 95 percent in the
more common locally run trials.[17] The nominal independence of town magistrates and jurymen, and their rights under Saxon Law, made the Polish courts

---

[13] Wiślicz, 'Społeczeństwo Kleczewa', 51; 'Township of Kleczew', 82.

[14] Some 88 percent of early modern Polish towns were small or medium-sized; about two-thirds
of towns in the same period were in private noble hands (Bogucka and Samsonowicz, *Dzieje miast,*
400; see also Maria Bogucka, 'Polish Towns between the Sixteenth and Eighteenth Centuries', in
J. K. Fedorowicz (ed.), *A Republic of Nobles* (Cambridge: CUP, 1982)). Although small towns were
usually private, there existed both small royal towns and quite large private towns (e.g. Rzeszów,
property of the magnatial Lubomirski family). After the drastic urban decline of the mid-17th-cent.
catastrophe, many once-important regional centers were reduced to the size of the smallest towns.

[15] Brian Levack, 'State-Building and Witch Hunting in Early Modern Europe', in D. Oldridge
(ed.), *The Witchcraft Reader* (New York: Routledge, 2002 [1996]); cf. Stuart Macdonald, 'Enemies
of God Revisited: Recent Publications on Scottish Witch-Hunting', *Scottish Economic and Social
History,* 23/2 (2003).

[16] Larner, *Enemies of God.*

[17] Levack, 'State-Building', 217.

importantly different from the Scottish commissions of justiciary; nevertheless the influence of local elites on these courts was considerable. We see this clearly, for example, in the totally different character and outcome of the trial at Chełmce to the other deputed trials of the Chęciny court in the same year (1665d; see Chapter 2). The sudden focus on superstition rather than malefice, and sentences of small fines rather than the stake, cannot be explained by a sudden change of heart among the Chęciny magistrates; rather, they responded to the wishes of the powerful nobleman Jan Tarło, whose serfs were the accused. Despite exceptions and qualifications, the nobility could and did use local small-town courts, especially deputed courts, as instruments of their own village administration.

CONFLICTING JURISDICTIONS

Most of those tried before small-town courts (and all cases before deputed courts) were enserfed peasants. Because the *szlachta* maintained almost proprietary rights over their peasant subjects, a serf could not stand accused before a town court without at least the tacit permission of her manor-lord. The appearance of class warfare discernible in some Polish witch-trials derives in part from this juridical situation: it is not that witches were especially prone to attacking their manor-lords, or that the *szlachta* were more superstitious, more keen to accuse than were the peasantry—it is just that, until the manor-lord came himself to suspect a woman of witchcraft, or came at least to take his subjects' suspicions seriously, there were few mechanisms by which she could come to trial. Village courts could and did try witches, not necessarily with the active participation of the manor, but absent the manor's agreement they could levy no punishment greater than a fine, penance, a flogging. Therefore, most peasant women accused of witchcraft before a town court may be assumed to have been suspected of witchcraft by their manor-lord or his representative, even in those many cases where the formal accuser was a fellow peasant. And, for the reasons already enumerated, a woman suspected or accused by the nobleman who had paid for the town court to travel to his village to try her was likely to be found guilty by that court. All this is to reiterate that the most crucial step on the road to the stake is the first one: once a community, or a nobleman, decided that a woman's reputation for witchcraft was sufficiently serious to warrant trial, they were committed to a procedure whose probable outcome they knew and hoped for. An accused witch, too often, was a witch condemned.

One corollary to this pattern is perhaps less obvious. The same factors which tended to increase the execution rate of accused witches in the countryside would simultaneously tend to limit the number of witches who came to trial, and the ability of trials to spread by denunciation. A nobleman could only bring to trial suspected witches under his own jurisdiction—his own serfs. Peasants could only successfully accuse women of their own village or its immediate vicinity, subjects of their own manor-lord. Because in the central areas of Poland noble patterns of land-tenure were characterized by small holdings of just a few villages or small towns, peasants must often have experienced themselves to be victims of malefice cast by a nearby neighbor belonging to a different feudal master. The sorts of quarrels and envies and tensions that led to witchcraft accusation knew no jurisdictional boundaries; and yet a woman just down the road, or a few fields over, would often belong to a different manor-lord. From the legal point of view, such a suspected neighbor might as well have been the citizen of a foreign country: unless the peasant victim could persuade her lord to persuade the suspect's lord to allow her to be brought to trial, nothing at all could come of such suspicions.

Indubitably, for the sake of neighborliness or because his subject's bad reputation reflected on his own, such a neighboring manor-lord must often enough have acceded to his neighbor's wish for a trial. Tomasz Wiślicz detects a 'class solidarity' among the nobility around Kleczew, who cooperated with each other, turning their subjects over to the court when denounced by the subjects of a neighbor.[18] Nevertheless, even in this witch-hunting area a determined persecutor like *pan* Wojciech Breza was able to bring thirteen women to trial, and ten to the stake, only because eight belonged to his own estate, while five belonged to an associate of his in Ślesin—none of the very numerous others who were denounced in this cycle of trials came before the court.[19] Elsewhere, neighboring manor-lords or leaseholders will have seen little reason to turn over their tenants for prosecution. Enserfed peasant subjects constituted a landowner's most valuable property. While he or she would be eager to rid their own villages of witches who had attacked the manor or other serfs, they need not always have agreed with neighbors that the problems on the neighbor's property could be traced to one of their subjects. Anna Markowa, a peasant woman whose successful appeal of a village-court conviction went first to the town court of Biecz and thence to the Superior Court in Kraków, was assigned a defense advocate who argued before the Biecz court that, as Markowa was the serf not of the noble plaintiff but of another noblewoman (who did not choose to agree that her subject was a witch), the court should have no jurisdiction over her (Biecz 1644).[20] More often, such jurisdictional quarrels would have prevented a trial from ever starting.

For a nobleman to accuse his neighbor's subjects of witchcraft could also be construed, by that noble neighbor, as an attack on his own property and honor. Manor-lords could go to considerable length to protect their subjects, although whether their motivations were economic, a matter of protecting their serfs as

---

[18] Tomasz Wiślicz, 'Religijność wiejska w Rzeczypospolitej szlacheckiej. Problemy i trzy przybliżenia', *Barok*, 11/2 (2004), 109.

[19] Wiślicz, 'Township of Kleczew', 75–6.

[20] Pilaszek, 'Apelacje', 115. In other criminal trials as well, defense counsel regularly argued that town courts had no jurisdiction over a serf accused without his feudal lord's consent (Mikołajczyk, 'Prawo do obrony', 407).

they would protect their other livestock, or rather a matter of preserving honor, it is difficult to say. Near Kalisz in the late seventeenth century, when the servants of one manor-lord attempted to capture a suspected witch from the neighboring lord's property, he and his servants protected her and beat up the party which had come to take her to court (Kalisz 1680).[21] Even after a trial had commenced a suspect's master could actively intervene. When Stanisław Zakrzewski, owner of part of village of Ćwiklina, accused two serfs belonging to the owners of the other half of the village, the witches' masters attempted to liberate them by force. During the night, the Ćwikliński brothers raided their neighbor's manor, and one of them fought his way into the chamber where the accused were being held. Barring the door behind him he said to the witches:

'Don't be afraid, because I have a stick and I won't let anyone get at you, and I have a knife to cut your ropes.' And sitting down with the witch, he would not allow the Court nor even the executioner to come in. (Płońsk 1699b)

Nevertheless, Zakrzewski seems to have had greater influence over the court, and the two witches were eventually burnt at the stake over their masters' protests.

Pilaszek notes that feudal lords not infrequently protested, via the noble *gród*-courts, against the verdicts of town courts which had sentenced their labor force to the stake. When the accused witch had practiced her malefice outside the holdings of her own master, he often chose not to believe the charges of witchcraft coming from neighboring nobility against his subjects.[22] Pilaszek has adduced two representative complaints to the *gród*-courts of Wielkopolska by noblemen unhappy with their neighbor's illegal prosecution of alleged witches under their jurisdiction. In one, Wojciech Kowalewski complained to the Poznań *gród*-court that the lord of a neighboring village refused to try his serf Helena Ratajka, known in the entire district (according to the plaintiff) as a witch (Poznań 1691). In the other, Dorota Żegocka, *starościna* of Konin, protested to the Konin *gród* that a leaseholder of one of her villages had put two women to torture as suspected witches despite her request that he put off such a trial in her husband's absence. The courts of all the neighboring towns declined to take the case, not wishing to fall out of the *starościna's* favor (Konin 1674). In both cases, jurisdictional conflicts between gentry worked to limit the possibility of a trial beginning.[23] Such conflicts would also severely limit the mechanism of denunciation. As we saw in Chapter 3, of a dozen or more women denounced by a witch under torture, often just one or two, or none at all, were brought to trial. In many such cases, I suspect, the others were subject to different manor-lords.

---

[21] Pilaszek, *Procesy*, 71–2, 259–61.
[22] Pilaszek, 'Apelacje', 132. In Lithuania, a considerable amount of the currently published 'witch-trial' material consists in fact of such noble protestations (Pilaszek, 'Litewskie procesy czarownic', 10).
[23] Pilaszek, 'Apelacje', 132–4.

THE CRIME OF CRIMES?

Summarizing both his own research and a great deal of recent work by others,[24] Brian Levack has recently developed a strong critique of the influential theory tying witchcraft to state formation and centralization. Scholars such as Christina Larner[25] and Robert Muchembled[26] treated witch-trials as a means by which the centralizing, bureaucratizing absolutist state could abrogate to itself judicial and administrative tasks previously performed by local gentry; they also used the trials as a means to undermine rural culture, 'disciplining' the peasantry to become citizens of a modern state. Under such theories, we should expect few trials in the Polish-Lithuanian Commonwealth, with its radical decentralization of power, its near total absence of a central bureaucracy, and its strong tradition of local noble autonomy. However, as Levack shows, the centralization theories accord poorly with the evidence. The takeover of witch-trials by secular courts across most of Europe in the sixteenth century did increase the number of cases, while the spread of torture and the inquisitorial procedure greatly increased conviction rates. But trials were not, for the most part, run by central authorities: on the contrary central authorities nearly everywhere acted to restrain the trials. Where they did so successfully, as in Spain and Italy under Inquisitorial administration, or France under the Parlement of Paris after 1604, conviction rates remained low and chains of denunciation rare. Trials were more frequent, more bloody, and longer lasting, where central state power was weak: 'it was the *failure* of the state to control local authorities and to supervise local justice that led to the great prosecutions of the seventeenth century'.[27]

Until the very late eighteenth century, nowhere in Europe did the state fail more abjectly to supervise local justice than in Poland. With its ideology of Sarmatian freedom and its political culture of *gminowładtstwo* (local-community self-government), the *szlachta* political class resolutely resisted all attempts at centralization, or even of effective national government.[28] Noble *gród*-courts or

[24] Notably Alfred Soman, *Sorcellerie et justice criminelle* (Brookfield, Vt.: Variorum, 1992); cf. Jonathan L. Pearl, *The Crime of Crimes* (Waterloo: Wilfrid Laurier University Press, 1999).

[25] Larner, *Enemies of God*; 'The Crime of Witchcraft in Early Modern Europe', in *Witchcraft and Religion* (London: Blackwell, 1984).

[26] E.g. Robert Muchembled, *Le Roi et la sorcière*; 'Satanic Myths and Cultural Realities', in B. Ankarloo and G. Henningsen (eds.), *Early Modern European Witchcraft* (Oxford: OUP, 1993).

[27] Levack, 'State-Building', 215–23; quotation at 219 (emphasis added). Levack has recently extended this argument explicitly to Poland, rightly arguing that Polish decentralization helps explain the large number of late trials in Poland. However, he fails to take into account how jurisdictional conflicts tended to limit the size of these trials. See Brian Levack, 'Witch-Hunting in England and Poland: Similarities and Differences', in R. Unger and J. Basista (eds.), *Britain and Poland-Lithuania* (Boston: Brill, 2008).

[28] On Polish-Lithuanian *szlachta* political culture, see esp. Andrzej Sulima Kamiński, 'The *szlachta* of the Polish-Lithuanian Commonwealth and their Government', in I. Banac and P. Bushkovitch (eds.), *The Nobility in Russia and Eastern Europe* (New Haven: Yale University

starościńskie courts, nominally beholden to the central government, were run locally, dominated by the better-off nobility of the region. Episcopal courts, which *were* quite centrally regulated by an organization bitterly opposed to secular control of witch-trials, never succeeded in regaining jurisdiction over witchcraft. Saxon-Law courts, especially those of private towns, operated largely without oversight; the Assessory Court attempts to reform or regulate small-town courts met with no success before the mid-eighteenth century. Small-town court magistrates were not quite the drunken, venal tools of local elites described in satire; trials often depict a careful attempt to arrive at the truth. Nevertheless, it is very clear that justice, in early modern Poland, was entirely local, administered by men who for the most part shared the concerns and fears of the local community.

Paradoxically, it was in small village courts, with their restorative-justice paradigm, and in the very largest cities, that witchcraft accusations and trials maintained their medieval character longest, with courts focusing on specific acts of malefice and assigning fines, whipping, or relegation as penalties. In the large cities and in the similarly very mild appeals courts, such an approach may be ascribed to the jurisprudential caution exercised by learned magistrates. More-over, the magistracy of large cities could display more autonomy *vis-à-vis* noble plaintiffs than could the courts of smaller towns, so dependent on the goodwill of their noble neighbors. But both village and large-town trials were the exceptions; the great majority of the accused were peasants or plebeians, tried before quite local magistrates.

In the absence of central regulation, we find in Poland what Levack would lead us to expect: scattered but quite numerous trials, high execution rates, and a tendency for witch-trials to continue long after they had been become a thing of the past in such centralizing states as France. But what we also find might be less expected: a near-absence of major witch-panics, or of run-away chain-reaction trials. The same extreme localism that made reform impossible also discouraged the spread of trials: a nobleman's near-autonomy on his own property, and *vis-à-vis* his own serfs, entailed a concomitant absence of rights over his neighbor's subjects. The decentralized character of Polish justice explains the high execution rate in Polish witch-trials, and their continued existence through most of the eighteenth century. It also explains the near absence, in Poland, of a witch-panic.

Witchcraft, traditionally, has been understood as the 'crime of crimes': a *crimen exceptum* so dastardly that the courts were justified, indeed duty-bound, to overlook the ordinary rules of procedure, the requirements for good evidence and trustworthy witnesses, in pursuing its prosecution and eradication. Demo-nologists espoused an uncompromising attack against the clear and present danger posed by the witchcraft conspiracy; law-books, following the *Malleus*,

Press, 1983); Stefania Ochman-Staniszewska, 'Od stabilizacji do kryzysu władzy królewskiej: państwo Wazów', in A. Sucheni-Grabowska (ed.), *Między monarchą a demokracją* (Warsaw: Wydawnictwo Sejmowe, 1994).

allowed testimony in witch-trials from people ordinarily excluded as witnesses, such as neighbors with a known grudge against the accused, or kin of the accuser, or women. Accused witches were tortured brutally until their testimony conformed to notions of witchcraft preconceived in the minds of their fanatical judges. A recognizable complex of attitudes and practices—an ideologically predetermined crime, more or less arbitrarily selected victims (that is, people accused of the crime), a guilty verdict more or less assumed, suspicion and rumor accepted as evidence, and association as grounds for guilt, a general public complicit or cowed into cooperation with the courts—has come to be called a 'witch-hunt' on the basis of this archetypical example, and has been found analogically in the Stalinist show-trials, the McCarthy hearings, and the procedures of the contemporary War on Terror.

This popular picture contains many grains of truth. Respected jurists did allow numerous exceptions to standard procedure on the grounds that witchcraft was a species of treason, and subject therefore to the relaxed rules of evidence allowable in treason cases. The standard legal formula that evidence of guilt must be 'as clear as the noonday sun' found its reversal in Bodin's injunction that, in witchcraft trials, the witch should not be acquitted unless the *accuser's calumny* is 'clearer than the sun'.[29] Procedures such as the water ordeal or dunking, already banished from ordinary jurisprudence for hundreds of years, continued to be countenanced and introduced into evidence in witch-trials. In certain times and places—North Berwick in the 1590s, the Bamberg and Würtsburg prince-bishoprics in the late sixteenth and early seventeenth centuries, Salem 1692, Kleczew in the last quarter of the seventeenth century—the merest suspicion could indeed lead, in remarkably short order, to execution for witchcraft.

And yet we have learned, over the last three decades of witch-trial scholarship, to treat with suspicion much of this narrative of witchcraze. As I have already noted, the tendency begun by Keith Thomas[30] and exemplified recently by Robin Briggs[31] has lead us to concentrate on what Peter Burke has called the 'unspectacular everyday persecution' of witches.[32] In the studies of the last several decades, witchcraft emerges not so much as the crime of crimes as a crime like any other, treated seriously but not fanatically by the courts.

One might also approach this question from the other side, as it were. Witchcraft was not, after all, the only crime for which the accused were habitually tortured—torture was the 'queen of proofs' for all serious criminal offences, in all regions where the Roman Law came to dominate jurisprudence in the sixteenth century. Nor was it the only crime treated as an 'offence against God's law', or

---

[29] Bodin, *Demon Mania*, bk. 4, ch. 5, p. 218.
[30] Thomas, *Decline of Magic*.
[31] Briggs, *Witches and Neighbours*.
[32] Peter Burke, 'The Comparative Approach to European Witchcraft', in B. Ankarloo and G. Henningsen *Early Modern European Witchcraft* (Oxford: OUP, 1993), 441.

the only crime to characterized by very high execution rates. As we have seen, in Poland the execution rate for witchcraft was lower than that for a whole host of other crimes, such as arson, rape, banditry, and murder.

Early modern law makes no clear distinction between what we might be inclined to see as naturally contrasting categories of crime: those that are religious and ideological and those that are social and 'real'. Despite the rhetorical uses to which the term 'witch-hunt' has been put in the twentieth century, witchcraft was not a 'thought crime' in the early modern period. It must be remembered, once again, that witches were accused of and tried for witchcraft: for a crime of magical harm. As a violent and harmful attack on others, witchcraft was just as social a crime as was murder—which itself, in transgressing the Fifth Commandment, was also a sin and a religious crime. The verdict formulae describing witchcraft as an offence against God's honor or the First Commandment (Słomniki 1674b; Nieszawa 1721a; Pyzdry 1740) must be read in this light: they make witchcraft not a *crimen exceptum*, but a crime like other crimes. Uruszczak, in the introduction to his edition of the criminal-court books of Nowy Wiśnicz, goes so far as to assert that the primary law followed in that court was the Decalogue: invoked not only against 'moral' or 'religious' crimes such as witchcraft and adultery but also against theft, banditry, and murder.[33] The formula *contra iura tam Divina quam humana* appears in verdicts for all sorts of criminal offences, most of which we would not now categorize as religious.[34] In a society that treated social peace as a fragile miracle, even ordinary non-supernatural squabbling between neighbors could be treated as 'an offense against the Lord God', as in a verdict of the village court of Jazowsko in 1731.[35] Witchcraft was a crime against society and a crime against God. In the next part of this book, I attempt to explore the web of meanings and symbols that entangled witchcraft with both peasant cosmology and the triumphant Catholic Christianity of post-Tridentine Poland.

---

[33] Uruszczak, *Acta Maleficorum*.
[34] Mikołajczyk, *Przestępstwo i kara*, 18–19; cf. Maisel, *Poznańskie*, 36.
[35] Grodziski, *Księgi sądowe*, item 92.

PART II

RELIGION

5

Healing and Harming

A która ma te przyprawki, jachać na granice
Powinna, gzło, w którym chodzi, wywrócić na nice.
Maściami się nasmaruje, a na ożog wsiędzie,
Śrzednim oknem wyskoczywszy, na granicach będzie.
Tam po polach i po miedzach czary zakopuje,
Sobie pożytki przywodzi, drugim ludziom psuje.

Whoever has the herbs, to go to the border
Should turn her shirt inside out,
Smear herself with ointments, hop on a broomstick
And jump out the window, right to the border.
They bury enchantments in the fields and the boundaries,
Bringing profit to themselves, but to others harm.

(*Sejm piekielny straszliwy* (1622), vv. 872–7)

What counted as witchcraft in early modern Poland; how was it imagined? We have seen the legal definitions and their changes through time; the sixteenth-century emphasis on provable magical harm giving way to a focus on treason or *crimen laesae majestatis divinae*, so that by the late seventeenth-century magistrates could condemn a witch who had 'opposed God, and wishing to liken herself to Him, dared to fly through the air' (Nowy Wiśnicz 1688b). The author of the *Witch Denounced* took a middle position, attempting to distinguish witchcraft from superstition, crime from misdemeanor:

Witchcraft takes place with offence against the Majesty of God and holy things belonging to him, and with harm to one's neighbour, either his possessions or his health. Whereas superstition, which also often occurs, lacks these two very evil characteristics.[1]

These definitions seem relatively straightforward. Moreover, as the epigraph to this chapter makes clear, popular literature of the early seventeenth century described behaviors of witches to a popular audience in terms recognizable throughout Europe. A witch is a woman who uses herbs for her nefarious craft; she engages in inversionary practices ('turns her shirt inside out'); by means of an

---

[1] *Czarownica powołana*, 5.

ointment and a broomstick she flies to the witches' meeting at 'the border'; through her buried enchantments, she steals 'profit' from others for her own good. All of these themes turn up again and again in the trials, suggesting that the author of the *Infernal Parliament* had an accurate understanding of popular notions of witchcraft.

And yet it could be extraordinarily difficult to know who was a witch, what counted as witchcraft. Witches used herbs: so did everyone else. From basic household remedies known to any housewife, to the more complex recipes of cunning-folk, to the expensive imported spices favored by medical doctors, botanicals formed the fundamental armamentarium of early modern healing. Witches stole milk from neighbors: ordinary peasant women engaged in counter-magic, protecting the milk of their cattle. To the outsider, or to the victim of counter-magic, such practices appeared identical to the magic attributed to witches. Witches met at night at the border, where they danced and feasted—ordinary peasant women at least occasionally met in the fields at night, for example on St John's Eve, where they danced and sang.[2] Witches worshipped and made offerings to the devil: ordinary peasant women took care not to offend the house-spirit, whom they fed with milk or groats (see Part III). Witches offended God by making illicit use of sacred things: so too, in the eyes of reforming churchmen of both Catholic and Protestant camps, did ordinary peasant women with their blessed candles against thunder, their blessed herbs against illness, their stolen water from the baptismal fonts; indeed most of the 'witches' of the *Infernal Parliament* or the *Devil's Lawsuit* performed nothing but ordinary peasant sacramental magic. Despite widespread and relatively stable popular assumptions about the nature of witchcraft, it was difficult to separate witchcraft from the indispensable practicalities of everyday village or small-town life. Ordinary practical knowledge blended imperceptibly into the more specialized knowledge of cunning-folk; and both could, depending on perspective and context, look very much like witchcraft.

In this and the following three chapters, I explore this problem of discernment, of definition, of naming. I have already argued that to become a witch

---

[2] Both Catholic and Protestant reformers repeatedly forbade the *Sobótka* or midsummer bonfire dancing as an occasion to give 'worship and prayer to the devil' or for 'great acts of witchcraft and error'. See Mikołaj Olszewski, *Świat zabobonów w średniowieczu* (Warsaw: Wydawnictwo Naukowe Semper, 2002), 183–5; S. Nasiorowski, *'List pasterski' kard.* (Lublin: Redakcja Wydawnictw Katolickiego Uniwersytetu Lubelskiego, 1992), 204; Marcin of Urzędów, *Herbarz Polski* (Kraków: Drukarnia Łazarzowa, 1595), 31–2; Mikołaj Rej, *Świętych słów a spraw Pańskich...* (Kraków: Matys Wirzbięta, 1556), fo. 228ᵛ. However, the humanist poet Jan Kochanowski defended midsummer dances as traditional, pious, and innocent; while the Catholic priest and historian Szymon Starowolski interpreted the bonfires as a Christian celebration memorializing the burning of pagan idols at the baptism of Mieszko I. See Jan Kochanowski, 'Pieśń świętojańska o sobótce', in J. Krzyżanowski (ed.), *Dzieła polskie Jana Kochanowskiego* (Warsaw: Państwowy Instytut Wydawniczy, 1952 [c.1585]); Szymon Starowolski, *Arka Testamentu zamykająca w sobie kazania niedzielna całego roku* (Kraków: W drukarniy Krzystofa Schedla, 1648), i. 485. Despite the disapproval of at least some clergy, such midsummer celebrations continued in Poland, as in most of Europe, throughout the early modern period.

meant to acquire a social and legal status: a woman was a witch insofar as she was thought to be such by her neighbors, her manor-lord, or the court. Formally speaking, a witch was always and only that person to whom the label 'witch' had come successfully to be attached through reputation, suspicion, accusation, and court-verdict. Such an account, however, leaves out the content: it gives us a pragmatics of witchcraft, but no semantics—what was *meant* by the accusation? What did the label 'witch' entail? Despite a stable core of motifs, the witch-label admitted of fuzzy borders and contested gray areas. Whether a given activity will have been labeled as 'witchcraft', or instead as superstition, or medicine, or even prayer, depended very largely on who was doing the labeling. Reforming clergy found diabolism or paganism or witchcraft almost everywhere. But these same clergymen, in their quarrels with secular authorities over jurisdiction, could reproach the latter as being incapable of distinguishing true witchcraft from ignorant superstition. Protestant reformers consigned the whole of traditional Catholicism to the category of witchcraft, which prompted seventeenth-century Catholic thinkers to distinguish more carefully than had their forebears between pious practice, excusable excess, forbidden superstition, and damnable witch-craft. Noble attitudes for the most part more closely resembled those of the peasantry than of the clergy. Treating witchcraft as a serious threat to order that must be ruthlessly extirpated, the *szlachta* nevertheless sometimes made use of women they understood to be 'witches' for their own purposes. Peasants, meanwhile, had their own fine distinctions, their own problems of perspective: what one person saw as entirely legitimate protective and counter-magical activity might look, to her neighbor, very much like aggressive witchcraft. The power to heal implied the power to harm; a blessing could hide a threat; a compliment could convey the evil eye. The social exchanges, the small gifts and favors that constituted and maintained village sociability, were also the media through which malefice was 'given' to its victims. 'Witchcraft' was not a single label with a single meaning, but rather a series of overlapping categories and oppositions, and these categories and oppositions, in turn, took up their place and their meanings in the context of overlapping theories of the world. Witches and witchcraft existed as part of a pluralistic universe.

THE PLURALISTIC UNIVERSE

In 1600, a thief stole a sizeable sum of money from the city coffers of Biecz. The city council took the following actions to recover the stolen funds: they arrested and questioned under torture one Maciej Mazurek, who died during interroga-tion without revealing the location of the stolen money; they commissioned and paid for the singing of two masses; they sent to Kraków, at great expense, for the learned 'doctor Fontan the astrologer'; at much less expense, they consulted a village cunning-woman, paying her in pepper and ginger; they consulted an

Orthodox priest or monk, who apparently had some reputation as a diviner; they also consulted a *mater diabolica*, in other words, a witch.[3] These actions exemplify the pluralistic world in which the councilmen lived: they were willing to try all options, including some we would classify as practical (interrogation of the suspected thief), religious (the masses, consultation with the Orthodox holy man), and magical. Under the magical category we may make further subdivisions: between 'high' or 'natural' magic (the Kraków astrologer), 'superstition' (the village fortune-teller), and 'diabolical witchcraft' (the *mater diabolica*). But from the perspective of the council itself, *all* its actions comprised practical, instrumental steps in the attempt to recover the stolen city funds.

The example of the Biecz city council demands that, for the purpose of interpretation, we set aside our own notions of the distinction between the practical-instrumental and the magical-religious-symbolic. While the council knew that sponsoring a mass was an entirely different sort of activity from torturing a prisoner, and both were different from consulting the stars or throwing wax on water, the distinctions made were not between the real and the supernatural, still less between the practical and the symbolic. Questions of efficacy did indeed enter into debates about the nature of magic and witchcraft and superstition and prayer, but the answers proposed to these questions were not our answers. As Stewart Clark has argued, interpretations of early modern witchcraft and demonology can hardly even begin until we set aside our own notions of scientific efficacy. Magic, Clark insists, 'is what, in particular cultural settings, it is construed to be'.[4] To attempt an interpretation of early modern Polish magic, we must discard modern distinctions between vain magic and efficacious technology without thereby discarding the notion of magic itself—it was a local category, with local definitions and limits which we will want to try to discover.

The mixture of what we might now characterize as 'science', 'religion', and 'magic' is especially evident in the arena of medicine, an arena, moreover, in which locally constructed delineations between indigenous versions of these categories were contested and discussed. A fascinating glimpse into popular healing is afforded by Jakub Kazimierz Haur's *Storehouse or Treasury of Wonderful Secrets of Landed-Gentry Economy*, a best-seller of the late seventeenth century which could be found on the (rather short) bookshelf of nearly every rural manor.[5] Haur's long tractate on folk remedies exemplifies 'medical pluralism': a practical, popular medicine that mixes learned and village remedies, empirical

---

[3] Franciszek Buczak, 'Śledzenie złoczyńców z pomocą czarów (Z rachunków miasta Biecza z r. 1600)', *Lud*, 16 (1910). Similarly, in 1452, the city councilors of Poznań made use of a cunning-man to recover stolen city funds; see Bylina, 'Magia', 43.

[4] Clark, *Thinking with Demons*, 216.

[5] Haur, *Skład Abo Skarbiec*. On its popularity, together with Haur's earlier, shorter *Oekonomia ziemiańska*, see Joanna Partyka, 'Książka rękopiśmienna na dworze szlacheckim', *Odrodzenie i Reformacja w Polsce*, 38 (1994).

and symbolic cures.[6] To the modern eye, it is difficult to see how some of Haur's cures differ from the sorts of things that could bring serious suspicion on a village cunning-woman. For example, one might rub an aching tooth with the dried tooth of a corpse, causing the sore tooth to dry up and fall out. A woman can prevent excessive blood-flow during her periods by tying a red string around her toe: a clear case of ligature. If a couple is having difficulty conceiving, the woman should mix spring-water with the ashes of a tree-branch on which swarming honey-bees have landed, and should drink this concoction morning and night, 'while participating in Marital association'. Epilepsy may be ameliorated with various herbs such as mistletoe and linden, but also by drinking a powder of dried bear or wild boar, taken in mare's milk; alternatively one may drink the powdered heart of a human corpse, in wine with sulphur.[7]

Our modern perception of some of these procedures as magical or superstitious can give no guidance as to their contemporary categorization. However, there can be no doubt that some of Haur's remedies, such as those using dried and powdered human remains, skirted the very edge of the category of magic as defined in his own time. Haur seems to have been aware of this problem, and prefaced his discussion of home medicine with a title that protests too much:

Concerning Farmers' Medicine, collected from Household Ingredients for People, who are far from Cities, Towns, and Doctors, concerning various illnesses, serving greatly for the use of the ill and for saving health: admonishing People lest they make use of Witchcraft, and Superstition, and all kinds of Nonsense, to the peril not only of their health but of their Souls, and that they should use only methods and remedies from the LORD GOD.[8]

In this and similar passages, Haur seeks to establish a safe middle ground for the home remedies he recommends. Unlike the expensive medicine of city doctors, they can be put together from household materials, by an ordinary nobleman-farmer or his wife. But more crucially, Haur insists somewhat strenuously that they are natural, to be distinguished sharply from the 'Satanic, Pagan, and non-Christian procedures and methods, by which many People, in vain, lose both their health and their Soul'.[9]

What sorts of 'Satanic, Pagan, and non-Christian procedures' does Haur have in mind, and how do they differ from his own 'Household Medicines that are certain, and proven in their effects'?[10] Despite Haur's construction of a series of nesting oppositions—natural vs. supernatural, Christian *vs.* Satanic, effective medicine vs. vain superstition or quackish charlatanry we must recognize that

---

[6] The notion of 'medical pluralism' is developed in David Gentilcore, *From Bishop to Witch* (New York: Manchester UP, 1992).
[7] Haur, *Skład Abo Skarbiec,* 435–6, 385–6, 98–9.
[8] Ibid. 379.
[9] Ibid. 380.
[10] Ibid.

all these oppositions were contested, unstable, and often enough simply ignored, even by Haur himself. His insistence on separating his own recommended practices from those of cunning-folk or witches rings all the louder insofar as he knows that not everyone would be able to discern a difference. In this as in other ways, he reflects the pluralistic, pious and practical, superstitious and devout and worldly character of his readership: the manor-lords, rural clergy, and small-town patriciate whose beliefs and attitudes shaped the witch-trials.[11]

As with healing, the production and processing of dairy, so central to the rural economy, displayed an inextricable admixture of religious, magical, and empirical practices. Valuable but easily spoiled goods, milk and its by-products were set about with anxiety, the focus of innumerable techniques for increasing and preserving production. The fermenting processes by which milk transforms into buttermilk, curds, farmers' cheese, and butter remain beyond perfect technological control even in modern hygienic conditions.[12] Satirists contemporary to the witch-trials saw the close connection between spoiled milk and witchcraft as an ignorant attempt to explain predictable mishaps in this tricky agricultural practice: 'The cows give no milk, or it won't turn to butter, . . . it's witchcraft . . .'[13] Modern scholarship has too often concurred on this point, imagining witchcraft accusation as a scapegoat for unhygienic practices, carelessness, and ignorance.[14] Such a stance is hermeneutically impoverished: people whose livelihood depended on a steady supply of milk were well aware of the need for hygiene and care in the preparation of dairy products. Nor did they, in Malinowskian fashion, use magic as a categorically separate supplement to fallible empirical practices. Rather, their distinction between natural and supernatural techniques tended to blur and mingle in complex ways. Haur's prescription for proper milking and for the storage of dairy is a perfect example of the seamless mixture of 'magic' and agronomy:

When the cows stand to be milked in the Dairy-barn, tied to the manger containing grass or feed, first sprinkle them with holy Water, then warm a [decoction of] blessed herbs, which should be ready prepared in a vessel, and wash their udders, drying them with a clean cloth, only after this should they be milked, three times a day according custom.

On Tuesdays and Thursdays, cense all the Cows in the Dairy-barn with these same herbs: in Summer, store milk in a cool place, so that it can sour slowly, the vessel containing the Milk should be uncovered to allow vapor to escape, but should be in such a place that dust doesn't fall into the milk.[15]

---

[11] On the largely shared worldview of rural *szlachta*, parish priests, the inhabitants of small towns, and the peasantry, see A. Zakrzewski, *W kręgu kultu maryjnego* (Częstochowa: Wydawnictwo WSP, 1995), 126–7; Wiślicz, 'Religijność wiejska', 87–101.

[12] Cf. similar accusations related to the similarly uncertain processes of brewing and distilling: e.g. Chwaliszewo 1511; Kalisz 1593; Kalisz 1616; Szadek 1632; Turek 1652b.

[13] *Wodka zelixierem*; after Baranowski, *Procesy Czarownic*, 62.

[14] Bohdan Baranowski, *Pożegnanie z diabłem i czarownicą* (Łódź: Wydawnictwo Łódzkie, 1965), 127.

[15] Haur, *Skład Abo Skarbiec*, 64.

Similarly, milk pails should be cleaned within the hour with clean water, heated with blessed herbs and nettles, and left to dry in a warm oven: otherwise they will spoil the next batch of milk.[16]

One could go through these recommendations line by line and, according to one or another standard, classify each one according to whether it belongs to the realm of 'magic', 'science', or 'religion'. Sprinkling the cattle with holy water might be religious (or superstitious or magical for a Protestant), the clean cloth and the hot water for washing the udders 'scientific', under which category we might also put the boiling of the milk pails and even perhaps the use of nettle, a mild antiseptic. Censing with blessed herbs might, again, count as magic or religion, although the smoke might have a hygienic effect and therefore be scientific; while the days chosen for this censing—especially Thursday, the stereotypical day for witches' gatherings and maleficent milk-theft—seems magical. Such an exercise is, however, misguided insofar as our goal is to understand Haur and his world. Whatever distinctions we might make are not the distinctions he makes. For Haur, none of the techniques are magical; instead, he brings religious material into complementary combination with customary practice and worldly common sense so as to form an effective set of legitimate techniques, recommended because they work.

However, even within Haur's frame of reference, not everyone would agree that all the techniques he espoused were entirely legitimate. To restore the production of a cow whose milk has been spoiled through witchcraft, Haur recommends washing the cow's udders, as well as all the vessels and tools used in dairy production, in a decoction of manure and burdock; this will cause the offending witch to 'tremble and itch' until she undoes her spell.[17] Although no witch-trials mention the use of burdock to such a purpose, the basic method of cooking milk-pails to cause pain to the witch was common (e.g. Kalisz 1580; Chęciny 1665b; Przecław 1675). The nettle for cleaning milk-pails appears in the trial of the cunning-woman Jagna of Żabikowo, who combined it with beeswax and blessed bread to fix witch-spoiled milk (Poznań 1549). More than a century later, another accused witch admitted that she knew something about the care of her own cattle and their milk: 'give the cows *biało zieło*[18] with bread so that the milk sours properly; I [also] collected *barwinek*[19] to get it blessed, but not for witchcraft, and I censed the cattle with it on Thursdays, . . . to get good profit from the cows' (Nowy Wiśnicz 1688c). Despite Haur's strenuous insistence that in caring for cattle and milk-production one must 'perform no sort of superstition' but trust in 'the Lord GOD',[20] his methods are very nearly identical with those that appear in witch-trials. Depending on context, intention, and minor differences in emphasis, the same techniques could be understood as good animal husbandry, as cunning or superstition, or as witchcraft.

---

[16] Ibid.   [17] Ibid. 469.   [18] Probably *postęp*, *Bryonia alba* L.
[19] Periwinkle, *Vinca minor* L.   [20] Haur, *Skład Abo Skarbiec*, 65.

The early modern Polish attitude toward herbs and their use may serve as a final example of ambiguity. Like healing and the protection of dairy (both practices making extensive use of herbs), herbal lore could partake of Christian piety, empirical medicine, superstition, and diabolical witchcraft. In literature, witches were masters of maleficent herbcraft: a devil in the *Infernal Parliament* boasts of the women he has corrupted toward witchcraft:

> I've turned good women into great witches.
> Teaching them symbols, they know our herbs as well;
> And go oftener to the border than to church.[21]

Polish witches were imagined to make use of herbs in their magic, and many accused witches confessed to such uses of herbs. Dorota of Siedlików, for example, confessed that she transformed herself into a milk-stealing cat by means of 'witches' herbs' (Kalisz 1613). Both elite and trial sources associated mandrake or its various local substitutes with 'magic-using women and old-wives who associate with devils'.[22] However, herbal knowledge was hardly confined to 'witches', however defined, nor to cunning-women. The accused witch Apolonia Porwitka claimed before the court that apothecaries bought herbs from her: 'I made no use of witchcraft, only of herbs, which I picked with other women and the apothecaries bought them from me' (Kalisz 1593). Haur's home remedies, both for people and livestock, consist primarily of herbs, and the Jesuit Benedykt Chmielowski provides a long list of effective herbs against witchcraft. The great Renaissance herbal-manuals of Marcin of Urzędów and Szymon Syreniusz catalogued the effects of many hundreds of herbs, foreign and local. At all levels of society herbs were believed to have medicinal properties, including the property of protecting against misfortune, witchcraft, and the devil (see Figure 5.1). Although some church reformers worried about superstitious herbal amulets, others felt free to recommend such amulets if the herbs had been blessed in church.[23] Syreniusz, Haur, and Benedikt Chmielowski all recommended such an amulet of *boże drzewko* (lit. 'god's little tree'; *Artemesia abrotanum* L., southernwood), as an excellent protection

---

[21] Ianuarius [pseud.] Sowirzalius, 'Sejm piekielny. Satyra obyczajowa', ed. A. Brückner (Kraków: Wydawnictwo Akademii Umiejętności, 1903 [1622]), 46, vv. 851–3. Cf. Swizralus, *Peregrynacja*, 170, v. 755: 'For I know all the herbs, which grow in the meadows.'

[22] Stefan Falimirz, *O ziolach y o moczy gich...* (Kraków: F. Ungler, 1534), fos. I.86ᵛ–87; cf. Marcin of Urzędów, *Herbarz Polski*, 201. In place of mandrake, Polish women were said to have used local roots such as belladonna, bryony, yellow-dock, or common iris. See Szymon Syreniusz, *Zielnik Herbarzem z języka Łacinskiego zowią* (Kraków: W drukarni Bazylego Skalskiego, 1613), 1378; Wacław Urban, 'Czary i mandragora w Tymbarku', *Odrodzenie i Reformacja w Polsce*, 49 (2005). At least one accused witch was said to be selling *pokrzyk* (mandrake or one of its substitutes) as a good-luck charm (Lublin 1643). See now Michael Ostling, "Witches' Herbs on Trial," *Folklore* 125 (2014), 179–201.

[23] Stanisław Bylina, *Chrystianizacja wsi polskiej u schyłku średniowiecza* (Warsaw: Instytut Historii Polskiej Akademii Nauk, 2002), 191; M. Plezia, 'Benedictio Gratiosae: Poznański formularz błogosławieństwa ziół z drugiej połowy XV w.', *Roczniki Humanistyczne*, 27/3 (1979), 87.

Figure 5.1. A female herb-gatherer with male doctors. From Stefan Falimirz's *O ziolach y o moczy gich* (Concerning herbs and their powers), Kraków 1534, fo. IV60ᵛ. Courtesy of the Folger Shakespeare Library.

against witchcraft and misfortune.[24] What had been condemnable superstition could be refigured as pious practice.

The Counter-Reformation church went quite far to accommodate and appropriate folk herbalism: herbs were blessed at the church on the Octave of Corpus Christi, sometimes on Pentecost (called *Zielone Świątki*, 'the green holiday'), and above all on the feast of the Assumption of the Virgin Mary, commonly called *Matka Boska Zielna* or 'Our Lady of the Herbs'.[25] In his programmatic pastoral

[24] Syreniusz, *Zielnik*, 370; Haur, *Skład Abo Skarbiec*, 455; Chmielowski, *Nowe Ateny*, iii. 259.
[25] Józef Rostafiński, 'Wpływ przeżyć chłopięcych Mickiewicza na obrazy ostatnich dwu ksiąg Pana Tadeusza oraz o święceniu ziół na Matkę Boską Zielną', *Rozprawy polskiej Akademii Umiejętności, Wydział Filologiczny*, 61/1 (1922); cf. Robert Scribner, *Popular Culture and Popular Movements in Reformation Germany* (Ronceverte, W. Va.: Hambledon Press, 1987), 33, on identical practices in Catholic Germany.

letter of the early seventeenth century, Cardinal Bernard Maciejowski permitted parish priests to distribute blessed herbs insofar as these were blessed 'not superstitiously, or for satanic purposes, [but] toward the health of spirit and body'.[26] By the time we reach Chmielowski's mid-eighteenth-century encyclopedia, blessed herbs and their use against witches and the devil have been entirely Christianized:

The reason why the devil fears herbs and flowers is this, that the Lord Christ is called the *Flower of Nazareth*, the *Lily of the Valley*, and his Most Holy Mother, when buried, was showered with flowers, so that [on the feast of her Assumption] each Year the Church of God blesses herbs, giving them power against witchcraft and devils.[27]

Thus the use of herbs could be grounds for suspicion of witchcraft, but could also be a fully orthodox method to protect oneself or one's cattle *from* witchcraft. As the accused witch Jadwiga Kryczka, who was eventually acquitted, noted in her own defense, the use of herbs need not imply witchcraft; herbs, she asserted, are good for people and animals (Sandomierz 1675). When the court asked Barbara Jewionka whence she knew the ingredient herbs for a love-magic bath, she responded: 'Just like other people use herbs, so do I. Besides, people bless all sorts of herbs' (Nowy Wiśnicz 1659; cf. Poznań 1603).

Thus whether the use of an herb was 'magical' or medicinal, witchcraft or piety, depended on all sorts of factors. According to witnesses, the accused witch Dorota Pilecka gathered herbs at the cemetery and mixed them in with her other herbs to have them blessed at Our Lady of the Herbs (Słomniki 1674b). To gather herbs before dawn was suspicious, especially as this could be combined with the gathering of dew and moisture which characterized maleficient milk-theft (e.g. Chęciny 1665d; Nowy Wiśnicz 1689a; Wyszogród 1718b). And yet a semi-elite writer such as Haur could insist that the herbs he recommends against witchcraft 'are to be collected before the rising of the Sun' and eaten raw, for their counter-magical powers to be fully effective.[28] Did such actions constitute witchcraft or counter-witchcraft, malefice or protection against malefice? The question allows for no determinate answer; imagined witches and the real peasants (and noblemen) who sought to protect themselves from such imagined witches used the same materials, often in the same ways.

---

[26] Nasiorowski, *'List pasterski' Maciejowskiego*, 203. Maciejowski's pastoral letter, written in 1601 when he was bishop of Kraków, came to influence the whole of Poland-Lithuania when he became archbishop of Gniezno; it was included in the texts of the important Catholic-Reformation Synod of Gniezno in 1628 (*'List pasterski' Maciejowskiego*, 9–11).

[27] Chmielowski, *Nowe Ateny*, iii. 260.

[28] Haur, *Skład Abo Skarbiec*, 455.

A COMMON LANGUAGE

A very few accused witches displayed sufficiently elaborate specialized knowledge to indicate their status as semi-professional cunning-folk. This is especially true of the long spells enclosed in aetiological myths characteristic of some early trials in Poznań and Kalisz. Apolonia Porwitka, who admitted that 'God be praised, I have some luck at blessing cattle and other things', demonstrated this facility in her charm to unbewitch fermenting beer. One should wash the brewing vats with a boiling mixture of millet to which have been added a shuttle and a spoon, while reciting the following:

By God's power, by the virgin Mary's power and by the help of all the saints, I have commanded winter grain and this spring grain, and I admonish here this curse and enchantment and these bugs from this cellar, from this beer and from these [brewing] vessels, and [from] the master and mistress [of the house] and all their vessels, [I expel] everything evil and all vermin and charms if they be in this beer and all evil things if there be here anything evil. Most Holy Virgin Mary I call you to myself, a miserable sinner, [asking] that you might intercede with your Most Beloved Son, so that the Lord Jesus might drive out and behumble the vermin from this beer or wine and from this cellar, as he behumbled the money-changers when they attacked his health, that through the power of Almighty God they might be swallowed up by the earth. In the name of the Father and Son and Holy Spirit, three times. (Kalisz 1593)[29]

In its complexity and length, and in its good knowledge of the Gospel and of Christian prayer, Apolonia's counter-magical charm goes well beyond the resources available to most ordinary women. It is less obvious how it differs from many of Haur's techniques, or how, in contrast to them, it partakes of 'Satanic, Pagan, and non-Christian procedures'. As with the examples of healing, care of cattle and milk, and herbcraft adduced above, Apolonia's spell suggests that despite attempts at demarcation, the boundaries between diabolical magic, natural technique, and Christian religion remained fluid and confused. Indeed the image of pluralism may be misleading: to a surprising extent, early modern Poles of both genders and most levels of education spoke a common symbolic language. Much of the uniformity, the sense of pattern discoverable in Polish witch-trial confessions, derives not from a common core of knowledge so much as from a common set of assumptions, tropes, metaphors, and structural relations, out of which both accusers and the accused could generate ever novel, but simultaneously always similar, accusations and confessions.

---

[29] Long narrative spells such as Apolonia's appear in only a handful of early trials: Poznań 1544a–b, 1549; Kalisz 1593, 1613.

In accusations, in protestations of innocence, and in confessions, it is usually clear that most people knew a great deal about what witches were supposed to do, and even how they were supposed to do it. Accusers and magistrates spoke formulaically of the witch having 'harmed people in their health and in other things, especially their cattle' (Brześć Kujawski 1691). The accused, with equal regularity and not always in response to such a statement, protested that they have 'never practiced witchcraft, never harmed anyone, neither their health nor their cattle' (Lublin 1700; Płońsk 1708a). In confessions these same themes are affirmed rather than denied, often with additions and elaborations: 'I've harmed cattle with a powder, which the bedamned devil gave me, both in the manor-herds and the village herds, for I sprinkled everything with that powder' (Kleczew 1690a). Taken together, these statements demonstrate little more than that all parties to witch-trials shared common assumptions about the targets of malefice: the health of human beings and cattle. But one can find common assumptions, common patterns, at a considerably finer level of detail as well.

Consider, for example, the accusations against Jadwiga Macowa (Nowy Wiśnicz 1688a). She was alleged to have fed the herb *barwinek* (Vinca minor L., periwinkle) to her cows. She admitted this, but insisted that the herb had been gathered 'on the meadow, not on the field-border'. *Barwinek* is to this day a common ingredient in the herb-garlands blessed on the feast of 'Our Lady of the Herbs' and fed to cattle, or made into a tea with which to wash their udders, in order to increase milk production and protect against witchcraft.[30] Jadwiga recognized, and denied, the central thrust of the accusation: not that she had fed this herb to her cows (as most of her neighbors probably also did as well), but that she had gathered the herb at the field borders. This is what witches do: rather than collect such *barwinek* on the meadow, in the commons, as all are allowed to do, she collects it on or near other peoples' fields, to steal the productivity of those fields and of the cattle who graze on them, and transfer it to her own cattle. Knowing; like her accusers, the sorts of things that witches are supposed to do, Jadwiga was able first to deny doing such things, and later to confess to them: under torture, she confessed to saying 'I take the profit from all the borders.'

Accused witches developed their confessions out of something at once more basic and more flexible than a finite set of standard spells or rituals. Rather than, or in addition to, a 'vocabulary' of standard tropes and clichés, accused witches and their accusers were proficient in what might be thought of as a 'grammar', a

---

[30] Lehr, 'Wierzenia demonologiczne', 140; Stanisława Niebrzegowska, *Przestrach od przestrachu* (Lublin: Wydawnictwo Uniwersytetu Marii Curie Skłodowskiej, 2000), 101; Piotr Köhler, 'Nazewnictwo i użytkowania roślin leczniczych na ziemiach polskich w XIX wieku na podstawie ankiety Józefa Rostafińskiego', in B. Kuźnicka (ed.), *Historia leków naturalnych* (Warsaw: Polska Akademia Nauk, 1993), 79.

set of assumptions and structural oppositions by which they could generate infinite variations on the general themes of witchcraft. Under torture, accused witches did not only or even usually parrot back to their interrogators what they thought was expected of them; they did not follow a script. Instead, they took up basic elements of common belief and improvised on them, added to them, elaborated, inverted, and modified them in ways that were not dependent on, and which cannot be taken as evidence for, knowledge of a unified body of stereotypes.

If protective magic focused on the policing of field-borders, witches violated these borders, sweeping rubbish from their own into other's fields (Krzemieniec 1731; Jazowsko 1748).[31] If ordinary households protected themselves from witchcraft by sharpening the demarcations of the homestead, hanging bundles of herbs over the doorways and windows of the home and barn, witches erased such boundaries. Even anti-superstition tracts such as the *Witch Denounced* countenanced the hanging of blessed bunches of fresh mugwort over doors against witchcraft.[32] These green herbs find their maleficient inversion in the mixed and muddled pots of filth, 'very mixed up, with ashes and some kinds of bones, very disgusting', that witches confessed to burying under thresholds (Nowy Wiśnicz 1632; cf. Bełżyce 1598a).[33]

This dynamic of variation and improvisation within the bounds of a common grammar is especially clear in the verbal spells recorded in many Polish witch-trials. Unlike the long narrative charm used by Apolonia Porwitka and her semi-professional ilk, most spells consisted of brief utterances accompanying ritual actions, and conforming to a relatively rigid analogical structure. These were the basic spells both of actually practiced folk-magic and of attributed, imagined witchcraft. Like proverbs, which can be entirely novel but nevertheless perfectly traditional, such spells could be accepted as genuine because they made use of and reproduced the fundamental structures, the oppositions and assumptions, of their audiences' worldview.[34] The spells confessed by Polish witches were probably often made up on the spot during interrogation, but they conformed to a traditional and expected set of structures.

---

[31] Cf. Dysa ('Witchcraft Trials', 101) on a similar trial in Krzemieniec in 1731.

[32] *Czarownica powołana*, 22; cf. Marcin of Urzędów, *Herbarz Polski*, 31: 'If mugwort is hung above gates, doors, entryways, and windows, then witchcraft will do nothing to that home.'

[33] For buried 'witchcraft' in the form of bones, vermin, toads, and so on, see also Kalisz 1613, 1616; Bydgoszcz 1638; Chęciny 1665c; Kleczew 1688; Nowy Wiśnicz 1688a–c; Kiszkowo 1761. See also Sowirzalius, *Sejm piekielny*, 47, vv. 876–7; Haur, *Skład Abo Skarbiec*, 455. The latter, in describing such buried witchcraft as composed of 'any old garbage', aptly describes the mixed and muddled disorder which, more than any specific ingredient, carried the symbolic freight of buried witchcraft.

[34] I take this notion of the *ad hoc* but nevertheless traditional proverb from Bourdieu's analysis of legal discourse in traditional North Africa. See Pierre Bourdieu, *Outline of a Theory of Practise*, tr. Richard Nice (New York: CUP, 1977).

The *content* of the spells recorded in Polish witch-trials is remarkably diverse, though some common phrases and symbols do crop up across a wide geography and over nearly two hundred years. The *structure* of these spells, however, is remarkably consistent over the same place and period. This does *not* imply that there was a secret society of witches (or of cunning-women) passing down and regulating magical knowledge. More plausibly, it implies that those who found themselves obliged, under torture, to describe what witches do, did so by drawing on a common body of folklore, a common repertoire of symbols, a common cultural logic of metaphor and analogy. This logic, the generative grammar of magic, allowed accused witches to create or imagine spells and rituals whether or not they had ever used such a procedure, and whether or not it had ever been taught to them. Just as native speakers of English easily create new, correct sentences in that language every time they speak or write, so any 'native speaker' of the general idiom of Polish peasant culture could generate 'correct'—in the sense of plausible, right-seeming—magical procedures, either in daily life or in the torture chamber.

I have already described several of these spells, and will have cause to describe more in further chapters; therefore I will only adduce a few here to illustrate this common structure.

A. For love:

Pani Zawadzka taught me to let a drop of blood fall from my heart-finger, into a drink, and give it to his honor to drink, saying the following words: 'Just as I cannot live without my blood, so you christened and called Jan, cannot live without me.' (Skrzynno 1639)

B. Also for love. A woman washed her body and mixed the water with the hearts of pigeons, then gave it to the prospective lover, reciting:

Just as it is hard for a pigeon without his mate, so let it be hard for him without a wife. (Rzeszów 1718)

C. For a positive outcome in a court-case before the Crown Tribunal. Bake the stolen Eucharist host into pancakes to give to the judges. While mixing the batter, recite:

Just as people crowd around the Most Holy Sacrament, in the same way let their graces the lord deputies of the court show favor in our cases. (Lublin 1732)

D. To destroy buildings. Take soil or dust from a whirlwind and sprinkle it on the buildings, reciting:

Just as this soil has toppled over, so will these houses topple over. (Lublin 1643)

E. To destroy the fertility of fields:

Place two chicken eggs on the field-border, so that the fields will be as bare as those eggs, and roll the eggs in ashes, so that the grain will be destroyed, as the eggs are destroyed in the ash. (Wyszogród 1705; cf. Bochnia 1679)

F. To cause a person pain:

Here I burn dried ash-tree leaves.
Just as they burn, and leave no ash,
So let his heart burn within him![35]

Despite their different purposes and the various materials used, all these spells conform to the same structure: 'Just as A is to B, so also let C be to D.' The standard Frazerian relations of sympathetic magic are present—pigeons are associated with love, blood with life, the Eucharist with favorable emotions, ashes with destruction or infertility.[36] However, the analogical structure of these spells implies not imitation and contagion in the Frazerian model, but difference. As Stanley Tambiah noted in his classic critique of Frazer's theory of magic, the analogical structure of magic rests on the absence of relation—it asks for, hopes for, exhorts, demands the creation of a relation which is understood to be lacking.[37] Unlike scientific analogies such as *sound:echo::light:reflection*, which find similarity to produce knowledge, magical analogies are rhetorical: they do not proceed by finding similarity but by finding difference, and 'evoking' or 'arguing for' or 'exhorting' similarity. Thus in the propagandistic relation *father: son::employer:worker*, the suggestion is that workers *should* treat their boss as a son *does* treat his father—with respect, obedience, and affection. But the analogy would not be made if employees did in fact so treat their employer; the deployment of such an analogy implies that one of the hoped-for relations is absent or amiss. A relation of similarity is not found but is *asserted*, in the hope that it will come to be. Thus the structure of the first spell for love may be written as *blood:essential for life::Zofia:(essential for life)*, where the fourth term, in parentheses, stands in a relation of opposition to its imputed analog. Blood really is essential for life, while Zofia, to her disappointment, is not at all essential to the life of Jan Podlodowski, the nobleman in whose manor she works as a cook. Quite the contrary, he ignores her entirely when not extorting sexual favors. The term in parenthesis is the exhorted outcome, while the parentheses themselves

---

[35] This last spell comes not from a trial but from Szymon Szymonowic's pastoral *Sielanki* (no. 15). The humanist poet derived the ritual of burning the leaves from Theocritus' *Idylls*, only replacing the laurel-leaves of the Hellenistic poem with indigenous *jasion* or ash. However, the form of the spell conforms precisely to those in the trials—suggesting that many levels of Polish society shared an implicit knowledge of the grammar of spells. For an insightful account of classical and popular motifs in this poem, see Władysław Szyszkowski, 'Pierwiastek ludowy w poezyi polskiej XV i XVI w (part 1)', *Lud*, 19 (1913), 128–9.

[36] The classic, still widely influential theory of sympathetic magic is laid out voluminously in James George Frazer, *The Golden Bough*, 3rd edn. (New York: Macmillan, 1935 [1912]), i, chs. 3–4. See Ch. 8 for further critique of this model and of its influence on the historiography of witchcraft.

[37] Stanley Jeyaraja Tambiah, 'Form and Meaning of Magical Acts', in M. Lambek (ed.), *A Reader in the Anthopology of Religion* (Malden, Mass.: Blackwell, 2008 [1973]). Tambiah's 'analogy of difference' closely resembles the concept of 'modeling' developed by Sanda Golopentia to understand the formulae of Romanian charms: Sanda Golopentia, 'Towards a Typology of Romanian Love Charms', in J. Roper (ed.), *Charms and Charming in Europe* (New York: Palgrave, 2004), 163–5.

A: For love

$$\frac{\text{blood}}{\text{essential for life}} : \frac{\text{Zophia}}{\text{(essential for life)}}$$

B: For love

$$\frac{\text{pigeon}}{\text{needs mate}} : \frac{\text{target}}{\text{(needs mate)}}$$

C: For favor before a court of law

$$\frac{\text{Eucharist}}{\text{attracts favourable attention}} : \frac{\text{legal case}}{\text{(looked upon favorably)}}$$

D: To destroy houses

$$\frac{\text{soil}}{\text{topples over}} : \frac{\text{houses}}{\text{(topple over)}}$$

E: To destroy crops

$$\frac{\text{egg-shell}}{\text{bare}} : \frac{\text{fields}}{\text{(bare)}}$$

F: For love

$$\frac{\text{leaves}}{\text{burn up}} : \frac{\text{heart}}{\text{(burns up)}}$$

Figure 5.2. The analogical structure of Polish spells.

indicate that the real or current relation is understood as one not of similarity, but of contrast.

Despite the very wide diversity of aims and materials used, and the considerable range in time and space of these spells, they all conform to this analogical structure (Figure 5.2). People crowd around the Eucharist in adoration, but so far the judges have not looked with favor on the party in a lawsuit. Egg-shells are bare and smooth, but the fields are full of growing grain—the worker of the egg-spell intends to remedy this situation. And so on. This simple and flexible structure of Polish spells helps explain how accused witches and others could produce well-formed, plausible, grammatically correct spells *ad libitum*, on the spot, and often under conditions of horrible pain.[38]

[38] The rhetorical or exhortatory nature of such charms rests on an assumption that the natural world is amenable to persuasion. This approach to 'nature as a text' has been emphasized by Michel Foucault in his reading of Renaissance systems of representation, in contrast to the modern understanding of

This consideration introduces an important element of uncertainty into our interpretation of the witch-trial confessions. Accused witches who describe detailed spells may have been confessing to things they really had done, or to things they had heard of other people doing, or to things that it was generally known that witches do: to know a spell does not mean that one has used the spell or intends to do so. A great deal of magical knowledge was widespread. Just as today everybody 'knows' that magicians say 'abracadabra' and 'hocus pocus'. so in early modern Poland everybody 'knew' that witches say 'biorę pożytek, ale nie wszytek' (I take the profit, but not the whole thing) to steal the cream and good milk from the udders of their neighbors' cattle (Kalisz 1584; Chęciny 1665b, 1665d; Nowy Wiśnicz 1688a; Słomniki 1700). People 'knew' this to be the case independently of whether or not anyone had ever really said these words. Knowing this, an accused witch could reproduce this spell while confessing under torture, or could modify it, transforming it into a spell not of theft but of counter-magical anti-theft—explaining that they took 'nothing from others, only what is mine, the profit and the whole thing (pożytek i wszytek) as it was before' (Kalisz 1584; cf. Chęciny 1665b).

THE CIRCULATION OF MOISTURE

'I take the profit, but not the whole thing.' This best-known and most widely attested formula of Polish witchcraft hints at the underlying structure of assumptions informing the imagination of witches in early modern Poland: 'profit', symbolized primarily as dew in the fields, alcohol in beer, and above all as milk in the udder and the breast, is a finite resource that can be stolen, sucked away, dried up. One finds the same notion elsewhere in Europe. Lyndal Roper speaks of an 'economy of bodily fluids' in the imagination of German witchcraft, where 'dry' and 'withered' old women were thought to suck away fluids naturally belonging to, and needed by, the young and fertile: fat, juicy infants wither away, the milk stolen from their mother's breasts constituting a reversal of proper nourishment roles.[39] Deborah Willis has developed a similar reading of English witchcraft imagined as inverted motherhood—suckling imps instead of babies, eating

---

signs as arbitrary. As Stuart Clark has pointed out, Foucault correctly characterizes the Renaissance Neoplatonists and Hermeticists, but not the Thomistic demonologists who largely opposed them. For someone like Del Rio, magic was a 'vain practice', efficacious only with the devil's help, precisely because inanimate objects, unlike demons, are unpersuaded by rhetoric. As Thomas Aquinas put the matter, 'we make signs only to other intelligent beings'. See Del Rio, *Disquisitiones*, bk. 3, pt. 2; Stuart Clark, 'The Rational Witchfinder: Conscience, Demonological Naturalism and Popular Superstitions', in S. Pumfrey *et al.* (eds.), *Science, Culture and Popular Belief in Renaissance Europe* (New York: Manchester UP, 1991), 240–5.

[39] Lyndal Roper, *Oedipus and the Devil* (New York: Routledge, 1994), 207–9; *Witchcraze*.

babies instead of nurturing them;[40] while Alan Dundes classically developed a global opposition between dry and wet—the latter symbolized by dew, milk, semen, blood, and wine—to explain the folklore of the evil eye.[41] Roper, Willis, and Dundes all draw on Freudian theory to explicate the connections between orality, consumption, and mother's milk central to this symbolic universe. While not discounting this approach, I have found it more useful to read the Polish material in terms of George Foster's notion of the 'limited good'—that there is only so much fortune, or prosperity, or fertility to go around, and one cannot acquire more than one's share except by stealing it from others. The image of the limited good may be treated as the key metaphor of the 'common language' of Polish witchcraft, while milk—its lack or overabundance, its theft and preservation—stands as the central synecdoche for the imagined activities of witches and the real practices of those who would protect themselves from witchcraft. Limited good also helps to explain what might be called the 'paradox of witchcraft'—the fact that everybody knows what witches do, and many people experience the effects of their malefice, although nobody admits freely to being a witch.

The anthropologist George Foster first proposed the image of the limited good to explain what he saw as universal features of peasant behaviors: suspicion and envy and social sanction against the more prosperous; a disposition to work less in response to increased yields rather than to benefit from them; various leveling mechanisms such as the sponsorship of festivals through which suspicious prosperity can be returned to the community. The image of the limited good suggests that all good things—not just wealth but also health and fertility, beauty and love, luck and honor, exist in 'finite quantity and are always in short supply'. Accordingly, a person can possess a superabundance of any of these goods 'only at the expense of others': all profit is gained at someone else's loss.[42] In an article inspiring my own thought, Raymond Kelly has brilliantly applied the concept of limited good to Melanesian beliefs about witchcraft and sexual relations.[43] The Etoro people of Papua New Guinea possess a 'tragic' view of life under which

[40] Deborah Willis, *Malevolent Nurture* (Ithaca, NY: Cornell University Press, 1995).

[41] Alan Dundes, 'Wet and Dry, the Evil Eye: An Essay in Indo-European and Semitic Worldview', in A. Dundes (ed.), *The Evil Eye* (New York: Garland Publishing, 1981). For an insightful reading of Scandinavian magic amenable to my own approach, see Jacqueline Van Gent, *Magic, Body and the Self in Eighteenth-Century Sweden* (Boston: Brill, 2009).

[42] George M. Foster, 'Peasant Society and the Image of the Limited Good', *American Anthropologist*, 67 (1965), 296–7. Foster clarified his formulation in response to early critique in 'A Second Look at Limited Good', *Anthropological Quarterly*, 45/2 (1972); for the application of Foster's notion to witchcraft, see Dundes, 'Wet and Dry'; Ralph A. Austen, 'The Moral Economy of Witchcraft: An Essay in Comparative History', in J. Comaroff and J. L. Comaroff (eds.), *Modernity and its Malcontents* (Chicago: University of Chicago Press, 1993).

[43] Raymond C. Kelly, 'Witchcraft and Sexual Relations: An Exploration in the Social and Semantic Implications of the Structure of Belief', in M. Lambek (ed.), *A Reader in the Anthropology of Religion* (Malden, Mass.: Blackwell, 2008 [1976]).

sexual acts are necessary but necessarily consumptive of life force or *hame*, through the reproductive loss of which a man grows old and eventually dies. A witch is a person who, through excessive sexual demands or spectral cannibalism, overconsumes *hame* without returning it to the community in the form of children.

The early modern Polish equivalent of *hame* was the moisture and fat which, at several levels and in several ways, nourished the body, the family, and the fields. Witches were above all those who stole moisture, either out of spite as when they 'dried up' or 'withered' a neighbor, or in order to seek illegitimate prosperity, as when they stole the 'profit' of their neighbor's dairy production. Whereas a central method of healing rituals involved drinking tinctures, washing in herbal decoctions, and being smeared with various ointments, that is, having moisture or fat added to oneself, a central method of malefice was to dry up the victim. As in the West, witches stole fat, juicy babies and burnt them; they kept the rendered fat for themselves to make witches' ointment; but used the dry ash or powder as a maleficient poison: the witches of Bochnia sprinkled a burnt and powdered *niewiniątko* (innocent one, infant) on the fields while reciting 'let the years be dry as this powder is dry; let no rain fall and no grain grow' (Bochnia 1679).[44] Indeed, in Poland, the sprinkling of dry powders was a characteristic method of malefice, and was almost never associated with medicine or healing. Dorota Gnieczkowa reported a spell for spoiling marriage involving the ashes of an owl (Poznań 1544a); and in a number of trials witches used powders of dried lizards, snakes, toads, mice, rooster-feathers, or human hair to destroy cattle and people, especially children (Kleczew 1626, 1629, 1662a, 1688, 1689b, 1690a, 1730; Opalenica 1652; Biecz 1655; Nowy Wiśnicz 1703; Wągrowiec 1708, 1725; Lublin 1739). The ashes of burnt human bones were seen as especially efficacious (Kleczew 1625; Lublin 1627; Chęciny 1665c; Bochnia 1679; Kamieniec Podolski 1716).[45]

Often the connection between dry ashes and infertility is clear and explicit (as in Bochnia 1679 or Wyszygród 1705, and see Figure 5.2 above). In another trial at Wyszogród, the fertility of the fields was destroyed with a powder of mushrooms and 'burnt dew', as literal an inversion of wet fertility as one could ask for (Wyszogród 1718b).[46] Humans and cattle could also be dried up by taking soil from a person's footprints or manure from cattle and drying it in the hearth fire (Poznań 1544a; Skrzynno 1639; Dobczyce 1687; Pyzdry 1719).

---

[44] Cf. the drought-causing dried-up infant corpse in Muszyna 1678. Of course, the 'witches' ointment' of baby fat and the 'witches' powder' of baby bones are a staple of western demonology from the time of Nider's *Formicarius* (*c.*1435) onward: for representative examples, see Alan Charles Kors and Edward Peters (eds.), *Witchcraft in Europe, 400–1700*, 2nd edn. (Philadelphia: University of Pennsylvania Press, 2001), 157, 160–2, 164–5, 323–4. The motif appeared in Poland as early as 1502, when a woman was accused before the Poznań ecclesiastical court of baking a live unbaptized baby to make an ointment (her case was dismissed). Adamczyk, 'Czary i magia', 150.

[45] Cf. Dysa, 'Witchcraft Trials', 30, concerning a powder of bones and teeth in a trial from Kamieniec Podolski, 1716.

[46] Dew could also be buried at the field-borders to cause drought or destroy the crops (Warta 1730).

Indeed, one could use the term 'to dry someone up' as a synonym for maleficient witchcraft in general, as when Zofia Filipowicowa allegedly asked her fellow house-maid to 'dry up (*ususzyć*)' her manor-lord's brother (Skrzynno 1639; cf. Poznań 1660). In the *Infernal Parliament* the demon Lelek, a servant of witches, explains his activity in the world: 'If I can, I take a person's soul/If I can't, I dry up his body.'[47]

Witchcraft entailed the unnatural and excessive loss of moisture; counter-magic, and healing more generally, involved the proper circulation of water in its double aspect as drink and as the medium for washing. Imbibed or bathed in, water restored the moisture stolen through witchcraft. But water also purified and cleansed; it was meant not only to be collected but also dispersed, taking illness and misfortune and enchantment away with it. Healing rituals often combined exorcistic motifs with cleansing, as when the one Marusza washed sick children to exorcize them of *kłobuchy*—evil spirits understood to cause disease (Kalisz 1616). Małgorzata Magierska washed a child in holy water; although in her trial this bath was said to have caused serious illness, the original intention must have been curative (Nowy Wiśnicz 1703; cf. Kalisz 1613; Lublin 1678). Jadwiga Macowa made explicit the symbolic connection between water, milk, and health when she gave children curative baths in buttermilk (Nowy Wisnicz 1688a). Indeed in the eighteenth century it was a common practice in noble families to bathe newborns in butter and blessed herbs, a sort of prophylactic exorcism against witchcraft and demons clearly indebted to the baptismal ritual.[48]

Although witches could and did dry up their victims from pure spite, as in many of the examples above, more often the goal was to obtain profit at another's loss. Contemporary sources understood such drying activities within the context of the limited good, as moves in a zero-sum game by which the moisture stolen from others accrued to the witch, nearly always in the form of milk and butter. The Jesuit preacher Aleksander Lorencowic captured this notion aptly, writing that a witch can make 'something of mine, which was as healthy as can be, slowly dry out and wither, while something of hers swells up'.[49] This elite characterization fits neatly with commoner conceptions: Zofia Skrzyneczka suspected witchcraft when her

---

[47] Sowirzalius, *Sejm piekielny*, 57, vv. 1173–4. Compare similar practices from Russia, where 'drying up' seems to have been the central metaphor for witchcraft, affecting everything from a field to a cow to a young wife: see Linda J. Ivanits, *Russian Folk Belief* (Armonk, NY: M. E. Sharpe, 1989), 65–8, 104; Worobec, *Possessed*, 66.

[48] Kitowicz, *Opis obyczajów*, 66. Such rituals persisted until recent times: in the Lublin region in the 19th cent., women still bathed their children in herbs; the bath-water was then thrown out into a stream, onto a strange dog, on the road, or onto an elderberry bush, so that the devil who lived underneath it could absorb the sickness. Kolberg, *Dzieła wszystkie*, xvii. 162–5.

[49] Lorencowic, *Kazania*, i. 154.

Figure 5.3. Milking and churning. From an anonymous *Kalendarz Wieczny* (Perpetual Calendar), Kraków, *c.*1600, p. 25. Courtesy of the Polish National Library.

cow stopped giving milk, and the calves 'dried up (*uschły*)' and died (Nowy Wiśnicz 1688a; cf. Toruń 1712).

Thus witches were, above all, thieves of milk. This was true across Europe: when the courtly poet Wezpazjan Kochowski wrote 'Here lies a famous witch, frightful to recall/Who milked a rope as if it were a cow', he drew on an image well known in the West; even Luther had called witches 'milk-thieves' in his *Table Talk*.[50] But while other images, especially those of flight and cannibalistic infanticide, replaced milk-theft in the West, it remained the central metaphor for witchcraft in Poland (Figure 5.3). Milk-theft appears in bishops' court documents from the fifteenth- and early sixteenth-century (trials in Gdańsk 1483; Wieluń 1476; Płock 1501),[51] while as recently as 2004 a man was accused of milk-theft publicly, after church, by his neighbor—he took her to court for defamation, and she apologized.[52] Although the main charge in most actual trials involved more serious sickness or death, milk-theft and milk-protection magic is a regular part of confessions as well as of witness's testimony, appearing

[50] Wespazjan Kochowski, *Nieproznujące proznowanie ojczystym rymem na liryka i epigramata polskie rozdzielone*, ed. K. J. Turowski (Kraków: Biblioteka Polska, 1859 [1684]), 309; cf. Baczko and Hinz, *Kalendarz pólstuletni 1750 1800*, 55. Kochowski alludes to a notion popularized by Geiler von Kayserberg's *De Emeis*: see Kors and Peters, *Witchcraft in Europe*, 238, 54, 63. On milk-theft in Germany, Scandinavia, and Scotland, see also Charles Zika, *The Appearance of Witchcraft* (New York: Routledge, 2007), 36–48; Stephen Wilson, *The Magical Universe* (New York: Hambledon, 2000), 106–9.

[51] Koranyi, 'Czary i gusła', 14–15; see also Szyszkowski, 'Pierwiastek ludowy (1)', 121–2.

[52] 'Pierwszy'.

in at least fifty trials (from Poznań 1544 to Uście Solne 1760).[53] So central is this trope to Polish witchcraft that the court adduced as evidence against one accused witch her possession of twelve pails of milk with thick cream, from only three cows (Muszyna 1678). Under torture, another accused witch denounced her neighbor, pointing out that 'she has plenty of butter from just one cow' (Kalisz 1613); conversely, the husband of another accused witch tried to prove his wife's innocence by claiming 'I have nine cows, but I don't have even a drop of milk, and my wife always used to say, "they call me a witch, even though I have to buy cheese"' (Nowy Wiśnicz 1688b).

In both demonology and confessions, increased milk featured as a primary motivation for witchcraft. Women were tempted to become witches when their cattle lost their milk; it was on such occasions, characteristically, that the devil appeared to offer his pact.[54] The devil promised butter (Kalisz 1613), or 'milkiness' (Pyzdry 1731). When Regina Wierzbicka saw milk flowing from another witch's staff, the latter told her that 'the devil makes that milk; when you give yourself over to him, you'll also have such milk' (Bochnia 1679).

Milk-theft, as understood and experienced in early modern Poland, was a real harm—it robbed especially the poor of one of their most important assets and sources of nutrition. Haur wrote that God, in his goodness, had created cows to feed the poor.[55] The mixture of economic and symbolic value placed on cows and their milk shows clearly in the testimony of a peasant in Jazowsko before the village court in 1667: 'I had only one cow which like a mother provided for myself, my wife, and my children; we ate only what she produced.'[56] As such testimony attests, the popularity and the persistence of this imagined crime has to do with its perfect articulation of the limited-good cosmology: milk was not only an important source of nutrition, but had a central place in the symbolic world as well. The dairy-yield of its milch-cow served as both an 'objective' and a symbolic index of a household's well-being.[57] The dried-up cattle, their profit stolen, metaphorically represented larger problems such as sickness in the household or generalized misfortune, so that milk-theft figures often even in those trials where it is not a central allegation. One can hardly find a better symbolic image of the 'drying out' represented and caused by witchcraft than that given by a cow

---

[53] This figure excludes a further twenty-nine trials featuring malefice against cattle rather than their milk, though milk-theft is likely implied in most of these as well. Milk-theft was also an ubiquitous accusation in the Ukraine and Ducal Prussia, on which see Dysa, 'Witchcraft Trials', 164–5; Wijaczka, *Procesy w Prusach*, 251–7.

[54] Ząbkowic, *Młot*, pt. 2, qu. 1, ch. 1. The same theme appears repeatedly in 19th-cent. Polish folklore: see Kolberg, *Dzieła wszystkie*, vii. 78–81.

[55] Haur, *Skład Abo Skarbiec*, 51.

[56] Grodziski, *Księgi sądowe jazowskie*, 37–8.

[57] Note that, although most peasant households kept several head of swine, malefice against swine figures hardly at all in the Polish witch-trials: I know of just two examples, both late (Pyzdry 1732 Kraków 1745).

near Opatów, which leaked milk from its tail and hooves, wasting away instead of nourishing the household.[58] Milk-theft stood simultaneously for itself and for a larger system of crimes and misfortunes.

Witches could steal milk in a large variety of ways. Suspicion fell on those who visited a barn in which a calf had just been born, or who attempted to steal such items as the afterbirth or manure from a cow that had just given birth (Słomniki 1674b; Nowy Wiśnicz 1689a; Szczekociny 1706). Other accused witches gathered herbs from the fields or the field-borders where cattle graze, again usually before dawn (Chęciny 1665d). They also gathered the grass and soil where cattle had walked out to pasture, especially at the first pasturing in spring (e.g. Słomniki 1674b; Nowy Wiśnicz 1688b and 1688d). It was in reference to such practices that the *Infernal Parliament* speaks of witches—

> Sweeping before the cows, when they come home
> Fetching milk to their own lairs from the barns of strangers[59]

—and it was against such practices that peasant women beat the cattle with Easter palms,[60] or caused them to step over a scythe or an axe on their way out to pasture.[61]

To protect milk from such theft, it could be filtered through blessed herbs (Chęciny 1665d);[62] through 'blessed cheese' (Chęciny 1665b); a cheesecloth boiled during Easter Mass (Szadek 1649a); or blessed bread (Poznań 1549); even through the stolen Eucharistic host (Lublin 1644; Lublin 1664). However, as the most common way to steal milk was to gather dew, the most common way to restore stolen milk was to restore moisture in the form of dew or river water. Merely to be up and around, particularly in the fields, of an early summer morning, could be grounds for suspicion of witchcraft. Witnesses against Justyna Rabiaszka claimed to have seen her gathering dew in the fields around dawn, while her daughter was alleged to fetch water from the river before dawn even in the summer, when morning came so early (Nowy Wiśnicz 1689a; cf. Klimkówka 1702c). Regina Frąkowa admitted that she gathered dew to 'sprinkle cows', smearing it on their horns, feet, and bellies (Słomniki 1700). Probably intended as a healing charm, Regina's dew collection looked suspiciously like milk-theft.

Such ambivalence was a general feature of counter-magic, which 'stole back' the moisture and milk removed by witchcraft. Such practices could be

---

[58] I take this image from Baranowski (*Procesy Czarownic*, 143), who cites APŁódź, AMOpatów sig. 1 fo. 193 as his source. As with many trials cited by Baranowski, he does not give a date or any other details.

[59] Sowirzalius, *Sejm piekielny*, vv. 892–3, 48.

[60] Bylina, 'Magia', 47. On the apotropaic magical use of such palms throughout Catholic Europe and even in Protestant Germany, see Robert Scribner, *Religion and Culture in Germany (1400–1800)* (Boston: Brill, 2001), 315; Wilson, *Magical Universe*, 34–5.

[61] Słomka, *Pamiętniki włościanina*, 205; cf. Scribner, *Religion and Culture*, 283.

[62] Cf. Niebrzegowska, *Przestrach od przestrachu*, 101–3, for the identical practice in the late 20th cent.

Christianized through the use of holy water rather than dew (Poznań 1544b; Kraków 1611; Kalisz 1613; Nowy Wiśnicz 1688c). But when cattle were washed from head to tail in water taken from a running source, such as a river (Kalisz 1584), from a well, before sunrise (Turek 1652b; Nowy Wiśnicz 1689a), or from a place of magical potency, such as the mill-wheel (Nowy Wiśnicz 1659);[63] it could be difficult to distinguish milk-theft from counter-magical cure. Jadwiga Głuchowa was accused of washing her cows all night before major holidays, and then pouring out the water on the crossroads (Chęciny 1665d). Was this witchcraft or its opposite? In practice, the distinction could become very blurry indeed. It was also relational: what I experience as counter-magic might look, to my neighbor, very much like witchcraft, especially if I am stealing back what is 'rightfully mine' from him.

Milk could also be filtered through or across an axe or scythe or a heated horseshoe, as when Katarzyna Kapuścina confessed that 'against enchanted milk I was taught to heat a scythe in the fire and lay it on top of the cheesecloth, and filter the milk through this' (Chęciny 1665c; cf. Warta 1679a; Szczekociny 1706).[64] Such rituals explicitly attacked the attacking witch, who would cut or burn herself when she attempted to steal the milk. In the aggression and willingness to cause harm of these counter-measures to witchcraft, one can see that the line between apotropaic magic and spiteful malefice begins to blur.

Witches plucked grass from the hoofprints of cattle to steal their milk, and hung soil from hoofprints or footprints in the chimney to 'dry up' their victims. Inversely, Jadwiga Macowa testified to drying up soil or grass from the hoofprints of her *own* cattle 'so that they should give more milk;' a practice we can interpret as an attempt to dry up the witch who was drying up the cattle—malefice in the name of healing one's own cattle (Nowy Wiśnicz 1688a). Similarly, a ritual aimed at the restoration of stolen milk involved stealing manure from the cattle of the suspected witch, mixing it with milk and yeast in an eggshell, and filtering the mixture through a cheesecloth boiled over wood stolen from the suspect's homestead. Finally, one adds the herb *wrotycz* (tansy, *Tanacetum vulgare* L.) to the filtered milk, while reciting 'By the Virgin Mary's power and the power of all the Saints, I take back my profit, that it should return to me just as this *wrotycz* returns' (Chęciny 1665b; cf. Kleczew 1624b). Although this ritual was presented by the accused witch, quite sincerely, as an attempt to regain witch-stolen milk, all of its elements adhere very closely to the popular

---

[63] According to the *Infernal parliament*, un-Christian peasants 'send their apprentices under the mill, for water' (Sowirzalius, *Sejm piekielny*, 47, v. 868). However, thoroughly Christian peasants still used mill-water to unbewitch milk in the late 20th cent. (Lehr, 'Wierzenia demonologiczne', 141).

[64] Cf. Haur, *Skład Abo Skarbiec*, 469. For similar rites in the 19th cent., see Kolberg, *Dzieła wszystkie*, vii. 89.

conception of how witches themselves stole milk. The neighbor who caught Maryna attempting to steal manure or wood from his homestead, and who would know herself not to be a witch, would not hesitate to accuse Maryna herself of witchcraft.

Milk-protection and milk-restoration rituals were indubitably really practiced, to a greater or lesser degree, by all peasant households. While the more elaborate spells may have been passed down from mother to daughter, the basic rituals were the common property of all peasants, male and female. Everybody fed their cattle crumbs from the Christmas Eve feast; everybody gave their cattle blessed herbs to eat at prescribed times of the year; everybody sprinkled their cattle with holy water at the first pasturing in spring; most hung blessed herbs in the stable or over the barn door. More elaborate practices, such as washing the cattle in a decoction of blessed herbs through the night of Holy Saturday, or censing them with the smoke of burning herbs, or washing them in water fetched before dawn, were also very common—many of these practices are still common today, or have died out only in the last few decades.[65] But no sharp line of demarcation can be made between

(1) protecting one's cattle from milk-theft;
(2) recovering the milk production of one's cattle, after it has been stolen or spoiled by a witch;
(3) increasing the profit of one's own cattle, ostensibly without stealing the profit from others; and
(4) harmful and selfish milk-theft.

All these activities blend imperceptibly into one another, so that one cannot speak clearly of 'white magic' versus 'black magic' or of 'defense' versus 'offense'. One woman's 'recovery' of her cow's lost milk must look, to an outsider, very like another woman's 'theft'—one might say that the best defense is a good offense. It follows that, while milk-magic was widely practiced, few or no practitioners thought of themselves as milk-thieves—that is, as witches. People were constantly doing all sorts of magic—*without there being any actual witches to do it against.* The imagined activity of thieves generated the real activities of protectors and recoverers, and the imagined rituals and spells of thieves generated the real rituals and spells of their adversaries. As Favret-Saada has commented of a similar situation in modern France, 'It is very likely that no one . . . throws spells, which does not prevent people from being hit by them.'[66]

If this picture of magic and counter-magic is correct, several interesting implications follow. First, we have another source for what I have been calling

---

[65] Such protective herbs did not always work. In 1601, a major fire was started in Nowy Targ by a woman censing her cattle with blessed herbs to protect them from witchcraft: Wijaczka, *Procesy w Prusach*, 251.
[66] Jeanne Favret-Saada, 'Unbewitching as Therapy', *American Ethnologist*, 16/1 (1989), 43.

the 'common language' of witchcraft confession. How does a person—whether accuser or confessing accused witch—know what real witches do? Easy: they take their own practices—justified, legitimate, defensive spells—and invert them to imagine the unjustified attacks or thefts perpetrated by witches. This is especially easy in that all counter-magical rituals are already inversions of the imagined rituals of witches: one knows that witches say 'I take the profit, but not the whole thing' precisely because, in counter-magic, one says 'I take back only my profit.' Secondly: it seems plausible that a great deal of magical practice must have constantly been taking place, without anyone ever having to think of themselves as a witch. When real women tried to steal their neighbor's milk, this could always be rationalized as defense, or as recovery, or as attempted reparation for milk previously stolen. Accordingly, there could be a great deal of witchcraft going on, without the necessity of any witches. Third: real counter-magical practice will have often been observed, and, since it so closely resembled the imagined practice of witches, upon which it was modeled as an inversion, this would provide a great deal of the evidence for witchcraft suspicion and accusation. Here, again, witches are found to be imaginary, but the imaginary witch produces real action, which in turn provides more evidence for imaginary witches. In such a context, it would be very easy to find constant, real evidence of witchcraft, and to know quite precisely what witches do.

BALD MOUNTAIN

The imagination of witchcraft in Poland, however, comprised more than consumption and overconsumption, drying up or hoarding the limited supply of health, prosperity and 'profit' in a circumscribed universe. It was also about sex with devils and demons; about acts of ritual desecration—the murder of babies, the murder of the innocent Infant in the Eucharistic host; about dances at the 'border' or at 'Lysa Góra', 'Bald Mountain'. In Chapters 6 and 7 we will have occasion to explore the developed stereotype of the witch as sacrilegious anti-Catholic; in Chapters 9 and 10 we will examine the complexities of the witch's relation with her demon lover. In this section, I provide a brief overview of the witches' meeting as it emerges in Polish witch-trials, and suggest that it can, in part, be understood in terms of the organizing metaphors of milk-theft and limited good. Despite the cosmopolitan provenance of the *sabbat* motif, bringing together literary inversionary stereotypes of the heretical secret society with Europe-wide folkloric themes of fairy visits, its local inflection derived in part from the common language through which the Polish witch was imagined and expressed.

As noted in Chapter 2, the developed *sabbat* motif may have entered into Polish jurisprudential consciousness via the description in Damhouder's influential *Praxis rerum criminalium*.[67] Within the first decades of the seventeenth century, descriptions of the diabolical feast could be found in popular literature, as in this witch's speech from the *Pilgrimage of Hobos*:

> I know many devils in hell, and where others sit
> They also know about me, I make sure of that.
> On Thursdays we get together, at the crossroads,
> Walking there not on our feet, but mostly on our heads.[68]

In sources as diverse as Marcin of Klecko's anti-Protestant *Slingshot against Ministers and All Heretics*, Gamalski's anti-witch-trial *Spiritual Warning to Judges*, and the ribald *Pilgrimage* and *Infernal Parliament*, the witches' meeting at Bald Mountain figured as a scene of ritual inversion, marginality, and carnivalesque orgy. As in the West, the *sabbat* provided, better than any other aspect of witchcraft, a coherent constellation of inversionary motifs with which to think about order, society, and the church.[69] The key to any interpretation of the *sabbat*-motif lies in its inversionary structure: 'we walk there not on our feet, but mostly on our heads'.[70] For the author of the *Infernal Parliament*, witches fly to 'granica'—the border or margin—by 'turning their shirts inside out': the inversion of clothing facilitates passage to the meeting which is itself a festival of inversion.[71] This structure of inversion, the *sabbat* as the opposite of all that is good or right or sacred or orderly, imparted to it a flexibility of function well-suited to every sort of moralizing discourse. As Stuart Clark has suggested, each particular reading of the topsy-turvy *sabbat* anti-structure instantiated 'an actual or symbolic inversion of a traditional form of life', providing a forum for reflection on order and its opposite.[72]

For the Catholic polemicist Marcin of Klecko, Bald Mountain was the Lutheran church in Poznań. 'Several dozen witches confessed under torture that several hundred devils danced with them, at Bald Mountain in Poznań; know then in what manner that [Protestant] Church was sanctified.'[73] In a chapter of his *Storehouse or Treasury* devoted to the dangers of immoderate drinking, Haur likened the dancing, drunkenness, and disorderly behavior frequently encountered in village taverns to the imagined excesses of the witches' gathering: 'wherever there's a Tavern, there bald Mountain is as well'.[74] The

---

[67] Damhouderius, *Praxis rerum*, cap. 61, sec. 115.
[68] Swizralus, *Peregrynacja*, vv. 772–5.
[69] I use the term *sabbat* in this and other chapters because of its wide currency in the scholarship of witchcraft. However, it should be kept in mind that the term is not found in Polish materials, which refer rather to 'gatherings', 'feasts', or simply '*Łysa Góra* [Bald Mountain]'.
[70] Swizralus, *Peregrynacja*, 171, v. 775.
[71] Sowirzalius, *Sejm piekielny*, 47, v. 873.
[72] Clark, *Thinking with Demons*, 81.
[73] Marcin of Klecko, *Procy na ministry i na wszystkie heretyki z piąćią Dawidowych kamieni w tobole* (Kraków: Wdowa Jak. Siebeneychera, 1607), 87.
[74] Haur, *Skład Abo Skarbiec*, 157–8.

author of the *Witch Denounced*, despite his conviction that Bald Mountain was an illusion born of melancholy, nevertheless described the gathering of witches as a heretical anti-mass: witches renounced God, Mary, and the saints, their baptism and all other sacraments; they entered into 'indecency' with devils, sacrificed newborn babies to him, and stole the Holy Sacrament for their satanic rites.[75] Chmielowski, to whom we owe the most complete Polish literary account of the Bald Mountain, repeats all these motifs but also develops more detailed theological and moral meanings: the witches' feast includes no bread (because it is a figure of the Body of Christ) and no salt (because it is used to bless holy water).[76]

By the beginning of the seventeenth century, the *sabbat*-motif had also begun to crop up in a limited way in witch-trials. In 1613 the accused witch Dorota confessed under torture that she had been carried away by her devil Kasparek to a 'marsh' where there were six other women and three devils—small, black, hairy beings dressed in red, with the heads of dogs. They danced, drank beer, and ate meat, but the beer was bad and the meat smelled rotten (Kalisz 1613). From this modest beginning, Bald Mountain grew to become one of the most common components of witch-trial confessions, especially in Wielkopolska. From the last quarter of the seventeenth onward, this motif figures in over half of those trials for which I have accurate records of accusation and confession.

The Bald Mountain of the witch confessions is a much simpler, more modest affair than anything found in demonology; it also encompassed very considerable variation. Most often it included a modest feast with dancing to music provided either by devils (Nowy Sącz 1670; Raciąż 1719) or by human musicians (Zbąszyń 1654a–b; Poznań 1669; Bochnia 1679; Zbąszyń 1681; Fordon 1682; Kleczew 1688; Nowy Koźmin 1690; Łobżenica 1692; Kleczew 1693, 1698; Nieszawa 1721a; Wągrowiec 1727, 1728a–b; Pyzdry 1740). As noted in Chapter 1, men figured in witch-trials largely as musicians at Bald Mountain, where they played cacophonous melodies on instruments such as the hoe, the plough, the needle, the moustache, the fish, or the fox's tail (Zbąszyń 1664b; Bochnia 1679; Kleczew 1688; Łobżenica 1690a–b, 1692; Pyzdry 1719, 1740; Nieszawa 1721a).[77] The feast could be very modest indeed. At Raciąż, Anna Ćwierciaczka said there were just two devils present—the fiddler and one other—and the feast consisted of pancakes that one of the witches had brought with her (Raciąż 1719). Sometimes the food was good, including meat and beer (Kleczew 1690a; Łobżenica 1692), or even vodka (Słomniki 1700). However, the food often was spoiled or rotten or, like fairy-food, turned into pig-shit or other unappetizing substances at dawn

---

[75] *Czarownica powołana*, 26, 31, 57–8.
[76] Chmielowski, *Nowe Ateny*, iii. 241.
[77] See also Wijaczka, 'Men', 78–81; *Czarownica powołana*, 58. A connexion between the musician motif and the pan-European legend of human musicians captured by the fairies should not be overlooked; see e.g. J. A. MacCulloch, 'The Mingling of Fairy and Witch Beliefs in 16th and 17th Scotland', *Folklore*, 32/4 (1921), 234–8.

(Kalisz 1613; Nowy Koźmin 1690; Nowe 1712a, 1718). Although witches were often provided with a diabolic dance-partner for their post-prandial revels, they never confessed to indiscriminate orgy: at most they lay with their devil-lover 'like a wife with her husband' (see Chapter 10).

The most famous Bald Mountain in Poland is Łysiec or Łysa Góra in the Świętokrzyskie (Holy Cross) mountains, site of an early Benedictine monastery. Scholars are still divided on the question whether pre-Christian practices at this site carried over into medieval and early modern collective memory.[78] Babia Góra (Old-Woman Mountain), a peak in the Beskidy mountain range near the headwaters of the Wisła, also derives its name from supposed assemblies of witches on its summit. But the numerous Bald Mountains of literature and folklore, as well as those which appeared in the confessions of accused witches, were usually local hills such as 'Rooster Mountain' (Zbąszyń 1654b), 'Goat Mountain' (Chęciny 1665b–c), or 'Titmouse Hill' (Nowy Wiśnicz 1688a–b). The term could be applied to almost any location, from a barn to a castle, a marsh to a forest. Most commonly, Bald Mountain happened 'at the border', the location symbolizing the marginality for which Bald Mountain itself served as synecdoche.[79] Bald Mountain could even imply an activity rather than a location; Gamalski, for example, calls the witches' meetings 'bald-mountainings (*łysogornice*)',[80] and in at least one trial the term appears to function as a euphemism for intercourse with the devil (Pyzdry 1719).

Witches did not always fly to Bald Mountain. Zofia Baranowa went in a dream (Lublin 1643); others went in carriages or buggies driven by devils in livery (Nowy Sącz 1670; Łobżenica 1692). However, by the late seventeenth century, night-flight to Bald Mountain figures in public insults, as when a woman of Przecław said of her neighbor that she 'was a witch and flew on a broom' (Przecław1675). Haur reported that horses, in contrast to cattle, are rarely enchanted, 'supposedly, because Witches don't ride to bald Mountain on Horses, but on Broomsticks'.[81] When accused witches did confess to flight, it could be without any apparent vehicle (Chęciny 1665b), or on 'devils' wings' (Chęciny 1665c), or on brooms and sabres (Bochnia 1679). The main means of

---

[78] Jerzy Gąssowski, 'Ośrodek kultu pogańskiego na Łysej Górze', in A. Oborny *et al.* (eds.), *Religia pogańskich Słowian* (Kielce: Muzeum Świętokrzyskie w Kielcach, 1968); Stanisław Bylina, 'Mesjasz z Gór Świętokrzyskich', *Odrodzenie i Reformacja w Polsce*, 33 (1988).

[79] In witchcraft confessions, the term Bald Mountain came to be applied to a neighboring village (Turek 1652b); a bush (Kleczew 1688); a castle, basement, or barn (Kleczew 1691b, 1730; Pyzdry 1731); behind the manor (Szkarszewy 1699c); the mill (Szczekociny 1706); the Jewish cemetery (Pyzdry 1740); or simply in someone's home (Pyzdry 1732). Most frequently, the location suggested wilderness or marginality: it was in the forest or wilderness (Lublin 1643; Wyszogród 1693, 1700a; Skarszewy 1700a; Płońsk 1709a); or most generically, 'at the border' (Zabłotów 1656; Nowy Wiśnicz 1688a; Kleczew 1690a). See also Karol Koranyi, 'Łysa Góra', *Lud*, 27 (1928), 60–1; Wijaczka, 'Witch and Sorcerer-Hunts', 118–20.

[80] Gamalski, *Przestrogi Duchowne*, 17.

[81] Haur, *Skład Abo Skarbiec*, 472.

flight to the Bald Mountain, however, was by means of witches' ointment: this could be made from dew (Słomniki 1700), from elderflower (Nowy Wiśnicz 1688a), or from "fatback and butter" (Kleczew ca. 1695),[82] or from dairy mixed with vermin: butter and white cheese mixed with herbs, snakes, and birds (Bochnia 1679), or 'various herbs, dairy, cheeses, butter, also reptiles, snakes, and birds' (Nowy Wiśnicz 1688b).[83]

A pattern thus emerges whereby the witches' ointment is, at least in part, the same thing as witches' riches—an overabundance of the symbolic goods of moisture: dew, cheese, milk, butter. Confessing witches knew what witches were supposed to steal, and applied this knowledge to their accounts of the witches' *sabbat*. I would like to end this section with a brief sketch of the development of Bald Mountain motifs from common knowledge of magic and counter-magic, and from inversion or exaggeration of the more prosaic imagined activities of witches. My point is not to discount the importance of demonological speculation in the development of the Bald Mountain stereotype, nor to discount the alternative possibility, associated with Ginzburg and his followers, that it represents deep and ancient patterns of interaction with the dead.[84] However, considerable detail about the *sabbat* could be generated out of the 'common language' of witchcraft that this chapter has explored.

Among those interrogated during the exceptionally large but also exceptionally mild trial of all suspicious peasant women enserfed to Jan Tarło, a certain Anna Wiązowa was accused of milk-stealing magic (Chęciny 1665d). She had allegedly been caught practicing the most typical magical technique attributed to Polish witches: gathering herbs before dawn in the meadows, muttering 'I take the profit, but not the whole thing (*biórę pożytek, ale nie wszytek*)'. Anna denied any wrongdoing; she *had* gathered dew, but had done so to repair the spoiled or bewitched milk of her own cattle: 'I went around collecting water because of an enchantment, when my cream didn't want to separate out and sour properly, and with this water I sprinkled the milk and recited three Hail Maries.' As I have argued above, the difference between witchcraft and ordinary activity turns on intention and perspective: witches gather dew to steal other peoples' milk, while good peasant women gather dew to restore the vitality and health of their bewitched cattle. Witches said 'I steal the profit, but not the whole thing'; good peasant women recited the Hail Mary. Anna Wiązowa's activity, at least as she represented it, was both pious and practical; it made use of the orthodox prayer for the legitimate purpose of protecting one's household from harm.

---

[82] The accused witch goes on to note that unfortunately her cat ate her supply of this tasty flying ointment.

[83] Cf. Koranyi, 'Łysa Góra', 63–4. On the symbolic implications of different alleged "recipes" for the witches' flight ointment, see now Michael Ostling, 'Babyfat and Belladonna: Witches' Ointment and the Contestation of Reality', *Magic, Ritual and Witchcraft* 11 no. 2 (2016).

[84] Carlo Ginzburg, *Ecstasies*, tr. Raymond Rosenthal (London: Hutchinson Radius, 1990).

Anna Wiązowa was dismissed without punishment of any kind. However, things could have turned out very differently. In two trials just a few weeks earlier, before the same court, similar allegations of milk-theft had led to interrogation under torture, during which the theme of dew-gathering underwent expansion, elaboration, and improvisation. Elżbieta Cackowa confessed that with her fellow witches she gathered dew in the fields and meadows and poured it into barrels at Goat Mountain. She did this out of malice, to cause drought, but also, it is implied, out of greed—the goodness or vitality or 'profit' in the dew was collected and hoarded by the witches (Chęciny 1665c). Ewa Krucka went even further. Like Anna Wiązowa, she had originally admitted to a spell which was an exact inversion of the witches' spell of milk-theft. She picked herbs and washed her cattle's udders in them, reciting:

I'm taking nothing more than the profit of my own cows, cream up to my waist, whey up to my feet, milk up to my knees. (Chęciny 1665b)

However, under torture this became, as with Elżbieta Cackowa, a story of the witches' *sabbat* and of dew-theft for drought. But now any sense of consumption or hoarding—anti-social and harmful activities which nevertheless have at least a comprehensible motivation—has been replaced entirely with pure spite and wanton caprice. Witches, Ewa explained, gather dew in barrels to stop the rain, because they dislike getting wet when they fly (Chęciny 1665b).

It is possible from the testimony of these three trials to construct a four-stage schema turning on common assumptions about the nature of moisture and its uses, and reflecting creative improvisation on this theme.

1. Anna Wiązowa's and Ewa Krucka's self-representations. Legitimate, conscientious, practico-religious use of dew and meadow-herbs, in combination with Christian prayer, to protect oneself and ones' household from witchcraft, or to undo the results of witchcraft.

2. The accusations against Anna Wiązowa. Illegitimate theft of dew, in combination with the universally known, characteristic spell of witches, in order to steal the cream and good milk from other people's cattle. This is the typical folk-view of witchcraft as the anti-social overconsumption of a limited good.

3. Elżbieta Cackowa's confession. Criminal theft of dew, in combination with the motifs of flight and Bald Mountain. Now the stolen moisture affects not just cattle but the weather as well, threatening the crops and the livelihood of the whole community. The basic theme of anti-social overconsumption remains in place but is expanded and deepened: the dew is collected by the collectivity of witches to bring profit to themselves at the expense of the entire village community.

4. Ewa Krucka's confession. Radically evil, transgressive theft of dew for no good reason. The witches steal dew and rain out of mere spite and thoughtlessness, because these life-giving substances, upon which the village economy and life itself depend, happen to be inconvenient to witches in their unproductive, pleasure-seeking flight on broomsticks.

All four accounts depend, for their comprehensibility, on a common cosmology of the limited good; and of moisture, figured as dew, rain, and milk, as the principal carrier of that good. The two interrogation accounts develop as elaborations of and improvisations on this basic stereotype of the milk-stealing witch. They do not replace the stereotype with another—the malefice-witch with the *sabbat*-witch, the popular witch with the demonological witch. Instead, they expand upon the stereotype's basic theme and follow things to their logical conclusion. Ewa Krucka's version appears to be unique—at least I have not found anything like it in other trials. And yet, clearly, she developed her version of what witches do with dew by drawing upon well-known themes and motifs. The Polish *sabbat* could be, in part, nothing more than a creative modification of the basic tropes and assumptions of early modern Polish cosmology.

Because a basic knowledge of herbcraft was common to nearly all accused witches, as also presumably to their accusers and even their judges; because everyone, from peasant women to Jesuit preachers to humanist poets, knew more or less what a spell was supposed to look like, and could therefore produce grammatically correct examples of spells in poetry or under interrogation; because the blessing of herbs against witchcraft, the filtering of milk against its theft, the whipping of cattle with Easter palms, the bathing of the sick and the pouring out of wash-water at the crossroads were all items in a repertoire of 'natural' medicine, counter-magic, and folk-Catholicism—a repertoire, again, common with small variations at every level of society—because of all these commonalities, it is not necessary or indeed useful to suppose that accused witches had special knowledge of any kind. They were not usually cunning-women nor even people of much magical reputation; on the contrary, most were ordinary women with ordinary knowledge. Both accusations and confessions were built out of a shared store of assumptions, oppositions, and analogies, forming a language out of which both ordinary women in their real rituals of counter-magic, and alleged witches in their imagined rites of destruction, could perform endless variations. In this chapter, I have set out and analyzed this common language and its implications. However, this account has been impoverished, indeed distorted, by a programmatic neglect of Christianity. Whatever else the accusers and victims of witchcraft may have been, and whatever other habits of thought shaped their actions and gave them meaning, they were also all Christians. The cosmology of the limited good, the common language of witchcraft, was part of, or was mixed with, the language and the cosmology of the church, and no account of witchcraft in Poland can be complete without an exploration of this master discourse. The 'Christianity' of Polish witchcraft, and the interpretative problems it raises, form the subject of the next two chapters.

6

Stealing the Sacred

Naydziesz takie złe ludzie, co Sakrament święty
Żydom i cżarownicom, w uściech swych przeięty,
Przedaią, bezbożnicy, ćiało i krew Pańską,
Uięci do pieniędzy chciwośćią szatańską.
O zakamiałę serca, łakomstwo bezecne!
O nieszczęsny rozumie i kupiectwo niecne!
Cżemu targuiesz tego za marny pożytek,
Którego iest kropla krwie droższa niż świat wszytek?

You'll find such evil people, who sell the holy Sacrament
To Jews and witches, having taken it in their mouths,
They sell the body and blood of the Lord: godless ones
Seized by a Satanic greed for money.
O rock-hardened hearts, indecent hunger!
Unlucky understanding, ignominious trade!
Why do you exchange, for a vain profit
That, of which one blood-drop is worth more than all the world?

(Sebastian Klonowic, *Worek Iudaszow* (1600), 139[1])

The beginnings of the narratives are nearly identical. A woman makes confession, either at Easter in her own parish or, more often, at the annual church fair (*odpust*) of some nearby parish where she is less likely to be recognized. At confession, she fails to mention her intention of stealing the communion wafer, the Body of Christ—and has thus already involved herself in the mortal sins of incomplete confession and communion without true absolution.[2] She attends mass, approaches the altar, and receives the host into her mouth from the hands of the priest (not touching it with her own hands—another mortal sin).

---

[1] Chs. 6 and 7 were enriched through the magnificent generosity of Dr Tomasz Wiślicz, who made available to me his transcripts of the Kleczew trials of 1669, 1688, 1691, and 1693, and Koranyi's MS copy of the Kleczew trial of 1730. Any shortcomings in the interpretation of these trials are, of course, mine alone.

[2] Piotr Skarga, *The Eucharist*, ed. and tr. E. J. Dworaczyk (Milwaukee: Bruce Publishing Co., 1939), 193; *The Roman Catechism*, tr. R. I. Bradley and E. Kevone (Boston: St Paul Edition, 1985), pt. 2, ch. 3, paras. 56–7; Trent sess. 13 canon 11; cf. 1 Cor. 11: 27–9.

But she does not swallow it: instead, after reciting the Our Father (with its deceptively simple and deeply problematic request that God provide the faithful with both His Incarnate Son and the temporal needs of their fleshly bodies— 'Give us this day our daily bread'), she spits the host into her kerchief or shawl and leaves the church. From here, accounts diverge. Some women take the stolen Eucharist home and use it to protect their cows from the milk-thieving schemes of witches. Others use it for love-magic, or to gain favor in a court case. Others sell it to the Jews, who are believed to require the Body of Christ for their own sinister purposes. Still others—witches themselves—throw it to pigs to create hail and storms, mix it with burnt frogs and vipers to create a poison, bury it enclosed in the rotting skull of a dead mare to bring death and disease to her feudal lord. Finally, a few re-enact the Passion by whipping and stabbing the host until it bleeds again 'that most Holy Blood, shed once for redemption of the human race by the Saviour of the world' (Kiszkowo 1761). The task of this chapter and the next is to interpret such narratives, which exist both in demonological and anti-Semitic polemics, in the verdicts of judges and in the testimony, both voluntary and extracted under torture, of accused witches. We will want to discover what they can tell us both about the beliefs and practices of the accused witches themselves, and of their accusers and judges: a key question will be to what degree these two groups diverge in their attitude toward the focal point of Catholic Reformation devotion and theology, the Most Holy Sacrament of the Eucharist.

CHRISTIAN MAGIC

From the early fifteenth century on, Polish synodal decrees display a constant preoccupation with the protection of sacramentalia from the laity and especially from women. Following the similar recommendations of the Fourth Lateran Council, provincial synods in Poznań (1420), Płock (1501), Łuck (1519), Gniezno (1602), Łowicz (1620), and Przemyśl (1641) directed clergy to carefully guard holy water, chrism oil, and the Eucharistic host from misuse or abuse. The synod of Chełmno in 1583 spelled out the nature of such abuse: sacramentalia must be guarded 'lest they be grasped by sacrilegious hands for the practice of sorcery'.[3]

This perceived need to prevent misuse of the sacraments and sacramentalia derived, ironically, from the very success of Christianization. Christian holy materials such as holy water, blessed herbs, and Easter palms had replaced older, pagan items as the mainstays of household magic by the fifteenth century.[4] Sticking Palm Sunday palms into the fields on Holy Saturday to drive away

---

[3] Jan Kracik, 'Chrzest w staropolskiej kulturze duchowej', *Nasza Przeszłość*, 74 (1990), 191; Adamczyk, 'Czary i magia', 243. The Polish church reflected worries found throughout Catholic Europe; see e.g. Gentilcore, *From Bishop to Witch*, 130–1.
[4] Bylina, 'Magia', 47.

vermin; carrying blessed 'thunder-candles' around the house at Candlemass to protect against lightning—such customs were well enough established to be condemned by learned clerics who saw such instrumentalist Christianity as almost worse than paganism.[5] Nevertheless, recommendations such as that of Mikołaj of Jawor, that women should replace their whispered spells during the gathering of herbs with recitations of the Our Father, are suggestive of the process by which popular culture assimilated official Christianity to its own needs.[6] As Aleksander Brückner presciently insisted long ago, 'one cannot speak of any strictly pagan remnants' in the superstitions attacked by fifteenth-century reformers; 'they have mixed entirely' with Christianity.[7]

Catholic critiques of superstition were appropriated and expanded during Poland's brief Reformation. What had been pagan or ignorant in the fifteenth century became, in the sixteenth, pagan, ignorant—and Catholic. Mikołaj Rej, the most eloquent of the early reformers, lampooned the blessing of Marian candles against thunder as a 'mistaken and pagan hope'.[8] Criticism of this kind presented a problem for the Catholic Reformation in Poland. On the one hand, the Catholic Reform sought to achieve a thoroughgoing monopoly over the sacred realm, and to cleanse the church of those excesses that provided Protestants with such excellent material for satire. On the other hand, the continuing attraction of the Catholic faith, especially among the common folk, lay above all in its rituals of protection and exorcism. What we find, then, is a double move in late sixteenth- and seventeenth-century Catholicism in Poland: toward austerity and toward exuberance, toward both the disciplining and the accommodation of folk practices.

The folk practices that the Counter-Reformation church sought either to expunge or to accommodate were deeply integrated into church ceremony—a fact sometimes rather overlooked by those who would assert the semi-pagan status of the early modern Polish peasant. What little we know about cunning practice makes it clear that most cunning magic borrowed liberally from the church: a cunning-women's 'spells' (which she called 'żegnania' or blessings— the same term was and is used for the act of crossing oneself) were made up in large part of sprinkling holy water, censing or bathing in blessed herbs, and multiple recitations of official church prayers. Dorota of Siedlików's ritual for blessing cattle against witchcraft consisted of sprinkling them with holy water

[5] Bylina, 'Magia', 40; *Chrystianizacja wsi polskiej*, 171–93; Aleksander Brückner, 'Przesądy i zabobony u ludu polskiego w wieku piętnastym', *Rozprawy Akademii Umiejętności: Wydział Filologiczny*, 24 (1895), 320–1; Olszewski, *Świat zabobonów*; on similar customs and critiques in Germany, see Scribner, *Popular Culture*, 32–8.

[6] Stanisław Bylina, 'Licitum—Illicitum: Mikołaj z Jawora o pobożności mazowej i zabobonach', in B. Geremek (ed.), *Kultura elitarna a kultura masowa w Polsce późnego średniowiecza* (Wrocław: Zakład Narodowy im. Ossolińskich, 1978), 156.

[7] Brückner, 'Kazania średniowieczne', 318.

[8] Rej, *Postylla*, fos. 304^v–305.

while reciting 'In the name of the Father and Son and Holy Spirit, by the Virgin Mary's power and the help of All the Saints' (Kalisz 1613).[9] Some variation of the formula 'By God's power, the Virgin Mary's power and the help of all the saints' turns up in numerous trials (Poznań 1544a–b; Kalisz 1584, 1593, 1613, 1616; Kleczew 1624b; Lublin 1664; Turek 1652b; Chęciny 1665b, 1665d), and is found in identical form in Polish village healing spells at the turn of the twentieth century.[10] Indeed our best evidence that Christian prayer formulae were well known to the women of small towns and villages in the sixteenth and seventeenth centuries comes from the testimony of such cunning-women or of ordinary women practicing *gusła* (superstition, enchantment)—officially illegitimate blessings or apotropaic rituals that borrowed their power from Christian symbols. That these same blessings and spells feature in witch-trials indicates the difficulty of distinguishing between witches, the enemies of God; recognized folk-experts standing in a position of uneasy rivalry with the church; or the ordinary village-women discussed in Chapter 5, with their counter-magical deployment of holy water, blessed herbs, and ritual invocation of the saints.

The difficulty inherent in such a distinction might be illustrated by the case of Katarzyna of Wojnicz, wife of a church organist, who specialized in exorcising *nocnice* or night-terrors (Nowy Wiśnicz 1662). Her method involved an inversionary recitation of the Hail Mary: 'You are not hailed, you are not full of grace, the Lord is not with you', and so on. Unsurprisingly, her accuser and the court treated this as a blasphemous spell 'of satanic inspiration', and Katarzyna was burnt at the stake as a witch. But she had confessed her exorcistic method to the court without any hint that she thought it was blasphemous or anti-Christian—as indeed, for her, it was not. The prayer was directed, after all, not to Mary but to the demons—*they* were not hailed, were not full of grace, were not blessed; accordingly they fell under the healer's power and could be driven out. What appears to be a Satanic prayer was intended as a proclamation that demons have no share in the protection or mercy of God.

For Catholic theologians, the distinction between superstitious abuse (cunning or magic) and orthodox devotion (religion)—the distinction between spell and prayer—often depended neither on the form nor the goal, but rather on indiscernible interior attitudes of the practitioner. To recite the Our Father a multitude of times, or as part of a cycle of rosary devotions, is licit and praiseworthy, even if in doing this one seeks temporal goods such as health. But the same actions, undertaken with the conviction that in themselves they will actually compel God, are magical and idolatrous, even if the intention is

---

[9] Such rituals were modeled closely on ecclesiastical protection against witchcraft. One Kleczew witch confessed that the local priest's cattle were immune to her maleficent witches' powder because 'he had his cattle driven into the church-yard, he performed a holy Mass and sprinkled the cattle with holy water; that helped him—else more of his cows would have died' (Kleczew 1690a).

[10] Inga Jaguś, *Lecznictwo ludowe w Królestwie Polskim na przełomie XIX i XX wieku* (Kielce: Kieleckie Towarzystwo Naukowe, 2002), 90–102.

praiseworthy, such as the shortening or lightening of a soul's torment in Purgatory. The difference may be expressed in terms of grammatical mood: a prayer is subjunctive and hortatory, magic takes the imperative.[11] Such a classification in terms of internal mood could hardly fail to generate borderline cases, and indeed it seems likely that most *guślarki* (whether by that term one means cunning-women or ordinary women healing their milk with the Hail Mary and some blessed herbs) understood their work to be more a matter of nudging or urging rather than compelling or command.

Seventeenth-century anti-superstition literature made no distinction between such healing spells and more nefarious uses of church materials. Nor, with the exception of narrowly focused writings such as the *Witch Denounced*, did it usually distinguish between witchcraft, cunning, and ordinary peasant superstition. The *Infernal Parliament*, quite possibly written by a minor church functionary and certainly reflective of orthodox post-Tridentine doctrine, complained of 'witches' who, on Great Saturday before Easter, 'cense their possessions with blessed fire, and send the apprentice to seven churches for holy water'.[12] The 'witches' who would do such a thing were rather ordinary village women: in fact the verse accurately describes an apotropaic ritual *against* witchcraft popular from the sixteenth to the nineteenth centuries.[13]

Indeed, most of the actions attributed to 'witches' in the *sowizdrzalski* literature amounted to the ordinary practices of ordinary peasant-women. Because of the semi-clerical authorship of much of this literature, witches are imagined to use church materials more than anything else in their craft:

> I tell one girl, to get strips of cloth from the church
> From the banners, the altar-cloth, however she can.
> 'Just as people follow those banners in crowds,
> So will they follow you—the devils as well!'
>
> . . .
>
> A third I teach, if she wants to get a man,
> To steal some hair, somehow, from his head.
> 'Also some wax from a baptismal candle, mix it
> with the hair to make a candle, burn it on Thursdays;
> As long as that candle burns
> So long will his heart yearn for you.'[14]

Such a use of sacramental materials for love-magic would have been understood as sinful by all concerned. But distinction between orthodoxy and magic,

---

[11] It should be clear from this that Frazer's classification of magic (mechanically efficacious) and religion (supplicatory) is indebted to Christian theological traditions, a problem to which I return in Ch. 8.

[12] Sowirzalius, *Sejm piekielny*, 47, vv. 884–5.

[13] Poznań 1549; cf. Kolberg, *Dzieła wszystkie*, liii. 392.

[14] Sowirzalius, *Sejm piekielny*, 50, vv. 962–5, 72–7.

between prayer and spell, was often much less clear. Despite efforts at demarcation, there remained a wide gray area over which Christians could legitimately disagree. For example, article 18 of the 'Declaration of the general synod of the under-clerks of the Podgórze region' distinguishes between those sacramental objects which may be distributed from the church, and those which may not:

Let nobody dare give wax from the church, strips [torn from the altar-cloth], baptismal water, moss from the roof, the bones of corpses, rust from the bells, *except for holy water, sprinkling [of holy water], herbs, mugwort*. For they use all these things to spoil property, to spoil marriages, to entice maidens and also young men.[15]

According to the article, beeswax, altar-cloth rags, and baptismal water, while legitimate and sacred in church, are only used by witches outside the church walls. In contrast, holy water and blessed herbs are legitimate sources of divine aid that may be used to protect oneself and one's homestead against demons or witchcraft.[16] The distinction (which is taken directly from Bishop Maciejowski's pastoral letter of 1601), could seem arbitrary, and points to the tension within the church between accommodation and critique of commoner piety.

OUR DAILY BREAD

In Poland, post-Tridentine indoctrination of the laity focused on the rote memorization of doctrinal formulae, accompanied by a hyper-scrupulous attention to the proper performance of rituals.[17] Archbishop Bernard Maciejowski's famous pastoral letter, which set the program for the Catholic Reformation in Poland, enjoined parish clergy to teach the catechism every Sunday, and to ensure that parishioners could cross themselves properly and recite the Lord's Prayer, the Hail Mary, and the Credo.[18] Maciejowski also attempted to bring lay use of sacramentalia and other para-liturgical items under control. While acknowledging that they may be used, according to the standard formula, 'for the health of the body and spirit', great care must be taken lest they be used superstitiously or be given to 'sathanicas'. All jocularity and wickedness must be eliminated during their administration, and they must be received with modesty, order, and piety.[19]

Such piety, however, tended to overflow the narrow bounds into which the clergy attempted to channel its flow. The church encouraged pious devotion to

---

[15] *Synod Klechów*, 224–5.

[16] Such blessed herbs continued to be used against witchcraft well into the 20th cent.; see Lehr, 'Wierzenia demonologiczne'.

[17] Jan Kracik, 'Katolicka indoktrynacja doby saskiej w parafiach zachodniej Małopolski', *Roczniki Teologiczno-Kanoniczne*, 20/6 (1973), 16–19.

[18] Nasiorowski, *'List pasterski' Maciejowskiego*, 195–8, 205.

[19] Ibid. 202–3.

images of the Virgin Mary or to the Passion of Christ, but also attempted to control such devotion—without much success. In the seventeenth-eighteenth centuries in the Kraków diocese alone there were twenty-seven officially sanctioned miracle-working images, mostly of the Virgin Mary; but there were also ninety-eight unofficial *imagiones gratiosae*.[20] Peasant-carved images of the crucified Christ, at crossroads and at field-borders, exorcized the landscape and claimed it for the Catholic Church; but they could also become the object of a folk-cult outside the control of, and therefore disapproved of by, the clergy and nobility. Both Haur and the author of the *Witch Denounced* suggested that such 'Passions' could become the object of unregulated devotions,[21] while Sebastian Klonowic complained in the *The Sack of Judases* that:

> Without their masters' permission [peasants] wander about,
> Tying straw ropes to God's Passion in the fields.[22]

The opposing tendencies toward control of the sacred and purification of the church, on the one hand, and toward accommodation or even encouragement of folk devotion, on the other, created in the post-Tridentine Polish church a profound ambivalence. If Protestantism brought about, as Roper puts it, a 'desomatization of the spiritual',[23] so that the sacred was no longer something to be touched, held, carried, imbibed, or, in its malevolent aspects, something that takes over and ravishes the flesh, nevertheless for Catholics spirituality remained profoundly embodied. Catholic writers were well aware that this bodily aspect of their faith remained one of its most attractive features; accordingly, in strong contrast to the fifteenth-century anti-superstition writers intent on a thorough spiritualization of the faith, Counter-Reformation reformers could not reject wholesale the embodied rites of their flock—attachment to which rites had to a large extent ensured the loyalty of that flock against the temptations of Reform. As Scribner has said in a similar context, 'the church's commitment to a sacramental view of religion made any hard and fast distinction between "religion" and "magic" almost impossible'.[24] The Catholic Church could not and did not wish to condemn ritualism wholesale, but nor could it countenance uses and abuses of church materials and prayers in ways that it increasingly viewed as superstitious, vain, and possibly diabolic.

---

[20] Bolesław Kumor, *Dzieje diecyzji krakowskiej do roku 1995*, 4 vols. (Kraków: Wydawnictwo św. Stanisław BM Archidiecezji Krakowskiej, 1998–2002), 571–6; see also Tomasz Wiślicz, '"Miejsca cudowne" w Małopolsce w XVI–XVIII wieku', *Kwartalnik Historii Kultury Materialnej*, 47/3–4 (1999).

[21] Haur, *Skład Abo Skarbiec*, 88; *Czarownica powołana*, 28.

[22] Sebastian Fabian Klonowic, *Worek Ivdaszow*, ed. K. Budzyk (Wrocław: Zakład Narodowy im. Ossolińskich, 1960 [1600]), 48.

[23] Roper, *Oedipus and the Devil*, 177.

[24] Scribner, *Popular Culture*, 15.

Nowhere, perhaps, is this ambivalence more evident than in the *pacierz*: the Our Father or Lord's Prayer. As the only prayer taught by Jesus himself, its orthodoxy was beyond question. Yet it could be used in a spell-like way, and its petition for 'our daily bread' and protection against 'the evil one' straddled the boundary between this-worldly and spiritual concerns. Indeed the text of the Our Father itself became a focus for discussion of the distinction between superstition and piety. The Roman Catechism provided a quite lengthy commentary on the fourth petition of the prayer: 'give us this day our daily bread'. Because this catechism was influential in Catholic-Reformation Poland, and because, unlike the works of theologians, it might be known to peasants and small-town judges, its commentary deserves careful consideration.

Our first parents in that first state did not need clothes, nor a house for shelter, nor weapons for defence, nor medicine to restore health, nor the many other things which are necessary to us for the protection and preservation of our weak and frail bodies . . . .

Occupied in the cultivation of that beautiful Garden of Paradise, their work would have been always blessed with copious delicious fruits, their labour never frustrated and their hopes never disappointed.

With the Fall, this state of affairs came to its end:

All things have been thrown into disorder and have undergone a sad deterioration. Among the evils which have followed upon that primeval transgression, it is not least that our heaviest cost and work and toil are frequently done in vain. This is either because the crops are unproductive, or because the fruits of the earth are destroyed by noxious weeds, by heavy floods, by storms, hail, blight, and drought. Thus is the entire work of the year often quickly reduced to nothing by the inclemency of the weather or the sterility of the soil.[25]

This catechetical teaching on the text 'Give us this day our daily bread' shows the church's, and indeed Christianity's, ambivalence toward 'the world'. It is permissible, we are told, to pray for the things of this life, for the preservation of our bodies, but only insofar as such preservation better enables us to achieve our ultimate end, 'the kingdom and glory of our Heavenly Father'. We thus pray for worldly things only insofar as these are necessary to 'achieve divine blessings'.[26] There is a great danger, here, of failing to pray 'as we ought',[27] nevertheless it is possible to distinguish between licit and illicit petitions:

To pray for temporal blessings as if they constitute one's supreme good and to rest in them as the ultimate end of our desires, seeking nothing else—this, unquestionably, is not to pray as we ought.[28]

The legitimacy of a prayer, or of other uses of Christian words and objects, depends on the intention and attitude of the petitioner. This seems clear enough,

[25] *Roman Catechism*, pt. 4, sect. 2, ch. 4, paras. 4–5.
[26] Ibid.
[27] Ibid. para. 3, quoting Romans 8: 26.
[28] Ibid. para. 3.

but becomes hopelessly tangled once one attempts to apply the distinction to actual cases.

The prayer itself could be used in a spell-like way: in divination (Skrzynno 1639), or in finding a thief (Poznań 1544a). Agnieszka Szostakowa, an alleged cunning-woman who won her case of defamation against those who called her a witch, was rumored to have advised others to protect their beer against harmful magic by donating a shilling to the church and reciting seven Our Fathers in memory of the seven joys of the Blessed Virgin (Przecław 1675). Such uses of the Our Father may seem clearly magical and superstitious, although the use in beer-protection is already ambiguous: might not the Lord's Prayer function here exorcistically, as it was meant to do? Is not beer, a grain-product treated primarily as food in early modern Poland, a kind of 'daily bread'? The church itself acknowledged the temporal efficacy of the Lord's Prayer, a tool provided by God for the well-being of humankind. Even the strongly reform-minded Stanisław of Skarbimierz, in the fifteenth century, grudgingly allowed 'that one may read the Lord's Prayer and the Symbol and give them to others as a medicine'.[29] Three hundred years later, after the Polish flirtation with Protestantism, Serafin Gamalski was prepared to be more generous:

Some prayers, appended to natural medicaments, are not forbidden, and indeed are beneficial, for it often occurs that efficacious things have no effect without Divine help. . . . And prayers by themselves, without the application of natural means, addressed to that Heavenly Medic the Omnipotent Lord, are good, so long as they are made *with faith alone, and trust in God.*[30]

Thus, when an accused witch denied any knowledge of witchcraft by declaring 'I don't know how to do anything except the Our Father' (Warta 1678b) she was not setting up a distinction between magic and religion, nor between *demonolatria* and Christianity. Rather, she was claiming that the only spell she knows is the one officially sanctioned by the church. For such women, the Our Father and other standard prayers were thought of as formulae of power that could be invoked to bring health or ward off harm.

The post-Tridentine Catholic Church struggled to encourage knowledge and use of such prayers, while guarding against what it saw as their abuse. The speaking of a prayer, but also the use of other church items such as thunder-candles, blessed herbs, or holy water, was 'magical' or 'pious' according to the intention of the user. Amulets—including those amulets, probably the majority, which include sacred objects such as words from the Gospels or a wax Agnus Dei—are superstitious, vain, and sinful insofar as they are understood to bring luck or protection from drowning or fire. But the same objects do in fact protect a person from evil spirits. And insofar as evil spirits are the bringers of bad luck,

---

[29] Olszewski, *Świat zabobonów*, 191.
[30] Gamalski, *Przestrogi Duchowne*, 11ᵛ–12.

death by drowning, and fire, such objects do in fact protect against them. It was a sin to use sacramentals and sacraments for temporal healing of the worldly body. On the other hand, as Lorencowic reminds his audience, citing Augustine, all sins of the body are symptoms of sins of the spirit.[31] And since sacraments and sacramentalia were expressly intended for the cure of souls, the distinction between temporal and spiritual healing could become very blurry indeed: recall that Archbishop Maciejowski permitted the use of sacramentalia 'for the health of the body and soul'. Secular authors such as Jakub Kazimierz Haur, as well, despite his frequent warnings against superstition, recommended paraliturgical remedies as the best medicine for temporal ailments. Since 'the hunting Satanic Ensnarer' lies in wait for one's soul during illness, one should, in addition to temporal medicine, 'strengthen and preserve oneself with the Holy Sacraments, according to the Faith of the Holy Roman Catholic Church, and Christian custom'.[32]

One finds, then, a sort of theological Catch-22 in elite attitudes toward superstition and piety: insofar as a person wears an amulet with no intention of thereby receiving luck or protection from harm, they will receive luck and protection from harm; if, however, such protection is their reason for wearing the amulet, it will not provide it or will provide it by demonic and mortally sinful means. One need not characterize the common people as materialistic or primitive or animistic or ignorant to appreciate that they were unlikely to follow the subtleties of such arguments. They recited the Lord's Prayer piously but also to keep their beer from spoiling; they wore their fragments of the Gospels or their Agnus Dei out of an undifferentiated desire both for the grace of God *and* for good fortune in their worldly undertakings.

No wonder some Catholic reformers could come to have an almost obsessive concern for the purity of ritual, prayer, and sacramentals, attempting to cleanse them from any temporal taint. No wonder too, that this quest for purity proved impossible. Stanisław Brzeżański reminded parish priests that *diabolus est simia operum DEI*, or in the Polish phrase, 'where the Lord God builds a Church, the devil builds a chapel', sneaking superstition into legitimate ritual and prayer.[33] The author of the *Witch Denounced* polemicized against 'crosses, holy words, pious prayers' used illegitimately: 'Such words are spoken toward the Devil's honor, although in themselves pious, because he has hidden his nooses and his words in holy things and in Sacraments, as a fisherman baits his hooks.'[34] And yet the same author, a little later, lists as legitimate means against demons and witches such materials as holy water and the Agnus Dei, 'because the church

---

[31] Lorencowic, *Kazania*, ii. 190.
[32] Haur, *Skład Abo Skarbiec*, 434.
[33] Stanisław Brzeżański, *Owczarnia w Dzikim Polu*...(Lwów: Drukarnia Kollegium Lwowskiego Societatis Jesu, 1717), fo. 24.
[34] *Czarownica powołana*, 28–9.

blesses them for this purpose.'[35] Less scrupulous authors such as Chmielowski, despite his Jesuit training, approved a long list of ecclesiastical medicines against witchcraft, effectively overturning the sort of careful distinctions attempted by Maciejowski:

Further *remedies* against witchcraft and devils include Palms blessed on Palm Sunday; carrying on one's person the Apostles' creed or blessed images of the Saints; sprinkling on oneself water blessed on Easter Saturday; grana from the Paschal, *that is* candles which are blessed every Year on Great Saturday; garlands [of herbs] from the Monstrance; the Gospel of the four Evangelists carried on oneself, or attached somewhere.[36]

Ordinary Christians, needless to say, could not be expected to distinguish the precise border between superstition and piety, if even the most educated priests could not reliably make the distinction. Learned Catholic distinctions between pious and orthodox uses of the church materials and their impious abuse as superstition or witchcraft, distinctions which rested on subtle adjudications between hope and assurance, intention and interior state, were not designed for easy application to actual pastoral practice.

BREAD MADE FLESH

If the church's attitude toward lay use of sacramentals was ambivalent and complex, its attitude toward lay use of the Eucharist was at once much more straightforward and problematic. On the one hand, the sin of sacrilege was easier to define and condemn than were the sins of superstition. To use the host for any sort of extra-ecclesial practice, one first had to steal it; and this theft of the sacred, sacrilege in the strict sense, was a mortal sin and capital crime irregardless of the thief's intended aims, knowledge or ignorance of church doctrine, or interior attitude. Whereas the distinctions between piety, superstition, and magic allowed for considerable variation and gradation of opinion within broad limits, the special status of the Eucharist was non-negotiable. Within what Miri Rubin has called 'the economy of the Eucharist',[37] all clergy shared an interest in maintaining the church's monopoly. The great Catholic Reformation Jesuit preacher Piotr Skarga considered the priestly transformation of bread and wine into divine Body and Blood to be the *raison d'être* of ordained clergy: following theological trends from as early as the thirteenth century, he asserts that all other sacraments can be performed *in extremis* by laymen and even women: only the Eucharistic consecration absolutely requires a priest.[38] The exclusive, prohibited character of

---

[35] *Czarownica powołana*, 82–3.
[36] Chmielowski, *Nowe Ateny*, iii. 260.
[37] Miri Rubin, *Corpus Christi* (New York: CUP, 1991), 334–42.
[38] Skarga, *Eucharist*, 146–9; Rubin, *Corpus Christi*, 36; cf. *Roman Catechism*, pt. 2, ch. 6, para. 34. Modern historians have sometimes overstated the economistic interpretation of Catholic

the Eucharist as God incarnate set it apart from the other sacraments, but also made it a concentrated conveyance of supernatural power.

However, the very same characteristics of the Eucharist which required its close regulation and restriction by the church—its character as God incarnate, its overwhelming power, far outstripping all other sacraments and sacramentalia—were characteristics that the church was eager to describe and promulgate: in doing so, the church necessarily advertised the instrumental usefulness of the Eucharist in the world. *Exemplum* literature from the high Middle Ages, when the doctrine of the Real Presence was in the process of institutionalization, encouraged belief in the miraculous temporal powers of the Eucharist, especially against illness. Clergy attempted to maintain a monopoly and discourage abuses; this was difficult insofar as the prohibited practices and the didactic miracles demonstrating Eucharistic power were practically identical.[39] Emphasis on the miraculous powers of the Eucharist, not only as spiritual food but also as protection against fire, flood, illness of every kind, and of course as the best and truest protection against evil spirits, became even more important in the Counter-Reformation. In Poland, as in the West, the miraculous powers of the Eucharist were the Catholic Church's most potent item of propaganda against the Reformed and their symbolic, commemorative, and decidedly non-miraculous Lord's Table. Partly in reaction to the Eucharistic controversies of the early sixteenth century, the Catholic Reformation saw a thoroughgoing affirmation and indeed expansion of high medieval Eucharistic piety, and a dogmatic reassertion of the full scope of Eucharistic miracles and graces.

Thus the church could not, as with other superstitions, scoff against extra-ecclesial use of the Eucharist as *vain* or *ineffective*; instead, it could only denounce such uses as sinful and criminal. Caesarius of Heisterbach, in his collection of *exempla* which was so important in propagating the doctrine of Real Presence in the thirteenth century, made this point unintentionally in his famous story of the woman who stole the host to improve her listless cabbage-patch. This sin brought down divine punishment, but the cabbages *did* improve: 'it became a torment to me as well as a remedy for the cabbages, as the devil can witness'.[40]

I will return to these issues below. The point to emphasize, as we encounter the Polish witches stealing the host for magic, is that their belief in its supernatural power need not be read as the ignorant appropriation of spiritual mystery for popular, materialistic ends. Quite possibly, Polish witches believed that the Eucharist was efficacious in healing and protection from evil for the same reason

theology of the Eucharist. See e.g. Ryszard Gansiniec, 'Eucharystia w wierzeniach i praktykach ludu', *Lud*, 44 (1959); Merall Llewelyn Price, *Consuming Passions* (New York: Routledge, 2003), ch. 3.

[39] Rubin, *Corpus Christi*, 336–9.

[40] Caesarius of Heisterbach, *The Dialogue on Miracles*, tr. H. Von, E. Scott, and C. C. Swinton Bland (London: George Routledge & Sons, 1929 [1223–4]), bk. 9, ch. 9.

their priests thought so: because it contained God incarnate, the Body and Blood of Christ. To determine whether this is so, and what such an interpretation might signify about Polish popular Christianity, will require both a close reading of particular trials and the interpretation of those trials in the context of miracle stories, host-desecration legends and accusations against Jews, and the general climate of Eucharistic piety in post-Tridentine Poland. Host-stealing is of interest not only because it is a rather frequent accusation in Polish witch-trials, but also because it illuminates the relationship—the points of agreement, but also points of conflict, misunderstanding, or category confusion—between elite and popular Catholicism in the witch-trial era.

In the mid-fifteenth century, the Gniezno episcopal court sentenced a peasant woman to severe, lifelong penance for her theft of the host, allegedly for beer-protection magic.[41] Although synodal decrees of the intervening years warn priests to guard the host against *maleficas mulieres*, the next trials for maleficent use of the Eucharist came nearly two centuries later (Nowy Wiśnicz 1643; Lublin 1644). By that date, legends of Christian women stealing the host to sell to the Jews had become well established, featuring in the host-desecration trials against Jews and accompanying anti-Semitic literature that proliferated from the mid-sixteenth century on.[42] With the development of witch-trials, such defamatory legends of the Jews combined with real host-magic and imagined diabolism to generate a stable, productive, and deeply anxiety-provoking motif of witchcraft accusation. By the seventeenth century, both magistrates and the common people understood there to be only two reasons to steal the host: for ritual desecration in a re-enactment of the Passion (either by Jews or, later, by witches at Bald Mountain) or for witchcraft.

The first questions asked by courts of host-thieves were 'for what witch-craft did you steal it?' and 'Did you sell it to the Jews?'—a precise summation of the two motivations considered likely. Katarzyna Koczanowiczówna, implicated as an accomplice in love-magic using the Eucharist, was asked by the court 'Whether you yourself ever stole Holy Communion, and whether you sold it to the Jews, or to some witch' (Rzeszów 1718; cf. Przemyśl 1630). Church robbers tried in Lublin in 1739, most likely intending only to steal saleable silver paraphernalia, appear to have knocked over the ciborium containing the consecrated hosts, and some of these went missing. The court asked them, under torture:

Fourthly, those eight or more consecrated Hosts that were taken: where did he take them, and to what profit, for what witchcraft, and was this witchcraft harmful to anyone, or not. *Fifthly,* in what place, with which persons did he use those acquired Hosts, whether he stabbed them or not, and who else knew about this.[43]

---

[41] Bylina, *Chrystianizacja wsi polskiej*, 129–30; Adamczyk, 'Czary i magia', 244.
[42] Hanna Węgrzynek, *'Czarna legenda' Żydów* (Warsaw: Wydawnictwo Bellona, 1995), 58–9.
[43] APLublin, AMLublin sig. 50 (Advocatalia) fos. 502–3. Two of the three robbers were Jews, a circumstance prejudicial to their case.

Nor only did the courts assume the worst in such cases. Fellow church-goers also treated any suspicious behavior surrounding the taking of communion as an attempt to steal the Eucharist for witchcraft. In Wyszogród, a woman observed her neighbor coughing the host into her hand, and began to yell: 'And you, what did you spit the Lord God out of your ugly face for, to what end?'[44] Before the woman could be apprehended, she had swallowed the host—nevertheless this became the beginning of a witch-trial. Anna Puchalina came under suspicion when, as a witness put it later in court, she rubbed her mouth with her shawl 'where she had the Lord Jesus on her lips' (Chęciny 1666). Jan Baran coughed into his hand after taking communion but quickly put the host back into his mouth, swallowed, and, insisting that 'I didn't do it for witchcraft', hurried from the church. This proved ill-judged; his attempted denial proved his real intentions. After a trial for sacrilege with intent to do witchcraft, the hand which had touched the host was cut off, and Jan Baran was burnt at the stake (Nowy Wiśnicz 1643). These trials, and the ease with which they were initiated, indicate a profound anxiety over the purity and power of the Eucharist in seventeenth–eighteenth-century Poland.

Of the 228 trials in my database for which the precise accusations are known, thirty-nine (or some 17%) include theft of the consecrated host among the accusations. Although they start somewhat late, the trials extend throughout the Polish witch-trial period, are geographically widespread, and diverse in character. The trials may conveniently be divided into two types, based on the nature of the initiating accusation. In what I will call *primary crimes*, theft of the host is either the main or one of the main crimes contained in the formal accusation that initiates a trial: the accused comes to trial, above all, for having stolen the host. Where host-theft was a *secondary crime*, it emerges during torture, always in conjunction with a large variety of other transgressions and abominations. This division is useful in that, although based on a formal criterion, it points toward juridical, symbolic and even theological differences between the two trial types. Where theft of the host was a primary crime, its intended use was most usually some minor magic: to bless the milk of one's cows, to curry favor, or gain love. In contrast, in trials where host-theft is a secondary crime, it represents just one component of what might be called a 'demonological complex' of transgressive behaviors: desecration of the host and of other sacred things; strong magic against the whole community (such as magic to bring hail, drought, or plague); malefice against humans (especially children) and livestock (especially cattle); renunciation of God, Mary, and the saints; baptism into

---

[44] Olszewski, 'Prześladowanie czarów', 497. Possibly, this is the same trial as the Wyszogród trial of 1718 (Wyszogród 1718a).

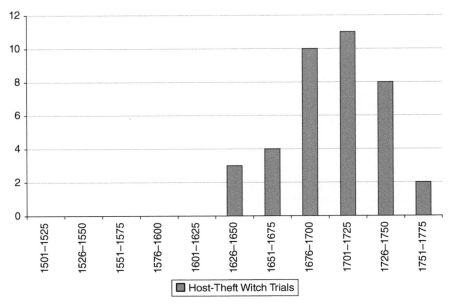

Figure 6.1. Chronology of host-theft witch trials.

service with the devil consummated with diabolical sex; and the *sabbat* at Bald Mountain.

Although the trials for host-theft and witchcraft all took place before town courts, one notes a difference in their judicial antecedents. Witch-trials featuring host-theft as a secondary crime were, from the perspective of court procedure, identical to those which did not have this feature. By the time an accused witch had confessed to stealing the host or using it for malefice, she would have already been sent to judicial torture because of other accusations of malefice. Host-theft and desecration confirmed the depth of the accused witch's depravity, and could lead to aggravation of the sentence by burning the hands of the witch who had 'dared to touch the Most Holy Sacrament with her hands' (Pyzdry 1699). But in such trials, host-theft in itself did not alter the legal nature of the case.

In contrast, there are indications that town courts were not fully persuaded of their jurisdiction over the primary crime of sacrilege. All of the Lublin primary-crime trials originate far from that city, and come to the city court by way of the Royal Tribunal, which regularly deputed criminal cases requiring judicial torture to the Lublin town court. Although the origin of most of these trials remains murky, it seems likely that small-town courts, local gentry, or possibly even regional noble courts sent the cases on to the Tribunal out of uncertainty as to

Trial	Type of Crime		Non-Harmful Magic		Harmful Magic (Malefice)		Themes	
	Primary	Secondary	Healing, milk, honey and wax	Love or favor	Against humans and livestock	Against crops; for bad weather or drought	Host-desecration	Bald Mountain
Przemyśl 1630	•			•				
Nowy Wiśnicz 1643	•							
Lublin 1644	•		•					
Lublin 1664	•		•					
Chęciny 1665c		•			•	•	•	•
Chęciny 1666	•							
Grudziądz 1666		•			•			•
Warta, ok. 1676		•			•			•
Kowalewo 1678b		•		•	•			•
Kleczew 1688		•					•	•
Kleczew 1689b		•			•			•
Albigowa 1690	•				•			
Kleczew 1690a	•			•	•		•	
Kleczew 1691b	•				•			
Kleczew 1693		•			•			•
Lublin 1697	•						•	
Lublin 1700	•		?	?	?	?		
Żerków 1702		•			•			
Wyszogród 1705		•			•		•	
Poznań 1708		•					•	
Grodzisk Wielkopolski 1710a		•					•	•
Szczerców 1716	?	?			•	•	•	
Brześć Kujawski 1717		•	?	?	•	?	?	•
Wągrowiec 1717		•			•		•	
Rzeszów 1718	•			•	•			

Figure 6.2. Features of 'primary' and 'secondary' host-theft witch trials.

Trial	Type of Crime		Non-Harmful Magic		Harmful Magic (Malefice)		Themes	
	Primary	Secondary	Healing, milk, honey and wax	Love or favor	Against humans and livestock	Against crops; for bad weather or drought	Host-desecration	Bald Mountain
Wyszogród 1718a	?	?			?	?	?	•
Pyzdry 1719		•			•		•	•
Wągrowiec 1719b		•			•		•	•
Wągrowiec 1727a		•			•	•		•
Wągrowiec 1727c		•			•	•		•
Wągrowiec 1728		•			•	•		•
Kleczew 1730		•			•			•
Lublin 1732	•				•			
Żerków 1732		•						•
Pacanów 1741	•		?	?	?	?	?	?
Wągrowiec 1741		•				•	•	•
Kiszkowo 1761		•				•	•	•
Tylicz 1763	•	?	?	?	?	?	?	?

Figure 6.2. *Continued*

how to deal with them.[45] We find a similar pattern in other towns, where town courts take over a primary-crime witch-trial either at the behest of the King's

---

[45] From 1670 the Crown Tribunal's jurisdiction over the Socinian heresy was expanded to include 'crimes against the Majesty of God' such as Jewish host-profanation. But even earlier, noble resistance to ecclesiastical jurisdiction over blasphemy led to the placing of that crime under the Tribunal's jurisdiction. This may help to explain the large proportion of host-theft in the Lublin witch-trials, which were often remitted to the town court from the Crown Tribunal. Marek Wajsblum, 'Ex Regestro Arianismi: Szkice z dziejów upadku protestantyzmu w Małopolsce', *Reformacja w Polsce,* 9–10 (1939), 91, 97; Hubert Łaszkiewicz, 'Sąd wojtowsko-ławniczy

local noble representative, the *starosta* (Pacanów 1741), or at the direct request of local clergy (Chęciny 1666; Kleczew 1691b). The trial of Regina Matuszka in Kleczew is the exception which proves the rule. Her accuser and manor-lord brought her to trial primarily because of malefice against his livestock; however, he testified that she had also stolen the Eucharist the previous year, avoiding prosecution by bribing the under-*starosta* with gifts of hens and honey: thus Matuszka's host-theft did not become a concern for the town court until coupled with maleficient witchcraft (Kleczew 1690a).[46]

The most salient distinction between primary-crime and secondary-crime host-theft, however, is theological: the two sorts of crime can be seen to correspond with the theological distinction between the Eucharist as Sacrament and as Sacrifice. This double nature of the Eucharist was a commonplace of Counter-Reformation theology, central to the Catholic claim to unique, direct access to the Real Presence incarnate in the fallen world. The great Jesuit preacher Piotr Skarga developed this theme repeatedly in sermons and popular writings. As sacrament, the Eucharist was the supernatural 'fount of all good and all heavenly gifts', and cure for every spiritual ill.[47] But the Eucharist derived its sacramental power from its obverse character as sacrifice: it produced redemption through repetition of the original act of redemption: 'every time we sacrifice to Him His own Passion, we renew His Passion, for our own absolution'[48] Only insofar as the Eucharist is a true sacrifice does it truly contain the Body and Blood of Christ, present in the world, and only through this renewed Incarnation and Passion is the Eucharist so effective a source of spiritual and temporal blessing.[49] Surprisingly, this complex sacramental theology is reflected in the two kinds of Eucharistic witch-trials. Women who used the host for healing their cows or to protect their milk against witchcraft made use of the Sacrament's supernatural efficacy against the devil and his minions. Judges who accused witches of treating the host with contempt and cruelty reflected the flip-side of devotion to the Eucharist as Sacrifice—a furious rage against Jews, heretics, and witches who would dare to treat the Body of Christ with insolence. The remainder of this chapter explores the theme of magical sacrament; Chapter 7 explores the passions unleashed by the imagined desecration of Christ's sacrificial Passion.

---

w Lublinie a trybunał koronny w drugiej połowie XVII wieku', *Roczniki Humanistyczne KUL,* 36/2 (1988).

[46] The honey, it should be noted, came from Matuszka's own hives, the fertility of which had been enhanced by her placing the Eucharist among the honeycombs.

[47] Skarga, *Eucharist,* 176; cf. *Roman Catechism,* pt. 2, ch. 3, para. 47, which Skarga seems to be following.

[48] Piotr Skarga, *Żywoty świętych starego i nowego zakonu na każdy dzień przez cały rok,* 12 vols. (Kraków: Wł. L. Anczyc i Spółka, 1881–9 [1579]), iii. 158 (Mar. 12).

[49] Skarga, *Eucharist,* 4, 179, 82. Cf. Lorencowic, *Kazania,* i. 148.

SACRAMENTAL MAGIC

In her magnificent study of the Corpus Christi festival in high-medieval Western Europe, Miri Rubin has shown how the Eucharist came, in the thirteenth-fifteenth centuries, to be the centerpiece of Christian worship, devotion, and doctrine, the bulwark and justification of clerical privilege, and the 'hinge around which things revolve'.[50] The Fourth Lateran Council in 1215 confirmed the doctrines of Real Presence and Transubstantiation which had been developing in the medieval schools; devotionally, the new feast of the Body of Christ, together with other para-liturgical practices and devotions, became central features of lay religious practice. This new prominence of the Eucharist brought about and was accompanied by two countervailing trends. On the one hand, 'magical' use of the host, always present in Christianity, gained new popularity: the Eucharist became a sort of arch-relic, access to which could bring about healing of sickness, protection from misfortune, and every sort of grace. On the other hand, new emphasis on the divinity really present in the Eucharist engendered a deep anxiety among theologians that such uses of the host showed insufficient awe for the Incarnate Word. In Poland as in the West, medieval sermons inveighed against those who ran from church to church on Sundays just to see the elevation of the host and to benefit from its blessing.[51] Practices such as the use of the host as a cure for blindness or sewed into one's clothes as an amulet against misfortune, which had been reported without condemnation by earlier churchmen such as Augustine and Gregory the Great, came to be regarded as superstition or worse.[52] But condemnations of superstitious host-magic stood in tension with concerns to promote the host as 'the source of every blessing'. Eucharistic field rogations, for example, featured the Blessed Sacrament carried in a monstrance around the borders of a community to ward off pestilence, hail, fire, and flood. In late medieval Germany, such Eucharistic rogations became so popular that provincial synods found it necessary to limit them to Corpus Christi or to emergencies such as fire and flood. However, some theologians defended rogations: God had provided the Eucharist to his flock as a defense against Satan, and it was devils, after all, who attacked Christian communities with pestilence, hail, fire, and flood.[53] In Poland, despite being forbidden in Maciejowski's Pastoral Letter, Eucharist rogation continued to enjoy wide popularity through the seventeenth century.[54] Preachers found themselves caught between a

---

[50] Rubin, *Corpus Christi*, 353.
[51] Bylina, *Chrystianizacja wsi polskiej*, 99–100.
[52] Gansiniec, 'Eucharystia', 83–4, 98; Rubin, *Corpus Christi*, 336–7; Bylina, 'Licitum—Illicitum', 141.
[53] Rubin, *Corpus Christi*, 291–2, 35, 341; Gansiniec, 'Eucharystia', 93–4; cf. Ząbkowic, *Młot*, pt. 2, ch. 7.
[54] Nasiorowski, *'List pasterski' Maciejowskiego*, 203–4.

desire to promote Eucharistic devotion, and an equal need to protect it from over-exposure, dishonor, or any hint of magic.

Post-Tridentine Catholicism, reacting to the sharply anti-Eucharistic theology of Zwingli, Calvin, and Socino, reaffirmed the full scope of medieval Eucharistic devotions, placing the Transubstantiated Body and Blood at the centre of theology and practice. Communion, previously annual for most lay parishioners, was now to be frequent—although the church also laid down strict, even impossible conditions for the reception of the host: purity of soul, purity of intention, concentrated devotion, and so on. The new order of Jesuits especially promoted the Forty Hours Devotion to the host, and made of the Eucharist, displayed in lavish monstrances, a central feature of urban and rural missions. Confraternities of the Sacred Sacrament, given over entirely to lay devotion to the host, sprang up in urban centers, including Kraków where it was organized under the active patronage of Piotr Skarga.[55] Corpus Christi processions, in which the host was paraded through the streets followed by the whole Catholic community, became occasions for the expression of community pride and solidarity, anti-Jewish or anti-Protestant riot, and Eucharistic magic—as when a woman in late seventeenth-century Lwów collected the soil behind the procession to cure herself of epilepsy.[56] The miraculous bleeding hosts at the Carmelite sanctuary of the Body of Christ in Poznań attracted pilgrims from all over Poland, and even from distant Ruś and Hungary. According to Jacek Wiesiołowski, these miraculous Eucharists and the church that housed them rivaled or even surpassed the wonder-working Marian image at Częstochowa as a focus of pilgrimage and miraculous healing; some 21 percent of these pilgrims were peasants.[57]

Piotr Skarga, whose *Sermons for Sundays and Holidays* and *Lives of the Saints* counted among the best-selling titles of baroque Polish publishing, put a Eucharistic stamp on the entire Catholic revival.[58] 'All our benefits, blessings, and happiness',

---

[55] Rubin, *Corpus Christi*, 354–6; L. Châtellier, *The Religion of the Poor* (Cambridge: CUP, 1997), 142; Wacław Urban, *Chłopi wobec reformacji w Małopolsce w drugiej połowie XVI w* (Kraków: Polskie Wydawnictwo Naukowe, 1959).

[56] Hanna Zaremska, 'Procesje Bożego Ciała w Krakowie w XIV XVI wieku', in B. Geremek (ed.), *Kultura elitarna a kultura masowa w Polsce późnego średniowiecza* (Wrocław: Zakład Narodowy im. Ossolińskich, 1978); Dysa, 'Witchcraft Trials', 163.

[57] J. Wiesiołowski, 'Funkcjonowanie poznańskiego kultu pątniczego w kościele Bożego Ciała (kon. XV-pocz. XVII wieku)', *Kronika Miasta Poznania*, 3/4 (1992).

[58] Archbishop Maciejowski recommended Skarga's sermons as an acceptable source-book for parish priests insufficiently educated to put together a proper post-Tridentine sermon of their own—a factor which helped Skarga's *Kazania* enjoy nine edns. between 1595 and 1792. Haur recommended Skarga's *Żywoty świętych* as an indispensible volume in every manor library, and it was the most-sold book in Poland through the mid-18th cent. Nasiorowski, *'List pasterski' Maciejowskiego*, 195; Haur, *Skład Abo Skarbiec*, 170; Partyka, 'Książka rękopiśmienna', Janusz Tazbir, *Piotr Skarga* (Warsaw: Państwowe Wydawnictwo "Wiedza Powszechna", 1978), 101. Even in this popular collection of saints' lives, Skarga returned again and again to the doctrine of the Real Presence, discussing it in conjunction with the hagiographies of St Basil, St John Chrysostom, St Ignatius, St Gregory the Great, St Leon I, St Anselm; St John of Damascus, St Epiphanius, St Augustine, and St Stanisław Kostka.

declares Skarga, 'find their source in this most intimate union with Christ.'[59] When Christ took on our 'corruptible human body' he used it for our benefit in every way. Not only did he, in incarnate form, work miracles, heal the sick, exorcize devils, and redeem humankind through his own bodily suffering; he also 'left his body for us here on earth in the Holy Eucharist to be ever at our disposal, that we might obtain through it every help, spiritual and temporal'.[60] These crumbs of divinity on earth are the best of medicines: 'There is no reason for sickness where the power of this food is permitted to become effective.'[61] If, during Jesus' earthly ministry, a mere touch of the Lord's garment cured fever, exorcized demons, made the crippled to walk and the blind to see, how much greater miracles might not be possible when one enters into that much more intimate contact of taking the flesh of Christ into oneself.[62] At the end of the seventeenth century, Skarga's fellow Jesuit Aleksander Lorencowic displayed equal eloquence in his encomium to the Eucharist as perfect food, medicine, and defense against evil:

But not only is this food delectable; it also provides a strange strength. For this reason it is often called Angelic bread, from the Jewish bread of strength, of health, for this Most Holy Sacrament gives strength and power against every kind of temptation and spiritual enemy. This food is a defense and a sword, and it is terrible to every enemy.[63]

The slippage between temporal and spiritual efficacy in such passages may be somewhat intentional and can hardly be avoided. The Eucharist is a food and a medicine, for the spirit but for the body as well. Indeed it represents the perfection of that 'daily bread' petitioned in the Lord's Prayer: a solace for the earthly body as it seeks the kingdom of God. Such an interpretation would be strengthened by Jesuit practices such as providing blessed (but not consecrated) hosts during rural missions, to heal peasants of physical illness; or the eating of the *opłatek* or blessed wafer at Christmas Eve, saving some for the cattle; or the convention, recorded by Chmielowski, that witches eat no bread at Bald Mountain since bread represents the Eucharist and Christ.[64] Skarga tells the story that Stanisław Kostka, a Jesuit novice who became the paradigmatic Polish Counter-Reformation saint, was fed the Eucharist by angels while he lay mortally sick in his lodgings in a Protestant household in Vienna. He recovered fully from his illness.[65] In such stories the host is manna from heaven, food, medicine: an unqualified blessing for body and soul. Not everyone would appreciate that Kostka, distinguished among other things by 'the beautiful flower of virginity', was uniquely chosen to receive so heavenly a cure for bodily affliction.

---

[59] Skarga, *Eucharist*, 179.
[60] Ibid. 182.
[61] Ibid. 183.
[62] Ibid. 186–7, 210; cf. *Roman Catechism*, pt. 2, ch. 3, para. 54.
[63] Lorencowic, *Kazania*, i. 149.
[64] Urban, *Chłopi wobec reformacji*, 243; Chmielowski, *Nowe Ateny*, iii. 241.
[65] Skarga, *Żywoty świętych*, xi. 202–3, paras. 13–24.

It should perhaps not surprise us to find that ordinary commoners took sermons, saints' lives, and indeed catechism at their word, and sought to harness the Eucharist's repeatedly proclaimed beneficent power to their own needs. Indeed, in the absence of most other kinds of reliable historical source-material recording peasant religiosity, our best evidence that the 'Eucharistic Turn' in Catholic Reformation theology had penetrated into the small towns and villages of early modern Poland derives, ironically, from the trials of witches accused for attempting to make use of the Eucharist's sacramental blessing.

What emerges from the testimony of women accused in primary-crime host-theft trials is a thoroughly Christian attitude toward the Eucharistic wafer, which both they and witnesses against them call 'the Lord Jesus' or 'the Lord God'. Host-thieves often take the time to say their prayers after stealing the Incarnate Word but before leaving the church. They have as good an understanding of the Eucharist as source of grace, benefit, and healing as does Skarga, as good an appreciation of its efficacy against devils as does Lorencowic, but they do not see that their use of it implies a desecration of the holy. Zofia Janowska, a young house-servant who stole the host in order to gain her master's love, naively confessed her intent to steal the host during her pre-communion confession (Rzeszów 1718). Maryna Białkowa made no attempt to deny that she had stolen the host for milk-magic, apparently not seeing anything wrong in this (Lublin 1664); while Regina Matuszka saw no harm in stealing the host for her beehives, saying, 'It's true, but I did good, I gave wax to the church' (Kleczew 1690a).[66] In such statements, the accused were attempting to put their crime in the best possible light; but one also gets the sense that they saw little wrong with their use of the sacrament for its intended purpose, as a source of blessing and a defense against evil.

Even where primary-crime host-theft had a more sinister purpose, magical use of the sacrament reflected its role as an object of universal adoration. To curry favor at the Crown Tribunal in a land dispute, the Ukrainian noblewoman Alexandrowa Mytkowa and her servant allegedly baked pancakes mixed with stolen Eucharistic hosts, with the intention of giving these pancakes to the officers of the court. While mixing the batter, they recited 'Just as a crowd goes to the Most Holy Sacrament, so also let the lords [deputies] of the court and the

---

[66] Regina's Eucharistic beekeeping, sinful but efficacious, echoes an exemplum from Caesarius of Heisterbach concerning 'bees who built a shrine for the body of the Lord'. As with the exemplum of the host-enhanced cabbages, it displays a profound ambiguity: the woman sinned in stealing the host for her bees, but the practice *did* have the hoped-for effect—'the Lord gave His blessing to all their work' (Caesarius of Heisterbach, *Dialogue on Miracles*, bk. 9, ch. 8). Polish bee-keepers were still stealing the host for their hives in the 19th cent. (Kolberg, *Dzieła wszystkie*, vii. 116). As creators of sweet honey for humans and wax for church candles, bees partake of the sacred in Polish folklore, and even in grammar: alone of the animal kingdom, bees, like human beings, 'pass away' instead of merely 'dying' (*umrzeć* rather than *zdechnąć*). Sebastian Klonowic placed theft from beehives alongside sacrilege and church robbery in his verse classification of crimes (Klonowic, *Worek Ivdaszow*, 103, 11).

lawyers be favorable to us' (Lublin 1732). In Rzeszów, the hapless house-maid
Zofia Janowska used a nearly identical spell, mixing the stolen host with her
spittle and water, giving this to her master, and reciting 'Just as a crowd gathers
around the communion, so let him gather around me, Christened and called
Zośka' (Rzeszów 1718). In one case, the host is used to suborn the course of
justice; in another, to incite romantic love. Such perversion of the sacrament's
power for the selfish satisfaction of temporal desires drew consistent condemnation
from demonologists.[67] And yet both instances are best read not as diabolical
inversion of Catholic sacramentality, but rather a misapplication, a particulariza-
tion, of the fully orthodox effects and aims of communion. In normal preparation
for communion, Christians committed themselves to reconciliation with, and
forgiveness of, anyone to whom they lived in a state of wrath or inimicability.
The kiss of peace ritualized this social and indeed sociable aspect of Eucharistic
devotion. Despite Catholic-Reformation efforts to emphasize the vertical love of
God rather than the horizontal love of neighbor effected and expressed by
the Mass, communion and the Eucharist itself remained powerful symbols of
amicability.[68] Alexandrowa Mytkowa and her collaborators abused this 'miracle
of the Mass' in their attempt to pervert the course of justice; but her very crime
attested to her orthodox understanding of the Eucharist as a vehicle for fellow-
feeling and the forgiveness of debts.

In like manner, Zofia's use of the host for love-magic made an explicit analogy
to the Eucharistic devotion encouraged by Catholic reformers. Her incantation
depends on such associations, and testifies to their currency: she wants, like the
host, to be 'crowded around' and adored. Her love-magic, though it used
the immaculate Body of Christ to satisfy the dishonorable, concupiscent needs
of the Christian's fallen body, is not best understood as a materialist appropriation of the sacred. Rather, it misapplies the universal amicability affected by
communion and focuses it inappropriately on a single person. Eucharistic love-
magic will have been understood by all concerned as a crime and a sin—but it
was a Christian sin.

To finish this chapter, I would like to look closely at the connections between
primary-crime host-theft and milk-magic, tying sacrilege to the themes with
which we began: milk, the circulation of moisture, and popular Christianity as an
arena in which temporal and spiritual well-being inextricably intertwined.
I suspect that the protection of milk and cattle against witchcraft was the most
common motivation for primary-crime host-theft: the uses to which the host was
put closely resemble, in intensified form, the counter-magical milk-charms
examined in Chapter 5. Eucharistic magic represented an escalation or intensification of the blessed herbs and holy water made use of universally with tacit

---

[67] Chmielowski, *Nowe Ateny*, iii. 245; Del Rio, *Disquisitiones*, bk. 6, ch. 2, sect. 1, qu. 1, no. 23;
bk. 3, sect. 1, qu. 3.
[68] John Bossy, *Christianity in the West: 1400–1700* (New York: OUP, 1985), 57–75.

church approval, and advocated, as a practice amenable to God, by such semi-elite writers as Haur.[69]

Regina Zaleska, a not particularly successful part-time cunning-woman in Opole Lubelskie who asked her own young son to steal the Eucharist at his first communion, appears to have intended it for some form of milk-protection magic (Lublin 1644). She had been hired in the past to unbewitch enchanted milk and butter, reciting 'By God's power, by the Lord God's help, [send] the enchantment onto a dog, onto a goat', but this spell, by her own admission, 'had, like usual, not helped at all'. Presumably she hoped for better results with the Eucharist.

Maryna Białkowa, a married peasant woman and no expert in cunning, used the Eucharist to protect the milk of her cows from witches. She confessed this freely before torture: Maryna went to communion in the parish church at Miastków Mazowiecki, but during auricular confession she failed to inform the priest of her immanent sacrilege. After confession she 'accepted the Lord Jesus, and having recited [her] prayers, left the church'. Over the next three Sundays, she filtered her cows' milk through the host wrapped in a kerchief, while reciting: 'you won't take this milk, you witches'. She seems to have seen nothing wrong with this, and advised her neighbors to do the same—leading eventually to her arrest for sacrilege and witchcraft (Lublin 1664). Although Maryna knew very well that in stealing the host she was handling, in her own words, 'the Lord Jesus', she appears to have had few qualms in doing so: her intended ends were good, and her means not too different from practices tolerated by the clergy. Did not preachers proclaim that the host was 'a defence and a sword, and it is terrible to every enemy'—and were not witches and devils the enemies of God and humankind? Why should ordinary villagers forgo the protections afforded by the church?

Maryna Białkowa's ritual of filtering milk through the Eucharist can also be understood as an extrapolation from similar practices using blessed (but not consecrated) bread. The cunning-woman Jagna of Żabików recommended the usual holy water and blessed herbs to protect milk against witches, but also advised that one should lead one's milch-cows over the table-cloth at which bread was blessed at Easter (Poznań 1544). At her second trial, the same cunning-woman advocated the filtering of witch-spoiled milk through blessed bread (Poznań 1549). When another accused witch boiled a cheesecloth outside church during Easter Mass, she most likely intended to draw the power of the elevated Eucharist into the cloth, to protect and increase the milk of her cows (Szadek 1649a). Similarly, the feeding of stolen Eucharists, baked into pancakes, to one's cows (as Krystyna Matysówna, herself under judicial torture for selling the Eucharist to the Jews of Sandomierz in 1639, accused her neighbor Anna of having done[70]) is an extension of non-Eucharistic milk-magic encountered in the trials: the accused witch Regina Smalcowa admitted that 'I used to make

---

[69] Haur, *Skład Abo Skarbiec*, 64–5.
[70] Wijaczka, 'Procesy o czary w regionie świętokrzyskiego', 29; Węgrzynek, *Czarna legenda*, 88.

pancakes with blessed herbs, so that the cows would give milk, and I heard about this from old mothers' (Nowy Wiśnicz 1688c; cf. Chęciny 1665d).

Feeding crumbs of the host to cattle finds its model as well in the practice, still standard today, of mixing the crumbs of the blessed Christmas Eve wafer or *opłatek* into livestock feed.[71] Although the anonymous author of the half ribald, half serious *Synod of the Under-Clerics* treats this as witchcraft—

> Women, even those who are quite devout,
> Bewitch with the *opłatki*, feeding them to cows.[72]

—it will have been an entirely standard and approved practice of most peasant women, and likely of their priests as well. Together with the practice of putting hay under the Christmas Eve tablecloth and later feeding this hay to the cattle, sheep, and horses, the extension of the ritual exchange of *opłatki* from the family circle to its animals had, indubitably, 'magical' content, in the sense that it was expected to affect temporal benefits. But it also, arguably, was a performance of social integration, and an expression of the insight in agricultural communities, that (as Bossy has commented in another context), religion involves 'the extension of social relations beyond the frontiers of merely human society'.[73] Maryna Białkowa and others who stole the host for their cattle or their bees, for the milk and honey in which peasant good fortune were measured, crossed a line recognized not only by the church and the courts, but by most other peasants and small-town agriculturalists—their accusers. But their action was fully in keeping with the symbolic logic, if not the law, of Catholic Eucharistic doctrine. Host magic, like the 'superstitious' use of holy water, blessed herbs, and the Lord's Prayer, stands as testimony to the strength and depth, not the weakness and superficiality, of peasant Christianity in early modern Poland.

---

[71] As early as 1409, the synod of Łęczyca condemned priests who went from house to house blessing pancakes (Kracik, 'Chrzest', 190). On the similar practice in pre-Reformation Germany, see Scribner, *Popular Culture*, 44.

[72] *Synod Klechów*, 198–9.

[73] Bossy, *Christianity in the West*, 13.

7

Broken Bodies

Grzechy czarownic są oprócz niezliczonych trzy naypryncypalnieysze: *Apostasia a DEO, Sodomia & sacrilegium.*

The sins of witches are innumerable, but the principal three are these: *Apostasy from God, Sodomy, and sacrilege.*

(Benedykt Chmielowski, *Nowe Ateny, albo Akademia Wszelkiej Sciencyi pełna* (1746), iii. 247)

Witch-trials for Eucharistic magic are relatively simple to interpret. Although a large store of comparative material must be brought to bear to render such trials intelligible, and although the adjudication of their status within Christianity depends on fine points of method and definition, the evidence from such trials has a solidity unusual to witch-trials. In primary-crime host-theft trials the accused usually did steal the host, and did so for the reasons given either by witnesses or by the accused herself, often voluntarily before torture. The record requires interpretation, but not much meta-interpretation; testimony is surely tendentious but probably not fabricated.

Secondary-crime host-theft trials present a different and more difficult set of interpretative problems. In these trials, accused witches admit under torture to torturing the Lord Jesus himself in Eucharistic form; to stabbing the wafer until it bleeds; giving it to devils at Bald Mountain; throwing it to pigs or burying it under a village cross to cause drought. Assuming, as we must, that Bald Mountain has no physical existence and that one cannot cause a wheaten wafer to bleed, we are left to interpret not actions but fantasies, not real (albeit magical) rituals but the imagined rituals of an imagined diabolical sect. The central question then becomes: whose fantasies, whose imagination?

According to some ways of thinking, this fantastic character of the confessions simplifies rather than complicates our interpretative task. If our goal is to understand the imaginative world of the accused witches themselves and their fellow peasants, there is nothing, in a sense, to interpret. The testimony does not reflect their own worldviews, but is instead read off, under circumstances of excruciating pain, from a demonological script. This script, in turn, like *sabbat* accounts in general, is predicated upon structural and rhetorical processes of inversion: it exemplifies John Bossy's dictum that to know what witches do, and how the devil was worshipped, 'one needed only to know what true religion was, and turn it inside out'.[1] Witches were imagined to desecrate the host, or draw blood from it or feed it to pigs, because such actions were the opposite of all that was thought to be good and right.

As Norman Cohn demonstrated long ago, variations on the theme of sacred bread and child-sacrifice are extremely ancient. First applied by Roman authors to early Christians and the misunderstood 'love feast' of their god's flesh and blood; subsequently taken up by Christian polemicists against Montanists, Bogomiles, Cathars, and especially Jews, accusations of sacrifice, cannibalism, and innocent blood mixed into ritual bread form part of a 'traditional stock of defamatory clichés'; a repertoire of inversionary atrocity-narratives.[2] Just as blood-libel trials against the Jews tell us nothing at all about Judaism but a great deal about the Christianity of accusers, the inversion narratives of Bald Mountain tell us about the imaginations of the magistrates and possibly of the demonological manuals which those judges may or may not have been exposed to: they cannot tell us much about the accused witches themselves.

In the early eighteenth century, Serafin Gamalski's *Spiritual Warning* precisely captured the epistemological argument against giving credence to the testimony of accused witches under torture:

Guilty of nothing, she confesses to everything, and sings out those things which they have stuffed into her head before torture (which is dishonorable). This is done either by the examining judges, or by the executioner and his assistants, or the guards, or the voice of the public, or even, one hears, by Confessors, who, incompetently questioning penitents, teach them and give them further occasion to lie.[3]

Gamalski compellingly exposes our historical difficulty. Can anything at all of the inversionary fantasy confessed by an alleged witch under torture be treated as originating in her own beliefs and worldview? Or is it all a matter of interpellation and suggestion by the magistrate, the public, the priest?

To interpret witch-trial testimony in this way is, I want to argue, to do a disservice to the accused witches, who had their own imaginative lives and who were, after all, perfectly capable of generating inversion narratives of their own. Accused witches might have their own ideas about 'what true religion is': in which case their inverted accounts might reveal to us—albeit through a glass, darkly—something about their relation to and understanding of their faith. While paying considerable attention to elite discourse, in this chapter I will also want to show that witches' accounts of their mistreatment of the Eucharist should be taken as some of the most direct, if inverted, evidence of popular

---

[1] Bossy, *Christianity in the West*, 137; cf. Clark, *Thinking with Demons*, 43–79.
[2] Cohn, *Europe's Inner Demons*, 56; See also Price, *Consuming Passions*, 32–6, 43–50; Frankfurter, *Evil Incarnate*.
[3] Gamalski, *Przestrogi Duchowne*, 14ᵛ–15.

Christian devotion that is available to the modern historian attempting to glimpse the practices of early modern Polish women. This is true because, I will suggest, the confessions of witches accused of host-desecration are their own co-creation, straying from the paths imagined by their interrogators. As in Chapter 6, I will first look at the theological and devotional background to host-desecration beliefs: the understanding of the Eucharist as a reinstantiation of Christ's self-sacrifice in the cross, and the corresponding view of those who torture or humiliate the host as participants in the Passion. I will then apply this context to a reading of the confessions, which emerge as anguished, inverted explorations of Christian piety.

SACRIFICE AND CRUCIFIXION

Scholarship on post-Tridentine Polish Catholicism has rightly emphasized its deeply Marian complexion, symbolized by the miraculous Madonna of Często-chowa, crowned Queen of Poland in 1656.[4] However, as the Eucharistic devotion discussed in Chapter 6 should indicate, popular piety was also deeply Christocentric, with a strong emphasis on the Passion. Polish baroque religious poetry took the Passion of Christ as a central theme, and even political verse, from the Zebrzydowski *rokosz* at the beginning of the seventeenth century to the Confederation of Bar in the late eighteenth century, made use of the Passion narrative, with a suffering Nation in the place of suffering Christ.[5] Devotional literature, especially Marcin Laterna's influential *Spiritual Harp*, included prayers to 'all the parts of the body of the Lord Jesus under torment' and meditations on the Five Wounds.[6] Hours of the Passion, popularized in the *Spiritual Harp* and by Confraternities of the Lord's Passion, traced the events from the Agony in Gethsemane to the Cross.[7] In music, vernacular 'Bitter Laments', modeled on funeral dirges, are a specifically Polish form dating from the late seventeenth century, performed during Lenten vesper services and in para-liturgical devotions.[8] The piety of Polish female saints focused almost obsessively on the Passion: the early seventeenth-century Benedictine St Magdalena Mortęska is described as meditating on the suffering of Christ unceasingly for three years.[9]

---

[4] Zakrzewski, *kręgu kultu maryjnego*; Wiślicz, 'Miejsca cudowne'; 'Religijność wiejska'.
[5] Janina Stręciwilk, 'Męka Pańska w polskiej literaturze barokowej', in H. D. Wojtyska and J. J. Kopeć (eds.), *Męka Chrystusa wczoraj i dziś* (Lublin: Katolicki Uniwersytet Lubelski, 1981).
[6] Stanisław Cieślak, 'Harfa Duchowna—modlitewnikowy bestseller jezuity Marcina Laterny (1552–1598)', *Nasza Przeszłość*, 93 (2000), 37; Jerzy Misiurek, *Historia i teologia polskiej duchowości katolickiej*, 3 vols. (Lublin: Redakcja Wydawnictwo Katolickiego Uniwersytetu Lubelskiego, 1994), i. 54–6, 165–74; Henryk Damian Wojtyska, 'Męka Chrystusa w religijności polskiej XVI–XVII wieku', in *Męka Chrystusa wczoraj i dziś*, 62–3.
[7] Cieślak, 'Harfa Duchowna', 37; Wojtyska, 'Męka Chrystusa', 62–3.
[8] Wojtyska, 'Męka Chrystusa', 67; Stręciwilk, 'Męka Pańska', 115.
[9] Wojtyska, 'Męka Chrystusa', 65, 75.

The very landscape bore testament to Passion piety, the ubiquitous Marian shrines sharing space with crucifixes (colloquially termed 'God's Passions') at roadsides and crossroads, property boundaries, and in the centres of villages. These were interspersed with the peasant-carved, decidedly folkloric 'Anxious Jesus' figures representing a tired, thorn-crowned Jesus resting on a rock with his head in his hands; such figures were extremely popular in rural areas from the fifteenth century.[10] On a grander scale, local Ways of the Cross and, from the late sixteenth century, *kalwarie*—Calvaries complete with a hill of the cross and built edifices recreating the site of the crucifixion—came to compete with Marian shrines as centers for pilgrimage. The first of these, Kalwaria Zebrzydowska to the west of Kraków, was founded by the magnate Mikołaj Zebrzydowski at the turn of the seventeenth century, and was quickly imitated by similar centers throughout Poland and Lithuania.[11]

This focus on the Passion is inseparable from Eucharistic devotion. From the fifteenth century, rural parishioners were reminded of the intimate connection between Host and Passion by murals of the suffering Christ in the niche where consecrated hosts were kept.[12] The elevation of the host in Mass, usually a joyous occasion, was met at Lenten vesper liturgies with 'Bitter Laments' about the suffering of Christ, sometimes accompanied by self-flagellation.[13] Mystical visions of the Christ-Child in the Eucharist, either as a beautiful little boy or as dismembered and bloody meat sacrificed for our sins, were known in Poland at least from the late fifteenth century from Mikołaj of Błonie's collection of sermons for Sundays and holidays.[14] Such visions could be popularized in drama, as in the Corpus Christi procession organized by the Jesuit academy in Wilno in 1633. Half theatre, half liturgy, it featured a tableau of 'Charlemagne, the Pope, and the Little Child in the Host'; a visual representation of Charlemagne's legendary vision, when observing the poor taking communion at Paderborn, that 'each one took a beautiful little Child into his mouth'.[15] The identification of the Eucharist with the Passion was so close that, in a trial in Szczerców in 1716, the court asks the accused why she stole 'God's Passion'.

---

[10] Bylina, *Chrystianizacja wsi polskiej*, 157, 161, and figures 52, 53, 61, 62; Jan Gintel (ed.), *Cudzoziemscy o Polsce* (Kraków: Wydawnictwo Literackie, 1971), i. 296; Wojtyska, 'Męka Chrystusa', 62, 70.

[11] Wojtyska, 'Męka Chrystusa', 65; Urban, *Chłopi wobec reformacji*, 253–4; Wiślicz, 'Miejsca cudowne'.

[12] Bylina, *Chrystianizacja wsi polskiej*, 80.

[13] Wojtyska, 'Męka Chrystusa', 66.

[14] Teresa Szostek, 'Exempla i autorytety w kazaniach Jakuba z Paradyża i Mikołaja z Błonia', in B. Geremek (ed.), *Kultura Elitarna a Kultura Masowa W Polsce Późnego Średniowiecza* (Wrocław: Zakład Narodowy im. Ossolińskich, 1978), 300. On the importance of such mystical visions in the West in connecting Passion to Eucharist, see Caroline Walker Bynum, *Holy Feast and Holy Fast* (Berkeley, Calif.: University of California Press, 1987), 60, 67, 246; Rubin, *Corpus Christi*, 343–4; Price, *Consuming Passions*, 31–2.

[15] Jan Okoń, *Dramat i teatr szkolny. Sceny jezuickie XVII wieku* (Wrocław: Zakład Narodowy im. Ossolińskich, 1970), 96.

Such identification of the sacramental Eucharist with the sacrificed body of Christ had its dark side. Intended to focus the Christian believer's attention inward, on his or her own personal responsibility for the suffering of incarnate divinity, it could also focus outward as rage against those who dare to scorn the Eucharist. In Poland as in Western Europe, the Corpus Christi procession brought into sharp focus the differences and antagonisms between Catholic and Protestant. Franco de Franco, one of the very few noble Protestants ever judicially executed during Poland's 'Reformation episode', came to trial not for heresy but for disrespecting the Eucharist.[16] But Eucharistic rage found its main target in the Jews, consistently represented by both clergy[17] and secular authors[18] as the murderers of Christ and of young innocent Christian children, Christ's image. Corpus Christi could become the occasion of anti-Semitic riots, as in Lwów in 1636;[19] however, host-desecration and ritual murder accusations came especially around Easter, with its intensive focus on the Passion and its close conjunction with Passover. Desecration of the host and blood libel are closely linked: both are attempts to re-enact the Passion of Christ through a renewed attack on his body— either literally in the transubstantiated host or metaphorically in the person of a pure and innocent child. Together, they represent a dark reflection of the heightened Eucharistic devotion promulgated in the late Middle Ages and re-emphasized in the Catholic Reformation. Visions of the Eucharist as a beautiful baby or as bloody and dismembered flesh, inspired devotion but also a desire for revenge. Blood-libel and host-desecration trials against Jews or witches therefore serve not only as indices of anti-Semitism or of demonological obsession, but also of the spread and penetration into the Christian populace of Eucharistic piety.

On this view, the proliferation of trials against Jews for host-desecration from the late sixteenth century onwards expresses the success of Tridentine Eucharistic devotion among the Christians of Poland. The first alleged instances of Jewish host profanation in Poland (in Poznań in 1399 and in Kraków, 1407) have the character of miracle stories: they expose simultaneously the iniquities of the Jews and the tremendous power of the Eucharist.[20] A trial in Sochaczew in 1556,

---

[16] Janusz Tazbir, 'Franco de Franco,' in *Reformacja w Polsce. Szkice o ludziach i doktrynie* (Warsaw: Książka i Wiedza, 1993); Wajsblum, 'Ex Regestro Arianismi', 316–36. The use of the Eucharist to focus and exacerbate Catholic/Protestant antagonisms in early modern Poland deserves closer attention than it has so far received.

[17] Skarga, *Żywoty świętych*, iii. 343–51 (on 'the martyrdom of the little boy Simon of Trent, tortured by the Jews', with comparison to an alleged similar crime near Wilno in 1574).

[18] Klonowic, *Worek Ivdaszow*, 29; 138; Haur, *Skład Abo Skarbiec*, 216–21; not to mention several polemics given over entirely to anti-Semitism, such as Przecław Mojecki's *O żydowskich okrucieństwach* (1598), Sebastjan Miczyński's *Zwierciadło Korony Polskiej* (1618), and Stefan Żuchowski's *Proces kriminalny o Niewinne Dziecię* (1713).

[19] Stefan Gąsiorowski, 'Proces o znieważenie hostii przez Żydów we Lwowie z roku 1636', *Nasza Przeszłość*, 82 (1994).

[20] Węgrzynek, *Czarna legenda*, 47–9. The chronicler Jan Długosz recorded these stories under the influence of his friend the Franciscan John Capistrano, a notorious Jew-baiter whose sermons had instigated blood libels and pogroms in Silesia.

instigated by the papal *nuncio* Aloisius Lippomino who was visiting nearby Łowicz, marks the first actual trial against Jews for profanation of the host. Thenceforward, despite repeated royal proclamations restricting prosecutions for host-desecration, secular authorities continued to express anxiety over the vulnerable Body of Christ in the Eucharist and prosecute His alleged tormentors.[21] A wave of anti-Semitic accusations of Eucharist profanation during the disastrous 1650s and 1660s culminated in a series of decrees of the *szlachta* in palatinate after palatinate, demanding expulsion of the Jews because 'they commit that abomination, the sacrilegious theft of the Most Holy Sacrament'.[22]

Such accusations were modeled on the story of the miraculous bleeding hosts at the Carmelite church of the Body of Christ in Poznań: a story that also provides the model for host-desecration in witch-trials.[23] A poor Christian woman who worked for a Jewish family was persuaded to steal three hosts on Friday, 15 August (a conjunction of the week-day of Christ's Passion and the feast of the Assumption of the Virgin Mary: this is also the day on which the host is confessed to have been stolen in at least three witch-trials). The Jewish elders gathered in the basement of a dwelling where, in order to 'execute their wrath on the body of Lord Christ', they laid the hosts on a table and pierced them with knives until they bled. The Jews became afraid and tried to destroy the hosts, finally throwing them into a ditch outside the Poznań walls. Next Sunday, just as the Eucharist was elevated in all the churches of Poznań, the three desecrated hosts also rose up, in response to which cows grazing nearby knelt down in worship. By 1540 more than a hundred miracles had been attributed to the bleeding hosts; in 1620, the table upon which the hosts had been stabbed was found, still stained with blood, and the site of the hosts' torment became a Chapel of the Most Holy Blood of Jesus Christ.[24]

In a controversial but important recent article, the anthropologist Joanna Tokarska-Bakir has asked to what degree one may treat 'the Jew as a witch and the witch as a Jew' in Polish culture. Tokarska-Bakir draws parallels between the demonization of witches and the demonization of Jews in Poland from the sixteenth through the twentieth centuries, noting, as I do here, their similar folkloric features and their similar function as the 'absolute other' against which

[21] Z. Guldon and J. Wijaczka, *Procesy o mordy rytualne w Polsce w XVI–XVIII w* (Kielce: Wydawnictwo DCF, 1995); Węgrzynek, *Czarna legenda*; Magda Teter, *Jews and Heretics in Catholic Poland* (New York: CUP, 2006).

[22] Zenon Guldon, 'Straty ludności żydowskiej w Koronie w latach potopu', in J. Muszyńska and J. Wijaczka (eds.), *Rzeczpospolita w latach Potopu* (Kielce: Wyższa Szkoła Pedagogiczna im. Jana Kochanowskiego, 1996), 302–3.

[23] After an early discussion by Jan Długosz, the Poznań miracle received elaborate treatment in a pseudonymously authored *History of the Wonderful Discovery of the Body of Christ* (1583) and in Tomasz Treter's *Sacratissimi Corporis Christi Historia et Miracula* (1609). See Węgrzynek, *Czarna legenda*, 49–52.

[24] Wiesiołowski, 'Funkcjonowanie'; Węgrzynek, *Czarna legenda*, 48–57; Piotr Bojarski, 'Nie godzi się, by wisiała: Zabytkową tablicę z antysemickim tekstem usunięto na polecenie abp. Stanisława Gądeckiego', *Gazeta Wyborcza* (May 30, 2005). On the motif of cattle kneeling before the elevated host, see also Caesarius of Heisterbach, *Dialogue on Miracles*, bk. 9, ch. 7.

the pious Catholic Pole was imagined.[25] Although these parallels are compelling, one must also note crucial differences: the Jews of Poland were a real social group, against whom host-profanation accusations involved a purely fantastic demonological ethnography. In contrast, there was no real group of witches, but there were real Christian women who sometimes really did steal the Eucharist. Host-profanation accusations against witches are therefore equally fantastic, but the work of fantasy in such trials moves, as it were, in the opposite direction. In the next two sections, I attempt to show that, whereas blood libel tells us nothing at all about Judaism, the secondary-crime host-theft trials can tell us something about the Christianity not only of the accusers but of the accused.[26]

HOST MAGIC IN THE MIRROR OF MALEFICE

To tease out a picture of the symbolic world of accused witches in secondary-crime trials, and the place of the Eucharist within that worldview, *in spite of and by means of* the inversion narratives they co-produce with their tormentors, let us look briefly at the manner in which the host was allegedly used for malefice, and the sorts of malefice it was allegedly used for.

Witches accused of using the host most often either buried it (in bed-chambers to cause illness to humans, in stables to kill cattle, in fields to cause drought and crop-failure), or made it into a powder with which they sprinkle their victims. Both burying and powder-sprinkling are standard procedures of imagined Polish witchcraft: the powder or ash symbolizing dryness while the burying of bones, vermin, and 'rubbish' undermines the order and borders upholding the well-regulated homestead (see Chapter 5). To introduce the most Holy Sacrament into combination with, for example, the rotting head of a mare (Kiszkowo 1761), vipers and snakes (Kleczew 1690a), the ashes of a burnt cat (Kleczew 1730), or pigs' brains, a mare's head, reptiles and vipers, and little red bugs (Kleczew 1691b) is to defile it utterly: quite apart from the maleficent purpose of such an action, it demonstrates witches' contempt and hatred for God. Such sacrilegious defilement is well attested in demonological sources. Already in the fourteenth century, Jews in France were accused of poisoning wells with a mixture of herbs, blood, urine, and the Eucharist: like so much of Jewish host-desecration

---

[25] Joanna Tokarska-Bakir, 'Żyd jako czarownica, 3–32; cf. Tazbir, 'Liczenie'.

[26] The relationship (and the differences) between Jewish host-profanation trials and witch-trials demands far greater attention than it has so far received. Host-profanation trials attracted the attention of polemicists, inspired debate in the regional dietines, led to calls for the expulsion of Jews from towns or whole palatinates, sparked off riots and attacks on Jewish neighborhoods. The far more numerous witch-trials had far less pronounced public effect, suggesting that, despite nearly identical inversionary motifs, witch-trials and host-profanation trials performed very different cultural work. I discuss this issue further in 'Imagined Crimes, Real Victims: Hermeneutic Witches and Jews in Early Modern Poland', in E.M. Avrutin, J. Dekel-Chen, and R. Weinberg (eds.), *Ritual Murder in Russia, Eastern Europe, and Beyond: New Histories of an Old Accusation* (Bloomington: Indiana University Press, 2017), 18–38.

stereotype, this is carried over into the discourse of witchcraft.[27] Chmielowski notes that witches use 'the Most Holy Sacrament, by God's permission, and holy Oil' for their ointment, mixed with the corpses of stillborn children.[28] The *Malleus* records an anecdote that combines the themes of burying, defilement, and Eucharist as Christ-Child. A witch stole the host and buried it, together with frogs and other things, in a jar in her stable. However, the next day a field worker, passing by, heard 'a voice as of a crying little child', and the witch was caught.[29] The trial testimony appears, then, to be a simple reflection of demonological tropes.

However, it is possible to discern the possibility of an indigenous discourse of host magic through the mirror of malefice, that is, through its inverted description in host-desecration trials. Where the *targets* of Eucharistic malefice can be identified, these are most often children (Warta 1676; Kleczew 1688; Kleczew 1691b, 1693; Szczerców 1716), cattle (Kleczew 1690a, 1730; Wyszogród 1705; Szczerców 1716), and crops through the creation of drought (Chęciny 1665b; Warta 1676; Pyzdry 1699; Kleczew 1730). The first two of these are of course primary targets of malefice in general; the third is rare in Poland, so the correlation of crop-destroying magic with the Eucharist deserves careful attention.

Children were targets of Eucharistic malefice in five of the trials. Anna Ratajka was originally accused of maleficient murder of her neighbors' children, before she confessed to helping steal and torture the Eucharist, and to poisoning her own child and giving its soul to the devil ((Pyzdry 1699; cf. Warta 1676; Kleczew 1693). In the opposite direction, Marjanna of Tuliszków first confessed to theft and torture of the Eucharist, and then added that this tortured Eucharist was used to kill the young son of her manor-lord, Wojciech Breza (Kleczew 1688); three years later, the same court tried another serf of the same master, again originally for host-theft but also, after torture, for attempts to 'spoil' the health of various noble children (Kleczew 1691b). Children and Eucharists are closely identified, as we have already seen: in theology and iconography which emphasized the Christ-Child in the host; in the symbolic equivalence of host-desecration and ritual murder in the accusations made against Jews; in the constellation of inversion stereotypes relating child sacrifice and cannibalism to mistreatment of the host. Of course torture, murder, sacrifice, and cannibalism of young children, as well as their use to make witches' powder and witches' ointment, are mainstays of demonology and folklore, and do not always appear in conjunction with the Eucharistic motif. Possibly, however, the children and Eucharistic magic are connected positively as well as negatively. Jacek Wiesiołowski surmises persuasively that the large proportion of children among those miraculously

[27] Rubin, *Corpus Christi*, 341.

[28] Chmielowski, *Nowe Ateny*, iii. 243–4; see discussion of this theme in Ostling, 'Babyfat and Belladonna'.

[29] Ząbkowic, *Młot*, bk. 1, ch. 5. This incident allegedly took place in the 1380s, and so considerably predates the *Malleus*, which adopts the defilement story into its own schema of anti-Christian witchcraft (Price, *Consuming Passions*, 55–6).

healed or saved from drowning by the Poznań Eucharists may be related to the motif of the Christ-Child in the Host.[30] The inversion narrative of malefice against children with the host *may* reflect, then, a tradition of healing children with the Eucharist.

A similar but less speculative argument can be made concerning confessions of Eucharistic malefice against cattle. Katarzyna Kozimińska confessed to stealing the host to bury in the barn to kill cattle (Wyszogród 1705), and we find the same theme in other trials (Kleczew 1690a, 1730). Women intending real malefice may have really used such methods, either on the principle that what can heal can harm, or through an implicit logic by which the buried and desecrated host calls down the wrath of God. Nevertheless, the connection with veterinary magic is clear enough: the accused may have produced her confession of Eucharistic malefice by inverting what she knew concerning the apotropaic use of the host to protect cattle. An accused witch who knew the Eucharist's power to protect milk and maintain the balance of blessing in the universe may, under torture, have flipped this knowledge upside down to create a confession of Eucharistic milk-theft and cattle-killing.

Finally, the host was buried in the fields to bring drought, or sprinkled on crops to destroy them. As noted, malefice against crops shows up rarely in the Polish witch-trials, despite the considerable emphasis given to it in demonology. Excepting host-desecration trials, I know of only six clear examples of crop or drought magic in Poland (Dobczyce 1634; Turek 1652b; Muszyna 1678; Bochnia 1679; Wyszogród 1718b; Lublin 1739). Of these, three share a tentative thematic association with Eucharistic magic in that the implement of drought-creation is a dead and dried-up child (Muszyna 1678; Bochnia 1679; Lublin 1739). Indeed the Bochnia trial began as an inquiry into ritual murder: the beggar-women witches were suspected of having kidnapped a 'little innocent child' to sell to the Jews.

Chmielowski, following Grillandus and Del Rio, declares that witches crumble the host and bury it in the fields to prevent bad weather.[31] Despite the positive outcome attempted, he understands this as an abuse of Eucharistic efficacy. Gansiniec records numerous examples, from Germany, Italy, and Switzerland, of the crumbled host being sprinkled on crops to strengthen and protect them.[32] We have already mentioned the ambivalence inherent in the exemplum of the cabbages fertilized with the Body of Christ, as also the conflicting views of churchmen concerning Eucharistic rogations of the fields to protect them from bad weather and from witchcraft. At the turn of the eighteenth century, Jesuit missionaries displayed the Eucharist in a monstrance and instructed the populace in devotional exercises, in order to bring rain to drought-stricken Bavaria—a

---

[30] Wiesiołowski, 'Funkcjonowanie', 157.
[31] Chmielowski, *Nowe Ateny*, iii. 245.
[32] Gansiniec, 'Eucharystia', 102–3.

textbook example of themes developed in Chapter 6, invoking the power of the divine bread to provide the daily bread of the Lord's Prayer. The missionaries offered this ritual as an alternative to the 'futile superstition to which some of the inhabitants were given'.[33] Such 'futile superstitions' may well have involved similar but unauthorized Eucharistic field-magic. After all, in his list of forbidden popular errors Del Rio enumerates the practice of sprinkling the Eucharist in the fields to rectify or protect against maleficent destruction of the harvest.[34] It seems likely that the rhetorical structures of witchcraft confession made—of a Christian but extra-ecclesiastical ritual to bring rain—an anti-Christian ritual to cause drought.

This speculative thesis gains some grounding in evidence from the witches who confessed to causing drought and weather magic with the host. Marjanna of Oporówko buried her stolen host under the 'Passion of Christ'—the *Boże Męka* or field crucifix between Jaksice and Oporówko—a strange place to desecrate the host, and more likely an unauthorized addition to standard fertility rituals incorporating these crucifixes (Kleczew 1730); Haur might have had something like this in mind when he complained of 'suspicious people, who practice superstition and witchcraft' at field crucifixes.[35] In three trials, the host was stolen during the feast of the Assumption of the Virgin Mary, a feast more popularly called 'Our Lady of the Herbs' (Warta 1676; Pyzdry 1699, 1719).[36] This is a feast of considerable ecclesiastical accommodation to popular needs, during which herbs were blessed for medicine, to protect the house from evil influences, and for the benefit of livestock and crops: the 'blessed herbs' that appear time and again in witch-trial testimony had been brought to the church and blessed by the priest on this day. Stealing the host on this particular day, and then burying it or sprinkling it in the fields seems, *prima facie*, like fertility magic rather than malefice. Although I have classified all these instances of host malefice as secondary-crime host-theft cases, and although in all of them the revelation of host-theft to cause drought emerges only under torture and usually in the context of the Bald Mountain motif, it is not improbable that they either did in fact steal the host for fertility magic, or were reporting, in inverted form, a well-known ritual practice. When an accused witch confessed to host-desecration under torture, she participated in the reimagination of herself as a diabolical enemy of God. But her confession may also have reflected real practices, practices grounded in lay appropriation of post-Tridentine Eucharistic devotion.

[33] Châtellier, *Religion of the Poor*, 102–3.
[34] Del Rio, *Disquisitiones*, 933; bk. 6, ch. 2, sect. 1, qu. 1, no. 23.
[35] Haur, *Skład Abo Skarbiec*, 89. Cf. the practice confessed to in Wągrowiec (1689), of gathering sand from under a field crucifix, for use in healing the sick.
[36] Referred to as such in the trials themselves, as *Matka Boska Zielna* (Mother of God of the Herbs) or *Najświętsza Panna Zielna* (the Blessed Virgin of the Herbs).

PASSION NARRATIVES

The analysis of host malefice presented here suggests that some of the maleficent uses of the host, recorded both in trial testimony and in demonology, might be distorted reflections of actual practices. Where witches kill children with the host, this reflects the particular suitability of the Eucharist, envisioned so often as the Christ-Child, for the miraculous healing of children. Burying the host in barns and stables to kill cattle reflects practices, known from primary-crime trials, of Eucharistic veterinary medicine, especially associated with cattle. Finally, burying the host to cause drought or hail and destroy crops reflects actual practices wherein the host *protects* crops from drought and hail. There is a danger, in analysis of this kind, of turning every alleged act of malefice into a misconstrued healing ritual. Such an apologetic for host-magic has not been my intention. I do think the analysis lends plausibility to the thesis that Eucharistic healing was widely practiced in Poland, and that such healing leaves diabolized traces in witch-trial testimony. However, I do not wish to maintain that the diabolization itself is solely an elite imposition, or that the accused themselves were incapable of making their own inversions. Healing magic is always ambivalent, as we have seen: to increase the productivity of one's own cow is to decrease that of one's neighbor; to bring rain to one's own fields is to cause drought somewhere else. It is not at all improbable that the women under trial believed that the Eucharist, used improperly or by the wrong person, could cause the inverse of what, in other circumstances, were its 'natural' functions of healing and benefit. But as with the dew and water and milk analyzed in Chapter 5, the divine bread was a polysemic, multivalent symbol—of innocence and of consumption, of blessing and of suffering, of Incarnation and of Passion. It was a symbol that accused witches, like any other early modern Christian, could take up and modify to their own ends.

Let us take a closer look at two trials where Eucharistic malefice is accompanied by particularly flagrant desecration, raising particularly difficult questions of interpretation. Both trials took place in villages to which the town court had been invited by the owner or manager; both exhibit the typical features of such deputed trials in Wielkopolska: Bald Mountain; large-scale denunciation of other women; an almost forgone sentence of death at the stake. Nevertheless, neither trial can be reduced to the reiteration of a stereotype or the playing out of a cultural script: above all, the unique sensibilities of the main accused, in each case, render such easy reduction impossible. Host-theft, the devil-pact, and the *sabbat* at Bald Mountain are elements of discourse, endlessly repeated, but they are also the building blocks out of which unique individuals create their unique narratives. Although I use these trials to make general points about the Eucharist in Polish belief and practice, the narratives presented here are as important for how they *differ* from standard models as for their conformity to such models.

The trial of the girl Marjanna, Kleczew 1688

Pan Wojciech Breza invited the Kleczew court to his village of Wąsosze to interrogate a young woman suspected of witchcraft. Marjanna, who the court record describes as a maiden some 15 or 16 years old, had recently gone into service as a *komornica* to one Jędrzej, a peasant tenant in Wąsosze and so a subject of *Pan* Breza.

Marjanna had been caught in the church of Ślesin, a small town near Wąsosze, in the act of tying some 'raw thread from her underwear' to the hands of statues of the Virgin Mary and St John. Jan Swiec of Ślesin, together with several unnamed women, confronted her and asked her what she was up to. While Swiec was untying the string from the statues' hands, Marjanna volunteered an extraordinary story. (The story comes to the trial record at third hand: from Marjanna to Jan Swiec, who told it to *Pan* Breza, who related it to the Kleczew court as part of his accusation.) She is said to have said that: 'a devil is following her, compelling her to have intercourse with him. Also when she slept with the other servant-girl behind the stove, the devil came to her and ordered her to scootch over, and he crawled in between them, saying, "scootch over, I'm going to sleep here."' The same devil came to her when she was watching over her master's fishing nets at the lake. The 'tempter' pointed at her with a whip, and told her to follow him home. He had the legs of a stork.

Marjanna appeared to believe herself to have been involuntarily initiated into a devil-pact: some time earlier, on the road from her home in Tuliszków to take up service in Wąsosze, she had met with a certain Regina who was a short time later burnt as a witch in Piotrkowice; Regina told her 'that you'll have things good, and don't you forget it'. In later testimony Marjanna elaborated this tale: Regina had bought her a glass of spirits at the inn in Ślesin during her journey to Wąsosze, and told her to drink it to the dregs; she did so, and immediately 'that tempter on stork's legs' appeared. Later still, under torture, she related that this same witch and a third woman, Katarzyna, tempted her saying '"you'll have things good, just join with us two together," and I got married to that tempter behind the old tavern past Slesin, and those two women were present'.

Under torture, Marjanna confessed to the making of poisonous powders from burnt frogs, lizards, and vipers. She had also been to Bald Mountain (in the town square of Ślesin) and she denounced a long list of fellow witches whom she had seen there. Of these, the four from Wąsosze were immediately brought in for interrogation during Marjanna's trial, while those from Ślesin came to trial soon after, accused by a townsman at *Pan* Breza's urging.[37] In subsequent rounds of torture, Marjanna and her co-accused confessed to a wide range of maleficent acts and atrocities: attendance at Bald Mountain; sex and feasting with devils; malefice against *Pan* Breza's horses and sheep using buried objects such as a mare's head, the corpse of a sheepdog, pigs' brains and hooves; magical murder of a priest (out of spite), and of a local peasant swain (out of jealousy). All the accused agree to the maleficient slaying of *Pan* Breza's son, but the means differ: for Kaszka Pastuszka this had been accomplished with a powder of human bones and wood from a coffin; Regina Czubatka said she did it with a buried mare's head and with nuts. Marjanna herself, however, told an extraordinary story of sacrilege, torture, and desecration—a story that simultaneously functions as a miracle-tale:

---

[37] Wiślicz, 'Township of Kleczew', 76; Hajdrych, 'Proces o czary w Wąsoszach'.

'When we were in the Church in Slesin together, I went to confession and took communion; [Regina Czubatka] told me to take the Most Holy Sacrament unobtrusively from my mouth; I did this and she unobtrusively wrapped it in a kerchief and took it; without waiting around we returned home to Wąsosze. On the other side of the ford, in the woods, she unwrapped it from the kerchief and began to stab it with a pin or needle, until a great miracle took place: blood trickled [from the host], and the kerchief was soaked with blood, then a little tiny child, naked, stood on her hand and wept heartily and mournfully, and then it disappeared, I don't know where. Later she wrapped up that kerchief with a string and wrapped it in the bed-linen in the manor-house of the youngest son of His Grace Sir Breza, which child she led to its death—no one else but her.'

In subsequent testimony through a total of four rounds of torture, Marjanna confirmed again that she stole the host to poison *Pan* Breza's son, but made no further mention of her vision of the baby in the sacrament. Regina Czubatka, tortured three times, confirmed that she had 'stabbed the Most Holy Sacrament, and hid this Most Holy Sacrament in the bed-linen of His Honor *Pan* Breza's son'. Nobody mentioned the vision of the baby in the Eucharist again, nor did the court refer to it in its verdict (which speaks only of the 'terrible sins' of the witches). The court consigned all five women—Marjanna of Tuliszków, Regina and Marjanna Czubatka, Kaszka and Regina the shepherdesses—to the stake.

Marjanna of Tuliszków's testimony is extraordinary and possibly unique; this does not detract from its historical significance. Tomasz Wiślicz, noting her freely given account of the devil on stork's legs who had been following her and forcing her into sexual acts, has suggested that she may have been mentally disturbed.[38] Such an interpretation is plausible, although hardly necessary. Perfectly sane early modern Polish women and men reported encounters with demons and devils all the time, not only when compelled to do so under torture—an issue we will return to in Chapters 9 and 10. Lacking the early modern worldview in which every hollow willow housed a demon, every pond the ghost of a drowned suicide-girl, while the mournful cry of treasure-bringing flying snakes with tails of sparks could be heard in the thunderstorm, we may feel compelled to interpret such encounters psychologically or symbolically (or both), but they will have seemed perfectly real to their tellers and audience. Nor does the possibility of mental disturbance preclude the possibility of interpretation. Let us take a closer look at her narrative. The devil on stork's legs and the repeated acts of coerced intercourse are either reflections of real incidents or of her own real fantasies and anxieties (by 'real' I mean simply that they were not imposed upon her, from outside, under interrogation): she supplied this information before ever coming to court, without torture, and she appears to have been attempting some ritual alleviation or expiation of this problem with the help of the Virgin Mary, when she was apprehended in Ślesin.

Marjanna came to the attention of the court when she was caught tying thread from her underwear to the hands of statues of the Virgin Mary and St John in the

---

[38] Ibid. 74; see now also the nuanced interpretation of this trial by Łukasz Hajdrych, 'Proces o czary w Wąsoszach'.

church in Ślesin. The source of the thread suggests the possibility of love-magic.[39] In the trial, however, this initial ritual is quite forgotten under the pressure of later and more scandalous testimony. She had been followed by, and forced into sex with, a devil with the legs of a stork: once when she was in the exceptionally vulnerable position of watching over fishing nets, alone, at the Wąsosze Lake; another time in what should have been a place of safety, her cozy bed behind the stove where she slept with another servant-girl. In subsequent testimony it transpired that she was very young, and had come to Wąsosze only recently to take up service in a peasant household, leaving her home in Tuliszków some 30 kilometers away. Her status—female, young, unmarried, very poor, an outsider with no local allies or kin—is utterly marginal, as low as it gets. The only way to sink lower would be to lose her virginity, her single possession of any cultural value. And this she did lose, or claimed to have lost, when, alone on the road to her new place of work some weeks prior to the trial, in a space *par excellance* of transition, liminality, and uncertainty, she fell in with a woman later burnt as a witch, who got her drunk, gave her a devil in the bottom of her glass of vodka, and then watched while the devil had sex with her behind the tavern outside Ślesin.

How shall we interpret this story? As fantasy: as anxious worry about what could happen in her new, insecure, semi-adult life? As even greater worry that she might want it to? As a retelling, in symbols, of an actual traumatic event—seduction or rape while on her journey, perhaps facilitated by the witch of Piotrkowice acting as a procuress?[40] Might not the strange ligature she made in church, with a specific piece of thread attached specifically to the hand of the Blessed Virgin, be an attempt on Marjanna's part to regain, or reclaim, or perhaps just preserve, her own virginity? Such questions cannot be answered, and I advance these suggestions very tentatively, as mere plausibilities.

Marjanna then told her story of having stolen and tormented the host together with Regina Czubatka. The account of stealing the host in a handkerchief is entirely standard, recalling the primary-crime trials discussed in Chapter 6: but what follows is not standard at all—at least not in witch-trials. Regina stabbed the host until it bled, and then a little child—obviously the baby Jesus—appeared, cried mournfully, and disappeared. Marjanna's own words signal the sort of source material she drew on for this account: 'And then a great miracle took place.' Although this scene recalls and might be based on stories of Jewish host-desecration,[41] it more clearly reflects Catholic *exempla* of medieval saints,

---

[39] Compare Zofia Filipowiczowa's use of 'a string from my underclothing', tied to a piece of aspen-wood and dried in the fireplace as part of a love-magic ritual (Skrzynno 1639), and cf. Lublin 1660.

[40] This story of Marjanna's meeting with the witch of Piotrkowice, despite its supernatural sequel, seems to recount a real experience. But it is *also* a widespread motif of witch-trials, possibly reflecting young women's fear of older women: see Roper, *Witchcraze*, 172.

[41] E.g, in Passau in 1478, Jews were accused of stabbing a communion wafer until it transformed into a young boy (Price, *Consuming Passions*, 37). In the 16th cent., identical stories were told of the Anabaptists: Gary K. Waite, *Eradicating the Devil's Minions* (Toronto: University of Toronto Press,

seeing the baby Jesus in the host, either as a beautiful little boy or as bloody and dismembered flesh, slaughtered for our sins—as when during Christmas Mass Gotteschalk of Volmarstein found in his hand 'no longer the appearance bread, but a most glorious infant, indeed, Him who is most beautiful in form compared with the sons of men on whom also angels desire to look'.[42] Her vision also recalls Skarga's paraphrase, in his *Lives of the Saints*, of John Chrysostom's twenty-fourth homily on the First Epistle to the Corinthians:

The three Kings kneeled down before this same Body, in the manger scene, with great fear and awe; and you see it, not in a manger, but on the altar, not in the arms of the Virgin, but in the hands of the priest.[43]

Marjanna might have known of such visions through *exempla* in sermons or from Corpus Christi dramas and processions. Her vision might be related to the miraculous Poznań hosts: Treter mentions a demon-possessed girl in the sixteenth century who was instructed by a vision of 'a most sweet little boy' to seek exorcism at the Carmelite sanctuary of the Body of Christ.[44] Considering the correlation of the Christ-Child with innocence and of demon-possession with sexual impropriety, such a story, had she some way of hearing it, might have spoken to Marjanna's own predicament.[45]

There exist, then, any number of literary, homiletical or dramatic source, any one of which Marjanna *may* have drawn on to produce her miraculous, inversionary confession. Inquiry into her source material must remain pure speculation; but what is not speculative—what is indisputable—is that this young, marginal, almost certainly illiterate peasant girl knew such stories of Eucharistic miracle from somewhere, and that she drew upon them in her trial to explain her own life: to herself as much as to the court. The bulk of Marjanna's further testimony followed more or less standard scripts: the malefice against children and cattle, attendance at Bald Mountain, demon-lovers. The desecrated host

---

2007), 166–78. Marjanna might have known similar tales, such as Skarga's anecdote of Jews torturing an *image* of the baby Jesus, from which miraculous, healing blood then flows (Skarga, *Żywoty świętych*, xi. 308–13).

[42] Caesarius of Heisterbach, *Dialogue on Miracles*, bk. 9, ch. 2. Skarga tells a considerably abbreviated form of a similar miracle in his *Life* of St Gregory the Great: Skarga, *Żywoty świętych*, iii. 148–9.

[43] Skarga, *Żywoty świętych*, i. 350; cf. i. 120.

[44] Wiesiołowski, 'Funkcjonowanie', 151, quoting Tomas Treter's *Sacratissimi corporis Christi historia et miracula* (1609).

[45] In witch-trials, possession and bewitchment functioned synonymously. However, at a higher social register possession could serve as an idiom through which to preserve the 'purity' of young women who might otherwise be found lacking in this virtue. Kałowski describes a young patrician maiden who had been seduced by a devil in the form of 'a handsome foreign bachelor', with whom she lived in sin for four years. She was freed from the influence of this devil, and retroactively returned to a state of marriageable purity, through the intervention of the wonder-working image of St Anthony at Łagiewniki: Marcin Kałowski, *Informacya o początkach y dalszym progressie Cudownego Mieysca Łagiewnickiego* (1723), quoted after Baranowski and Lewandowski, *Nietolerancja*, 126.

remained part of this picture: however, though the court sought and obtained repeated confirmation, from Marjanna and Regina, that they stole the host, made it bleed, and hid it in Franciszek Breza's bed-linen to kill him, nobody mentioned the crying baby in the host again. The Kleczew court sought to judge a witch for witchcraft, not a Christian visionary. Whatever leading questions may have brought Marjanna to speak of stealing the Eucharist in the first place, her account of the mournfully lamenting Christ-Child must be treated as her own; it is extraneous, going well beyond what the court may have been seeking. Might not Marjanna, who emerges from all this as a devout if disturbed young girl, have drawn upon the symbolism of the innocent child, crying and bleeding, to mourn her own loss of innocence?

The trial of Anna Ratajka and others, Pyzdry 1699

Tomasz Orzechowski, noble land-agent of the village of Wierzbocice in central Wielkopolska, invited the town court of nearby Pyzdry to the village to try the 'true and Brazen Witch' Anna Ratajka. The trial began with a formal oath of accusation against Anna by three male peasants of the village, who accused her of maleficent murder of their young sons.

On the basis of this accusation, Anna Ratajka was put to torture. She admitted nothing, but cried out 'Most Holy Virgin Mary—Most Holy Sacrament—Image of Studzianna!'[46] And later: 'Have mercy, for the sake of the Most Holy Virgin and the Most Holy Sacrament.' However, at her second session of torture, Anna confessed to witchcraft, which she had learnt from Jagna Łakomianka of Wierzbocice, who presented her to a *szatan*, with whom she took part in a wedding against her will. The devil forbade her to mention Jesus or the Virgin Mary, or to cross herself. There follows, during this second and a third session of torture, a cascading series of denunciations of all the witches Anna had met at Bald Mountain. From Wierzbocice and four other local villages she denounced a total of twenty-one women and one man, and admitted that 'there are many witches almost everywhere'. Of these, three women of Wierzbocice eventually came to trial and were sentenced alongside Anna Ratajka.

During these same sessions of torture, Anna Ratajka also admitted to a number of crimes: she killed a cow and some pigs, and her colleagues persuaded her to bring her own child to Bald Mountain, where she killed it with a powder and gave it body and soul to a devil. But Anna attributed the worst crime to one of the witches she had denounced, Jagata Korfunka. According to Anna, 'she stole the Lord Jesus at the church fair in Biechów, and whipped [Him] all the way to Bald Mountain, so that the blood flowed'. This host was made into a powder, with which Jagata caused drought and destroyed the crops in the fields.

---

[46] The 'Image of Studzianna' is a wonder-working painting of the Virgin Mary in the small town of Studzianna, notable for its anomalous iconography: Mary is seated at table with Joseph and a toddler Jesus. A cheap broadsheet print of this image could be purchased at church-fairs and similar venues from about 1678, and may have been a specific against witchcraft: a written amulet dated 1682, the possessor of which 'need fear no witches and no bewitchment', is claimed to have been brought 'from Rome to the Most Holy Virgin of Studzianna'. See Tadeusz Seweryn, *Staropolska sztuka ludowa* (Warsaw: Wydawnictwo Sztuka, 1956), 19; Pilaszek, *Procesy o czary*, 412–13.

The court's verdict listed the witches' crimes: the killing of Szymon's and Kazimierz's sons, the maleficent murder of several calves, horses, and pigs, the making of witch's powder from a dead man's shirt and frogs burnt to ash, attendance at Bald Mountain. The court paid special attention to the matter of the stolen and desecrated hosts, and expressed its outrage terms more fervent than are usual in Polish witch-trial verdicts:

'And what is more, and terrible to relate and describe (Heaven and Earth tremble and are afraid), [Jagata Korfunka] stole the Most Holy Sacrament of the Body and Blood of Christ two years ago during the church fair in Biechów at the Feast of the Annunciation to the Most Holy Virgin; she burnt it into a powder, with which she destroyed the fruits of the harvest. Quite terrible and no less a crime, both Anna and Jagata renounced and abandoned God, their Creator and Redeemer, also the Most Holy Virgin, Mother of Christ, in whom everyone places all his hope, and all the Saints; and caring nothing but nothing for God or for Salvation, forsaking Heaven, they took Devils, traitors and swindlers of Humankind, as their protectors; listened to their treacherous counsel, had business with them, and did everything that the devils' demanded of them.'

Anna Ratajka, Jagata Korfunka and three others were sentenced to death at the stake. Because Jagata Korfunka had 'dared to touch the Most Holy Sacrament with her hands' the offending extremities were first coated with tar and sulfur, and burnt.

Anna Ratajka's testimony from Pyzdry is more difficult to interpret than that of Marjanna in Kleczew. If the details of Marjanna's testimony stand out as anomalous or unique, Anna Ratajka's testimony displays a near-perfect conformity to the 'demonological script'. Her trial could almost be used as the type sample of a classical, continental witch-trial: starting with a concrete and limited accusation of malefice at the village level against a single woman, it quickly expands via the *sabbat* trope and through the mechanism of denunciation into a large-scale trial involving four women accused sex with devils, weather-magic, child-sacrifice, and profanation of the host. Maleficent murder of a few children is transformed into an attempt, as in Jewish blood libel, to re-enact deicide: whipping the Christ-Child in the host until it bleeds. Under torture, Anna's inversionary description of Bald Mountain closely resembles the Jesuit Benedict Chmielowski's literary narrative of ritual inversion in his mid-eighteenth-century encyclopedia—a narrative Chmielowski derives not from the observation of Polish witch-trials but from western demonological sources:

Witches renounce their faith; renounce the Lord Christ, His Most Holy Mother, their Guardian Angels; taking henceforth the devil as their guardian. They take confession for no purpose but to steal the host, spitting and stamping on the Most Holy Sacrament.... They take various things from churches and use them indecently and with contempt.... They make a holy Mass for the devil; submitting to him, [and promising] never to adore the Most Holy Sacrament, but to rip, scratch, and spit on Images and relics of the Saints, and to treat indecently crosses, blessed salt, and blessed herbs.... Obtaining the Most Holy Sacrament either during Communion or by theft, they stamp upon it before the devil.[47]

[47] Chmielowski, *Nowe Ateny*, iii. 242–3. Cf. Ząbkowic, *Młot*, pt. 1, ch. 2; Del Rio, *Disquisitiones*, bk. 2, qu. 16; bk. 5, sect. 16. The tradition of host-desecration at the *sabbat* goes

Moreover, the unwontedly elaborate verdict suggests that some member of the Pyzdry court may have been particularly interested in host-desecration, or particularly well-versed in demonology, lending credence to the supposition that Anna's confession came as a response to (unrecorded) leading questions and prompts.

Nevertheless Anna Ratajka's relation to the Eucharist is her own: it displays a singular devotional attitude quite at odds with the narrative of diabolism into which it comes to be shaped. In great need of spiritual strength while undergoing torture, Anna cried out for help to 'the most blessed Virgin Mary, the Most Blessed Sacrament, the [holy] Image of Studzianna!' 'Have mercy, by the Most Holy Virgin and the Most Holy Sacrament.' Although the court focuses on sacrifice (of children and of the Eucharist), Anna has her own, entirely orthodox, relation to the host as sacrament. She calls upon it to give strength in a moment of spiritual danger: in this case, bearing overwhelming pain, but also attempting to resist the mortal sin of bearing false witness.[48] Anna's invocation of the Eucharist might specifically refer to the miraculous Eucharists of Poznań, just as her invocation of the Blessed Virgin refers to a specific holy image; however, more likely this is an invocation of the Most Holy Sacrament as such. When, in subsequent torture, her spirit now broken, Anna described the desecrated Eucharist as 'the Lord Jesus . . . whipped all the way to Bald Mountain, until blood flowed from it', this statement must be read in light not only of the demonology to which it conforms so closely, but also in terms of Anna's earlier expressed Eucharistic piety.[49] As with her confession to the sacrifice of her own child, host-desecration may be understood as what Anna imagined once it became clear to her that the court demanded her to describe atrocity: it is the worst thing she can think of. Execration of the host is thus not just an inversion of Tridentine Catholic Christianity; it is an inversion of Ratajka's *own* Christian belief and thus a testimony to her faith.

back at least to Nider's *Formicarius* (*c*.1435), if not earlier: see Kors and Peters, *Witchcraft in Europe*, 157, 61.

[48] Ratajka's invocation of the Holy Sacrament may also have worked as an oath. Compare the testimony of Katarzyna Ratajowa (Lublin 1700), who believed herself to be the victim of a frame-up: 'For God's sake I don't know, have mercy on me that I don't know, those others here made it up although they did it themselves, remember that, by the Holy Sacrament.'

[49] This is true even though the courts could wrest such confessions of desecration from the accused with a disheartening regularity: in three of the Wągrowiec trials (1708, 1719b, 1727), the tortured witches made nearly identical confessions of whipping the host 'until the blood flowed from it'.

8

Piety in the Torture Chamber

Moi łaskawi panowie, proszę nie każcie już cielska mego dręczyć, gdyż jakom
Pana mojego dziś przyjmowała, ten mi niechaj przy śmierci mojej ze mną
będzie, więcej nie powiem tylko com powiedziała i z tym na śmierć idę.

My gracious sirs, please do not require my body to be tormented anymore, since
I accepted my Lord today [in communion]; let Him be with me at my death;
I will say no more, only what I've already said, and I go with that to my death.

(Anna Przybeła, who had confessed to stealing the Eucharist,
before her third session of torture, Warta c.1676)

A long-standing problem in the study of European witchcraft has to do with the
relation of alleged witches to Christianity. Few scholars treat seriously the old-
fashioned thesis, itself merely a transvalued revision of demonological motifs,
that witches and witchcraft represent the remnants of a still-active underground
pagan or pre-Christian religion. But the anti-thesis is equally unsatisfactory: as
evidence accumulates that the men and women accused of witchcraft held a
variety of beliefs and assumptions, and performed a variety of practices, deeply at
variance with mainstream Christianity, it becomes difficult to maintain that the
witch-trials were merely a product of clerical fantasy, the accusations mechanically produced from a discourse of inversion and binary opposition. Witch-trials
bring into focus, then, a central problem in the historiography of early modern
Christianity in general: to what extent, and in what sense, were the common
people 'Christian' and what shall we mean by that term?

The study of early modern popular religion is largely the study of silences and
whispers: it is an attempt best characterized by the words of the dedicatory poem
to Natalie Zemon Davis's *Society and Culture in Early Modern France*: 'She
listens. . . . You speak sometimes too soft.'[1] Such voices are quiet enough
among commoner townsmen, fainter yet in the countryside. They fade into
near silence when we attempt to hear the voices of village women. Worse, they

---

[1] Natalie Z. Davis, *Society and Culture in Early Modern France* (Stanford, Calif.: Stanford
University Press, 1975), p. xiii.

are muffled, filtered, distorted, nearly drowned out in the babble of the louder, more articulate, more authoritative voices of official religion.

The problems attendant upon hearing such popular voices are well known. Baptismal records and wills are reticent and formulaic. Sacramental confession leaves few records, while confession manuals reflect ecclesiastical concerns about magic sometimes shaped by classical models wildly at variance with the actual practices of the people confessing.[2] Visitation records and synodal decrees focus primarily on perceived departures from orthodox Christianity. The 'ethnography of popular Protestantism' so well exploited by Scribner, an ethnography carried out by pastors examining the customs of their flock in order to eradicate those customs, provides us with a wealth of detail about calendrical rites, life-cycle ritual, weather-magic, apotropaic charms. But as with visitation records, such ethnography focuses on the exotic, the different, the superstitious, the 'wrong'— and thus can tell us little about how or whether such practices were integrated into or understood as part of commoner Christianity.[3]

In Poland the place of 'Protestant ethnography' is taken up by Catholic anti-superstition literature such as the *Witch Denounced*—in which we learn, principally, that among Polish peasant-women 'superstitions are as numerous as grains of sand'.[4] The literature of pastoral reform reiterates such claims. Stanisław Brzeżański's catechetical handbook sums up his attitude toward popular religion in the title: *The Sheepfold in the Savage Field* figures the rural peasant, and the peasant-woman especially, as untamed, ignorant, and as dumb as a wild beast— she has nothing to say, certainly nothing worth listening to. Although Brzeżański blames indifferent noble landlords for this state of affairs, he does not hesitate to claim that the Catholic peasantry 'have become so un-used to the Lord's Church, that they have nearly turned back into pagans'.[5] To make his point, Brzeżański recounts an interview with a peasant who cannot name the three persons of the Trinity, getting only as far as the Father and the Son.[6] Although Brzeżański describes this exchange as a real event, it closely resembles many other pastoral dialogues with the village idiot, who invariably doesn't 'know how to cross himself or recite the Lord's Prayer' or, after the Trinity has been explained to him by analogy to a candle made up of tallow, wick, and flame, brightly responds that he understands: the Trinity 'is a candle!'[7] Such stories must be understood as

---

[2] Bernadette Filotas, *Pagan Survivals, Superstitions and Popular Cultures in Early Medieval Pastoral Literature* (Toronto: Pontifical Insitutue of Medieval Studies, 2005).

[3] Scribner, *Religion and Culture*, 276, 323.

[4] *Czarownica powołana*, 5.

[5] Brzeżański, *Owczarnia*, fo. 5ᵛ.

[6] Ibid. fos. 6–6ᵛ.

[7] Rubin, 'Lud w polskim', 136; Francois Paulin Dalerac, *Memoires du Chevalier de Beaujeu contenant ses divers voyages...* (Amsterdam: Les héritiers d'Antoine Schelte, 1700), 185. See the very nearly identical story, from late 15th-cent. England, in Thomas, *Decline of Magic*, 165. For a collection of such anecdotes and comments drawn from all over Europe over several centuries, see Richard Fletcher, *The Conversion of Europe* (London: HarperCollins Publishers, 1997), 508–10.

part of the rhetorical construction of the countryside as a savage field in need of missionary work.

However, the imputed ignorance and paganism of the Polish peasant derive not only from the demands of rhetoric—they originated, as well, from real differences in religious concern. Brzeżański's perception of paganism among his flock arises from his own ritualistic hyper-scrupulosity: one peasant-woman is a 'pagan' and a 'heretic' for having inserted the phrase 'holy ghost' into the Hail Mary; others are 'superstitious' because of the way they cross themselves, while those who kneel improperly during prayer are likely candidates for demon-possession: 'Devils often request of Exorcists', we are told, 'that they might be allowed to enter into those who kneel on just one knee in church.'[8] Similarly, his peasant interlocutor is, to Brzeżański's standards, irredeemably ignorant because he can't correctly name the persons of the Trinity (and 'concerning the Sacraments, remedies, and other teachings of the Church, don't even ask'), and yet the peasant's speech is full of piety: he hopes, for example, that 'the Lord God will bring lighter serfdom-obligations', so that he will have time to spare for the care of his soul.[9] In fact, what Brzeżański and others like him often took to be ignorance or paganism may have simply reflected a reasonable confusion concerning what even the most devout and knowledgeable Christians acknowledged to be difficult mysteries of the faith. Concerning a 'pagan' among his parishioners who could not understand the doctrine of the resurrection of the flesh, since bodies rot after death, Brzeżański commented: 'many of the parishioners, in pagan fashion, hold to similar hidden infidelities against the articles of Holy Doctrine'.[10]

What counts as Christianity, and who counts as a Christian? Should reformers such as Brzeżański adjudicate such questions? Peasants who knew the Lord's Prayer and recited it in petition for their daily bread, or who knew what sorts of herbal decoration were appropriate for the Green Holiday (Pentecost), and Our Lady of the Herbs (Assumption of the Virgin Mary), or who avoided bathing in rivers until the water had been baptized and exorcized by the Feast of St John the Baptist, or who knew that the sign of the cross could protect them from devils, demons, and ill-fortune of all kinds, need not have known the details of the doctrines of the salvation narrative to which they adhered. Contemporary scholars have sometimes too easily described such an attitude as one of ignorance, this-worldly materialism, or a semi-pagan animism. Even sympathetic scholars of early modern Polish popular religion have been quick to describe the Christian peasant as someone who 'lacked even a normal interest in what he believed', learning just enough to attain the 'supernatural and temporal ends which he required'.[11] The testimony of accused witches challenges us to rethink the

---

[8] Brzeżański, *Owczarnia*, fo. 23.
[9] Ibid. fo. 6.
[10] Ibid. fo. 26ᵛ.
[11] Kracik, 'Katolicka indoktrynacja', 14.

Christian experience of early modern commoner men and women, and to treat elite evaluations with greater care than has been common heretofore.

Stanisław Bylina, while acknowledging the universal participation in Christian ritual by the end of the Middle Ages, insists that such participation need not imply 'profound reception of Christian concepts or values'.[12] One wonders what sort of evidence could possibly be adduced to demonstrate such a 'profound reception', or whether such an integrated Christian piety could be found outside of holy orders or intentional religious communities in any era, in Poland or elsewhere. 'Christianity' here becomes an ideal type, impossible in our post-lapsarian condition: in this sense, *all* Christians are a little bit pagan. As the great church historian Jerzy Kloczowski put the problem in his discussion of the degree of 'Christianization' in medieval Poland: 'the ideal of a truly Christian community has never been attained and is indeed unattainable'.[13] No one has ever been a Christian; as St Paul puts the matter, 'There is none righteous, no, not one' (Romans 3: 10). If a person or a populace are Christian only insofar as they have fully accepted and integrated the true message of the Gospel, then Christianity has never been tried. Accordingly, while scholars of various eras speak of this or that period—the fifteenth-century attacks on superstition; the sixteenth-century Reformations, the seventeenth-century confessionalization, eighteenth-century missionization of the countryside—as moments of achievement in the history of Christianization, it is never ultimately achieved. Christianization is a 'process without end', a total but exceedingly gradual transformation not only of exterior practices but of the entire interior person. According to this model, Poland achieved Christianization only by the end of the nineteenth century, if ever at all.[14]

The historical judgments going into this sort of account are intertwined with, indebted to, and ultimately indistinguishable from theological judgments: the history thus recounted, for all its scholarship, is a sort of sacred history. Recent important anthropological work about the 'Christianization' of non-Christian peoples[15] has stressed the spatial and temporal metaphors by which Christianity both breaks away from and maintains ties with the previous religion, which becomes a meaning-producing 'other', a shadow-religion always ready to reseduce the potential backslider from Christian rigor. Missionaries spoke pessimistically in terms of Christianity being 'put on like a new robe over a soiled body'; a superficial, outward veil inadequately covering an unchanged heathen interior.[16]

---

[12] Stanisław Bylina, *Człowiek i zaświaty* (Warsaw: Instytut Historii Polskiej Akademii Nauk, 1992), 4.

[13] Jerzy Kloczowski, *A History of Polish Christianity* (Cambridge and New York: CUP, 2000), 20.

[14] L. Milis, 'La Conversion en profondeur: Un processus sans fin', *Revue du Nord*, 68 (1986).

[15] Birgit Meyer, *Translating the Devil* (Edinburgh: Edinburgh UP, 1999); Joel Robbins, *Becoming Sinners* (Berkeley, Calif.: University of California Press, 2004).

[16] Wolfgang Kempf, 'Ritual, Power, and Colonial Domination: Male Initiation among the Ngaing of Papua New Guinea', in C. Stewart and R. Shaw (eds.), *Syncretism/Anti-Syncretism* (New York: Routledge, 1994), 111.

Ethnographers often echo this sort of language while inverting the value signs, seeking 'authentic' tradition beneath the Christian practice and thus, as Joel Robbins has noted, reinscribing Christian constructions of paganism and superstition while neglecting the Christianity of the people under study.[17]

Scholars of early modern popular Christianity in Europe have not always escaped entanglement with such categories and metaphors. Even Robert Scribner, whose work did so much to complicate easy Enlightenment historiographies of Reformation as an exorcism of 'the magic of the medieval church',[18] and whose sensitive exploration of the sacramental system of traditional Catholicism problematized any easy equation of Catholic ritual to magic[19]—even Scribner reinscribed popular religion with Christian assumptions about its adequacy. He quoted with approval Valerie Flint's definition of magic—'preternatural control over nature by human beings, with the assistance of forces more powerful than they'—and religion—'recognition by human beings of a supernatural power on whom they are dependent, to whom they show deference and are obligated'.[20] But he did not seem to notice that Flint's dichotomy comes from Frazer, while Frazer's definitions are borrowed from Enlightenment reworking of Protestant polemic; this polemic in turn is largely dependent on the sort of distinction between 'vain practice' and true piety which so exercised Catholic theologians from Thomas Aquinas to Martin Del Rio—and which was central to the theological discourse around witchcraft. Again, without belaboring the point, I want to insist that the basic assumptions that make such an interpretive move seem both easy and natural derive from Christianity itself and its persistent self-perception as a religion constantly just emerging from this-worldly pagan magic.

A good deal of the recent work in religious studies concerns the problems raised by exporting concepts and terms developed in the history of Christianity—belief, the supernatural, magic, scripture, even 'religion' itself—into other religions (or whatever they are to be called).[21] 'Witchcraft' and 'magic' especially can be problematic exports: rejected by many scholars as systematically misleading in non-Christian contexts.[22] The point of these and of similar studies has been that

---

[17] Robbins, *Becoming Sinners*, 27–34.

[18] Robert Scribner, 'The Reformation, Popular Magic, and the "Disenchantment of the World"', *Journal of Interdisciplinary History*, 23/3 (1993); Scribner, *Religion and Culture*, 275–301.

[19] Scribner, *Popular Culture*, 34, 38–9.

[20] 'Disenchantment', 476–7; Valerie Flint, *The Rise of Magic in Early Medieval Europe* (Oxford: OUP, 1991), 3.

[21] From a very large and growing bibliography, see esp. Malcolm Ruel, 'Christians as Believers', in M. Lambek (ed.), *A Reader in the Anthropology of Religion* (Malden, Mass.: Blackwell, 2008 [1982]); and Jonathan Z. Smith, 'Religion, Religions, Religious', in M. Taylor (ed.), *Critical Terms for Religious Studies* (Chicago: University of Chicago Press, 1998). A discussion of these issues which was important for the formation of my own thinking has been their application to the category of 'Hinduism'; see Vasudha Narayanan, 'Diglossic Hinduism: Liberation and Lentils', *Journal of the American Academy of Religion*, 68/4 (2000).

[22] The activities and abilities glossed as 'witchcraft' by anthropologists are often understood to be legitimate, indeed necessary attributes of powerful people in some cultures, while 'magic' can end up

Christian or post-Christian ('secular') notions, such as the privileging of 'faith' over 'empty ritual', 'spirit' over 'law', 'spirit' over 'matter', and 'religion' over 'magic', have profoundly distorted our interpretations of the non-Christian religions of the world.

I want to suggest, however, that distortion begins at home. Post-Reformed Christianity forms the 'background religion' of the contemporary academy, shaping assumptions, providing categories, suggesting the sorts of questions to be asked. Despite the worries on the part of many scholars that the Christian presuppositions upon which distinctions between 'magic', 'superstition', and 'religion' rest make it a poor export, my own argument is, in a sense, the inverse. Because of its Christian provenance and presuppositions, the distinction is especially unhelpful for the study of Christians: it is an insider definition, privileging particular insider positions. We must use the terms 'magic' and 'superstition', since, in Latin and in their various vernacular cognates, they are contemporary, indigenous terms used by demonologists, pastors, magistrates, witches, and their accusers. But we should not mistake them for scholarly categories—in doing so, we end up repeating what Hildred Geertz famously accused Keith Thomas of doing in his *Religion and the Decline of Magic*: 'taking part in the very cultural process he is studying' by interpreting early modern magic (or religion) in terms and through categories that themselves developed out of early modern discourse on magic.[23]

Scholars must resist this tendency to take on the categories of Christian theology when examining the Christian past: this is especially true for those areas, such as Poland, that somewhat pride themselves on the comparative 'recentness' or 'shallowness' of their conversion—a conversion that took place at least nominally over a thousand years ago, and which has profoundly shaped all institutions ever since. By resisting the pull of these assumptions, we see Polish witchcraft in a different light. Cunning-folk did not 'use' Christianity for their own ends; rather they were Christians who tried to heal their neighbors in the name of the Father, Son, and Holy Ghost.[24] Ordinary peasants did not perform a thinly Christianized magic; rather, they protected themselves from Christian devils by means of Christian holy objects. Even those witches who confessed to the most radical rejection and abomination of Christianity—who worshipped the devil, or who trampled the Eucharist and threw it to pigs—may be seen, in

as a residual category filled with whatever the scholar can't place in the categories of religion or of empirical technique. Among a large literature, see Geschiere, *Modernity of Witchcraft*; Lerner, 'Magic, Religion and Secularity'. Ronald Hutton has concisely summarized the historiography of scholarship on this issue in relation especially to Mediterranean religions: Hutton, *Witches*, 98–106; see now also Hutton, *The Witch: A History of Fear* (New Haven: Yale University Press, 2018).

[23] Hildred Geertz, 'An Anthropology of History and Magic: Two Views', *Journal of Interdisciplinary History*, 6/1 (1975), 74.

[24] In addition to the material and arguments adduced in Ch. 6, see David Elton Gay, 'On the Christianity of Incantations', in J. Roper (ed.), *Charms and Charming in Europe* (New York: Palgrave, 2004).

fragmented hints and inversion narratives, in their involuntary cries under torture, beseeching the Virgin or God's Passion or the Eucharist for succor, as pious Christian women.

Of course, I do not want to suggest that every use of the host was pious, or that everyone who used it had a deep appreciation for its sacramental character and effects. For some, surely, it can have been little more than a source of power, no more meaningful or holy than any other source. It would be ridiculous to argue that the man tried for church robbery in Nowy Sącz in 1639 was acting in a Christian manner when he supplemented his good-luck amulet (a handkerchief containing 'a piece of blessed sausage, a piece of blessed bread and a piece of blessed ham, . . . not for witchcraft, but because it works well to carry [such a thing] for luck') with a second amulet of seven freshly stolen consecrated communion wafers.[25] The noblewoman Alexandrowa Mytkowa, baking the Eucharists into pancakes to sway the Tribunal to her side in property litigation, displays an equal disregard for Christianity, under any definition of that term. And it is impossible to rule out that some of the uses for the host reported under torture in secondary-crime trials, as poison for children and livestock, as a means of bringing hail and drought, might not have some basis in actual practice. Ritual transgression and inversion of the holy is not always a fantasy.

However, only by accepting the possibility that accused witches thought of themselves as good Christians can we understand their action as something other than ignorant superstition; only then can we catch a glimpse of what they thought themselves to be doing. Christian women such as Maryna Białkowa who stole the host for what theologians would describe as 'temporal' ends were disobeying the rules of the church; in this institutional sense, clearly, they were bad Christians. But in their own terms, it is hard to see how such actions bespeak an adulterated Christianity. On the contrary, I would argue that the trials in which host-stealing forms the primary crime are one of our best sets of data to show a deep, committed, if not fully orthodox, Christianity among the early modern Polish commoner women. Regina Zaleska, who most probably did ask her son to steal the host, appears to have been a somewhat amateur cunning-woman who had tried her hand at the healing of horses and the removal of witchcraft from butter and milk. Both she and Maryna Białkowa made use of information that was 'in the air'—both in the sense that it was more or less common knowledge and in the sense that it followed easily, could readily be extracted, from standard church teaching about the host as a defense against misfortune and the diabolic. Regina Matuszka in Kleczew stole the host not only for personal profit, but also to increase the production of wax from her honey-combs that she could donate to the church. Even Zofia Janowska and Alexandrowa Mytkowa, using the Eucharist for love or favor, were drawing upon its

---

[25] Tomasz Wiślicz, *Zarobić na duszne zbawienie* (Warsaw: Wydawnictwo Neriton/Instytut Historii Polskiej Akademii Nauk, 2001), 173.

symbolism of reconciliation: their sin, I have suggested, lay in attempting a particularistic application of what Bossy has called 'the social miracle of the mass'.[26]

Those trials which centered around the Bald Mountain motif are most easily read as inversions of, travesties of, what is right and good: God exchanged for Satan, orgy for sexual virtue, abuse and torture of the host taking the place of its proper veneration and adoration. This world turned upside down is extensively explored in elite demonology, almost to the exclusion of ordinary maleficent magic; a conclusion often taken from this demonological emphasis is that trials featuring these inverted structures are essentially top–down, elite impositions on popular culture. Under such assumptions, it follows that these trials can tell us a great deal about elite attitudes, but very little about popular witchcraft or popular Christianity. Chmielowski's account of the *sabbat*, cribbed from half a dozen western demonologists, makes clear that the orgiastic, devil-worshipping, Eucharist-profaning witch is a cosmopolitan product of the discursive habits, as well as the reading and citation practices, of elite authors.

Nevertheless, the elite discourse is not so totalizing as to fully exclude the voices of the accused witches themselves, who, after all, were themselves perfectly able to produce and reproduce fantasies of transgression and sin through a discursive structure of binary opposition and inversion. The extraordinary testimony of Marjanna of Tuliszków points to her folkloristic, but nevertheless deep, and indeed orthodox, Catholic faith. We don't know what sort of question, whether leading or not, elicited her initial description of the Christ-Child appearing from the stabbed and mistreated host; we do know that her answer went beyond whatever might have been wanted.

Marjanna's confession implies both devotion to the host as the body of Christ and devotion to Jesus as the innocent child. I have tentatively suggested that this young girl, away from home for the first time—adolescent, in a new and hostile home, possibly the object of somebody's unwanted (or ambivalently wanted and feared) carnal interest, possibly raped or seduced on the road from Tuliszków to Wąsosze after having been made drunk by a chance acquaintance, might have seen in the 'heartily and mournfully crying' little child, stabbed and bleeding (as she may have been 'stabbed' and have bled in a sexual attack), a deeply meaningful metaphor of her own plight. If this interpretation is too far-fetched (I find it no more than plausible), it remains to interpret what she saw and did, or thought she saw and did or chose to report having seen and done, and we cannot do this sufficiently by reference to the demonological script forced upon her. At the very least, and for whatever psychological purposes of her own, Marjanna bears testimony to the infiltration of Eucharistic images from *exempla* and sermons into the religious life of the very lowest levels of Polish society. Even Anna Ratajka's testimony, seemingly so scripted, should be read in light of her evident

---

[26] Bossy, *Christianity in the West*, 57–75.

devotion to the Eucharist as an inversion not just of elite attitudes, but of her own attitude as well.

Both types of Eucharist-stealing witch-trial, far from demonstrating, on the one hand, the parasitic animistic beliefs of a somewhat materialistic peasantry, and on the other hand, the obsessions of the elite, give us the most direct evidence we have that Polish common women of the seventeenth and eighteenth centuries had absorbed post-Tridentine devotion to the Eucharist and adopted it as their own. The very names by which the accused denote the Eucharist give some indication of their beliefs and attitudes. For the court scribes, the Eucharist is most often simply the 'Most Holy Sacrament'. The accused witches, for their part, expressed a variety of titles for the Eucharist that collectively indicate a deep knowledge of Eucharistic piety and doctrine. The Szczerców witches, asked by the court why they stole 'God's Passion' answer that they stole 'The Lord God' for malefice (Szczerców 1716). For both Maryna Białkowa in Lublin and Anna Ratajka in Pyzdry, the host is simply 'the Lord Jesus'; for Anna Przybeła in Warta, it is 'my Lord' (Warta 1676). Marjanna of Oporówko displays a considerable knowledge of at least the terms of Catholic doctrine in testifying that she stole 'God's Transubstantiation' (Kleczew 1730). Clearly, and in strong contrast to the endless complaints of pastors bemoaning peasant ignorance, something of elite Eucharistic doctrine was getting through to the women accused of witchcraft. Reina Bartoszowa Misiakówna, wife of the blacksmith of Popielowo (Kleczew 1693), testified that 'I couldn't see [the host] when it was elevated during Mass' after she had sold her soul to the devil—an attribute of witches still repeated in nineteenth-century folklore.[27] Appearing in testimony from a tiny village in the late seventeenth century, it indicates the importance of devotion to the elevated host already in this period.[28] Anna Przybeła's extraordinarily eloquent speech to her judges and tormentors in Warta (quoted as the epigraph to this chapter), indicates that among the very women accused of, and testifying to, the worst excesses against the Most Holy Sacrament, one can find clear expressions of deep and fully orthodox understandings of the graces brought about by consumption of the Body of Christ.

For Maryna Białkowa as much as for Piotr Skarga, the Eucharist is a true fragment of the Incarnation—she calls it, matter-of-factly, 'The Lord Jesus': for both, too, it is the best defense against spiritual harm. For Anna Ratajka, or for Marjanna of Tuliszków, as much as for Benedykt Chmielowski, execration of the host is the worst possible sin: in confessing to it, they are not just participating in elite discourse but also, paradoxically, making a confession of faith.

---

[27] Kolberg, *Dzieła wszystkie*, vii. 78; cf. Gentilcore, *From Bishop to Witch*, 244; Waite, *Devil's Minions*, 166–78.

[28] Similarly, the devil of a witch in Fordon berated her for attempting to take communion. And 'when the Most Holy Sacrament was raised, he wouldn't let me look at it, but covered my eyes and made me look at the ground' (Fordon 1695).

It may seem misguided, even obscene, to hear Christianity in the confessions of accused witches under torture—to amplify the soft voice of early modern peasant-women's religiosity by the means of the rack or the strappado. Gamalski warned that an accused witch, 'guilty of nothing, confessed everything, and sings out those things that they have stuffed into her head'.[29] Such warnings must be taken seriously, lest we participate in a 'bloody ethnography', whereby through torture the court 'borrows the voice of the victim to double its own voice'.[30] William Cavanaugh argues that pain robs its victim of language and of the community built in language:

Those in great pain are reduced to inarticulate screams and moans...Pain does not merely resist language but actually destroys it, in extreme cases reducing the sufferer to sounds he used before he learned to speak.[31]

Although we must not forget that the portrait of witchcraft and Christianity developed in Chapters 6–8 is built on confessions under torture, I cannot fully accept Cavanaugh's account of the inarticulate torture victim. Accused witches had voices; we can hear them. Their very screams and moans were not prelinguistic but were cultural and religious: 'I'm not guilty of anything, my soul to God' (Lublin 1644); 'I'm innocent for God's sake, I beg you . . . I'm innocent, have mercy on me a sinner . . . Unjustly, unjustly, by God's mercy I beg you . . . I don't know, I don't know, take care for the sake of Jesus Christ' (Lublin 1664); 'Have mercy, for the sake of the Most Holy Virgin and the Most Holy Sacrament' (Pyzdry 1699); or simply 'Jesus Mary!' (Lublin 1732). These are Christian screams and moans, testimonies of faith screamed out at the very moment of imputed diabolism, paganism, divine treason, demonolatry, and desecration of the Body of Christ. Painful though it is to hear these voices, we ought to listen to what they have to say.

---

[29] Gamalski, *Przestrogi Duchowne*, 14ᵛ–15.

[30] William Cavanaugh, *Torture and Eucharist* (Cambridge, Mass.: Blackwell, 1998), 35. I borrow the term 'bloody ethnography' from Ronald Hsia's characterization of ritual murder trials: Ronald Po-Chia Hisa, *Trent 1745: Stories of a Ritual Murder Trial* (New Haven: Yale University Press, 1992).

[31] Ibid. 34.

PART III

DEMONOLOGY

9

A Candle for the Devil

Piękny-c diabeł niemiecki i foremny, sztuczny,
Jedno nazbyt poważny, a do tego buczny.
Włoski zaś foremniejszy, jedno za pieszczony,
Do tego barzo słaby na dalekie strony.
Polski dobry i sprawny, a do tego śmiały
I na kłopot cierpliwy, i na nędze trwały.

Your German devil's handsome, attractive and contrived,
But not very serious, and vain besides.
The Italian devil is pretty but coddled
When far from home he's easily addled.
The Polish devil is clever and resolute
Patient in trouble, tenacious when destitute.

(*Nędza z Biedą z Polski idą* (1624), vv. 467–72)

I have been arguing that the accused Polish witches, like their accusers and judges, were pious Christians. The Polish witch inhabited a crossroads world where the peasant cosmology of limited good, of blessing conceived as dew and milk, intersected with more mainstream Catholic symbols of the sacred such as the Eucharist and the story of Christ's Passion that it embodied. If one listens carefully to confessions, one learns as much about Christianity as about witchcraft: one is offered a rare window into the religious conscience of early modern Polish women.

The devil, as always, is in the details and, as devils do, complicates the picture I have been developing of the pious Polish witch. So far in this book the devil has avoided our direct attention: glimpsed in a curse or eaten with a gift of bewitched parsnips; fleetingly encountered at Bald Mountain; he has haunted the margins of our story without taking center-stage. This may be appropriate, for the devil of the witch-trials is shifty and elusive, an unsavory local character rather than the Prince of Hell. Nevertheless, we will need to pin him down: to understand the imagined witch, we must also understand her imagination of the devil to whom she was accused of giving her allegiance. If the last several chapters have largely dealt with the cosmopolitanism of the Polish witch, her participation in universal Catholic devotion, the next two chapters pay more attention to witch as indigene, her world informed by neighborhood folklore. The path from the crossroads leads outward to pan-European elite demonology, but also in toward the village with its house-demon living cozy behind the stove. In Polish witch-trials, when accusers, the accused, witnesses, and magistrates spoke of 'devils' (*diabli, czarci, szatany*) and 'evil spirits' (*złe duchy*), what sort of creature did they have in mind?

OUR GOOD POWERS OF EVIL

A long tradition of Polish scholarship asserts that in Poland, in contrast to other Christian cultures, the devil is an ambiguous figure of fun—an easily fooled foil for the clever peasant in legends, or, as in the epigraph to this chapter, himself the embodiment of peasant tenacity and cunning. Only lightly Christianized, Polish devils are looked on with some affection: to borrow the title of a popular article on peasant-carved devil figures, they are 'our good powers of evil'.[1] Mischievous but ultimately sympathetic, such 'playful demon-sprites' reveal an earthy Slavic tolerance lightly disguised in Christian diabolical dress.[2] With specific reference to the Polish witch-trials, Janusz Tazbir has contrasted the ludic Polish devil to western figures of fear, and has noted the 'weakness' of Polish demonology in the Reformation period.[3] Others have followed Tazbir's lead, drawing a connection between what they take to be the relatively mild Polish witch-trials and the comic Polish devil.[4] Maria Bogucka has described the Polish devil as 'domesticated', in strong contrast to the western imagination of 'an ominous demon very dangerous to people, a really powerful ruler of hell'.[5]

Such exceptionalism exaggerates the distance between Polish and western devils—the latter of which could be just as comical, ribald, or foolish as their Polish equivalents.[6] Conversely, Polish devils could be very frightening indeed: Marjanna's devil-suitor, who followed her about on his stork legs and forced his attentions upon her, does not seem to have been a figure of fun. The ribald devils in the *Infernal Parliament* or *Pilgrimage of the Hobos* were often played for laughs, but other genres depicted the devil differently. In his study of the seventeenth-century sermons of Bernarnd Gutowski, for example, Janusz Drob finds no trace whatever of the popular ambivalent devil: in Gutowski's Franciscan imagination,

---

[1] Zuzanna Pol, 'Nasze dobre złe moce', *National Geographic Polska*, 54/3 (2004).

[2] Michał Rożek, *Diabeł w kulturze polskiej* (Warsaw: Polska Akademia Nauk, 1993), 188. Such a depiction of the Polish devil and the national exceptionalism it underwrites were first popularized in Kazimierz W. Wójcicki, *Zarysy domowe*, 4 vols. (Warsaw: M. Chmielewski, 1842), esp. iii. 185–9.

[3] Janusz Tazbir, *Myśl polska w nowożytnej kulturze europejskiej* (Warsaw: Nasza Księgarnia, 1986), 148, 57; Tazbir, 'Procesy o czary', 158.

[4] Bylina, 'Magia', 42; *Człowiek i zaświaty*, 167; Karpiński, *Kobieta*, 321.

[5] Maria Bogucka, *The Lost World of the 'Sarmatians'* (Warsaw: Polska Akademia Nauk, 1996), 176, 88.

[6] From a large, uneven literature, see Darren Oldridge, *The Devil in Early Modern England* (Phoenix Mill, Glos.: Sutton Publishing, 2000), which has the virtue of emphasizing the diversity of English devils.

the devil figures always and only as infernal tempter, animated by an unquench-able hatred for humankind.[7] But tricksterlike, the devil eschewed consistency even within a single genre or text. The sixteenth–seventeenth-century collections of Jesuit *exempla* anthologized by Mariusz Kazańczuk roil with humorous or foolish devils, but also with terrifying spirits of destruction: a whiff of brimstone is never absent from even the most comical anecdotes.[8]

The author of the *Witch Denounced* can indulge a chuckle at 'a certain Ruthenian' who lit two candles in church: one for God, the other 'so that the devil might do me no harm'.[9] The same author dismisses with a witticism a long tradition of Polish anti-superstition literature, condemning the common people for leaving food to the house-demon on Thursday evenings.[10] While texts such as the *Devil's Lawsuit* treat such a practice as witchcraft and diabolism, the recita-tion of 'prayers to the devil's honor' and sacrifice to demons,[11] the *Witch Denounced* author dismisses such practices with a literary smirk: 'They don't wash dishes on Thursdays. Why? They know, I also know but I won't say.'[12] But the same author could strongly denounce as 'stinking of heresy' those among the common folk who 'don't believe that the Devil is really so vile or so damned'; and could describe child-killing devils waiting to pounce on a mother who forgets to wear her crucifix.[13]

In later Polish folklore, the devil is most often a mild trickster—but even here there are variations and contradictions. Legends of the devil fooled by a young peasant-man or an old peasant-woman, who takes advantage of the devil's powers to gain riches but manages to keep his or her soul, are peppered throughout the sixty-eight volumes of Kolberg's folklore compendium.[14] But the same collection includes the devil met by witches when the new moon

---

[7] Janusz Drob, 'Model człowieka wieku XVII w kazaniach Bernarda Gutowskiego', *Roczniki Humanistyczne KUL*, 29/2 (1981).

[8] Kazańczuk, *Historie dziwne i straszliwe.* See e.g. the early 17th-cent. story of a devil tricked out of its pact by a wily peasant lad—the same story shows up as a folktale in 19th-cent. ethnography. *Historie dziwne i straszliwe*, 56–7; Kolberg, *Dzieła wszystkie*, x. 221–2.

[9] *Czarownica powołana*, 78. This is one version of a still popular proverb; and the anecdote is often told, not of a Ruthenian swain but of King Władysław Jagiełło. For a detailed account of the proverb and its history, see Krzyżanowski, *Mądrej głowie*, i. 87–9.

[10] The *skrzat* or *uboże* or *domowik* (or, as a 15th-cent. Polish–German dictionary calls them, the 'lares familiares *skrzathkovye*, which we call little people') took food esp. at Maundy Thursday in exchange for the fortune he brought to the home. Condemnation of this remnant of pre-Christian ancestor cults formed a repeated theme of 15th-cent. anti-superstition literature. Bolesław Erzepki, 'Przyczynki do średniowiecznego słownictwa polskiego I. Glosy polskie wpisane do łacińsko niemieckiego słowniku drukowowanego w roku 1490', *Rocznik Towarzystwa Przyjaciół Nauk Poznańskiego*, 34 (1908), 95; Brückner, 'Średniowieczna poezja łacińska', 25; 'Kazania średniowieczne', 320, 41, 45.

[11] *Postępek*, 117; cf. Sowirzalius, *Sejm piekielny*, 56–7, vv. 1161–2.

[12] *Czarownica powołana*, 6.

[13] Ibid. 4, 83.

[14] e.g. Kolberg, *Dzieła wszystkie*, iii. 153, viii. 43–76, ix. 12–13, xiv. 43, 210, 24–47, xv. 26, xix. 20. This is, of course, a worldwide folklore motif, illustrated by *Rumpelstiltskin* or *The Devil and Daniel Webster* or even, slightly modified, by the Brer Rabbit stories.

falls on Sunday, who grants them milk stolen from neighbors in return for their souls, and tears their heads off if they try to rescind the pact.[15] Kolberg and others also chronicle the numerous child-stealing *mamuny*, cattle-drowning *topielcy*, vampiric *zmory* and *strzygony* who populated the anxious imaginations of the Polish peasants—not to mention the apotropaic herbs and crosses, Marian images and amulets used to ward off the devil and his minions.[16] The foolish or mischievous devil represents just one aspect of a complex and polyvalent character. The folklorist Adam Fischer, more open to ambiguity than those historians such as Tazbir and Bogucka who have drawn on his work, writes of an ambivalent devil, derived from the mixture of the 'one-time friendly house-spirit', the terrifying Christian devil of the early Middle Ages, and the 'weak and comic' devil of the late Middle Ages.[17]

One example of this polyvalent devil may stand in for many others, leading us into the complex relationship between literary tropes, folklore motifs, and the confessions of witches. In a collection of jokes and anecdotes from the sixteenth century, we find the following story. An old widow was worried how to get her harvest in. The devil appears, and offers to help with the harvest in return for her soul; the woman agrees that if this *szatan* can complete the three tasks she will assign him, her soul will be his. First she commands him to bring in the produce from the fields and store it in her barns; second, to gather, chop up, and stack a supply of firewood to last through the winter. The devil completes these tasks without difficulty, and asks what the third task will be:

And the woman, who had eaten radishes that morning, farted (pardon the expression) with a great voice, and said: 'Devil, catch that fart as fast as you can and twist it into rope. If you can't, our deal is off and you'll not have my soul!' The devil, who had never gone to that school where they teach how to twist ropes from farts, departed from the woman, for he could expect to get nothing from her.[18]

In comic literature at least, a poor old widow—the stereotypical candidate for the devil-pact—could make use of the devil's services without endangering her soul. In a back-handed compliment to female cunning, the anonymous author concludes that 'the female nation is always shrewd; they can dupe the devil himself'.[19] In witch-trials themselves, we sometimes find similar diabolical servants—Barba Marczynka's devil helped her hoe her garden, while Ewa Urbańska's devil chopped wood and plowed the fields (Skarszewy 1699c, 1700b). But in a twist on the folktale, such devils could demand constant labor, strangling cattle if not given

---

[15] Kolberg, *Dzieła wszystkie*, vii. 78–81.
[16] Mikołaj Rybkowski, 'Dyabeł w wierzeniach ludu polskiego. (Z okolic Biecza)', *Lud*, 9 (1903); Lehr, 'Wierzenia demonologiczne', 118–20.
[17] Adam Fischer, 'Diabeł w wierzeniach ludu polskiego', in *Studia staropolskie ku czci Aleksandra Brücknera* (Kraków: Krakowska Spółka Wydawnicza, 1926), 209.
[18] *Facecje polskie z roku 1624*, ed. A. Brückner (Kraków: Akademia Umiejętności 1903 [1624, 1570]), 148–9.
[19] Ibid.

other work to do—malefice understood here as the inverse of their domestic chores (Chojnice 1691; Łobżenica 1692; Skarszewy 1700a). Most often, however, devil-servants were treasure-hauling imps, violating the limited good of the peasant moral economy by stealing grain and milk from neighbors. While the devil in the anecdote gathered grain from the woman's own fields, devil-familiars stole it from others.

The *Infernal Parliament* provides a portrait of such a devil in a speech delivered by *Latawiec* before the gathered devils:

> I get, it's true, plenty of groats and milk from good wives,
> But in return I must provide them with human goods.
> In the barns of strangers I thresh peas and wheat,
> Sometimes I collect so much I can hardly move;
> Or money, if I find some, or steal it from someone—
> Wherever I live, I must bring profit to the household.[20]

Latawiec clearly resembles the prosperity-maintaining house-spirits condemned in fifteenth-century sermons, and dismissed as superstition in the *Witch Denounced*.[21] He also closely resembles the hobgoblins and pucks of Europe as a whole, mischievous but benevolent if given milk to drink.[22] And he resembles (indeed, shares a common name), with the treasure-hauling demons of several trials. Eva Lenartka denounced others for having a '*latawiec* in the attic' who brings them money (Warta 1679b; cf. Kalisz 1580); while Marianna Karabinka's *latawiec* flew out of her chimney with sparks in its tail, bringing her gifts of milk and grain (Warta 1679a).[23] In 1677, the wife of the Klimkówka *wójt* brought a defamation suit against a villager who had said she 'gets things from devils' (Klimkówka 1677b).[24] Much more serious were the consequences for the accused witch Anna of Żelazno, who complained bitterly that, ever since youth, 'they've called me a witch and said I had a devil who helps me work'. She had aroused such suspicions

---

[20] Sowirzalius, *Sejm piekielny*, vv. 994–1003.

[21] Indeed his colleague *Nocny Lelek* (nightjar or goatsucker, a nocturnal bird associated with milk-theft and witchcraft throughout its European range), refers to this tradition directly: 'they don't give food to the poor on Thursdays, instead, with their unwashed dishes, they leave it all for us'. Ibid. vv. 1161–2, 56–7. On treasure-bringing demons in German-speaking areas of eastern and north-eastern Europe, see now Johannes Dillinger, 'The Dragon as a Household Spirit: Witchcraft and Economics in Early Modern and Modern Sources', *Magic, Ritual and Witchcraft*, 10 no. 2 (2022).

[22] Burchard of Worms condemned such milk-drinking, prosperity-bringing, sometimes treasure-stealing imps as early as 1000 CE; Reginald Scot lampooned the bowl of milk set out for 'Robin Goodfellow' in the 16th cent.; while in the 17th cent. Thomas Heywood noted the similarity between eastern European 'Diuels . . . called Kottri or Kibaldi' and the beings 'such as wee/Pugs or Hob-Goblins call'. J. T. McNeill and Helena M. Garner (eds.), *Medieval Handbooks of Penance* (New York: Columbia University Press, 1990 [1938]), 335; Katharine Briggs, *The Anatomy of Puck* (London: Routledge & Paul, 1959), 19–20; Thomas Heywood, *The Hierarchy of the Blessed Angells: Their Names, Orders and Offices; The Fall of Lucifer With His Angells* (London: A. Islip, 1635), 574; cf. Wilson, *Magical Universe*, 408–9 for similar beliefs throughout Europe.

[23] The sparking tail is a feature of the Polish *latawiec* and *skrzatek*, as well as similar beings from Estonia to Romania. The verb *skrzyć się*, 'to spark', used in witness testimony against Marianna describing her *latawiec*, amounts to a folk etymology for the treasure-hauling *skrzatek*.

[24] Compare a trial in Fordon (1682), where the accused allegedly owned 'white *plenniki*, which fetched them grain from various places'. *Plennik* might be roughly translated as 'fertile little thing'.

because she worked hard, 'for which reason I've earned my bread, but they say that a devil brings it to me' (Łobżenica 1692).

What in literature amounted to a feeble joke, a ribald and light-hearted dig at the cunning of old women and their tendency to flatulence, could in trials be a matter of life and death. Witches did confess to devil-servants not unlike those found in folklore or ribald verse, but such equivalence did little to ameliorate the trials. And yet we should note the fairy-quality of many of these devils: their double or even triple nature as infernal beings, remnants of the pre-Christian house-demon, pan-European hobgoblin or treasure hauler. It is worth noting that in some trials, as in most literary sources, the devil dressed as in foreign, German clothes (Nowe 1647, 1671; Nowy Sącz 1670, 1684; Łobżenica 1686, 1692; Kleczew 1728, 1730; Pyzdry 1731; Żerków 1732).[25] But in other confessions, the witch's devil, like a sprite or *krasnoludek*, dressed all in red (Kowalewo 1678b; Nowy Wiśnicz 1689a; Nowe Koźmin 1690; Pyzdry 1699, 1731; Nowe 1699, 1704b, 1706, 1709b; Nieszawa 1721b).[26]

When, then, we encounter 'devils' in the Polish witch-trials, we must exercise some caution. The being so labeled may be the benevolent house-demon who protects the farm from harm; or the morally ambivalent treasure-hauler or grain-stealer, who similarly provides prosperity to the household but does so at the expense of others; or, finally, the Christian devil—whose assistance in this world always comes with a heavy price in the next. Most often, it is some combination of several of these.

THE DEVIL FROM KRZEMIEŃ

In Chapter 3 we looked briefly at the trial of Regina Lewczykowa, accused of witchcraft for having told her neighbor Wojciech to 'eat a devil' (Lublin 1698). A year after their quarrel, Wojciech's leg and back suddenly began to hurt him sharply—a common symptom of witchcraft in south-eastern Poland and Ukraine.[27] Wojciech's subsequent symptoms, however, were less typical. He had been possessed by an 'evil spirit', which, as he said, 'spoke through me': 'I was not in myself'. After exorcism by a priest failed to alleviate his symptoms, Wojciech traveled some 50 kilometers to Pilaszowice, to be bathed in herbs by a cunning-man. A friend accompanied him on this journey, and later testified before the Lublin court concerning what had happened during Wojciech's exorcistic bath:

---

[25] Janusz Tazbir, 'Obraz heretyka i diabła', in *Szlaki kultury polskiej* (Warsaw: Polskie Wydawnictwo Naukowe, 1986 [1981]).

[26] The terms *krasnoludek* and *krasnal*, which may be translated both 'pretty people' and as 'red people' (in reference to their red caps), do not seem to have been current in the early modern period; but the color symbolism was already present. On red as the color of Slavic 'demons', see Kazimierz Moszyński, *Kultura Ludowa Słowian*, 3 vols. (Warsaw: Książka i Wiedza, 1967–8 [1934]), ii/1. 623–4.

[27] Dysa, 'Witchcraft Trials', 154–7.

In that bath it began to speak through him in these words: 'Ah, old woman of Krzemień, I didn't have any business for you here, ah, old women, release me, I say, I'm not from hell, I'm an unbaptized soul.' People asked him there about things they had lost, but he answered, that 'I don't know, only one from hell [knows that sort of thing],' and he also said, 'Lewczykowa bought me, from a woman of Krzemień.'

Kiszka's testimony appears to have had no effect on the outcome of the trial: Regina supplied a considerable number of character witnesses, on the strength of whom the court dismissed the case, requiring only an expurgatory oath. Despite its inconsequence for Lewczykowa's trial, I find Kiszka's brief statement to be among the most interesting texts from the entire corpus of Polish witch-trial testimony. In a few sentences, he raises serious questions about the ontological status of the 'devil' possessing Wojciech Koziełek. By extension, he raises questions about all the other devils encountered in other witch-trials, and complicates further our understanding of the Christian experience of witches and their accusers.

'I'm not from hell, I'm an unbaptized soul'—*iam nie zpiekła, jam nie krzceniec*. The term *niechrzczeniec* could be used literally to mean any unbaptized person, such as an adult pagan or Jew, as in a sermon by Marcin Białobrzeski[28] reminding his congregation that without baptism one cannot enter the Kingdom of Heaven. More often, however, as clearly stated here, the term meant an infant who had died without baptism, as in the Catechism by the same author.[29] In this second meaning, it was closely associated with witchcraft and demons: a fifteenth-century manuscript herbal, for example, lists *nyeskrzczenecz* as the Polish vernacular for *Mandragora officinarum*, the characteristic herb of witchcraft.[30]

John Bossy has explored the central place of baptism in traditional European Christianity. Baptism was the crucial sacrament for integrating the newly born infant, not only into the church and into the ranks of the saveable, but into society. Indeed, in traditional Christianity to be capable of salvation is to be social: through baptism one becomes integrated into the network of kinship relations through which the benefits of Christ's atoning sacrifice were understood to flow.[31] The unbaptized, not having been thus integrated into society, were

---

[28] Marcin Białobrzeski, *Postylla ortodoxa...*, 2 vols. (Kraków: Drukarnia Łazarzowa, 1581), 143.

[29] Marcin Białobrzeski, *Katechizm ALBO Wizerunk prawey wiary Chrześciańskiey wedle Nauki Pana Iezusa Chrystusa* (Kraków, 1566), 186.

[30] Rostafiński, *Średniowieczna Historya*, 810. In Poland, real mandrake root was rare, but its various substitutes have been treated ritually as children; the herb *przestęp* or *postęp* (*Bryonia alba*, bryony) was sometimes fed or washed in milk, like a little baby. This same herb has the characteristics of a treasure-hauling demon or house-spirit; it brings its owner increased prosperity, esp. increased dairy milk. See Moszyński, *Kultura Ludowa*, ii/1. 336; Kolberg, *Dzieła wszystkie*, vii. 78.

[31] John Bossy, 'Blood and Baptism: Kinship, Community and Christianity in Western Europe from the 14th to the 17th Centuries', *Studies in Church History*, 10 (1973); Bossy, Christianity in the West, 14–19.

undomesticated, wild, foreign; indeed, in a sense, inhuman.[32] One senses the outrage and despair of parents whose dead infants were thus relegated to the anti-social margin. One should not be surprised, then, to find that baptism was the most popular sacrament, sought out without the usual nagging and browbeating needed to get villagers to confession, or to marry in church. Stanisław Brzeżański, discussed in Chapter 8, spent most of his *Sheepfold in the Savage Field* complaining about peasant ignorance and indifference. Not so with baptism: somewhat to his own surprise, Brzeżański's versified catechism on the proper means of baptism had proven extremely popular.[33] This strong concern to baptize as quickly as possible constitutes one of a very few areas where we can show that folk religion agreed in full with elite priorities. Polish women of the sixteenth through eighteenth centuries were terrified that their babies, so prone to early death, might be claimed by devils or indeed become devils themselves.

Although post-Tridentine Catholicism removed much of the 'horizontal' focus on kinship from baptism, it preserved the notion that the unbaptized infant could not be saved. Provincial synods and pastoral letters reminded parish priests that, like suicides, stillbirths and unbaptized infants were to be refused Christian burial on hallowed ground.[34] Instead unbaptized infants were to be buried in the fields or under a *Boże Męka* or 'God's Passion'—the field and roadside crucifixes encountered in Chapter 7. They were thus ritually and spatially set outside the borders of society and of the church.[35] The crucifix placed over their bodies (the same crucifix which was so popular at crossroads and borders in general, as protection against the evil spirits associated with such places) may be understood simultaneously as an expression of grudging hope for their salvation and as an exorcism: like the stake through the vampire's heart, it was meant to keep their soul from wandering or harming others. (In 1673, the parish priest of Miłówka caused a chapel to be built on the site of an old crucifix before which many peasants had seen the ghosts of unbaptized infants kneeling in prayer.[36]) In

---

[32] Stephen Wilson has noted that in the Mediterranean region (both Catholic and Orthodox), unbaptized children are referred to as Turks, Moors, or barbarians. The equivalence of the unbaptized to fairies, and their vulnerability to fairy-theft, is of course a pan-European motif. Wilson, *Magical Universe*, 184, 215–17, 24.

[33] Brzeżański, *Owczarnia*, fo. 35.

[34] Parents protested, as in a village trial for incest between first cousins (1732), wherein the woman's mother insisted repeatedly that when she baptized the dying child of the incestuous union, the veins behind his ear were still pulsing faintly. Although a suspiciously large number of other witnesses insisted on the same point, the parish priest denied church burial since the infant 'had not been perfectly baptized'. Grodziski, *Księgi sądowe jazowskie*, item 95.

[35] Kracik, 'Chrzest', 192; Nasiorowski, *'List pasterski' Maciejowskiego*, 207; see also, for Protestant Germany, Scribner, *Religion and Culture*, 314, 31; cf. Wilson, *Magical Universe*, 211–12.

[36] Seweryn Udziela, 'Z kronik kościelnych. I. Kronika w Miłówce', *Lud*, 16 (1910). In an infanticide trial in Nowy Wiśnicz in 1658, the mother confessed to burying her child at the riverbank, ostensibly to save the costs of burial, 'since we know that such children are not buried in the cemetery, but under a crucifix (*Boże Męka*) in the fields'. See Uruszczak, *Acta Maleficorum*, 194–5.

practice they could also be buried under lone-standing lindens, a tree sacred to the merciful Virgin Mary, who had sheltered under its branches from Herod's soldiers. Such a site seems particularly apt, but such trees were also associated with paganism, demons, and ghosts, so that it was often necessary to sanctify and exorcize them with a small Marian image.[37] In folk practice as in orthodox theology, where the doctrine of the *limbus infantium* (limbo, literally the 'threshold of the infants') remained sufficiently undefined to allow some hope that unbaptized infants might escape damnation, their place was at the borderland between the demonic and the sacred, the wilderness and the domesticated.[38]

The unbaptized dead came to supplant, or to mix with, the malicious spirits of field and forest, stream and marsh. For example, Haur asserts that 'concerning the *Topielec*, who inhabits Rivers, doing harm to People and drowning Cattle, one should know that his nature comes from a pregnant Woman who has drowned'.[39] Here the *topielec*, more commonly understood as a water-sprite or as the soul of a drowned man, becomes the soul of an unborn infant killed by its suicide mother.[40] Similarly, in later folklore, both a suicide maiden and her unbaptized child could become the *mamuny* or *boginki* or *mawki* who avenge themselves on the living by stealing any infant children not yet protected by baptism.[41] The theme of the unbaptized *latawiec* or *skrzat* or *poterczę*, a bird chased by hail and lightning, flying before the storm and crying *chrztu, chrztu* (baptism, baptism!), is widespread throughout Poland and Ukraine. Should one encounter such a demon, reciting the formula of baptism will save it and cause it to disappear.[42] As late as the 1960s, a poll in rural east central Poland found that about 15 percent of those surveyed thought the 'spirits of the air' which bring hail and thunder were the ghosts of unbaptized babies.[43]

[37] Moszyński, *Kultura Ludowa*, ii/1. 326, 527–30; Niebrzegowska, *Przestrach od przestrachu*, 86.

[38] Beliefs concerning an old linden tree outside the village of Modlnice in the 19th cent. perfectly captured the liminal, sacred but demonic character of such sites. The villagers believed that the linden had miraculously sprung from the lindenwood staff of St Wojciech, missionary to the Prussians and embodiment of the victory of Christianity over paganism: accordingly they had placed an image of the saint under the tree. But they also speculated that the small chapel under the tree was 'pagan', and was haunted by the condemned souls of the stillbirths and children who died unbaptized buried in its shade. Kolberg, *Dzieła wszystkie*, vii. 59–60.

[39] Haur, *Skład Abo Skarbiec* 100.

[40] The ethnographer Urszula Lehr found precisely the same belief among the peasants of southern Małopolska in the 1970s (Lehr, 'Wierzenia demonologiczne,' 120–2). According to Brückner, the beautiful *rusalki* or water-nymphs of Ruthenian folklore were also often associated with unbaptized children, to the extent that the term *rusalka* came to be synonymous with *poterczat* or stillbirth. Aleksander Brückner, *Mitologia polska*, ed. S. Urbańczyk (Warsaw: Polskie Wydawnictwo Naukowe, 1985 [1924]), 308.

[41] Kolberg, *Dzieła wszystkie*, xxxi. 98; Brückner, *Mitologia polska*, 318; Lehr, 'Wierzenia demonologiczne', 127–9.

[42] Kolberg, *Dzieła wszystkie*, vii. 60–1; Edmund Kolbuszewski, 'Materyały do medycyny i wierzeń ludowych według opowiadań Demka Żemeły w Zaborzu w pow. rawskim', *Lud*, 2/2 (1896), 160; Moszyński, *Kultura Ludowa*, 399; Lehr, 'Wierzenia demonologiczne', 132–333.

[43] Bohdan Baranowski, *W kręgu upiorów i wilkołaków* (Łódź: Wydawnictwo Łódzkie, 1981), 115–16.

Since failure to properly baptize an infant had such disastrous consequences, both priests and the laity paid extraordinary attention to this sacrament. Already in the fifteenth century, miracle-registers at pilgrimage sites described dying babies who had revived just long enough to receive baptism, and therefore salvation.[44] Such miracle stories also appear in seventeenth-eighteenth century Jesuit sermons and in the registers of early modern Marian shrines.[45] The Council of Trent, the Roman Catechism, and episcopal pastoral letters repeated earlier injunctions, reminding the laity that in an emergency baptism could be performed by any Christian layman or even a woman. If no Christian women were present, then a heretic 'or even a Jew, a Turk, or the crudest pagan, with no belief in baptism' could carry out the rite, and it would be considered valid so long as such a person, himself damned, said the formula correctly and with the intention of 'doing what Christians do'.[46]

When one considers the degree to which the Tridentine reforms concentrated on the consolidation of Catholic ritual efficacy, and on the reservation of sacramental power to the clergy, these almost ecumenical gestures towards laywomen and heretics seem quite extraordinary. In the context of hyperscrupulous ritualism that characterized the Catholic Reformation in Poland, where even crossing oneself incorrectly could be a sign of paganism, baptism could be done almost anywhere, with almost any material. So long as the liquid used contained water, it need not be holy or even clean, and it could be some adulterated substance such as wine. One could wash whatever part of the infant was available, using only enough water to wash the smallest finger. In an era of ever-elaborating ritual, the emergency baptism was simplicity itself: 'I baptize you in the Name of the Father and Son and Holy Ghost, Amen.'[47] Such attention to practical exigency points to the Catholic Church's real concern that, as Brzeżański puts it, 'not a single soul in the whole world should be condemned eternally out of ignorance of the baptism ritual'.[48] But it also suggests the pressures exerted by the laity who wanted to ensure that their children should not be turned into demons. Some indication that the church

---

[44] Aleksandra Witkowska, *Kulty pątnicze pietnastowiecznego Krakowa* (Lublin: Wydawnictwo Towarzystwa Naukowego Katolickiego Uniwersytetu Lubelskiego, 1984), 190–4.

[45] Kazańczuk, *Historie dziwne i straszliwe*, 74–5; Wiślicz, 'Religijność wiejska', 116–17; cf. Wilson, *Magical Universe*, 226–9. Jesuit tales could also frighten with their description of demon-like unbaptized infants, such as a baby-ghost who visited its infanticide mother repeatedly, biting her breasts, until she confessed her sin in church. Jan Kwiatkiewicz, *Suplement rocznych dziejów kościelnych* (Poznań, 1706), 945; quoted after Kazańczuk, *Historie dziwne i straszliwe*, 71–2.

[46] Quotations from Brzeżański, *Owczarnia*, fo. 36, who follows Trent session 7 can. de consec. dist. 4, ch. 24; cf. *Roman Catechism*, pt. 2, ch. 1, paras. 24–5; Nasiorowski, '*List pasterski' Maciejowskiego*, 210–11.

[47] Brzeżański, *Owczarnia*, fos. 38–9.

[48] Ibid. fo. 35ᵛ.

was responsive to lay anxiety about demon-children may be found in Adam Opatovius's *Tractatus de sacramentis*, in which he considered whether an infant could be baptized by throwing it into a river or well. He ruled that such a baptism was forbidden (as it killed the child), but would be sacramentally efficacious if the baby was still alive at the moment it came in contact with the water.[49] Polish scholars have seen this as a hypothetical case, illustrative of the hyper-scrupulosity of Catholic Reformation liturgists. But I think another interpretation is called for: Opatovius responded to a very real, indeed practical question: whether infanticide mothers could express maternal self-sacrifice in the moment of murder, ensuring the salvation of their newborn infants even as they damned themselves to hell.[50]

At folk and elite levels, baptism theology intertwined intimately with demonology. In such a context, Wojciech's unbaptized 'devil' may not be as exceptional as it first appears. Marianna Karabinka's *latawiec*, like its nineteenth-century descendents a small fiery bird with a tail of sparks, had been seen to fly in and out of her home (Figure 9.1). Neighbors assumed this was her familiar or treasure-hauler, out on its rounds stealing milk from other people's cows and grain from their fields. Although the *latawiec* is not always imagined as an unbaptized soul, Marianna drew explicitly on this tradition to deflect the charges against her: 'and even if that *latawiec* was in my home, what of it? In whatever home there has been an unbaptized child, you'll often find a *latawiec*' (Warta 1679a). Marianna used the limbo-child aspect of *latawcy* to deflect the charges against her; if a *latawiec* happened to dwell in her home, this was only because some previous tenant of the house had committed infanticide.[51] Similarly, the husband of young Fenna Dudzianka, who had run away from home, threatened that his mother would send '*chowańcy* alias *latawcy*' to fetch her back by force. This mother already had a reputation as a witch: among other rumors, it was said that the current drought was caused by a dried-up dead child which she had hung in her doorway to keep the rain-clouds away. Later, the court made a search of her house to find her *latawiec*; it is probable that they meant to find its physical manifestation as the baby's corpse (Muszyna 1678).

The most spectacular account of unbaptized devils comes from the late, complex trial before the Crown Tribunal between the noble Mytko and Pogorski families of Ukraine: a trial interweaving motifs of devil servants, stillbirths, and

---

[49] Adam Opatovius, *Tractatus de Sacramentis* (1642), 116; cited after Kracik, 'Chrzest', 195.

[50] Cf. Wilson, *Magical Universe*, 225–6.

[51] In similar vein, a devil haunting a house in Oksza in 1649 sought to avenge the blood of innocent children killed by the previous tenant, an abortionist. This Catholic devil demanded proper burial of the dead infants buried under the stove, but the Protestant citizenry of Oksza refused such a 'pagan' practice. Wijaczka, 'Procesy o czary w regionie świętokrzyskiego', 66–7; Kazimierz Bem, 'The Devil Went Down to Oksa: Demonic Visitation and Calvinist Piety in Mid-Seventeenth Century Poland', *Reformation and Renaissance Review* 23 (2021), 48–67. For a similar occurrence involving a *lotaniec* in the early 20th cent., see Dżwigoł, *Polskie ludowe słownictwo mitologiczne*, 19.

Figure 9.1. A bird-like devil or demon. Illustration to Matthew 15: 22, from the *Biblia* of Jan Nicz Leopolita, Kraków, 1561, p. Bbiii. Courtesy of the Polish National Library.

the symbolic equivalence of Eucharistic hosts with innocent children. The Crown Tribunal remitted several serfs of the Mytko family to the Lublin city court to be interrogated under torture, together with a list of questions, including: 'whether they used the corpses of the dead, or stillborn babies (*potyrczęta*) and what did they use them for'; and further, 'Whether they made any sort of offerings to devils, or whether someone else [made such offerings] in their presence, and what did they offer: children or something else, and what happened to that offering... and how many such offerings of children to the devil were made.' Later in the trial, one of the accused testified that others had dug up a stillbirth. She was said to have said: 'for this stillbirth which we have dug up, give the devil the child of *pani* Mikołaiowa's sister' (Lublin 1732).

Arguably, one may detect in this testimony, as in that of Fenna Dudzianka in Muszyna, the convergence and mixture of two traditions regarding witches' treatment of infants. The first holds that witches sacrifice infants to Satan for a variety of theological reasons: as innocents, they typologize the baby Jesus; as unbaptized souls, they are under Satan's power in any case; as the objects, in good Christian society, of the greatest love and care, their mistreatment by witches represents the ultimate inversion of Christian and indeed natural law. The second treats dead infants as the unnatural dead, therefore as a species of evil whose powers can be harnessed for malefice; this tradition also makes use of the physical remains of dead infants, as also of their coffins or soil from their graves, as particularly potent variants of the human remains, coffin splinters, and grave-soil used in malefice more generally (e.g. Kielce 1605; Lublin 1627; Bochnia 1679; Kleczew 1688; Lublin 1739).[52] However, Wojciech's unbaptized demon provides a clue that the stillborn children had quite another purpose: they were identical to, or the source of, the devil Ichnatek who was sent to murder the Pogorskis' lawyer. The convergence between the cosmopolitan and the local notions comes with the words that Katarzyna attributes to *pani* Alexandrowa Mytkowa: 'for this *poterczę* which we have dug up, give the devil the child of Pani Mikołaiowa's sister'. The statement incorporates western demonological notions of child-sacrifice with the Slavic notion of dead infants as demons: because one unbaptized baby has been dug up—and thus, as it were, removed from the devil's realm—another must be provided in its place. Child-sacrifice is not, here, the abominable devil-worship depicted in demonology; rather it is a more straightforward economic transaction. One child is given for another.

In the eighteenth century, Chmielowski noted that 'simple people call [shooting stars] *latawcy* or *diabły*, because in their simplicity, ignorant of the causes of things, they impute all extraordinary things either to GOD or to the devil'.[53] As so often, Chmielowski got things backward. It was the church, not the people, that insisted that whatever was not done naturally must be done by God or, with God's permission, by the Devil, there being no other allowable options. The 'simple people' had a considerably more complex cosmology. Their 'devils' *were* devils—that is what they called them, and we must take this labeling seriously. But they were many other things besides: helpers about the home, protectors of fortune, thieves of other people's grain or milk, errand-boys. Despite clear pre-Christian roots in the ancestor spirits of the Slavs, these were not 'pagan' spirits in any meaningful sense. They had been Christianized, if not always in the manner hoped for by the church—not just as devils, but as purgatorial spirits or as the wandering souls of unbaptized infants. Peasant attitudes toward these 'pre-Christian nature spirits' show not the 'shallowness' of Christianity that some historians have

---

[52] 17th-cent. Muscovite accused witches, according to their trial testimony, used earth or rocks removed from graves, and thereby invoked the power of the impious dead and unbaptized children. See Ivanits, *Russian Folk Belief,* 93–4.

[53] Chmielowski, *Nowe Ateny,* i. 163–4.

found in them, but the contrary: a profound internalization of the church's doctrine of limbo, and of the sacrament of baptism. Stanisław Kiszka's report of the words of the devil from Krzemień attests to the common people's understanding that baptism was the gateway to society, to personhood, and to salvation: *extra ecclesia non est salus.*

10

Demon Lovers

Widma, oczami wartowana tyłą,
Co rosę z kwiatów na śmietanę cyrka;
Jęcząca w górze nieochrzczona dusza;
Latawiec, gwiazda, co kobiet wysusza,
Litość i twrogę budzą na przemiany.

The witch, with eyes in back,
Who gathers dew from flowers to make cream;
The unbaptized soul, wailing in the sky;
Latawiec, the shooting star, who withers women
Incite terror and pity by turns.

(Severyn Goszczyński, *Zamek Kaniowski*
(1828), vv. 271–5)

In an important late essay on religious experience, Clifford Geertz asked what ought to be a central question of any humanistic scholarship that takes seriously both the autonomy of individual thought and the social construction of the self: 'Where does culture stop and the rest of the self begin?'[1] The question cannot be answered, but must be posed if we are to avoid two equally unsatisfactory frameworks: a simplistic model of individual autonomy or the collapse of the subject into a figment of discourse.

The problems raised by this question become acute in the interpretations of those subjectivities recorded under the extremely asymmetrical power-relations of the witch trial: a context in which powerful literate men imposed their definitions of witchcraft, religion, and criminality onto illiterate peasant-women. And yet, even in the extremity of this impossible situation, the accused witches sometimes found ways to express their own subjectivities, shaping their testimony as a mixture of stereotyped demonological tropes and deeply personal narrative. By their emphases, their silences, their willingness to confess to certain things and reluctance to confess to others, their additions and modifications, the accused witches translated demonological stereotypes into a local idiom. Despite all the dreary repetition of motifs in Polish witch trials (motifs that often can be found almost without modification right across Europe

---

[1] Clifford Geertz, *Available Light* (Princeton: PUP, 2001), 204.

and in the New World) Polish witches were not subsumed into demonological categories; they did not become mere figments of discourse but, taking on or accepting parts of that discourse, they amended it and made it their own.

In this chapter I trace the negotiation between the self and culture, and between cosmopolitan and indigenous cultures, in terms of a single motif: that of diabolical copulation. As elsewhere in Europe and its colonies, Polish witches were imagined to promise not only their souls, but their bodies as well, to the lustful attentions of devils. And, as has been shown to be true elsewhere in Europe and its colonies, individual accused witches could and did take this most intimate imposition of elite categories and build from it a narrative of their own lives.[2]

The confessions, and my argument, lead in two directions. First, toward a consideration of the manner by which many Polish witches managed to uphold a self-image of sexual propriety while simultaneously confessing to diabolical sex: it happened but they didn't enjoy it. Second and conversely, confessions to taking pleasure in demonic sex lead away from the issue of subjectivity toward *indigenization*: the process by which accused witches assimilated elite conceptions of devils and demons into local categories, and thereby transformed them. The 'devils' with whom some Polish witches admitted to having sexual relations, like the devil-servants discussed in the previous chapter, were not always devils in senses that could be accepted or even recognized by the theologically orthodox.

WILLING FLESH, WEAK SPIRITS

The Judeo-Christian tradition of demon lovers begins with the account, in Genesis, of the generation of giants before the flood: 'When people began to multiply on the face of the ground, and daughters were born to them, the sons of God saw that they were fair; and they took wives for themselves of all that they chose' (Gen. 6: 1–2, NRSV). The Septuagint translated Hebrew *bᵉnē hā ᵉlōhīm* not as 'sons' (υἱοί) of God but as 'angels' (ἀγγέλου) of God,[3] a usage followed by Jubilees 5.1 and Flavius Josephus' *Antiquities of the Jews* 1.3.1, which interprets the giants of Genesis 6: 4 as the offspring of angels 'accompanying with' human women. The pseudepigraphical Book of Enoch, an important source for early Christian accounts of the fallen angels, expands upon this narrative and influentially relates demon sex to the origins of witchcraft and magic: the angels, lusting after the daughters of men,

took unto themselves wives, and each chose for himself one, and they began to go in unto them and to defile themselves with them, and they taught them charms and enchantments, and the cutting of roots, and made them acquainted with plants. (Enoch 6.1–2, 7.1)[4]

---

[2] Concerning the construction of the self in European witch-trials, see esp. Sabean, *Power in the Blood*; Roper, *Oedipus and the Devil*.

[3] John Wevers, *Notes on the Greek Text of Genesis* (Atlanta, Ga.: Scholars Press, 1993), 75–6.

[4] I have relied on R. H. Charles's translations of Jubilees and Enoch, with his excellent notes (both London: Society for Promoting Christian Knowledge, 1917).

Augustine of Hippo, while denying that the 'sons of God' in Genesis 6 are fallen angels, left open the possibility of such intimate spirit–body interactions:

Nevertheless it is the Testimony of Scripture (which tells us nothing but the truth) that angels appeared to men in bodies of such a kind that they could not only be seen but also touched. Besides this, it is widely reported that *Silvani* and *Pans*, commonly called *incubi*, have often behaved improperly towards women, lusting after them and achieving intercourse with them. These reports are confirmed by many people, either from their own experience or from the accounts of the experience of others, whose reliability there is no occasion to doubt. Then there is the story that certain demons, whom the Gauls call *Dusii*, constantly and successfully attempt this indecency.[5]

Augustine thus introduced the theme of diabolical sex on the basis not of biblical exegesis or theological speculation, but of a sort of ethnographic interpretation of Roman (*silvani*), Greek (*panites*), and Celtic (*dusii*) nature spirits, incorporating all these into a general category of Christian devils: the *incubi*.

In the thirteenth century, Thomas Aquinas took up the problem of demon sex in an attempt to harmonize scriptural narratives of embodied angels with Aristotelian categories of spirit and matter.[6] For Aquinas, angels do not possess material bodies: they can, however, *assume* bodies of condensed air, 'not for themselves, but on our account'. They can even capture a man's 'seed' as a succubus, imparting it to a woman in incubus form, and thus generate monstrous children.[7] For medieval philosophers following Aquinas, the nature of demonic bodies and the possibility and mechanism of procreation with human beings became standard problems against which to prove one's skill at scholastic dialectic.[8] The *Malleus Maleficarum*, however, accomplishes a profound shift. Sex takes central stage as both the most hideous crime and the primary motivation of witches. 'Everything is governed by carnal lusting, which is insatiable in [women] . . . and for this reason they even cavort with demons to satisfy their lust.'[9] Previously the demons had lusted after women: now they merely take advantage of the insatiable lust of the women themselves. Institoris noted his own shift in emphasis; it is central to what he understood to be the *new* crime of witchcraft. 'Present day sorceresses', according to their own testimony, 'no longer subordinate themselves to this wretched form of slavery against their will, as has hitherto been the case, but do so of their own accord for their own physical pleasure (a most foul thing).'[10] Women did not submit to the erotic attentions of

---

[5] Augustine, *City of God* 15.23.

[6] Walter Stephens, *Demon Lovers, Witchcraft, Sex, and the Crisis of Belief* (Chicago: University of Chicago Press, 2002).

[7] Thomas Aquinas, *Basic Writings of Saint Thomas Aquinas*, ed. and tr. A. C. Pegis (New York: Random House, 1945), i. 493–4: 1.51.2–3.

[8] Stephens, *Demon Lovers*, 58–61; Clark, *Thinking with Demons*, 190.

[9] Institoris, *Malleus*, pt. 1, qu. 6, 170. Ząbkowic's tr. omits pt. 1 of the *Malleus*, thus lacks this passage.

[10] Ibid. pt. 2, qu. 1, ch. 4, pp. 307–8; Ząbkowic, *Młot*, pt. 1, ch. 4.

devils in order to gain the powers of malefice; rather, they perform acts of malefice because this is a condition, imposed by devils, for their continued erotic attentions. As Erik Midelfort has commented, the *Malleus* depicts witchcraft 'almost exclusively as a crime of female lust'.[11]

Although later works of demonology did not follow Institoris's controversial insistence on extreme female concupiscence, they did incorporate his categorization of diabolical sex as one of the four principal sins of witches, along with renunciation of the faith, the devil-pact, and the sacrifice of infants.[12] The general trend of elite demonology from the *Malleus* onward defined witchcraft as a type of treason against God rather than harm against one's neighbor, apostasy rather than malefice: and diabolical sex sealed the diabolical pact. As a bride consummated the marriage contract by submitting sexually to her new husband, so a witch consummated her pact with the devil by submitting sexually to him.

This sexual aspect of witchcraft proved widely influential: in Poland, as we have already had cause to mention, Chmielowski considered the three principal sins of witches to be apostasy, desecration of the host, and 'Sodomia'—by which he must mean diabolical sex.[13] In his introduction to the *Hammer*, Ząbkowic makes diabolical sex the last and worst of witches' crimes: 'they openly take up alliance with *szatany* and shamelessly associate with them, feast, and (what is ugly even to mention), take part in carnal intercourse with them'.[14] Even the author of the *Witch Denounced*, who thought most women accused of witchcraft were either innocent or were mere *zabobonnice* (superstition-workers) and not true *czarownice* or witches, admitted the existence of true witches and described their crimes in terms closely reminiscent of the *Malleus*: in addition to heresy, apostasy, blasphemy, and sacrilege, witches 'indulge in gross indecency with devils'.[15] According to theological consensus, witches could not perform the malefice they stood accused of without demonic assistance. Sex is a corollary, binding the witch to the demon in marriage and generating reciprocity. Worked out most thoroughly in Del Rio's *Disquisitiones*,[16] the relationship of magic, demonic pact, and demon sex commanded the consensus of elite thinking about the mechanics of witchcraft: Chmielowski puts the matter delicately when he says that a familiar spirit can only be summoned by 'promising him some indecent thing'.[17]

What is the relationship between this widespread elite stereotype of diabolical sex and the confessions of actual accused witches in trials? This question requires refinement into two correlative questions. First, does the literary discourse have

[11] Midelfort, 'Heartland', 115.
[12] Institoris, *Malleus*, pt. 1, qu. 2, 120.
[13] Chmielowski, *Nowe Ateny*, iii. 245; probably after Del Rio, *Disquisitiones*, bk. 2, qu. 15.
[14] Ząbkowic, *Młot*, fo. 5.
[15] *Czarownica powołana*, 26.
[16] Del Rio, *Disquisitiones*, bk. 2; Clark, *Thinking with Demons*, 466–71.
[17] Chmielowski, *Nowe Ateny*, iii. 238.

any echo in the oral traditions, the folklore, of the peasants and townspeople who constitute both the main accusers and, overwhelmingly, the accused, in witch-trials? Did 'the people' believe in human intercourse with devils? Second, what is the causal relationship between elite discourse and the confessions of accused witches? Did the accused, under the ministrations of the torturer and via leading questions, participate in the construction of a stereotype that was foreign and repugnant to them? Or, on the contrary, did the accused share some version of the stereotype, so that torture forced them to take on an identity they recognized as applicable to others, if not to themselves? Where does demonology stop and the rest of the self begin?

Recent scholarship on witchcraft has tended to reject the approach of nineteenth-century romantic historiography, which took seriously the demonological account of wild demonic sex while naturalizing it, preserving the structure while reversing the signs. For Jules Michelet 'the sorceress' was a beautiful, openly sexual young woman, punished for daring to transgress the prudish limits of an anti-sexual church; some modern Pagans persist in treating the accused witch as sexual rebel.[18] All recent historians assume that demon sex is fantastic, but a minority, such as G. R. Quaife and Lyndal Roper, suggest that the fantasy could originate with accused witches themselves. For Quaife, fantasies of ravishment by an overpowering devil may have grown out of peasant-women's unsatisfactory sex-lives; Roper, more subtly, finds echoes of female sexual anxieties played out in the narratives of demon sex.[19]

In sharp contrast, most contemporary scholarship treats the construction of the 'woman wailing for her demon lover', the sex-crazed witch, as a fantasy imposed on the accused witch, who is forced to embody an imaginary inversion, a dark mirror-image, of the newly emerging ideal of the chaste, subservient wife.[20] Sigrid Brauner takes Quaife to task for a historiographical version of blaming the victim: he repeats the demonological pattern by taking male fantasies of sexual assault and projecting them onto the accused witches.[21] Walter Stephens, the most recent exponent of this school, sums up its main points eloquently: 'The idea that witches copulated with demons was characteristic of scholarly fantasies about witchcraft, while it was foreign to the oral imagination of the illiterate village and countryside.'[22] Demonological accounts of demon sex 'represented the forcible imposition of literate ideas about spirituality and

---

[18] Glenn William Shuck, 'The Myth of the Burning Times and the Politics of Resistance in Contemporary American Wicca', *Journal of Religion and Society*, 2 (2000) Kristen J. Sollée, *Witches, Sluts, Feminists: Conjuring the Sex Positive* (Berkeley: ThreeL Media, 2017).

[19] G. R. Quaife, *Godly Zeal and Furious Rage* (New York: St. Martin's Press, 1987), 101–5; Roper, *Oedipus and the Devil.*

[20] Brauner, *Fearless Wives*, 20–4; Muchembled, 'Satanic Myths'; Jackson, 'Witches, Wives, and Mothers'.

[21] Brauner, *Fearless Wives*, 21.

[22] Walter Stephens, 'Incredible Sex: Witches, Demons, and Giants in the Early Modern Imagination', in K. Jewell (ed.), *Monsters in the Italian Literary Imagination* (Detroit: Wayne State University Press, 2001), 154.

corporeality over a popular culture' in which such distinctions were not important. Although opponents of witch-trials such as Johann Weyer dismissed
accounts of sex with demons as old wives' tales or the heated imaginations of
irrational, unlettered womenfolk, most modern scholars locate the heated imagination and the irrationality in the elite, literate writers on witchcraft. Stephens
states categorically that such sexual 'narratives were never told independently of
physical and psychological torture, and that they were constructed dialogically
through defendants' responses to standardized leading questions'.[23] Under torture, women accused as witches had to conform their identities to male fantasies
of demonic ravishment.

This view allocates the blame where it belongs: it also has the unintended
consequence that, in researching and studying that most female of early modern
crimes, we end up talking mostly about men. We are told that, since statements
about sex with the devil were coerced, they had nothing to do with the woman's
own belief structure and everything to do with the beliefs and fantasies of the
torturer and judges. Women, we are told, have nothing to say—at least nothing
recoverable, nothing that comes from themselves; they also, apparently, have no
erotic fantasy life of their own. To talk about sex with devils, then, is to talk about
demonology as an early modern literary male discourse; women, once again, are
silenced. A praiseworthy refusal to participate in the violence of representation
becomes a refusal to talk about accused women or their experience at all. To treat
confessions of diabolical sex as *only* the 'production, in the mouths of the
persecuted, of the fantasies gradually elaborated by their persecutors' is, as
Roper notes, to ignore the real concerns and subjectivities of the women
confessing.[24] And yet, as I argued in Chapters 7 and 8 in relation to host-
desecration, accused witches made use of elite discourse to think about themselves, and could bend such discourse to their own self-expression.

WITCHES, WHORES, AND THE DEVIL'S COLD NATURE

With these concerns in mind, let us turn to an examination of demon sex in the
Polish witch-trials. Sexual relations with devils could be volunteered, as in the
teen girl Marjanna's extraordinary narrative of a demonic stalker (Kleczew 1688,
discussed in Chapter 7), or Zofia Baranowa's spectral lover Paweł: a mix of her
dead husband's ghost and a demon (Lublin 1643). Most often, however,
accounts of such relations emerged gradually during interrogation under torture.
Assumed rather than dwelt upon, diabolical sex rarely emerges as a central
concern in the Polish witch-trials; nevertheless it comprises an element in a

---

[23] Stephens, 'Incredible Sex', 156.   [24] Roper, *Oedipus and the Devil*, 230.

large number of trials, as a stereotypical component of either the pact or Bald Mountain.

Diabolical sex was often only hinted at as an element of pact narratives. Jadwiga Gedkówna, young and unmarried, encountered the devil in a manner that recalls a folktale. Caught by a thunderstorm while out in the fields, she fell to the ground in terror. Too frightened even to recite the Our Father, she instead gave her soul over to the devil, who immediately appeared in the form of a 'youth' who embraced her, but his hands were cold (Wyszogród 1690). Others were slightly more explicit, such as Zofia Kowalka, who had 'her own Jasiek, I had a wedding with him, four years ago. Old Dyska gave me that Jasiek, she said to me: "you'll have things good, just marry him." He visits me and has lain with me, but he's cold as ice' (Wielki Koźmin 1690). Katarzyna Mrowczyna's devil took the form of a 'black peasant'. She had christened herself to service with this devil, had renounced God and the Virgin Mary, and 'once that spirit Marcin lay next to her and had relations with her like a husband with his wife, but his member was cold' (Słajszewo 1695; cf. Łobżenica 1692; Pyzdry 1719, 1731; Nieszawa 1721a).

In these accounts, sex plays a marginal role. The devil, most often named Jaś or Marcin, appears at a time of crisis in the forests or in the fields, or is given to the witch in an object of some kind. There is a strong folktale quality to some of these narratives; the manner in which the demon appears at a moment of crisis or despair, promising safety and riches, exactly parallels the foolish devils of legend.[25] Sex consummates the pact, which is understood in terms of a wedding contract, but it is not enjoyable because the devil is icy to the touch. There is none of the lasciviousness of some demonology: sex is referred to euphemistically, as a mere 'embrace', or 'relations' or, peculiarly, 'bald mountain'. As Briggs has said, 'sexual possession of witches by the Devil at the moment of apostasy was almost exclusively an expression of power, involving pain rather than pleasure'.[26]

It is in the context of the Bald Mountain motif that we expect, and find, the most frequent descriptions of diabolical sex, and the clearest indication of its elite provenance. Regina Stokarka was originally accused of malefice against goats, cattle, and human beings. But Regina's confession, given after what the Kleczew court records as 'two or three hours' of torture, refers to none of this malefice but instead to attendance at Bald Mountain, apostasy, and diabolical sex:

At bald mountain we eat, we drink tasty things, we dance, we bring beer in a sack from the tavern. A devil lays with me, like a husband. . . . Matuszka told me to renounce the Blessed Virgin, she said to me don't mention the Lord God and the Blessed Virgin, you'll have a different Lord and he showed up so quickly, he drank with us and danced. I slept with him just like with a husband, when midnight came he embraced me and went away, when

---

[25] Cf., on this point, Gentilcore, *From Bishop to Witch*, 248–53.
[26] Briggs, *Witches and Neighbours*, 385.

Table 10.1. Witch-trials featuring sexual relations with a demon or devil

Trial	Region	Trial	Region
Nieszawa 1550	Royal Prussia	Wągrowiec 1695b	Wielkopolska
Kalisz 1613	Wielkopolska	Fordon 1698	Wielkopolska
Braniewo 1637	Royal Prussia	Kleczew 1698	Wielkopolska
Braniewo 1642	Royal Prussia	Nowe 1698	Royal Prussia
Lublin 1643	Małopolska	Wyszogród 1698	Mazowsze
Poznań 1645	Wielkopolska	Żywiec 1698	Małopolska
Kleczew 1646a	Wielkopolska	Płońsk 1699a	Mazowsze
Kleczew 1646b	Wielkopolska	Pyzdry 1699	Wielkopolska
Kleczew 1646c	Wielkopolska	Skarszewy 1699c	Royal Prussia
Kleczew 1646d	Wielkopolska	Nowe 1701b	Royal Prussia
Kowalewo 1647	Royal Prussia	Nowe 1701e	Royal Prussia
Opalenica 1652	Wielkopolska	Nowe 1701f	Royal Prussia
Zbąszyń 1654a	Wielkopolska	Nowe 1704b	Royal Prussia
Praszka 1665	Wielkopolska	Wyszogród 1705	Mazowsze
Poznań 1666	Wielkopolska	Nowe 1706	Royal Prussia
Kleczew 1668	Wielkopolska	Grodzisk Wielkopolski 1707a	Wielkopolska
Poznań 1669	Wielkopolska	Wągrowiec 1708	Wielkopolska
Braniewo 1670	Royal Prussia	Fordon 1709	Wielkopolska
Kleczew 1670a	Wielkopolska	Nowe 1709b	Royal Prussia
Klimkówka 1677b	Małopolska	Nowe 1712a	Royal Prussia
Kowalewo 1678b	Royal Prussia	Nowe 1718	Royal Prussia
Bochnia 1679	Małopolska	Wyszogród 1718a	Mazowsze
Łobżenica 1686	Wielkopolska	Nowe 1719a	Royal Prussia
Kleczew 1688	Wielkopolska	Nowe 1719b	Royal Prussia
Nowy Wiśnicz 1688b	Małopolska	Pyzdry 1719	Wielkopolska
Gniezno 1689a	Wielkopolska	Raciąż 1719	Mazowsze
Kleczew 1689b	Wielkopolska	Wągrowiec 1719b	Wielkopolska
Nowe 1689	Royal Prussia	Nieszawa 1721a	Wielkopolska
Kleczew 1690a	Wielkopolska	Nieszawa 1721b	Wielkopolska
Kleczew 1690b	Wielkopolska	Wągrowiec 1725	Wielkopolska
Nowe 1690	Royal Prussia	Czerniewo 1727	Royal Prussia
Nowy Koźmin 1690	Wielkopolska	Kleczew 1730	Wielkopolska
Wielki Koźmin 1690	Wielkopolska	Pyzdry 1731	Wielkopolska
Wyszogród 1690	Mazowsze	Pyzdry 1732	Wielkopolska
Kleczew 1691b	Wielkopolska	Żerków 1732	Wielkopolska
Łobżenica 1692	Wielkopolska	Kleczew 1734	Wielkopolska
Wielki Koźmin 1692	Wielkopolska	Wągrowiec 1735	Wielkopolska
Kleczew 1693	Wielkopolska	Nowe 1747	Royal Prussia
Kleczew 1695	Wielkopolska	Kiszkowo 1761	Wielkopolska
Słajszewo 1695	Royal Prussia		

I confessed [in church] he beat me, but he never wounded me, I prayed to him prettily 'My blessed Jasienieczek'[27] and he disappeared and didn't beat me. (Kleczew 1690a)

This is about as explicit as *sabbat* narratives get in Polish trials. Instead of the indiscriminate orgy, the wild libidinous outpouring of chaotic transgression envisioned in demonology and visually depicted with such aesthetic verve by the Polish Jan Ziarnko,[28] one finds a modest feast, dancing, and 'weddings' with the attendant demons. Anna Szymkowa married and subsequently 'had business with' her devil Bartek at Bald Mountain (Nieszawa 1721a); Barbara Kaczmarka attended a 'meeting' at a fellow witch's cottage, where she married her *pokuśnik* Jan. He was a 'poor dog' dressed in black, with horse hooves, and Barbara slept between him and her human husband in their marital bed (Pyzdry 1732). Anna Ratajka wedded her *szatan* 'against her will', and denounced a neighbor for having a 'sweetheart' who 'dresses in Red' (Pyzdry 1699). Most accused witches offered the barest confession of diabolical sex, referring briefly to their devil 'husbands' (Bochnia 1679; Kleczew 1691b, 1730; Wyszogród 1698). Often we find not even a euphemistic mention of sex—as 'business' or 'association'—nor even of marriage; where they could, witches confessed only to receiving a 'sweetheart' or 'beau' or 'bridegroom' to dance with at the feast (Kalisz 1613; Praszka 1665; Nowy Wiśnicz 1688b; Kleczew 1690a; Raciąz 1719).

These fragmentary accounts reveal several things about the imagination of demon sex. First, although accused witches confessed to intercourse with demons, their partners in this endeavor were decidedly folkloric, and only ambivalently diabolical. Referred to as a *diabeł* or *czart* or *pokuśnik* but also as a 'poor dog' or simply as a 'sweetheart', and with common peasant names such as Marcin (Gniezno 1689a; Słajszewo 1695; Nowe 1706), Kasparek (Kalisz 1613; Braniewo 1643, 1684; Nowe 1689), or Jaś (Kleczew 1690a, 1728; Wągrowiec 1695b; Nowy Koźmin 1690; Wielki Koźmin 1690: Jaś is also the stereotypical name for the young peasant hero of folk love songs);[29] they are dressed as peasants or noblemen or army officers, or as Germans, 'all in red'—the color of gnomes and sprites.

Second, the accounts are extremely reticent, and focus less on sex than on marriage. In demonology, the pact was often understood as an anti-baptism or as an oath of fealty; but in Polish trials it is almost always interpreted in conjugal terms. The witch gives herself to her diabolical 'bridegroom' precisely as a women gives herself, body and soul, to her terrestrial husband: after which it is entirely natural that she should say, with Regina Stokarka, that she 'slept with

---

[27] *Jasienieczek* is a diminutive of *Jaś*, itself a diminutive of *Jan*.

[28] Ziarnko (*c.*1575–*c.*1630), a burgher of Lwów, spent his artistic career in Paris, where he etched the famous frontispiece to Pierre de Lancre's *Tableau de l'inconstance des mauvais anges* (1613).

[29] See Jan Stanisław Bystroń, *Polska pieśń ludowa* (Chicago: Rada Polonii Amerykańskiej, 1945), examples at 28–33, 40–5, 50–2, 55–6, 71–2. According to Wiślicz, of the forty-eight 'devils' described in the Kleczew trials between 1682 and 1700, thirty-one were named Jan, Janek, or Jaś; these were also the most common devil names in the trials at Nowe (Wiślicz, 'Township of Kleczew'; Wijaczka, 'Witch and Sorcerer-Hunts').

him as with my husband' (Kleczew 1690a). Sex is the consummation of the pact
with the devil, just as sex with one's husband consummates and makes irrevoca-
ble an ordinary marriage.[30] When Polish accused witches found themselves
forced to confess to sex with devils, they did so in a way that maintained their
self-image as decorous and upstanding women, confining sexual relation to the
marital bed.

Third—and this is the aspect of confession I want to elaborate—the very
reticence of Polish witches on the subject, their refusal to go into detail even
where it might have hastened the end of torture, may in itself be understood as an
act of resistance and as an attempt to maintain a prized aspect of their self-
identity. Lyndal Roper has noted the relative willingness of accused witches to
confess to—identify with or recognize in themselves—the most extreme forms of
malefice: envy and its destructive potential were things they could understand
and accept as part of themselves. Roper contrasts this to the tendency in these
same confessions to deny sex with devils, to minimize the number of times they
had engaged in sexual intercourse, or to reduce this number at the free confession
after torture.[31] Roper's insight is comparable to the Polish cases: women who
confessed to desecrating the host, bringing storms or droughts to their village,
and killing their neighbors' cattle and children, said as little about diabolical sex
as was strictly necessary. In a context of almost total constraint, an accused witch
could nevertheless 'determine how she will play out the role which circumstance
has thrust upon her. She dies deciding her own identity, sealing her own fate.'[32]

Dorota of Siedlików, for example, admitted before torture to a number of
cunning practices, malefice with buried bones, and the possession of a *szatan*
named Kasparek who helped her find lost objects; under torture she confessed to
sex with this *szatan*, but then attempted to revise the story. Kasparek tried to lay
with her and 'strangle' her, but she recognized him by his cold hands and made
the sign of the cross, whereupon he flew out the window (Kalisz 1613). Other
accused witches, again and again, emphasized that their diabolical trysts were
violent, unwelcome, and unpleasant. Like Dorota, they focused on the icy
coldness of their demon lovers: cold hands (Wyszogród 1690), cold body (Wielki
Koźmiń 1690); and especially his 'cold one' or 'cold member' (Łobżenica 1692;
Słajszewo 1695; Skarszewy 1699). Despite the contention of the *Malleus*—that
demons can satiate the lusts of human women by creating a body 'appropriate in
qualities like heat'[33]—Polish accused witches emphasized their devils' icy nature,
and thereby the extreme unpleasantness of their sexual relations.

---

[30] On the pact as a marriage and sex as its consummation, see Martin, 'Devil and the Domestic',
79–83; Roper, *Witchcraze*, 94.

[31] Roper, *Oedipus and the Devil*, 204, 16, 21 n. 18. 'Even when conviction was a certainty, these
accused witches still tried to minimize the extent of their sexual involvement with the devil' (*Oedipus
and the Devil*, 216).

[32] Jackson, 'Witch as a Category', 326.

[33] Institoris, *Malleus*, pt. 2, qu. 1, ch. 4, 314.

In maintaining such a distinction, Polish accused witches made use of a widespread demonological trope. The claim that the devil's penis and semen are cold and give pain was a commonplace of the literature from which the *Malleus* conspicuously dissented.[34] Chmielowski, for example, claimed that the bodies with which devils seduce women 'are cold, because GOD does not allow the devil to warm them'.[35] It is not possible to reconstruct how a village woman of Mazowsze or Wielkopolska came to learn these elite conceptions of the devil's sexual organs: here as so often one is tempted to attribute such knowledge to the unknowable leading questions of her examiners. What is clear, however, is that she appropriated the motif and used it to her own ends. In doing so, accused witches held on to their honor as women and (as many of them were) as wives. As erring humans, they seem to be saying, they had fallen to temptation in committing maleficent crimes of wrath, envy, and greed, but they had maintained control over their lust: they would confess to being witches, but not whores.

It is relevant, here, to recall that the two most common and most severe insults against a woman in early modern Poland were *kurwa* and *czarownica*: whore and witch—and that these were often combined. Polish civil court records are peppered with such insults. Although witnesses often showed the circumspection characteristic of early modern Polish court testimony ('I don't know if they called each other Witches, I don't know if [she] called Nowinska a whore'[36]), women in the streets were less guarded in their language. An exchange between two commoner women of the Lublin suburbs may be taken as typical: when Olexina yelled 'whore, Witch, you went to old village women for Enchantments', Janowa responded 'you're the Same. . . . you're a younger whore than I am'.[37] Townswomen yelled in the street 'here goes the whore, the witch, the fat cow';[38] 'Whore, thief, witch';[39] 'You whore, witch, hag!'[40] Such public assaults on honor had to be defended: by violence or by the protestations before the court that have caused these insults to be recorded. They rarely resulted in witch-trials, though the trial of Elżbieta Stepkowicowa for witchcraft began as a defamation suit against her neighbor who had, as Elżbieta complained, 'bewhored me and called me a witch' (Nowy Sącz 1670).

To call a woman a whore did not, usually, amount to accusing her of actual acts of prostitution, but neither was it an empty insult. To call a woman a whore

[34] Pierre de Lancre, *Tableau de l'Inconstance des mauvais anges et demons* (Paris, 1613), cited after Quaife, *Godly Zeal*, 98–9; Nicolas Rémy, *Demonolatry*, tr. E. A. Ashwin (London: J. Rodker, 1930 [1595]), bk. 1, ch. 6; Del Rio, *Disquisitiones*, bk. 2, qu. 15. On this motif, see also Roper, *Witchcraze*, 94–8.

[35] Chmielowski, *Nowe Ateny*, iii. 213.

[36] APLublin, AMLublin sig. 61 fos. 119–20 (1713).

[37] APLublin, AMLublin sig. 210 fo. 144ᵛ (*c*.1637).

[38] Wijaczka, 'Witch and Sorcerer-Hunts', 103.

[39] Pilaszek, *Procesy*, 328.

[40] APLublin, AMLublin sig. 226 fo. 477ᵛ. For other examples, from Lublin, Nieszawa, and Kraków, ibid. 354, 71, and APLublin, AMLublin sig. 50 fo. 227; sig. 107 fo. 445.

was to assert that she acted like a whore, or rather, that she acted as whores were understood or imagined to act. The insult implies that she sleeps around, or that she flaunts her assets in an immodest manner, or it ascribes to her other, ancillary traits of the imagined whore: lewdness, drunkenness, vulgarity, slovenly house-keeping, and so on. The same can be said of the insult 'witch'. It need not (and usually did not) constitute a concrete accusation of malefice, but rather drew on the image of the imagined witch to suggest that the woman so insulted was quarrelsome, envious, spiteful, sharp-tongued. While the one insult implies an excess of sociality, an indiscriminate mixing of self with others in a manner that undermines personal honor, the other implies anti-social behavior but concedes that the target of the insult has a certain power—as when Wojciech Koziełek commented of Regina Lewczykowa, with a mixture of admiration and fear, that 'the devil himself is afraid of her' (Lublin 1698). The frequent combination of the two insults might best be interpreted not as equivalence but as complementarity: to call a woman a whore *and* a witch was to impute to her *both* of these constellations of negative traits; to attack her character from two directions—it is comparable to the contemporary insults 'bitch' and 'slut' which, when combined, describe their target as both anti-social and overly social, both 'pushy' and 'easy'.

Thus, when Polish accused witches, under torture, confessed relatively quickly to the crimes of witchcraft, but made every attempt to deny the accusation of diabolical sex or, if that failed, to make clear that it was unwilling, undesired, and painful, they were staking their claim to a partial share of the honor they had lost through the process of the trial. At the point in the proceedings when such confessions were made, there was usually no possibility at all that the accused would escape death at the stake; they could still, however, avoid declaring themselves to be whores. The resolute refusal to declare one's own guilt in the face of unimaginable pain, or, where this proved impossible, to modify that guilt in certain directions through selected emphasis of particular demonological tropes, may be best read not as an attempt to save one's own life but rather to save the meaning of that life; to preserve one's subjectivity and to ensure that one will be remembered aright.[41] If the trope of demon-sex was indeed, as Stephens argues, usually a forced imposition on accused witches, this does not mean that they were powerless to resist or to modify, to deflect, the implications of this imposition. They gave themselves sexually to devils, but they did so unwillingly; they refused to be subsumed into the discourse of overwhelming female lust. They could be spiteful, violent, and maleficent, but (tied to the strappado, hung in the air, helpless) they never lost control.

---

[41] Cf. Diane Purkiss, *The Witch in History* (New York: Routledge, 1996), 145. Refusal of the demonological narrative may be understood as what Erving Goffman called a 'character contest': even under torture, some witches found that they could 'act so as to determine the traits that will thereafter be theirs; they create and establish what is to be imputed to them': Erving Goffman, *Interaction Ritual* (Garden City, NY: Anchor Books, 1967), 238.

A WARM NATURE

There were exceptions. Proving the rule, and reflecting the different coin in which male honor was measured, the rare male witch confessed more readily of his frolics with demonesses. Grzegorz Klecha married a 'sweetheart' at Bald Mountain named Jaśkowa (a feminization of the traditional Jaś). 'She was young and dressed in red, with a crown, because in that place they mostly dress in red, and wear crowns' (Nowy Koźmin 1690). Jan Figulus, an alleged musician at Bald Mountain, seems almost to brag about his young she-devil in her pretty cotton frock. It was 'a greater pleasure to have her than to have other women, but she was cold' (Łobżenica 1690b). Nor did women always refuse to express sexual yearning. The herb-seller, alcoholic, and (it is implied) prostitute Zofia Baranowa expressed longing for her dead husband through demonic fantasy. Without torture, she described her 'Paweł' as cold like a corpse and smelly: nevertheless, she had lain down with him often, unforced. Despite his horns and lack of nostrils, he resembled her dead husband Stanisław to such a degree that when he first appeared she cried 'but you died!' He responded: '"Tsk, don't worry, I am still alive to you", and he appeared to me in the shape of my husband, because I loved that husband of mine' (Lublin 1643).

Zofia's expression of love for her devil-ghost is exceptional, if not wholly unique.[42] But details of some other trials suggest that demonic sex was not always an elite imposition, not always forced or unpleasant, nor was sex with a devil always sex with the Devil. Katharzyna Kozimińska, for example, described her devil as 'wanting me to treat him as a husband'—but she also describes him as a small creature fed on milk who she 'hid up high, behind the stove' (Wyszogród 1705). Dorota of Siedlików, who resisted the demon-sex narrative, described her Kasparek as a *latawiec* who gave her a feather to make witch's ointment: he also demanded 'boiled millet groats with milk' in exchange for the prosperity he would bring to her (Kalisz 1613). Agnieszka Jakóbka's devil, 'a simple, poor peasant' who nevertheless 'dressed in red', had sex with her repeatedly. Exceptionally, she confessed that 'I loved that devil and he loved me as well. I took great pleasure in him, for his nature was warm.' He also demanded 'milk to drink' (Nieszawa 1721b).

All three accused witches describe a reciprocal relation with their devils. The devil provides (or at least promises) wealth or butter or grain or 'good things', while the witch provides her soul, symbolized by sexual submission. So far this is entirely standard. But in these confessions, the witch also provides her devil with food. And this is food of a specific kind: milk, or in

---

[42] Compare a similar confession from a century later. Elżbieta Pasturka's devil came to her 'in my imagination, as I wanted a friend'. Asked why she accepted the devil, she answered 'only for bodily pleasure, as she could not get a lover' (Nowe 1747). Further on this theme see Michael Ostling, "Speaking of Love in the Polish Witch Trials," in L. Kounine and M. Ostling (eds.), *Emotions in the History of Witchcraft* (London: Palgrave), 155–171.

the case of Dorota, milk cooked up with millet groats. Katharzyna adds the detail that she hid her devil 'up high, behind the stove'.

Milk and groats, as we saw in Chapter 9, are the food given to house-demons and treasure-haulers in return for their legitimate maintenance (or illegitimate increase) of a farmstead's productivity.[43] They typically live behind the stove (like Katharzyna's Stanisiek),[44] and they are often called *latawcy* (like Dorota's Kasparek). They appear as a small hairy man, as a cat, or snake, or, especially under the title of *latawiec*, 'the flying one', as a bird—note that Kasparek gave Dorota a feather with which to make her witch's ointment.[45] It was concerning such beings, ambivalently house-spirits and treasure-haulers, that Pietro Duodo, the Venetian envoy to the court of Zygmunt III in 1592, wrote that in Lithuania they set a bowl of milk out in the chamber to feed the 'demons who, in order to more easily seduce people to their false cult, enter into close intimacy with them: they serve people in the cultivation of the fields and in other domestic affairs'.[46]

In Chapter 9, we encountered *latawiec* as common name for the ghosts of unbaptized infants who, in bird form or as a shooting star, flee before the thunder-storm crying *chrztu, chrztu!*—'baptism, baptism!' But the same name, and sometimes the same ontological status as an unbaptized infant, attaches to treasure-hauler demons, who fly with sparking tails through the chimney with their stolen grain or money (Warta 1679a, 1679b; Mokrze 1723).[47] Indeed in Polish demonology, *latawiec* also translated Latin *incubus*, the demon lover of witches—a strange choice of terms, as the *incubus* is an icy cold spirit of the air, while the *latawiec* a fiery flying bird or serpent, with a warm nature.[48] When a Kleczew witch encountered a beautiful

---

[43] Compare the *skrzatek czart* or 'hobgoblin devil' fed on groats with milk and butter (Grodzisk 1710a), or the Nowe devils, who constantly promise prosperity but must instead themselves be fed with groats (e.g. Nowe 1689).

[44] In the *Infernal Parliament* the treasure-hauling *Latawiec* complains 'In my old age I'd rather live here [in hell], Than in a box behind the chimney, though they feed me groats.' Sowirzalius, *Sejm piekielny*, vv. 998–1000; compare Kolberg, *Dzieła wszystkie*, xvii. 202; Fischer, 'Diabeł', 205.

[45] Demon-helpers appeared not infrequently in birdlike form (Kalisz 1616; Lublin 1678; Łobżenica 1692; Fordon 1692). In later Polish folklore the *latawiec* and the *skrzatek*, both often understood as the ghosts of unbaptized infants, similarly appear in birdlike form: Kolberg, *Dzieła wszystkie*, xv. 25–7; Moszyński, *Kultura Ludowa*, ii/1. 735.

[46] Eugenio Albèri (ed.), *Le Relazioni degli Abasciatori Veneti al Senato durante il secolo decimosesto*, vi (Florence: self-published, 1862), 333.

[47] In the last of these cases, the accused had to flee her village after her house burnt down twice in succession—its thatch ignited, the neighbors claimed, by the fiery tail of her visiting *latawiec*. Cf. *Sejm piekielny*, vv. 970–1000, and for very similar motifs from eastern Germany and the Baltic, see now Dillinger, "The Dragon."

[48] The *Devil's Lawsuit* e.g. characterizes *latawiec* both as a minor house-demon, the special servant of witches, and as a spirit constantly frustrated in its desire to keep company with humans 'for the Lord God did not allow him to have a real body, only an illusory one, in which he can do nothing... many have told us that he spoils human marriages. But this no wise man believes. Only illusions are all those Jncubi and Succubi, for a ghost cannot conceive child.' *Postępek*, 20, 100–1; cf. Swizralus, *Peregrynacja*, 173–4, vv. 862–7. I review the history and consequences of translating *incubus* as *latawiec* in Ch. 11.

male *latalec* (Kleczew 1646b), was this an unbaptized ghost, a treasure-hauler, an *incubus,* or all three combined?[49] In witchcraft confessions, was an imagined local demon sexualized through assimilation to the lascivious Christian devil? Or did the elite *incubus* encounter a sexual motif already present in the folkloric treasure-hauler?

Allow me to approach this question obliquely, by way of comparative folklore. Nineteenth-century Russian folklore includes the winged 'fiery serpent' or *zmei* who, scattering sparks before himself, or appearing as a shooting star, flies to the homes of peasant women for sexual trysts.[50] The form of this being relates him closely to the Polish *latawiec,* his manifestation as a shooting star relates him to unbaptized ghosts, while his erotic encounters relate him to the *incubus.* In his monumental study of Russian magic, W. F. Ryan dismisses the sexual motif as a late import from the West.[51] While such an interpretation is not impossible, one is struck by the correlation of the erotic motif, the appearance as a flying fiery bird or snake, the function as a treasure-hauler or thief, and the ontological status as an unbaptized spirit in the folklore of a wide cultural area encompassing the Balts, Slavs, and peoples of the Balkans. Folk demons are extraordinarily fluid, with motifs and functions overflowing the categories into which both early modern demonology and contemporary folklore attempt to contain them.[52] Though it would therefore be futile to establish the essential identity of *latawiec* or any other imagined sprite or fairy, the complex of unbaptized child, shooting star, treasure bringer, and seducer of women appears commonly if in various combinations among the Polish *skrzat, latawiec,* and *koltek;* the Russian *leshii* and *zmei;* the South-Slavic *zmai;* the Slovakian *škràt,* Estonian *puuk, kratt,* and *pisuhänd;* the Lithuanian *kaukas;* the Latvian *pukis;* and the Romanian *zburător.*[53] Possibly elite *incubi* had infected the imaginations of the peasantry from the Baltic to the Balkans

---

[49] Cf. the *latoperz* ("flying feathered thing") that carried Petronella Bartkowa to Bald Mountain (Kleczew 1680b). At the other end of the social scale the young noble victim of love magic Magdalena Gładyszówna admitted to sexual trysts with a *latawiec* (Kraków 1644). In contrast, the Carmelite mystic Anna Maria Marchocka (1603–52) recalled how, as a young girl, she had the habit of rising very early and praying in a grove. Her mother became suspicious that she might 'have an assignation with a *latawiec*'. Here the same questions apply: what sort of being did Anna's mother worry about—clearly a sexual devil, but was this also an unbaptized ghost? Anna Maria Marchocka, *Żywot y wysokie cnoty W. Matki Teresy od Pana Jezusa Marchockiey,* ed. J. Augustynowicz (Lwów: Drukarnia J. K. Mci Societatis Jesu, 1752), 12, 26.

[50] Ivanits, *Russian Folk Belief,* 43, 156–7.

[51] W. F. Ryan, *The Bathhouse at Midnight* (University Park, Pa.: Pennsylvania State University Press, 1999), 135.

[52] S. I. Johnston, 'Defining the Dreadful: Remarks on the Greek Child-Killing Demon', in M. Meyer and P. Mirecki (eds.), *Ancient Magic and Ritual Power* (Leiden: E. J. Brill, 1995); cf. Dżwigoł, *Polskie ludowe słownictwo mitologiczne,* 13–24. on the wide and overlapping range of meanings of *latawiec, skrzat,* and their cognates.

[53] For Poland, see Kolberg, *Dzieła wszystkie,* xvii. 74; Kolbuszewski, 'Materyały do medycyny', 163; Leonard. J. Pełka, *Polska demonologia ludowa* (Warsaw: Iskry, 1987), 19–20, 49–50. For Russia, see Ivanits, *Russian Folk Belief,* 70, 81, 109, 75. For Estonia, Lithuania, and Latva, see Ülo Valk, *The Black Gentleman* (Helsinki: Soumalainen Tiedeakatemia, Academia Scientiarum Fennica, 2001), 194; Aleksander Brückner, *Starożytna Litwa,* ed. J. Jaskanis (Olsztyn: Pojezierze, 1979 [1904]), 56–7, 213; Kolberg, *Dzieła wszystkie,* xl. 67–8; and Dace Veinberga (pers. comm.). For Romania, see Golopentia, 'Romanian Love Charms', 180; Wilson, *Magical Universe,* 216. For the Slavic world as a whole, see Moszyński, *Kultura Ludowa,* ii/1. 463–5, 635, 53, 68. As Moszyński

by the nineteenth century, when most of the folklore concerning such beings was collected—and yet one wonders why, in such a case, the cold sexual demon of the literary tradition would so usually combine with the treasure-hauling fiery bird and unbaptized souls of East and East-Central Europe.

Moreover, we have a few unequivocal examples of their combination in the early modern period. Writing around 1600, the Belorussian petty-nobleman, Calvinist, and local official Teodor Jewłaszewski recalled encountering in his youth a being that he called a латавес (*latawiec*): a 'fiery person' who attacked him and who, according to a friend, often flew to visit the cottage of a local peasant-woman. For the rest of his life, Jewłaszewski suffered from nightmares and sleep-paralysis—a condition his doctors diagnosed as caused by the demon encountered in his youth, which the doctors called an инкубус (*incubus*).[54] Jewłaszewski's narrative corresponds closely with the Russian folktale of the flying serpent recorded three centuries later, but also with the sometimes sexual, sometimes unbaptized treasure-haulers of, for example, the Warta trials: and it directly chronicles the combination of elite *incubi* and popular *latawcy*.

Around the same time, but near the opposite border of Poland, the accused witch and procuress Anna Chociszewska confessed to having had a *latawiec*, with whom she 'eats and drinks', since she was 12 years old. She, rather than the court, introduced the term. When the court asked whether their relation was sexual, Anna displayed a remarkable understanding of the range of associations this entity could embody:

> I don't have any relations of the flesh with him, I don't lie with him, as many *latawcy* lie with women and throw them out of bed and beat them. *Also* she confessed, that when I still had my late husband, he [the *latawiec*] also came to her, but my husband didn't know about that, however I never lay with him, because the children that I have I conceived with my husband. (Poznań 1582a)

Most extraordinarily, Anna's confession explicitly relates the sexual *latawiec* with the theme of unbaptized babies. When, as a young girl, she told her mother of the *latawiec*'s visits, her mother immediately 'rode to Wągrowiec and had her aunt Hanna Janeczkowa exhumed, who had been buried pregnant, but it was too late, for she had already decayed'.[55]

In folklore gathered over the last century and a half, as in early modern sources, both textual and from the trials, *latawiec* combines an array of features and functions: he is a youth who ravishes women and 'dries' them with his fiery warmth; he is a fiery bird or fiery snake who flies through the air shedding sparks; he is a being

---

and Brückner both note, most of these beings share motifs with the Skandinavian and English *pugs* and *pucks* and *pooks*, and with the Germanic *skratts* and *kobolds*.

[54] Teodor Jewłaszewski, 'Uspaminy', in *Pomniki memuarnai literatury Belarusi XVII st.* (Minsk: Navuka i Tekhnika, 1983 [*c.*1604]), 34.

[55] On women buried pregnant as a source of demons or vampires throughout Europe, see also McNeill and Garner, *Medieval Handbooks*, 339–40; Wilson, *Magical Universe*, 214.

of uncertain provenance, sometimes a devil *sensu strictu*, but sometimes an unbaptized infant, haunting the place of its murder (Warta 1679a) or visiting its living cousin (Poznań 1582a). He is assimilated to benevolent house-demons, but more often to the more ambivalent treasure-bringing demons who increase one's prosperity only by reducing that of one's neighbors, just as a witch achieves her high milk-yields by stealing the milk of neighboring cattle.

Paweł Gilowski, a theologian from Małopolska who, over a long career, moved from Catholicism through Lutheran and Calvinist positions to Anti-Trinitarianism, inveighed against what he saw as mistaken conceptions of *latawcy*. In a passage of his reformed *Katechizm*, he attempted to defend their theological status as infernal devils devoted to seduction, against what he considered to be local superstitious accretions. Witches live with *latawcy* 'in obscenity', motivated not by sex but 'for their temporal advantage, which they gain from these demons, who stealing money or grain from others, bring it to them, to the damnation of their souls'.[56] However, following Augustine, Gilowski confirms that *latawcy* can 'heat the lusts of women', and correspond to the *incubi* and *succubi* of demonology. This creature

appears, among other deceits, as a youth, who recommends himself to some woman, especially one desirous of debauchery, and it befriends her and binds her, not without gifts, to enter into debauched relations with it, or also, in the person of a wonderful maiden, they also deceive men.

However, one must avoid falling into

great stupidity; for the things rumoured about them by the people, that *Latawcy* are supposed to come out of little children in their graves, where the child died in the womb along with its mother and was buried—this is an old wives' tale and slander of Satan, that his cunning should not become known.[57]

Gilowski complains of the 'stupidity of the people' for believing exactly what Anna Chociszewska believed and confessed to: that her demon companion was an unbaptized infant. But just as with Benedykt Chmielewski's similar complaint against the 'simplicity' of the people who equate shooting stars with unbaptized ghosts (see Chapter 9), it seems that Gilowski has things backward. It is only because he equates the *incubus* to the native *latawiec* that he sees local imaginations of its origination as ignorant or confused. *Latawiec* is both more and less than an *incubus*; when Gilowski and others translate the philosophical term with the folkloric one, they change the semantic content of both.

Throughout this chapter, my intention has been to capture something of the beliefs, imaginings, and experiences of accused witches. I have wanted to reject

---

[56] Paweł Gilowski, *Wykład Katechizmu Kościoła Krześćijańskiego, z Pism swiętych dla Wiary prawdźiwey utwierdzenia, a fałszywey się ustrzeżenia* (Kraków, 1579), ch. 5, art. 5, fos. 161ᵛ–162ᵛ.
[57] Ibid. Compare *Postępek*, 20.

the approach of many scholars which, through what might charitably be characterized as misguided scrupulosity, banishes accused witches themselves from the study of witch-trials, rendering them mere figments of elite discourse. But I have also wished to avoid the opposite approach, which makes of witch-confessions primarily a source for folklore and a basis for the recovery of popular, or even pre-Christian or archaic, religious forms. I have no interest in establishing what *latawiec* is in fact—a question absurd to ask and impossible to answer: as a creature of the imagination, he is whatever he is thought to be. Instead I have explored the construct of *latawiec* as a way of exploring, and opening up, the mixed and hybrid nature of early modern Polish devils. I have attempted to make plausible the contention that Polish accused witches, in confessing to sex with a devil, need not have imagined themselves to be confessing to sex with a diabolical, anti-Christian being. On the contrary, they may often have understood themselves (and in a handful of cases demonstrably did so understand themselves) to be confessing a relationship well established in the local worldview: a reciprocal relationship involving sex and the exchange of gifts—milk and butter for the devil, increased fortune and fertility for the witch. Accused witches such as Dorota of Siedlików, Katharzyna Kozimińska, and Agnieszka Jakóbka, and possibly others such as Zofia Baranowa, confessed to sex with what they usually called a devil, but this lexical identity obscures rather than reveals the substance of their imagined relationship. Although these confessions were extracted under torture, they did *not* accomplish the erasure of popular conceptions and its replacement with elite discourse. Polish accused witches confessed to sex with the devil, but the devil they admitted to having sex with was an indigenized one, a domesticated member of the peasant household. Any evaluation of the meaning of demon lovers in early modern Poland must take into account that the lover in question was not, usually, understood to be a principal of evil. Instead, he was something far more ambivalent: part nature spirit or fairy, part house-demon or baby ghost, part treasure-hauling fetish.

11

Translating the Devil

Szło dwóch w nocy z wielką trwogą
Aż pies czarny bieży drogą
Czy to pies?
Czy to bies?

Two walked by night in great dread
When they saw a dog on the road ahead
Is it a dog?
Or is it a devil?

(A. E. Odyniec and Juliusz Słowacki,
'Nie wiadomo co, czyli romantyczność',
from Odyniec's *Poezye* (1832), 90)

'The devil often makes of himself an *Incubus* or *succubus, alias* (as they call it here in Ruthenia) a *latawiec* or *latawica.*' This assertion, from Chmielowski's eighteenth-century encyclopedia, takes *latawiec* to be the local, vulgar version of the universal, Latin term *incubus*.[1] When someone 'here, in Ruthenia' says *latawiec*, they are denoting or referring to a specific, determinate entity by its local name. There is no important difference, Chmielowski assumes, between the vulgar expression and the educated Latin. Although the literal meanings and etymology of the two terms differ markedly from one another (*latawiec* from *latać*, 'to fly', so 'the flying thing'; *incubus* from *incubare*, 'to lie over, lie upon', hence 'he who lies upon women'), their reference is identical. They pick out and point to the same creature.

And yet such direct translation is impossible; it carries with it connotations not intended by the translators. Gilowski complained against the 'stupidity' of the people, who believe *latawcy* originate as the souls of unbaptized infants. Yet this stupidity of the people was an artifact of Gilowski's own attempt at translation: the people think *latawcy* are unbaptized souls, while Gilowski knows that

---

[1] Chmielowski, *Nowe Ateny*, iii. 208. Concerning the Christian antecedents of the Polish *latawiec*, see also Krzysztof Bracha, 'Latawiec, z katalogu imion rodzimych duchów i demonów w źródłach średniowiecznych', in W. Iwańczak and S. Kuczyński (eds.), *Ludzie-Kościół-Wierzenie* (Warsaw: Wydawnictwo DiG, 2001). Although Bracha's approach is rather different from my own, our conclusions are concordant.

incubi—which he translates into Polish as *latawcy*—are not. If there is a mistake, it lies with the learned scholar rather than with the people whose significations he finds deficient. Gilowski's interpretation of local beings in terms of biblical and patristic texts, through which the *latawiec* becomes equivalent to the *silvani* and *panites* discussed by Augustine and thence to the *incubi* developed in later theological speculation, renders the local description false and superstitious. However, to speak of Gilowski as mistaken and 'the people' as correct is to reify the 'folkloric' *latawiec* over against the learned *incubus*, and so again to miss the point. Both are constructs, neither has anything resembling the sort of objective referent by which one might say, with little worry about mistranslation, that a *malum* is a *jabłko* is an *apple*. Every translation is an interpretation and a compromise; each translation choice carries a host of unintended consequences. In this chapter, I explore the problems and effects of translation, taking *latawiec* as our primary example. In a wider sense, the problems besetting the translation of the devil in Poland point toward a central theme of this book: the contested interpretation of imagined beings and practices: devils, witches, witchcraft, magic, and Christianity.

The term *latawiec* or its close variations can be traced to the fifteenth century, appearing first as a marginal gloss on the Latin terms *incubus* and *succubus*. A collection of manuscript sermons from the Augustinian house in Kraków, dated 1477, associates the *lathalecz* with devils of carnal sin: 'Hec videns diabolus qui inimicus spiritualis humano generi est [in margin: lathalecz] qui specialius laborat in his peccatus sodomiticis . . . accubus, incubus, succubus, cacodemon, calodemon.'[2] A manuscript herbal of the same decade equates *latawecz* with the Greek *efialtes*, which may be understood either as a sexual *incubus* or as the personification and cause of nightmares.[3] Similarly, Stefan Falimirz's Renaissance herbal compendium extols the virtues of the diamond, which 'helps against Latawcy and other apparitions' and 'drives away vain dreams'.[4] In the Latin–Polish dictionary appended to his sixteenth-century commentary on Saxon law, Jan Cervus of Tuchola translates both *succubi* and *incubi* as *lathalci*.[5] Later in the same century, as we have seen, Gilowski and the author of the *Devil's Lawsuit* used *latawiec* to the same purpose. While the *Lawsuit* treated *latawiec* as a real demon with an illusory body, the Catholic priest and former natural magician Stanisław Poklatecki insisted on the reality of corporal contact with *latawcy* in refutation of Agrippa, Weyer, and Cardano who, to his mind, 'declare overhastily that all

---

[2] K. Czaykowski and J. Łoś, 'Zabytki augustiańskie', *Materyały i Prace Komisyi Językowej Akademii Umiejętności w Krakowie*, 2/3 (1907), 324. Still earlier, an anonymous Silesian manuscript of 1454 'Contra incubum alis latalecaem' [sic] describes methods for avoiding such a demon: Bracha, 'Latawiec', 251–2.

[3] Rostafiński, *Średniowieczna Historya*, ii. 510.

[4] Falimirz, *O ziolach*, fo. IV 46ᵛ; cf. Marcin Siennik, *Herbarz, to iest zioł tutecznych postronnych y zamorskich opisanie co za moc maią* . . . (Kraków: Mikołaj Szarffenberg, 1568), 324.

[5] Jan Cervus, *Farraginis actionum iuris ciuilis et prouincialis saxonici, municipulisque Maydeburgensis* (Kraków: Officina Ungleriana, 1540), 323ᵛ.

writings and tales of *latawcy* are inventions and fairy-tales'. On the contrary, Poklatecki insists, '*latawcy* are evil spirits from the lower levels of the satanic species, who, taking on themselves unreal bodies invented from air, in the character of a man or of a woman, associate uncleanly in carnality with human beings'.[6]

The Catholic Poklatecki, Reformed Gilowski, and the anonymous author of the *Devil's Lawsuit* might disagree with each other on certain points of demonology. However, they all fully integrate the term *latawiec* into the pan-European learned discourse concerning the reality of *incubi*, the possibility and manner of their interactions with humans, and the problem of the generation of human progeny from a demon father. They all fully identify the entity denoted by the term *latawiec* with the entity denoted by the terms *incubus* and *succubus* in the standard texts on the subject, such as Augustine and Aquinas. Similarly, as we have already seen, Ząbkowic used the term *latawiec* consistently to translate the very numerous references to *incubus* demons in the *Malleus*, an equivalence enshrined in the *Thesaurus Polono-Latino-Graecus* by the Jesuit lexicographer Grzegorz Knapiusz.[7] It would seem that we may treat *latawiec* simply as the Polish word for *incubus*.

But *latawiec* was something else in Poland before it came to be integrated into translations of or commentaries on learned Latin texts. The process by which *latawiec* came to translate *incubus* is permanently irrecoverable, but texts such as the anonymous Augustinian sermon, with its *lathalecz* scrawled in the margin next to *incubus,* imply that Polish writers cast about for a local entity whose features, to some extent, corresponded to the features attributed to the *incubus* in Latin discourse. Such correspondence, however, could never be total: the *incubus* itself was, after all, the product of millennia of demonological speculation, and its denotation was not stable even in learned Latin texts. Thus the translation involved a partial correspondence, and the entity chosen to take up the semantic burden of *incubus* carried with it a remainder of what it had been before. This 'remainder' did not disappear once the integration of the entity into learned discourse had been accomplished; on the contrary, meanings and connotations carried over from the folkloric substratum come to adulterate and infect the 'learned' definition, while conversely learned concerns and controversies come to color the 'folkloric' definition. Insofar as the Polish term came to be accepted as a translation of the Latin, both were permanently changed. It is rather as if, in English-language demonological discourse and trial literature, *incubus* had come to be regularly translated as *puck* or *brownie* or *hobgoblin*: the mischievous English spirit of the homestead would be diabolized, but would not the sexual demon take on a puckish coloration?

---

[6] Stanisław z Gór Poklatecki, *Pogrom: Czarnoksięskie błędy* (Kraków: Jakub Siebeneycher, 1595); quoted after Rosenblatt, *Czarownica powołana*, 25; see also Roman Bugaj, *Nauki tajemne w Polsce w dobie odrodzenia* (Wrocław: Zakład Narodowy im. Ossolińskich, 1976), 143–7.
[7] Cited after Berwiński, *Studia o gusłach*, i. 194.

Some inkling of the complexities involved in the trajectory by which *incubus* became *latawiec* may be gleaned from a close reading of early modern Polish writers who, instead of relating to scholastic or post-scholastic demonology, use *latawiec* to render biblical terms. Marcin Bielski's humanist *Chronicle or History of the World* uses the term *latawiec* to describe the 'sons of God' who engendered the giants in Genesis 6: 4—the starting point ever since Augustine for discussions of demonic sexuality: 'From Cain's nation also came great people, Giants strong and valiant, ... who worked harm in the world (Josephus writes that they were conceived from *Latawcy*).'[8] In his exegesis of the book of Revelation, the Protestant Mikołaj Rej commented on the fall of Babylon in Revelation 18. After the ruination of Babylon, it becomes:

'A haunt of every foul spirit, a haunt of every foul bird.' Here little explanation is needed, since we see and hear of such things, that those little devils that we call *latawcy* (which lead folk here [in Poland], knowing little of God, astray from their faith, tricking them by their deceptions and cunning) commonly like to visit and inhabit such ruins and abandoned places. Here also bats, owls, screech-owls and other foul birds of the night and of darkness commonly take shelter.[9]

Bielski refers to the first book of the Christian Bible, Rej to the last. But the two texts are intimately connected in traditional exegesis via the Book of Isaiah and its vivid description of the ruination of Babylon and Edom (Isa. 13: 19–22, 34: 11–15). Rej alludes to these passages of Isaiah, when he expands the 'foul spirits' and 'foul birds' of Revelation (*spiritus immundi* and *volucres immundae* in the Vulgate) to include owls, bats, screech-owls, and *latawcy*.[10] For it is in Isaiah that one meets the ostriches and jackals, the hawk and the hedgehog, the vultures and screech-owls, and the goat-demons who inhabit the ruins of Babylon and Edom. Institoris, following Augustine via the *Etymologies*, draws these strands together, connecting the Hebrew goat-demons, the Greek *panites*, and the *incubi* of speculative demonology:

'Ostriches,' says Isaiah, 'will live there, and shaggy people will dance there' (understand 'demons' in the place of 'shaggy people'). Hence, the gloss says, '"Shaggy ones" are hairy forest people, who are *incubones* or satyrs, certain varieties of demons.' ... To the same effect St Isidore ([*Etymologies*] Bk. 8 last chapter) says 'Shaggy ones, who are called *Panites* in Greek and *incubi* in Latin.' Hence, they are also called *incubi*, from the verb *incubare*, that is, to commit sexual misconduct.[11]

---

[8] Marcin Bielski, *Kronika tho iesth Historya Swiata na sześć wiekow, a cztery Monarchie, rozdżielona z rozmaitych historykow*...(Kraków: M. Siebeneicher, 1564), 4ᵛ.

[9] Mikołaj Rej, *Apocalypsis To iest Dziwna sprawa skrytych taiemnic Pańskich*...(Kraków: Maciej Wirzbięta, 1565), 148.

[10] Cf. Klonowic, *Worek Ivdaszow*, 229; 74, describing the dark of night: 'When the nightjar flies, and the winged mouse/Night-crows, *Latawcy*, and horned owls.'

[11] Institoris, *Malleus*, pt. 1, qu. 3, 126–7. Ząbkowic's *Młot* lacks this passage.

Thus Isaiah is made to speak of the sexual demons who are the lovers of witches, the same as those who engendered the Giants (as Bielski says Josephus says), the same as those who live in all ruins, not only those of Babylon and Edom but in Poland as well (as Rej says)—that is, *incubi*, that is, *latawcy*. The *incubi* of the time before the flood are the same as the *incubi* of the end-times, and they are both the same as the *incubi* who, in early modern Poland, hide in ruins, fly about with screech-owls and bats, and associate sexually and otherwise with witches.

So says the gloss. But let us review: Bielski and Rej and Institoris are mistaken. Josephus did *not* say that *latawcy* engendered the Giants, nor that *incubi* nor even *daemonia* did so; he says, following the Septuagint, that angels (ἄγγελοι) did so—an interpretation rejected by Augustine and by the Vulgate. Revelation 18 speaks of demons and unclean spirits and winged things, not, as Rej suggests, of *latawcy*. Isaiah describes various sorts of unclean bird, the female demon *lilith*, and the *sĕ'īrīm* (he-goats, wild goats, goat-demons?). The Septuagint translates the last term as *daimonia*, the Vulgate as *pilosi* (hairy ones), the KJV as *satyrs*. Wujek, translating the Vulgate, renders *pilosi* with what appears to be his own neologism, *kosmacze* (hairy ones)—perhaps recalling the appearance of devils in Orthodox Christian iconography as small hairy creatures.[12] Augustine spoke not of *incubi* but of *silvani*, *panites*, and *dusii*.

My point is not to privilege the older texts or the classical languages. The biblical *sĕ'īrīm* are no more or less real than the later demons, and it is unhelpful to conceive of their transformation from Hebrew to Greek to Latin to Polish as the result of a series of mistranslations. To even speak of mistranslation is to miss the point—that point being the mere fact of the translation itself. Each translation was an act of comparative ethnography, an attempt to gloss not just a foreign *term* but a foreign *thing*: each translation is accomplished through reference to some locally imagined spirit or creature or demon. Although some translations (such as the Vulgate's *pilosi* or Wujek's *kosmacze*) tended toward a literalist caution, most translations simultaneously interpreted and appropriated biblical imaginations to local settings, so that Greek, and Celtic, and Hebrew, and Polish demons become associated and intermixed. Thus the fiery bird and treasure-hauler of popular Polish fairy-lore, a being associated with the family and with the home (as an unbaptized infant, but also via the remnant ancestor cult of house-spirits), comes to be equated to the biblical hairy goat-demon, symbol of the desert, of ruination and chaos: and both these essentially popular creatures meet in the abstracted, theologized *incubus*, that spirit with a body of condensed air who takes advantage of women's overwhelming lust to lead them into damnation.

Wolfgang Behringer, analyzing the mixture of Christian demonology with local imaginations of fairies and ghosts in sixteenth-century southern Germany, writes that

---

[12] Dysa, 'Witchcraft Trials', 54.

the Christian idea of demons fitted seamlessly together with the popular belief in malevolent spirits, even though a certain 'surplus' of popular notions was left over, which stuck out beyond the tight contours of Christian theology . . . The Church tried to trim away these 'excesses' (these 'superstitions' in the literal sense of the word), in order to preserve a basic faith in harmful demons.[13]

One finds such an attempt to 'trim' the *latawiec* into the parameters of the *incubus* in Gilowski's catechism, and to a lesser degree in the *Devils' Lawsuit*. Other texts, such as Pokłatecki's *Pogrom* or Ząbkowic's translation of the *Malleus*, take no notice at all of local meanings and thus see no need to purge *latawiec* of those meanings. Most Polish texts, and all of the trial testimonies, are deeply ambiguous. *Latawiec*, and indeed also *bies, czart, diabeł, pokuśnik, szatan, skrzabeł* and all the other terms used to describe the entities encountered by a Polish witch at Bald Mountain or in the attic, at the field-border or in her chamber, is a composite character, such a mixture of Christian demons with local spirits that neither witch, nor judge, nor poet, attempts to delineate where one begins and the other ends. As Berwiński said of Polish witches, so too of Polish 'devils'—they were born at the crossroads, at the intersection between local folk-culture and global Christianity. The theologically naïve small-town magistrates who judged most Polish witch-trials never inquired as to why Dorota of Siedlików's *szatan* asked for milk porridge, the food of house-demons, or why Katharzyna Kozimińska hid her *diabeł* in the house-demon's traditional place behind the stove, or whether the warm 'nature' of Agnieszka Jakóbka's demon-lover might not imply the hot and drying, woman-withering *latawiec* rather than *incubus*, that cold spirit of the air whose illusory body, by God's will, can generate no heat. Nor did anyone ever seem to ask why the devils at Bald Mountain so often dressed in red. Indifferent to these subtleties, they did not 'trim' popular conceptions down to their proper Christian cores.

We should follow this lead of the Polish magistrates, and affect a naiveté that came to them naturally. A given *szatan* was not a house-demon, pure and unchristianized, but neither was it a theologically orthodox infernal devil. It was neither and both; it was itself, a mixture whose mixedness is perceived by modern scholars and, in a different way, by the occasional reforming theologian or critic of superstition, but *not* by the witches and judges for whom it was a real, living being. This mixing goes both ways: house-demons undergo a process of diabolization, but at the same time devils are domesticated.

I have concentrated on *latawiec* because of his central place in the early modern Polish literary tradition and his association with the *incubus* and with unbaptized children. But a similar analysis could be done of the other devils (or demons, or fairies, or imps) encountered in the Polish trials. The anonymous fifteenth-century

---

[13] Wolfgang Behringer, *The Shaman of Oberstdorf*, tr. H. C. Erik Midelfort (Charlottesville, Va.: University Press of Virginia, 1998), 95. I explore Behringer's argument in the context of global Christianity in 'Where've All the Good People Gone', in M. Ostling (ed.), *Fairies, Demons, and Nature Spirits: 'Small Gods' at the Margins of Christendom* (London: Palgrave, 2017), 1–53.

'Sermon of a Polish Hussite', studied by Brückner, condemns *sortilegiantes* who ask, immediately after the birth of a child, '*quid natum est, an masculus vel femina,*' to protect the newborn '*ab infirmitate que vocatur wlgariter* nocznicze'.[14] The educated and reforming author understood *nocznicze* (literally 'night-ones, little night things') to be an illness of newborn infants, but to the village-women whom he described as *sortilegiantes* they seem to be demons: the preacher condemned the women for misrecognizing a natural infirmity as demonic possession.

The ambiguity need not be resolved: we still use terms such as *nightmare* or *cauchemar*—originally demons cognate to the Polish *mara* and *zmora*—to denote the condition or illness or affliction of bad dreams or night-terrors.[15] In the late seventeenth century the ontological status of such nightmares remained ambiguous; the accused witch Katarzyna of Wojnicz, it will be recalled, healed children suffering from *nocnice* by addressing them with an inverted version of the Hail Mary (Nowy Wiśnicz 1662), while the aristocratic poet Walerian Otwinowski, translating Ovid, glossed the night-gods summoned by Circe as 'the *szatany* of the night, those that the witches call *nocnice*'.[16] Even *szatan* is ambivalent: clearly the biblical Satan, he or it is also a *nocnica*, while Duńczewski's popular almanac makes of *szatan* the witch's impish servant: 'a sort of familiar and affectionate ghost, which can be found in their bosoms or in the corners of the home'.[17] The devils of the confessions refused categorization: they were big tough peasant lads who hid behind the witch's knee or in her hair; they were an evil influence given in food, appearing suddenly as a fiery bird, or a wet chicken, or a little man with the head of a dog, or a handsome German youth in fine foreign dress. Any attempt to insist on a particular categorization, to fix these demons with a singular meaning and form, was doomed to failure. More importantly, few actual participants in the Polish witch-trials attempted any such categorization; they were dealing, after all, with shape-shifting beings of the ontological borderlands, and did not usually feel inclined to determine exactly what such beings were, or where they came from.

Folklore, like demonology, is a science of categorization. One wishes to find and establish the name and function and appearance and status of each different demon; to specify them, arrange them into hierarchies and classes.[18] History and ethnography, on the other hand, should strive for faithfulness to the source rather than for precision. Or rather, a precise account of the beliefs and experiences of witches and

---

[14] Aleksander Brückner, 'Kazania husyty polskiego', *Pracy Filologiczne*, 4(1892), 574–5.

[15] On the *mara* or *mora* in early modern Poland, see Syreniusz, *Zielnik*, 740. On its complex etymology (including translation issues cognate to those we find with *latawiec*), see Alaric Hall, "The Evidence for *Maran*, the Anglo-Saxon 'Nightmares'", *Neophilologus* 91 (2007): 299–317.

[16] Otwinowski, *Księgi Metamorphoseon*, 576.

[17] Baczko and Hinz, *Kalendarz półstuletni 1750 1800*, 55.

[18] Johnston, 'Defining the Dreadful', 371. Folkloric work undertaken by Baranowski and his student Janusz Pełka frequently resorted to describing folk beliefs about demons as 'mistaken' or 'confused' when they fail to conform to predetermined schema—in this, Baranowski resembles the demonologists he derides. More recent Polish folk demonology, while continuing the futile task of categorization, recognizes the flimsiness of such constructions. Baranowski, *W kręgu upiorów*, 114–15, 314–15; Dźwigoł, *Polskie ludowe słownictwo mitologiczne*, 7–8; Pełka, *Polska demonologia*.

their accusers, a rigorous account, *requires* vagueness and indeterminacy—because these beliefs and experiences were themselves vague and indeterminate. Polish witches had sex with devils, but the connotation and even denotation of 'devil' differs from trial to trial, witch to witch, even, for a single accused witch, from moment to moment as she fit her testimony to the magistrate's questions while also struggling to maintain her self-respect and a self-image she could live with. The devils thus constructed refuse to fit into comfortable categories, frustrating our desire to place them inside or outside Christianity or Slavic mythology, local village culture or pan-European demonological discourse.

Ever since Ginzburg's pioneering study of the witchcraft beliefs among the Friuliani of north-eastern Italy began to draw the attention of historians outside Italy, it has become less and less possible to treat the devils and other characters peopling witchcraft confessions as the product of Christian fantasies only.[19] Ginzburg discovered that the 'witches' prosecuted by the Roman Inquisition in this area understood themselves to be *benandanti*: men and women destined by special birth to fly out at night four times a year to engage in aerial battles with witches and to thereby ensure the fertility of the crops. After Ginzburg, other scholars have found similar formations elsewhere: Henningsen showed that the witches' meetings in Sicily were originally visitations from the fairy-like 'ladies from outside';[20] Klaniczay discovered 'shamanistic elements' in Hungarian witch-trials;[21] and Behringer, as mentioned above, explored southern German confessions as expressions of beliefs in the traveling revenant dead.[22] While these studies have made limited and cautious claims linking witchcraft beliefs with underlying cults of the dead or of fairies, others have gone further. Éva Pócs interprets the witchcraft confessions in Hungary and Slovakia in terms of medium-like contact with the dead and with fairies.[23] She draws on Ginzburg's own later work, in which he has claimed to find in witch-beliefs and confessions 'an underlying Eurasian mythological unity' of shamanism, animal metamorphosis, and mediation between the living and the dead.[24]

In doing so, in privileging underlying, hidden paganism in what are ostensibly more or less Christian confessions, Ginzburg comes to resemble the Inquisitors whose interrogations of the Friulian peasantry form the source material for his scholarship. If we are to avoid such retroactive ratification of the inquisitorial

---

[19] Carlo Ginzburg, *The Night Battles*, tr. John and Ann C. Tedeschi (Baltimore: Johns Hopkins University Press, 1983 [1966]).

[20] Gustav Henningsen, '"The Ladies from Outside": An Archaic Pattern of the Witches' Sabbath', in B. Ankarloo and G. Henningsen (eds.), *Early Modern European Witchcraft* (Oxford: OUP, 1993 [1987]).

[21] Gábor Klaniczay, 'Shaministic Elements in Central European Witchcraft', in M. Hoppál (ed.), *Shamanism in Eurasia* (Göttingen: Edition Herodot, 1984).

[22] Behringer, *Shaman of Oberstdorf.*

[23] Éva Pócs, *Between the Living and the Dead*, tr. Szilvia Rédey and Michael Webb (Budapest: Central European University Press, 1999).

[24] Ginzburg, *Ecstasies*, 267.

point of view—as I think we must for both ethical and methodological reasons—
we must accept witchcraft confessions in all their dissatisfactory mixedness. We
may look for hidden meanings, or folkloric traces, but must read these in
conjunction with the surface narratives of devil-pact and diabolical *sabbat*. But
even at this surface level, it is not difficult to see strong overlays of fairy-belief, or
of belief in contact with ghosts of various kinds, in witch-confessions from all
over Europe. Even Norman Cohn, who traced the *sabbat*-stereotype to a standard set of defamatory clichés directed first against heretics and Jews, noted that
some of the demons of early witch-trials were clearly fairies—sometimes even
named 'Robin Goodfellow'.[25] Erik Midelfort has emphasized the plurality and
fluidity of supernatural beings in pre-Reformation Germany, and characterizes
the sixteenth century as an era of 'demonization of the world' whereby such
creatures came to be consolidated into more-or-less orthodox devils.[26]

Surprisingly, the best comparative examples of devil–fairy intermixtures come
from the British Isles—perhaps these are simply the best studied. Katherine
Briggs noticed decades ago that in Scottish witch-trials, the devils with whom
witches entered into pacts often resembled both fairies and (what amount to the
same thing) the spirits of the untimely dead.[27] In an important recent article,
Stuart Macdonald has fleshed out this claim: 'instead of the details we would
expect in a portrait of the great enemy of God and humanity, what we find are
elements than in places are suggestive of a fairy or elf'.[28] From the elite point of
view, spiritual beings could only be angelic or demonic; James VI insisted that
visits to fairyland were in fact 'delusions of the devil'.[29] However, the common
people seem to have tended to assimilate devils to fairies, rather than the reverse.

Through a survey of this Scottish material alongside folklore and witch-trial
sources from England, Emma Wilby has shown convincingly that the witch's
familiars that are so important in British witchcraft (and which so closely
resemble the *latawcy* and *chowańcy* and *szatany* of many Polish trials) bore
close relations to fairies. In appearance, function, and sometimes even in name
(imp, puckling, Robin), they resembled hobgoblins rather than the devils of
standard Christian imagery.[30] Despite elite insistence that witches consorted

---

[25] Cohn, *Europe's Inner Demons*, 137–41, 59, 70–1.

[26] H. C. Erik Midelfort, 'The Devil and the German People', in D. Oldridge (ed.), *The Witchcraft Reader* (New York: Routledge, 2002 [1989]), 242; cf. Scribner, 'Disenchantment'.

[27] Katherine M. Briggs, 'The Fairies and the Realms of the Dead', *Folklore*, 81/2 (1970), 85–8; see also MacCulloch, 'Mingling of Fairy', 234–8.

[28] Stuart Macdonald, 'In Search of the Devil in Fife Witchcraft Cases 1560–1705', in J. Goodare (ed.), *The Scottish Witch-Hunt in Context* (Manchester and New York: Manchester UP, 2002), 46; cf. Martin, 'Devil and the Domestic', 83.

[29] *Demonologie*, bk. 3, ch. 5; after MacCulloch, 'Mingling of Fairy', 240.

[30] Emma Wilby, 'The Witch's Familiar and the Fairy in Early Modern England and Scotland', *Folklore*, 111/2 (2000), 286–8. See now also her *Cunning Folk and Familiar Spirits* (Brighton: Sussex Academic Press, 2005).

with infernal devils, in the popular view a witch had to do with 'a fairy which could be a familiar which could be a devil which could the Devil'.[31]

The close similarities of this British situation to what I have been describing in Poland should not blind us to the important differences. In England, elite literary sources insisted that *fairies are devils* (much more rarely, they insisted that fairies should be distinguished from devils).[32] In Poland, there was never, at the elite level, any literary separation of fairy and devil: from the very beginning, literature treated the named supernatural beings believed in by the common people as species of devil. There was no Polish equivalent of *A Midsummer Night's Dream*—and therefore, also, no Polish *Hierarchies of the Blessed Angells*. Works such as the *Devil's Lawsuit* or the *Infernal Parliament* treat all non-angelic supernatural beings as devils, but they do not *polemicize* on this point. With no elite literary tradition of fairies against which reforming clergy could react, one finds no insistence on the issue, and few attempts at precise definitions beyond occasional sneers regarding the stupidity of the common people. One cannot imagine a pious English cunning-woman saying, like a pious Polish cunning-woman in the nineteenth century, that 'Marynka had only good devils; for that reason she also went to church.'[33]

English-speaking demonologists and theologians insisted strongly and frequently that entities such as imps and pucks and goblins and fairies and elves and leprechauns were 'nothing but' devils, that they were devils in fact. But such a statement is very different from the process which took place in Poland, whereby a native 'folkloric' term comes to substitute for and translate a theological term. To say 'X is nothing but Y' is to acknowledge the prior assumption of their difference. It is to say that, in spite of popular or ignorant misconceptions, entities believed to belong to different categories in fact belong to just one category, and that the non-demonic features alleged to obtain in the popular category in fact do not so obtain. The theological category thus comes to encompass the popular category, without remainder—this, at least, is the rhetorical intention of statements such as 'fairies are demons' or 'the gods of the Pagans are devils'. With the partial exception of Gilowski, Polish ecclesiastical authors did not follow such a polemical procedure. The substitution of *latawiec* for *incubus* was not an assertion of this sort, as it does not include the necessary context of assumed difference. Precisely because terms like *brownie* or *puck*

---

[31] Wilby, 'Witch's Familiar and the Fairy', 302.

[32] William Bradshaw, in *A plaine and pithy exposition of the second epistle to the Thessalonians* (1620), 123, considers 'Goblins, Fayries, walking Spirits etc.' to be diabolical phenomena characteristic of Catholic periods. In contrast, John Webster in *The displaying of supposed witchcraft* (1667), 287, 'allowed for "middle creatures" who "because of their strange natures, shapes and properties, or by reason of their being rarely seen have been and often are not only by the common people but even by the learned taken to be Devils, Spirits or the effects of Inchantment and Witchcraft"' (both quoted after Clark, *Thinking with Demons*, 239, 361).

[33] Kolberg, *Dzieła wszystkie*, xv. 142.

remained, in English, distinct from terms like *incubus* or *devil*, the latter terms preserved, for the most part, their theological senses and were not fully integrated into folk conceptions of nature spirits and sprites.[34] In Poland, on the contrary, a preference for translation into local terms, substituting local demons for 'theological' ones, mixed the meanings of both. Translating the devil meant, above all, combining the Christian theological entities with local notions of grain-stealers, unbaptized ghosts, and house-demons, and neither the Christian nor the aboriginal being ever came to dominate in this inextricably hybrid creature.

We are left, once again, at the crossroads, in the company of that cosmopolitan indigene, the Polish witch. A faithful portrait of this imaginary creature, and of the women who came to embody her through accusation, interrogation, and confession, must remain at the crossroads, refusing to explain the witch either in terms of elite Christian demonology or an underlying Slavic folklore. The Polish witch, like the devil she did not really worship, was a twilight creature: her place, as the *Devil's Lawsuit* puts it, was 'at the border'.

---

[34] Terry Gunnell, "How Elvish Were the Álfar?", in Andrew Wawn, Graham Johnson, and John Walter (eds.), *Constructing Nations, Reconstructing Myth* (Turnhout: Brepols, 2007), 111–30; Michael Ostling and Richard Forest, '"Goblins, owles, and sprites": Discerning early modern English preternatural beings through collocational analysis,' *Religion* 44/4 (2014), 547–572.

Conclusions

The methodological stance and theoretical concerns of this book may best be characterized by a juxtaposition of quotations from the two scholars who have had the greatest influence on my thinking about religion and culture.

On the one hand, Jonathan Z. Smith opens his *Imagining Religion* with a famously radical, albeit characteristically gnomic passage. Reflecting that human-kind has, for the entirety of its discoverable history, imagined all manner of gods, demons, cosmogonies, afterlives, Smith declares that nevertheless we have had

> only the last few centuries in which to imagine religion. . . . That is to say, while there is a staggering amount of data, of phenomena, of human experiences and expressions that might be characterized in one culture or another, by one criterion or another, as religious—*there is no data for religion*. Religion is solely the creation of the scholar's study. It is created for the scholar's analytic purposes by his imaginative acts of compari-son and generalization. Religion has no independent existence apart from the academy.[1]

I understand Smith to be insisting that, as 'religion' is a category invented by scholarship in order to facilitate the comprehension, originally by European Christians, of religious 'others', scholarship is free to formulate the definition and boundaries of the category in whatever ways seem most likely to best serve this task of comparative interpretation. Religion is not out there in the world; it is, rather, a construction imputed to events, beliefs, and behaviors as a herme-neutical tool or explanatory device.

Smith's relocation of the category 'religion' from the world to the imagination implies freedom, but it also implies responsibility—especially in conjunction with our awareness of the category's colonial pedigree. Because the category is ours to construct rather than to discover, it behooves us to construct it in such ways as to distort as little as possible the imagined realities (the 'religions') of the people we study. This brings me to my other quotation, or rather dictum, from Clifford Geertz. He asserts that, while recent scholarship has been fascinated with the 'representation of 'The Other' (inevitably capitalized, inevitably singular)', our task must be to understand 'others', uncapitalized and plural.[2] That is, while 'religion' was invented so that Christians could understand Buddhism, Judaism,

---

[1] Jonathan Z. Smith, *Imagining Religion* (Chicago: University of Chicago Press, 1982), p. xi.
[2] Geertz, *Available Light*, 95–6.

'primitive religions', and so on, a more fruitful and less distortionary approach is to try to understand what Buddhists, Jews, Christians, and the various other indigenes of the world are doing, and why. Scholars must ask the historiographical questions about the conditions under which categories such as 'religion' and 'witchcraft' were developed, and the uses to which such categories were put. But we cannot allow an interest in discourse or in representations to overshadow the central interpretative task—which is to understand the lives and actions of historical others: the people themselves, uncapitalized and plural.

It is a central contention of this study that the opportunities and problems created by treating religion as an imagined category can very fruitfully be brought over into the study of witchcraft. Like religion, witchcraft is the product processes of second-order reflection, comparison, and generalization by which both early modern demonologists and modern historians and anthropologists organize and categorize diverse folk-cultural behavior and beliefs from all over the world. As with religion, witchcraft has recently come in for criticism insofar as the European category, imposed elsewhere, has led to distortion and confusion rather than increased understanding. But unlike religion, witchcraft is a category doubly imagined: in the scholar's study but also within the indigenous context of the culture in which it is feared and punished.

The word 'witchcraft' describes an 'impossible crime': there are no real witches, in Poland or elsewhere, except insofar as that role is successfully ascribed to persons (by the community, by demonologists, by magistrates, by historians). While 'religion' is a category constructed through comparison and categorization of real, concrete behaviors, dispositions, artifacts, and utterances—albeit behaviors and utterances often directed toward imaginary or at least invisible supernatural beings—witchcraft is constructed from the very beginning. Whereas scholars may fruitfully postpone questions about the ontological status of gods, demons, or angels while studying beliefs or behaviors related to such entities, the witch, as a category related to persons, must be rejected as the first step of any serious interpretation. The witch is imagined, but the consequences, for real people imagined by their community to be witches, are all too real. Accordingly, the study of witchcraft differs from the study of most other religious phenomena, in that it begins with a rejection, a denial (rather than a bracketing or a disregard) of the reality of the category.

Earlier generations of scholars have responded to this imaginary status of the witch, the impossibility of her crime, by treating witchcraft beliefs as an emblem of ignorance, fanaticism, the dangers of religion in general and Christianity in particular. One can appreciate the sincere moral outrage of this brand of scholarship, while also noting its tendency to demonize the demonizers—in particular its use in anti-Catholic polemic and in the construction of the 'primitive'. More perniciously to my mind, the tendency to attribute witchcraft belief to scapegoating mechanisms absolves the scholar from any serious attempt to interpret, or to understand, the experiences of the parties involved in witch-trials, both as accusers and as accused. We end up, again, studying the construction of the 'Other' rather than the lives of others.

A countervailing tendency in recent years—to treat the imagined witch as a dark reflection by which we might glimpse the real, true, underlying religion of the common-people—carries equal dangers. Scholars have sometimes, in effect, agreed with the demonologists while reversing the value-judgments: 'witches' really were residually pagan, and this is a good thing. Others, while refraining from discovering paganism in the witch-trials, have agreed with early modern elites at least insofar as they treat the peasantry's Christianity as fragmented, magical, or superstitious. Witch-trials become a window past or through Christianity to an animistic or shamanistic substratum of age-old peasant religion.

A pervading theme of this book, pursued in Part II and problematized in Part III, is to complicate these sorts of position. Educated elites and reformers were perfectly correct in pointing out that much of rural Christianity was at variance with orthodox doctrinal norms. From a purely historical point of view they were also correct, though less often than they believed, in attributing those characteristics of rural religion which they labeled as 'superstitious' or 'magical' or 'Satanic' to a syncretic residuum of pre-Christian, pagan practice. But they were neither correct nor incorrect in asserting that those who partook of such practices were themselves therefore pagan. Or to put the same point otherwise, the secular scholar of religion cannot adjudicate, and should not take sides, in what is essentially a theological question about what counts as true Christianity. We may note the use of such socially ascribed labels, we may attempt to evaluate whether accused witches understood themselves to be Christian, and what this might have meant to them. But from the standpoint of the secular study of religion, theological categories such as 'true Christianity' or 'correct religion' have no meaning. Without access to a transcendent Authority, the secular student of religion must treat the self-identification of practitioners as authoritative.

As Charles Stewart has shown in his important study of folk-demons and Christian devils over two millennia of Christianity in Greece, 'pagan' folk tradition has lived alongside and intermingled with Christianity for a very long time. He thus finds it necessary to reformulate 'Christianity' as everywhere syncretic and synthetic, nowhere 'pure'—or rather, its pure form is an ideal construction realized nowhere.[3] In Poland and elsewhere, scholars have rather too often agreed with the judgment of the demonological, or pastoral, or anti-superstition literature which contrasts rural religion with this imaginary ideal type, and found the former necessarily wanting. By treating *both* Christianity and witchcraft as equally imagined categories, I hope in this work to have provided a more nuanced, less evaluative account of their interactions. I do this through

---

[3] Charles Stewart, *Demons and the Devil* (Princeton: PUP, 1991).

analysis of Polish trials, Polish customs, Polish texts, but I think the conclusions will have relevance to studies of Christianity elsewhere in Europe or the world.

Ultimately, however, I have wanted to show not only how the western Christian imagination of witchcraft played out and became localized in Poland, but how individual accused witches imagined their own stories. The story told here is less about the interpenetration of 'center and periphery' on a European scale than it is about the margin between culture and the self. By 'imagining witchcraft' I have wanted to denote the stereotypes and 'synthetic images' by which accusers, judges, theologians, and poets imagined the witch as terrifying Other; but I have also wanted to explore the ways in which the accused imagined and reimagined themselves, in resistance to such stereotypes but also by and through them. Witch-trials are very nearly our only source for the voices of early modern Polish peasant-women, the only place where they talked about themselves. They spoke unwillingly, compelled through unimaginable torture. Accused witches were forced to declare themselves to be the worst kind of criminal, guilty of the worst abominations. Nevertheless, through and under and around the 'demonological script', they told their judges a great deal that was true, or that at least bore some resemblance to what they wished to think about themselves. They managed to talk about love and loss; they managed to express resentment and spite but also yearnings, fears, fantasies of their own; they displayed themselves, often, to be people of great courage and assertiveness. Many, as well, imagined and represented themselves as women of deep Catholic piety—and they did this through the very act and in the words of rejection of that piety. The notion of 'imagining witchcraft' intends to convey this double process: the imagination of witches by their accusers and magistrates (and more widely, by demonological theory or even by modern scholarship), and the strategies of representation employed by the accused witches themselves. Through these self-representations, we get a glimpse beyond imagination into the real world of the early modern Polish women imagined by their neighbors to be witches.

Appendix: Witch-Trials in Poland, 1511–1775

ABBREVIATIONS

AAL KGL	Archiwum Archidiecezjalne w Lublinie, Konsystorz Generalny Lubelski
ADK	Archiwum Diecezjalne w Kielcach
AdŁomża	Archiwum dawne w Łomży (pre-war)
ADT	Archiwum Diecezjalne w Tarnowie
AGAD	Archiwum Główne Akt Dawnych
AKMK	Archiwum Kurii Metropolitalnej w Krakowie
AmBydgoszcz, AmLublin, etc.	Akta miasta Lublina, Akta miasta Poznania, etc.
ANK	Archiwum Narodowe w Krakowie
APLublin, APPoznań, etc.	Archiwum Państwowe w Lublinie, Archiwum Państowe w Poznaniu, etc.
APMP	Archiwum Państwowe Miasta Poznania
APPotockich	Archiwum Publiczne Potockich
ArchGdańsk	Archiwum w Gdańsku (pre-war)
ARN	Archiwum Radziwiłłów z Nieborowa
ASA	Akta Sądu Asesorskiego (pre-war)
BBaw	Biblioteka Baworowskich
BJ	Bibioteka Jagiellońska
BPAU/PANK	Biblioteka PAU / PAN w Krakowie
BPTPN	Biblioteka Poznańskiego Towarzystwa Przyjaciół Nauk
BTarnowski	Biblioteka Tarnowskich (pre-war)
KcKrzemieniec	Księga czarna Krzemieniecka
KgLublin, KgPoznań, etc.	Księgi grodzkie Lublina, Księgi grodzkie Poznania, etc.
LNNBU	L'vivska Natsionalna Naukova Biblioteka Ukrainy
MHDW	*Monumenta Historica Dioceseos Wladislaviensis*
NBLDU	Naukova Biblioteka L'vivskoho Derzhavnoho Universytetu
PANKraków	Polska Akademia Nauk, Oddział w Krakowie
SDDBC	Sądy Dominialne Dóbr Biskupstwa Chełmińskiego
SWPN	Sąd Wyższy Prawa Niemieckiego
TsDIA (Kyiv)	Tsentral'nyi Derzhavnyi Istorychnyi Arkhiv Ukrainy, Kyiv
TsDIA (Lviv)	Tsentral'nyi Derzhavnyi Istorychnyi Arkhiv Ukrainy, Lviv

Note that many archival records listed were destroyed during World War II. Others have undergone extensive recataloging in the post-Communist era. It has not usually been possible to update the archival references of older published sources.

Trial	Published Source • Archival Source
Chwaliszewo 1511	Ulanowski, *Acta iudiciorum*, item 1660; Adamczyk, 'Czary i magia', 205–206
Trześniów 1529	Polaczkówna, *Najstarsza księga*, item 709; Wiślicz, *Regesty spraw*, item 2
Poznań 1535	Ulanowski, *Acta iudiciorum*, item 1837; Koranyi *'Czary i gusła'*, 21
Poznań 1544a	Łukaszewicz, *Obraz historycznostatystyczny*, ii., 275; Kolberg, *Dzieła wszystkie*, xv. 15, 240–241; Worończak, 'Procesy o czary', 50–55 • APPoznań, AmPoznań sig. 474, ff. 83v–86v
Poznań 1544b	Maisel, *Poznańskie prawo*, 213; Worończak, 'Procesy o czary', 55–56 • APPoznań, AmPoznań I/168, ff. 88v–90
Poznań 1549	Worończak, 'Procesy o czary', 57 • APPoznań, AmPoznań I/168, f. 148v
Nieszawa 1550	*MHDW* v., 5; Wijaczka, *'Próba zimnej wody'*, 78
Poznań 1559	Łukaszewicz, *Obraz historycznostatystyczny*, ii., 123–124; Kolberg, *Dzieła wszystkie*, xv. 15, 239–240; Maisel, *Poznańskie prawo*, 213 • APPoznań, AmPoznań sig. I/639 ff. 22–23
Poznań 1567	Maisel, *Poznańskie prawo*, 213 • APPoznań, AmPoznań sig. I/639 f. 43v
Grudziądz 1568	Wijaczka, 'Procesy o czary przed sądem miejskim', 88–95
Grudziądz 1569	Wijaczka, 'Procesy o czary przed sądem miejskim', 96
Torki 1572	Ulanowski, *Acta iudiciorum*, items 3845, 3846, 3850–3852; Wiślicz, *Regesty spraw*, item 3
Wągrowiec 1578	Moeglich, 'Procesy o czary', 48• APPoznań, AMWągrowiec sig. I/13, f. 157
Kalisz 1580	Baranowski, *Najdawniejsze procesy*, 13–23; Guldon, 'Radomska czarownica', 169–172 • APPoznań, AmKalisz sig. I/158, ff. 17–29
Poznań 1582a	Maisel, *Poznańskie prawo*, 213 • APPoznań, AmPoznań sig. I/639 ff. 216v–218v
Poznań 1582b	Maisel, *Poznańskie prawo*, 213 • APPoznań, AmPoznań sig. I/640 ff. 40–40v
Kalisz 1584a	Baranowski, *Najdawniejsze procesy*, 24–26 • APPoznań, AmKalisz, A. Decr. sig. 1 ff. 43–44
Wara 1585	Łysiak,*Księga sądowa wsi Wary*, item 262; Wiślicz, *Regesty spraw*, item 4
Kalisz 1587	Baranowski, *Najdawniejsze procesy*, 27–29 • APPoznań, AmKalisz, A. Decr. sig. 1 ff. 67–68
Kraśnik 1587	Zielińska, 'Kraśnika sprawy', 94 • APLublin, AmKraśnik sig. 1, f. 62v
Kalisz 1593	Baranowski, *Najdawniejsze procesy*, 30–38 • APPoznań, AmKalisz, A. Decr. sig. 1 ff. 102v–107
Żywiec 1595	Komoniecki, *Chronografia*, 106; Pilaszek, *Procesy o czary*, 402
Bełżyce 1598a	Klarner, 'Sprawy o czary', 468
Bełżyce 1598b	Klarner, 'Sprawy o czary', 467
Bełżyce 1600	Klarner, 'Sprawy o czary', 468–469
Wschowa ca. 1601	Bukowska-Gorgoni, 'Procesy o czary', 160–161
Kraków 1601	Bukowska-Gorgoni, 'Procesy o czary', 160–161 • ANK SWPN sig. I–27 ff. 1283–1285
Iwkowa 1602	Płaza, *Księga sądowa wsi Iwkowej*, item 284; Wiślicz, *Regesty spraw*, item 5

Kasina Wielka 1602	Ulanowski, *Acta iudiciorum*, item 2801; Wiślicz, *Regesty spraw*, item 6
Poznań 1603	Pilaszek, *Procesy o czary*, 107, 209, 288–90, 389, 446 • APPoznań, AmPoznań sig. I/662 ff. 145–149
Kielce 1605	Szanser, 'Ustrój miasta Kielc', 32; Wijaczka, 'Procesy o czary w regionie świętokrzyskiego', 38
Poznań 1607	Pilaszek, *Procesy o czary*, 295 • APPoznań, AmPoznań sig. I/664 f. 20
Grabowiec 1608	APLublin, KgGrabowiec sig. 77, ff. 415–416
Kazimierz 1610	Mikołajczyk, 'O pławieniu czarownic', 128 • ANK AmKazimierza sig. 266 ff. 340–344
Poznań 1610	Pilaszek, *Procesy o czary*, 402 • APPoznań, AmPoznań sig. I/665 f. 248
Siary 1610	Ulanowski, *Acta iudiciorum*, item 7109; Wiślicz, *Regesty spraw*, item 7
Kazimierz 1611	Mikołajczyk, 'O pławieniu czarownic', 128 • ANK AmKazimierza sig. 267 ff. 13–14
Kraków 1611	Kracik and Rożek, *Hultaje*, 111 • ANK AmK sig. 267, ff. 13–14
Kalisz 1613	Baranowski, *Najdawniejsze procesy*, 39–55 • APPoznań, AmKalisz, A. Decr. sig. 1 ff. 176–182
Bereznicza 1616	NBLDU VR no. 518iii, f. 91v
Ekonomia Samborska 1616	Dysa, *Istoriya z Vid'mamy*, 126 • NBLDU VR no. 518iii, f. 91
Kalisz 1616	Baranowski, *Najdawniejsze procesy*, 56–66 • APPoznań, AmKalisz, A. Decr. sig. 1 ff. 191–194
Kobylin 1616	Łukaszewicz, *Krótki historyczno-statystyczny opis*, i., 74; Baranowski, *Procesy czarownic*, 129–130
Klimkówka 1618	Łysiak, *Księga sądowa kresu klimkowskiego*, item 145; Wiślicz, *Regesty spraw*, item 10
Ptaszkowa 1618	Ulanowski, *Acta iudiciorum*, item 4110; Wiślicz, *Regesty spraw*, item 9
Gniezno 1619	Pilaszek, *Procesy o czary*, 209, 245, 249 • APPoznań, AmGniezno sig. I/30 ff. 886–926
Wielki Koźmin 1621a	Wijaczka, 'Oskarżenia i procesy', 199 • APPoznań, AmWKoźmin sig. 12 f. 22
Wielki Koźmin 1621b	Wijaczka, 'Oskarżenia i procesy', 199 • APBydgoszcz, AmNowe sig. 1 f. 336
Krościenko 1622	Rafacz, 'Podejrzenie', 302–303 • ANK Kg Kraków, vol. 47 ff. 1955–1956
Nowy Wiśnicz 1622	Kaczmarczyk, 'Przyczynki', 330; Pilaszek, *Procesy o czary*, 302, 343
Chojnice 1623	Pilaszek, *Procesy o czary*, 426
Borek 1624	Łukaszewicz, *Krótki historyczno-statystyczny opis*, ii., 38
Kleczew 1624a	Hajdrych, 'Wizja świata', 39, 128, 156, 211 • BPTPN, ms. 859 ff. 1v–5
Kleczew 1624b	Hajdrych, 'Wizja świata', 39, 47, 128, 156, 197, 212, 214 • BPTPN, ms. 859 ff. 5–8v
Nowe 1624	Wijaczka, 'Witch and Sorcerer-Hunts', 105 • APBydgoszcz, AmNowe sig. 1 f. 336

(Continued)

(*Continued*)

Trial	Published Source • Archival Source
Kleczew 1625a	Hajdrych, 'Proces czarownicy Anny', 5–12; 'Wizja świata', 35, 39–54, 208, 239–241 • BPTPN, ms. 859 ff. 9–13v
Kleczew 1625b	Hajdrych, 'Wizja świata', 46, 70, 106 • BPTPN, ms. 859 ff. 13v–15v
Kozienice 1625	Siarczyński, *Obraz wieku*, i., 45
Kleczew 1626	Hajdrych, 'Wizja świata', 48, 129, 156, 206, 207, 211 • BPTPN, ms. 859 ff. 16–20v
Lublin 1627	Zakrzewska-Dubasowa, *Procesy o czary w Lublinie*, 11–12 • APLublin, AmLublin sig. 141 ff. 198–204
Łekno ca. 1628	Wijaczka, 'Oskarżenia i procesy', 200
Wielki Koźmin 1628	Wijaczka, 'Oskarżenia i procesy', 200 • APPoznań, AmWKoźmin sig. 12 f. 28–29
Kleczew 1629	Hajdrych, 'Wizja świata', 172, 198, 211, 212 • BPTPN, ms. 859 ff. 20v–21v
Bydgoszcz 1630	Malewski, 'Procesy o czarnoksięstwo', 78–80 • APBydgoszcz, AmBydgoszcz sig. 211, f. 44
Przemyśl 1630	Teter, *Sinners on Trial*, 176–199
Lublin 1631	Riabinin, *Jeszcze o czarach*, 3–4; Kowalska-Cichy, *Magia i procesy o czary*, 46–47 • APLublin, AmLublin sig. 207, f. 320
Nowe 1631	Jacek Wijaczka, personal communication.
Szadek ca. 1632	Bukowska-Gorgoni, 'Procesy o czary', 161
Kraków 1632	Bukowska-Gorgoni, 'Procesy o czary', 161 • ANK SWPN sig. I–31 f. 381
Nowy Wiśnicz 1632	Uruszczak, *Acta Maleficorum*, 41–46 • ADT AmWiśnicz sig. LN XXIII, ff. 37–44
Wielki Koźmin 1632	Wijaczka, 'Oskarżenia i procesy', 201–202 • APPoznań, AmWKoźmin sig. 7 ff. 7–8
Wola Żarczycka 1633	Wiślicz, *Regesty spraw*, item 12 • ZPJP # 173
Dobczyce 1634	Ulanowski, *Acta iudiciorum*, item 3157; Wiślicz, *Regesty spraw*, item 13
Lwów 1634	Dysa, *Istoriya z Vid'mamy*, 43 • TsDIA (Lviv), fond 52, op. 2, no. 302, ff. 145–156
Klimkówka 1636	Łysiak, *Księga sądowa kresu klimkowskiego*, item 399; Wiślicz, *Regesty spraw*, item 14
Klucz lipnicki 1636	Wiślicz, *Regesty spraw*, item 15 • APPrzemyśl, Zbiór Szczątków Zespołów z XVIII i XIX w. sig. 1 f. 2v
Braniewo 1637	Pilaszek, *Procesy o czary*, 394, 423–4, 437 • BPAU/PANK sig. 2796 v. 3 ff. 126v–127
Grudziądz 1637	Wijaczka, 'Procesy o czary przed sądem miejskim', 96–97
Lublin 1637	Kowalska-Cichy, *Magia i procesy o czary*, 64–68 • AAL KGL sig. Rep 60 A XXV, ff. 191–196v, 206–207
Radoszyce ca. 1638	Bukowska-Gorgoni, 'Procesy o czary', 163
Sambor ca. 1638	Bukowska-Gorgoni, 'Procesy o czary', 161

Braniewo 1638	Pilaszek, *Procesy o czary*, 441 • BPAU/PANK sig. 2796 v. 3 f. 127
Bydgoszcz 1638	Janiszewska-Mincer, 'Bydgoski proces o czary', 110–124 • Biblioteka PAN w Kórniku ms. 1037
Chełmno 1638	Biskup, *Ziemia chełmińska*, 149–151 • APToruń sig. 322, items 502, 506, 522
Kraków 1638a	Bukowska-Gorgoni, 'Procesy o czary', 163 • ANK SWPN sig. I–31 ff. 1156–1157
Kraków 1638b	Bukowska-Gorgoni, 'Procesy o czary', 161 • ANK SWPN sig. I–31 f. 381
Braniewo 1639	Pilaszek, *Procesy o czary*, 425, 438 • BPAU/PANK sig. 2796 v. 3 f. 127v
Skrzynno 1639	Zakrzewska-Dubasowa, *Procesy o czary w Lublinie*, 13–20 • APLublin, AmLublin sig. 38, ff. 113–116
Kleczew 1640	Hajdrych, 'Wizja świata', 142, 206 • BPTPN, ms. 859, f. 24v–25v
Braniewo 1642	Pilaszek, *Procesy o czary*, 427, 434, 438, 441 • BPAU/PANK sig. 2796 v. 3 ff. 127v–128
Kleczew 1642	Hajdrych, 'Wizja świata', 105, 117 • BPTPN, ms. 859, f. 224r–226r
Żarnowiec ca. 1643	Bukowska-Gorgoni, 'Procesy o czary', 163–164
Braniewo 1643	Pilaszek, *Procesy o czary*, 420–421 • BPAU/PANK sig. 2796 v. 3 f. 128
Kraków 1643	Bukowska-Gorgoni, 'Procesy o czary', 163–164 • ANK SWPN sig. I–32, ff. 286–288
Lublin 1643	Zakrzewska-Dubasowa, *Procesy o czary w Lublinie*, 20–26 • APLublin, AmLublin sig. 140 ff. 50–51, 60–64v
Nowy Wiśnicz 1643	Uruszczak, *Acta Maleficorum*, 98–102 • ANK AmWiśnicz, ADT sig. LN XXIII, ff. 102v–105
Wągrowiec 1643	Moeglich, 'Procesy o czary', 50 • APPoznań, AMWągrowiec sig.I/21, f. 25
Biecz ca. 1644	Bukowska-Gorgoni, 'Procesy o czary', 164–165
Braniewo 1644	Pilaszek, *Procesy o czary*, 295, 447 • BPAU/PANK sig. 2796 v. 3 f. 128v
Kraków 1644	Bukowska-Gorgoni, 'Procesy o czary', 164–165 • ANK SWPN sig. I–32, ff. 464–465
Lublin 1644	Ostling, 'Nieznany proces o czary', 191–204 • APLublin, AmLublin sig. 143 ff. 122–132
Pilica ca. 1645	Bukowska-Gorgoni, 'Procesy o czary', 165
Biecz 1645	Mikołajczyk, 'Przestępstwa przeciwko religii', 232 • ANKAkta dominialne 6, ff. 148–149
Kowalewo 1645	Wijaczka, 'Procesy o czary przed sądem sołtysim', 103 • APToruń AmKowalewo sig. 5 ff. 83–83v
Kraków 1645	Bukowska-Gorgoni, 'Procesy o czary', 165 • ANK SWPN sig. I–32, ff. 567–569
Poznań 1645	Łukaszewicz, *Obraz historycznostatystyczny*, ii., 323; Kolberg, *Dzieła wszystkie*, xv. 15, 239–240
Wola Żarczycka 1645	Podgórski, *Wola Żarczycka*, 34; Wiślicz, *Regesty spraw*, item 17 • ZPJP, # 65
Braniewo 1646	Pilaszek, *Procesy o czary*, 456 • BPAU/PANK sig. 2796 v. 3 f. 128v

(Continued)

(Continued)

Trial	Published Source • Archival Source
Kasina Wielka 1646	Ulanowski, *Acta iudiciorum*, item 3294; Wiślicz, *Regesty spraw*, item 18
Kleczew 1646a	Hajdrych, 'Wizja świata', 105, 162, 177 • BPTPN, ms. 859, f. 228r–231v
Kleczew 1646b	Hajdrych, 'Wizja świata', 106, 162, 177, 188, 202 • BPTPN, ms. 859, f. 236r–240r
Kleczew 1646c	BPTPN, ms. 859, f. 240v–242v
Kleczew 1646d	Hajdrych, 'Wizja świata', 177 • BPTPN, ms. 859 ff. 231v–234
Kleczew 1646e	Hajdrych, 'Wizja świata', 117, 154, 177 • BPTPN, ms. 859 ff. 266–268
Nowy Sącz 1646	Sygański, 'Wyroki Ławicy Nowosandeckiej', 457
Czukiew 1647	Wiślicz, *Regesty spraw*, item 19 • TsDIA (Lviv), fond 142, op. 1, no. 1, 202–203
Kasina Wielka 1647	Ulanowski, *Acta iudiciorum*, item 3306; Wiślicz, *Regesty spraw*, item 20
Kowalewo 1647	Wijaczka, 'Procesy o czary przed sądem sołtysim', 103–108 • APToruń AmKowalewo sig. 6 ff. 8–11v
Turek 1648	Milewski, *Pamiątki historyczne*, 346–352; Wijaczka, '*Próba zimnej wody*', 98, 100–101
Szadek ca. 1649a	Bukowska-Gorgoni, 'Procesy o czary', 165–166
Szadek ca. 1649b	Bukowska-Gorgoni, 'Procesy o czary', 166–167
Kraków 1649a	Bukowska-Gorgoni, 'Procesy o czary', 165–166 • ANK SWPN sig. I–32 ff. 818–819
Kraków 1649b	Bukowska-Gorgoni, 'Procesy o czary', 166–167 • ANK SWPN sig. I–32 ff. 819–821
Sidzina 1649	Wiślicz, *Regesty spraw*, item 21 • BJ ms. 9092 f. 53
Czukiew 1651	Wiślicz, *Regesty spraw*, item 22 • TsDIA (Lviv), fond 142, op. 1, no. 1, ff. 241–3
Kasina Wielka 1652	Ulanowski, *Acta iudiciorum*, item 3369; Wiślicz, *Regesty spraw*, item 23
Łódź 1652	Zand, *Z dziejów*, 58–59 • AGAD, AmŁódź sig. 5/6 ff. 181v–182v
Opalenica 1652	Wojcieszak, *Opalenickie procesy* • APPoznań, AmOpalenica sig. I/5 ff. 17–18
Turek 1652a	Wyporska, 'Witchcraft, Arson and Murder', 46 • APPoznań, AmTurek sig. I/30
Turek 1652b	Wyporska, 'Witchcraft, Arson and Murder', 46–53 • APPoznań, AmTurek sig. I/30, ff. 14v–21v
Nowe 1653	Wijaczka, 'Witch and Sorcerer-Hunts', 128–129 • APBydgoszcz, AmNowe sig. 1 ff. 334–335
Piątkowa 1653	Wiślicz, *Regesty spraw*, item 24 • APRzeszów, Akta gminny Błażowej sig. 98 f. 128
Kleczew 1654	Hajdrych, 'Wizja świata', 179 • BPTPN, ms. 859 ff. 283–284v
Zbąszyń 1654a	Adamczyk, 'Zbąszyń', 85–86
Zbąszyń 1654b	Adamczyk, 'Zbąszyń', 85
Biecz 1655	Mikołajczyk, 'Jak obronić oskarżona', 389–410 • ANKAkta dominialne 6, ff. 216–247

Miechów 1656	Pilaszek, *Procesy o czary*, 455 • BJ sig. 86 f. 67v.
Zabłotów 1656	Semkowicz, 'Dwa przyczynki', 386–390 • KgHalicz sig. 147, ff. 1963–1967
Sanok 1657	Klint, 'Miłość, mężobójstwo i praktyki magiczne', 183–197 • TsDIA (Lviv), fond 15, op. 1, no. 169, ff. 1498–1513
Bydgoszcz 1658	Malewski, 'Procesy o czarnoksięstwo', 80–81 • APBydgoszcz, AmBydgoszcz sig. D I, f. 6, f. 141
Nowy Wiśnicz 1659	Uruszczak, *Acta Maleficorum*, 212–240 • ANK AmWiśnicz, ADT sig. LN XXIII, ff. 204–42
Ekonomia Samborska 1660a	Wiślicz, *Regesty spraw*, item 25 • NBLDU VR no. 514iii, f. 49
Ekonomia Samborska 1660b	Dysa, *Istoriya z Vid'mamy*, 204; Wiślicz, *Regesty spraw*, item 26 • NBLDU VR no. 514iii, f. 65v
Ekonomia Samborska 1660c	Wiślicz, *Regesty spraw*, item 27 • NBLDU VR no. 514iii, f. 68
Ekonomia Samborska 1660d	Wiślicz, *Regesty spraw*, item 28 • NBLDU VR no. 514iii, f. 81v
Ekonomia Samborska 1660e	Wiślicz, *Regesty spraw*, item 30 • NBLDU VR no. 514iii, f. 94
Ekonomia Samborska 1660f	Wiślicz, *Regesty spraw*, item 29 • NBLDU VR no. 514iii, f. 82
Lublin 1660	Zakrzewska-Dubasowa, *Procesy o czary w Lublinie*, 26–54; Kowalska-Cichy, 'Nieopublikowane fragmenty procesu', 27–31 • APLublin, AmLublin sig. 109, ff. 273v, 274v, 275v, 277, 278v–281, 282v, 284–288, 290–292v
Opalenica 1660a	Wojcieszak, *Opalenickie procesy*
Opalenica 1660b	Wojcieszak, *Opalenickie procesy*
Poznań 1660	Pilaszek, *Procesy o czary*, 60–61, 320–21, 366–73 • APPoznań, AMPoznań sig. I/642 ff. 84, 86, 96–101, 157–8
Lublin 1661	Zakrzewska-Dubasowa, *Procesy o czary w Lublinie*, 26–54; Kowalska-Cichy 'Nieopublikowane fragmenty procesu', 27–31 • APLublin, AmLublin sig. 169, ff. 117v, 120–121, 122v–127, 264v–268v, 277v–280, 337–229v, 342, 345v–346v
Kleczew 1662a	Hajdrych, 'Wizja świata', 132 • BPTPN, ms. 859 ff. 27–29, 259–260v
Kleczew 1662b	Hajdrych, 'Wizja świata', 132, 178 • BPTPN, ms. 859 ff. 263–264v
Łobżenica 1662	Wijaczka, 'Proces o czary we wsi Młotkowo', 170 • APBydgoszcz, AmŁobżenica sig. 11, ff. 13v–15v
Nowy Wiśnicz 1662	Uruszczak, *Acta Maleficorum*, 241–260
Ekonomia Samborska 1664a	Dysa, *Istoriya z Vid'mamy*, 129; Wiślicz, *Regesty spraw*, item 31 • NBLDU VR no. 514iii, f. 235
Ekonomia Samborska 1664b	Wiślicz, *Regesty spraw*, item 32 • NBLDU VR no. 514iii, f. 240v
Lublin 1664	Zakrzewska-Dubasowa, *Procesy o czary w Lublinie*, 54–57 • APLublin, AmLublin sig. 140 ff. 206–208

(Continued)

(*Continued*)

Trial	Published Source • Archival Source
Poznań 1664	Pilaszek, *Procesy o czary*, 289–90 • APPoznań, AmPoznań sig. I/643 ff. 44–45
Wizna 1664	Jarnutowski, 'Miasto Wizna', 357–358 • AdŁomża AmŁomży sig. 16, f. 144
Chęciny 1665a	Wijaczka, 'Procesy o czary w regionie świętokrzyskiego', 39–40 • BJ ms. 5476, f. 41
Chęciny 1665b	Wijaczka, 'Procesy o czary w regionie świętokrzyskiego', 40–45 • BJ ms. 5476, ff. 41v–43
Chęciny 1665c	Wijaczka, 'Procesy o czary w regionie świętokrzyskiego', 45–50 • BJ ms. 5476, ff. 43–44v
Chęciny 1665d	Wijaczka, 'Procesy o czary w regionie świętokrzyskiego', 50–55 • BJ ms. 5476, ff. 45–46v
Chełmno 1665	Biskup, *Ziemia chełmińska*, 149–151 • APToruń sig. 322, # 506
Praszka 1665	Baranowski, 'Wielki proces', • AGAD, AmPraszka sig. 2, ff. 76–83
Chęciny 1666	Wijaczka, 'Procesy o czary w regionie świętokrzyskiego', 56–58 • BJ ms. 5476, ff. 46–56v
Grudziądz 1666	Wijaczka, 'Procesy o czary przed sądem miejskim', 97–98
Poznań 1666	Pilaszek, *Procesy o czary*, 289, 356, 430 • APPoznań, AmPoznań sig. I/643 ff. 61–74
Ekonomia Samborska 1667	Wiślicz, *Regesty spraw*, item 33 • NBLDU VR no. 515iii, f. 26
Kleczew 1668	Hajdrych, 'Wizja świata', 132, 160, 178, 179 • BPTPN, ms. 859 ff. 36–39v
Klimkówka 1668	Łysiak, *Księga sądowa kresu klimkowskiego*, items 691–692; Wiślicz, *Regesty spraw*, items 34–35
Łęczyca 1668	Rafacz, 'Sprawy karne', 562, 564 • ArchGdańsk sig. 717, f. 147
Poznań 1669	Pilaszek, *Procesy o czary*, 54, 288, 289, 404, 409, 420 • APPoznań, AMPoznań sig. I/643 ff. 137, 148, 153–65
Braniewo 1670	Pilaszek, *Procesy o czary*, 420, 425–6 • BPAU/PANK sig. 2796 v. 3 f. 125
Bydgoszcz 1670	Malewski, 'Procesy o czarnoksięstwo', 80–81
Kleczew 1670a	Hajdrych, 'Wizja świata', 133, 186 • BPTPN, ms. 859 ff. 270v–272v
Kleczew 1670b	Pilaszek, *Procesy o czary*, 349; Hajdrych, 'Wizja świata', 106, 133, 155, 179, 186, 203 • BPTPN, ms. 859 ff. 202r–204v
Nowy Sącz 1670	Sygański, 'Wyroki Ławicy Nowosandeckiej', 457–458; Uruszczak, 'Proces czarownicy', 196–203 • ANK, Acta maleficorum miasta Nowego Sącza sig. 116, ff. 399–419
Jędrzejów 1671	Karwowski, 'Gniezno', 198
Nowe 1671	Wijaczka, 'Witch and Sorcerer-Hunts', 105, 123–124, 127 • APBydgoszcz, AmNowe sig. 1 ff. 336–338, 344, 346, 349
Kleczew 1672	Hajdrych, 'Wizja świata', 133, 178, 198, 203 • BPTPN, ms. 859 ff. 184r–187v

Krzywin 1672	Rafacz, 'Sprawy karne', 562
Lwów 1672	Dysa, *Istoriya z Vid'mamy*, 44 • TsDIA (Lviv), fond 52, op. 2, no. 311, ff. 408–433
Kłodawa 1673	Rafacz, 'Sprawy karne', 562, 564; Woźniakowa, *Sąd Asesorski*, 339–340 • AGAD, ARN sig. 52 f. 261–6; ASA no. 399 ff. 261–266
Lwów 1673	Dysa, *Istoriya z Vid'mamy*, 199 • TsDIA (Lviv), fond 52, op. 2, no. 311, f. 496
Konin 1674	Pilaszek, *Procesy o czary*, 259–260 • APPoznań, KgKonin sig. 66 f. 255
Słomniki 1674a	Siarkowski, *Materiały do etnografii*, 84–85
Słomniki 1674b	Siarkowski, *Materiały do etnografii*, 85–87
Braniewo 1675	Pilaszek, *Procesy o czary*, 450 • BPAU/PANK sig. 2796 v. 3 f. 129
Fordon 1675	Pilaszek, *Procesy o czary*, 209, 425 • APBydgoszcz, AmFordon sg. 5 ff. 1ff.
Lipno 1675	Lasocki, 'Szlachta płońska', 41
Przecław 1675	Krzyczyński 1932, 'Święcenie wody i soli', 109–10
Sandomierz 1675	Wijaczka, 'Procesy o czary w regionie świętokrzyskiego', 55–56 • APKielce AmSandomierz sig. 11 ff. 77v–78, 88
Łobżenica 1676	Wijaczka, 'Men standing trial', 73–74 • APBydgoszcz, AmŁobżenica sig. 11, f. 89v
Warta 1676	Baranowski and Lewandowski, *Nietolerancja i zabobon*, 193–194 • AGAD, AmWarta sig. 46 ff. 529–533
Klimkówka 1677a	Łysiak, *Księga sądowa kresu klimkowskiego*, item 775; Wiślicz, *Regesty spraw*, item 37
Klimkówka 1677b	Wiślicz, *Regesty spraw*, item 38
Fordon 1678	Pilaszek, *Procesy o czary*, 361 • APBydgoszcz, AmFordon sg. 5 f. 11
Kleczew 1678a	Hajdrych, 'Wizja świata', 198 • BPTPN, ms. 859 f. 188r
Kleczew 1678b	Hajdrych, 'Wizja świata', 178 • BPTPN, ms. 859 ff. 172r–175v
Klimkówka 1678	Łysiak, *Księga sądowa kresu klimkowskiego*, item 797; Wiślicz, *Regesty spraw*, item 39
Kowalewo 1678a	Wijaczka, 'Procesy o czary przed sądem sołtysim', 114–115 • APToruń AmToruń sig. 8911 f. 17–18
Kowalewo 1678b	Wijaczka, 'Procesy o czary przed sądem sołtysim', 108–114 • APToruń AmToruń sig. 8911 f. 9–17
Lublin 1678	Zakrzewska-Dubasowa, *Procesy o czary w Lublinie*, 57–60 • APLublin, AmLublin sig. 144 ff. 69–73
Muszyna 1678	Piekosiński 1889, 357–361, # 18; Wiślicz, *Regesty spraw*, item 40
Warta 1678a	Baranowski and Lewandowski, *Nietolerancja i zabobon*, 181–183 • AGAD, AmWarta sig. 46 ff. 441–442
Warta 1678b	Baranowski and Lewandowski, *Nietolerancja i zabobon*, 193–194; Adamczewska, 'Magiczna broń', 7–8 • AGAD, AmWarta sig. 46 ff. 134–135v
Bochnia 1679	Kaczmarczyk, 'Opisy', 45–53
Fordon 1679	Pilaszek, *Procesy o czary*, 345, 420 • APBydgoszcz, AmFordon sg. 5 ff. 16–23

(Continued)

(*Continued*)

Trial	Published Source • Archival Source
Kleczew 1679	Hajdrych, 'Wizja świata', 178 • BPTPN, ms. 859 ff. 189r–194v
Łobżenica 1679	Wijaczka, 'Men standing trial', 79–80 • APBydgoszcz, AmŁobżenica sig. 11, ff. 137–138v
Warta 1679a	Baranowski and Lewandowski, *Nietolerancja i zabobon*, 183–185; Adamczewska, 'Magiczna broń', 8–9 • AGAD, AmWarta sig. 46 ff. 441, 456–457
Warta 1679b	Baranowski and Lewandowski, *Nietolerancja i zabobon*, 185–189 • AGAD, AmWarta sig. 46 ff. 437–439
Fordon 1680	Pilaszek, *Procesy o czary*, 345 • APBydgoszcz, AmFordon sg. 5 ff. 54–59
Kalisz 1680	Pilaszek, *Procesy o czary*, 71–2, 261 • APPoznań, KgKalisz sig. 259 ff. 113–113v
Kleczew 1680a	Wiślicz, 'Township of Kleczew', 86–87; Hajdrych, 'Wizja świata', s. 198, 203 • BPTPN, rkps 859, f. 194v–199
Kleczew 1680b	Hajdrych, 'Wizja świata', 198 • BPTPN, ms. 859, f. 212r–214r
Kleczew 1680c	Hajdrych, 'Wizja świata', 151–152 • BPTPN, ms. 859, f. 176r–177r
Łobżenica 1680	Wijaczka, 'Men standing trial', 82–83 • APBydgoszcz, AmŁobżenica sig. 11, ff. 403–403v
Lublin 1681	Zakrzewska-Dubasowa, *Procesy o czary w Lublinie*, 60–66 • APLublin, AmLublin sig. 144 ff. 130–138
Zbąszyń 1681	Adamczyk, 'Zbąszyń', 86
Czukiew 1682	Wiślicz, *Regesty spraw*, item 45 • TsDIA (Lviv), fond 142, op. 1 sig. 4, ff. 30, 46
Fordon 1682	Pilaszek, *Procesy o czary*, 347 • APBydgoszcz, AmFordon sg. 5 ff. 50–54
Kleczew 1682	BPTPN, ms. 859, f. 34r–35v
Klimkówka 1682	Łysiak, *Księga sądowa kresu klimkowskiego*, items 849–850; Wiślicz, *Regesty spraw*, items 43–44
Fordon 1683	Pilaszek, *Procesy o czary*, 431 • APBydgoszcz, AmFordon sg. 5 f. 77
Klimkówka 1683	Łysiak, *Księga sądowa kresu klimkowskiego*, item 890; Wiślicz, *Regesty spraw*, item 46
Braniewo 1684	Pilaszek, *Procesy o czary*, 458 • BPAU/PANK sig. 2796 v. 3 f. 129
Chełmno 1684	Biskup, *Ziemia chełmińska*, 149–151 • APToruń sig. 322, # 522
Łobżenica 1684	Wijaczka, '*Próba zimnej wody*', 103 • APBydgoszcz, AmŁobżenica sig. 11, f. 304v
Tuliszków 1684a	Wawrzeniecki, 'Przyczynek', 173
Tuliszków 1684b	Wawrzeniecki, 'Przyczynek', 173
Dobczyce 1685	Udziela, *Świat nadzmysłowy*, 4
Kleczew 1685	BPTPN, ms. 859, f. 207r–210r
Podzamcze Lubelskie 1685	Kowalska-Cichy, *Magia i procesy o czary*, 100 • APLublin, Akta jurydyki Podzamcze sig. 3, f. 801v
Warta 1685	Baranowski and Lewandowski, *Nietolerancja i zabobon*, 189–190 • AGAD, AmWarta sig. 46 ff. 291–292

Kazimierz Biskupi 1686 — Wiślicz, 'Township of Kleczew', 67 • AGAD, KmKazimierz sig. 4 f. 107

Łobżenica 1686 — Wijaczka, 'Proces o czary we wsi Osowo' • APBydgoszcz, AmŁobżenica sig. 11, ff. 458–462v

Czukiew 1687 — Wiślicz, *Regesty spraw*, item 48 • TsDIA (Lviv), fond 142, op. 1 sig. 4, ff. 225–228

Dobczyce 1687 — Mikołajczyk, 'Przestępstwa przeciwko religii', 231 • PANKraków sig. 594, ff. 1–3v

Warta 1687 — Baranowski and Lewandowski, *Nietolerancja i zabobon*, 190–191 • AGAD, AmWarta sig. 46 f. 290

Kleczew 1688 — Hajdrych, 'Wizja świata', 48–50, 135–138 • BPTPN, ms. 859, ff. 146–151

Nowy Wiśnicz 1688a — Kaczmarczyk, 'Proces o czarostwo', 303–309 • ANK AmWiśnicz sig. IT IT2059, ff. 10–17

Nowy Wiśnicz 1688b — Kaczmarczyk, 'Proces o czarostwo', 309–312

Nowy Wiśnicz 1688c — Kaczmarczyk, 'Proces o czarostwo', 312–316

Nowy Wiśnicz 1688d — Kaczmarczyk, 'Proces o czarostwo', 316

Dobczyce 1689 — Udziela, *Świat nadzmysłowy*, 5; Mikołajczyk, 'O pławieniu czarownic', 121–129 • PANKraków sig. 594, ff. 105v–107v

Gniezno 1689a — Wijaczka, 'Jak się pozbyć matki', 539–555 • APPoznań, AmGniezno sig. I/35, ff. 1040–1056; sig. I/70, ff. 371–377, 384–394

Gniezno 1689b — Wijaczka, 'Jak się pozbyć matki', 553 • APPoznań, AmGniezno sig. I/70 415, 417, 430

Kleczew 1689a — Wiślicz, 'Township of Kleczew', 86; Hajdrych, 'Wizja świata', 136, 142 • BPTPN, ms. 859 ff. 99–101v

Kleczew 1689b — Wiślicz, 'Township of Kleczew', 86; Hajdrych, 'Wizja świata', 137, 154, 187, 243–247 • BPTPN, ms. 859 ff. 132–135

Kleczew 1689c — Wiślicz, 'Township of Kleczew', 86; Hajdrych, 'Wizja świata', s. 36, 69 • BPTPN, rkps 859, f. 97–102

Nowe 1689 — Wijaczka, 'Witch and Sorcerer-Hunts', 105, 107–109, 111, 117, 121, 123–4 • APBydgoszcz, AmNowe sig. 130 ff. 52, 106; sig. 131 ff. 5–6, 8, 12, 13, 48

Nowy Wiśnicz 1689a — Kaczmarczyk, 'Proces o czarostwo', 316–321

Nowy Wiśnicz 1689b — Kaczmarczyk, 'Proces o czarostwo', 321–322

Wągrowiec 1689 — Moeglich, 'Procesy o czary', 51–2 • APPoznań, AMWągrowiec sig. I/25, ff. 1–3, 12–14

Albigowa 1690 — Wiślicz, *Regesty spraw*, item 49 • APPrzemyśl, Akta wsi Albigowy sig. 1, f. 34–35

Czukiew 1690 — Wiślicz, *Regesty spraw*, item 50 • TsDIA (Lviv), fond 142, op. 1 sig. 4, ff. 296–297

Kleczew 1690a — Hajdrych, 'Wizja świata', s. 106, 137, 198, 208 • BPTPN, rkps 859, f. 106–110v

Kleczew 1690b — Hajdrych, 'Wizja świata', s. 137–138 • BPTPN, rkps 859, f. 121–122v

(*Continued*)

(*Continued*)

Trial	Published Source • Archival Source
Łobżenica 1690a	Wijaczka, 'Men standing trial', 74–75 • APBydgoszcz, AmŁobżenica sig. 11, ff. 521–532v
Łobżenica 1690b	Wijaczka, 'Proces o czary we wsi Młotkowo', 162; 'Men standing trial', 75–77 • APBydgoszcz, AmŁobżenica sig. 11, ff. 532v–534v
Lublin 1690	Kowalska-Cichy, *Magia i procesy o czary*, 102–103 • APLublin, KgL (Relationes) sig. 133, ff. 539–540
Nowe 1690	Wijaczka, 'Witch and Sorcerer-Hunts', 109, 111, 114, 117, 121, 130–131 • APBydgoszcz, AmNowe sig. 131 ff. 17, 20–21, 23–28
Nowy Koźmin 1690	S.X., 'Kilka słów'; Rosenblatt, *Czarownica powołana*, 20; Wijaczka, 'Oskarżenia i procesy', 202–207
Wągrowiec 1690	Moeglich, 'Procesy o czary', 52 • APPoznań, AMWągrowiec sig. I/25, ff. 3–4
Wielki Koźmin 1690	Łukaszewicz, *Krótki historyczno-statystyczny opis*, i., 76; Kolberg, *Dzieła wszystkie*, xv. 15, 246; Wijaczka, 'Oskarżenia i procesy', 208–209
Wyszogród 1690	Olszewski, 'Prześladowanie czarów', 493–494, 497–498
Brześć Kujawski 1691	Olszewski, 'Prześladowanie czarów', 491–493
Chojnice 1691	Pilaszek, *Procesy o czary*, 172, 356–7, 426 • APBydgoszcz, AmChojnice sig. 136 ff.79–83
Kleczew 1691a	Wiślicz, 'Township of Kleczew', 86; Hajdrych, 'Wizja świata', 153–154 • BPTPN, ms. 859 ff. 154–155
Kleczew 1691b	Hajdrych, 'Wizja świata', 138–9, 208, 210 • BPTPN, ms. 859 ff. 138–145v
Łobżenica 1691	Wijaczka, 'Men standing trial', 82–83
Poznań 1691	Pilaszek, *Procesy o czary*, 26–61 • APPoznań, KgPoznań sig. 759 ff. 133–134v
Warta 1691	Baranowski and Lewandowski, *Nietolerancja i zabobon*, 191–193 • AGAD, AmWarta sig. 46 ff. 136–138
Fordon 1692	Pilaszek, *Procesy o czary*, 139, 345, 420, 423 • APBydgoszcz, AmFordon sg. 5 ff. 107–118, 124
Łobżenica 1692	Wijaczka, 'Proces o czary we wsi Młotkowo', 163–170; Wijaczka, '*Próba zimnej wody*', 83–84 • APBydgoszcz, AmŁobżenica sig. 11, ff. 570–578, 584–588v
Wielki Koźmin 1692	Gagacki, 'Widok miasta Koźmina', 114–118; Kolberg, *Dzieła wszystkie*, xv. 15, 243–244; Wijaczka, 'Oskarżenia i procesy', 207–208
Czukiew 1693	Dysa, *Istoriya z Vid'mamy*, 202; Wiślicz, *Regesty spraw*, item 52 • TsDIA (Lviv), fond 142, op. 1, no. 5, ff. 60–61, 68v
Kleczew 1693	Hajdrych, 'Wizja świata', 178, 199 • BPTPN, ms. 859 ff. 112–114v
Uniejów 1693	Baranowski, *W kręgu upiorów*, 27
Wągrowiec 1693	Moeglich, 'Procesy o czary', 53–4 • APPoznań, AmWągrowiec sig. I/25, ff. 6–12
Wyszogród 1693	Olszewski, 'Prześladowanie czarów', 500

Fordon 1694	Pilaszek, *Procesy o czary*, 420 • APBydgoszcz, AmFordon sg. 5 ff. 185
Nowy Dwór 1694	AP Gdańsk sig. 544 f. 15
Piątkowa 1694	Półćwiartek, *Wybór źródeł*, 231, # 37; Wiślicz, *Regesty spraw*, item 53 • APRzeszów, Akta gmimny Błażowej sig. 98 ff. 141–142
Kleczew ca. 1695	Pilaszek, *Procesy o czary*, 447; Hajdrych, 'Wizja świata', 162 • BPTPN sig. 895 ff. 162v
Fordon 1695	Pilaszek, *Procesy o czary*, 428, 430 • APBydgoszcz, AmFordon sg. 5 f. 104
Łobżenica 1695	Wijaczka, 'Men standing trial', 77–78 • APBydgoszcz, AmŁobżenica sig. 11 ff. 620–620v
Słajszewo 1695	Guldon, 'Proces czarownicy', 150–161 • Biblioteka Miejska w Bydgoszczy sig. III/158
Wągrowiec 1695a	Moeglich, 'Procesy o czary', 54–5 • APPoznań, AmWągrowiec sig. I/25, f. 15
Wągrowiec 1695b	Moeglich, 'Procesy o czary', 55–6 • APPoznań, AmWągrowiec sig. I/25, f. 17
Czukiew 1696	Dysa, *Istoriya z Vid'mamy*, 125; Wiślicz, *Regesty spraw*, item 55 • TsDIA (Lviv), fond 142, op. 1, no. 5, ff. 173–174v
Wągrowiec 1696	Moeglich, 'Procesy o czary', 57 • APPoznań, AmWągrowiec sig. I/25, f. 18
Fordon 1697	Pilaszek, *Procesy o czary*, 420 • APBydgoszcz, AmFordon sg. 5 ff. 158
Klimkówka 1697	Łysiak, *Księga sądowa kresu klimkowskiego*, item 1092; Wiślicz, *Regesty spraw*, item 56
Lublin 1697	Kowalska-Cichy, *Magia i procesy o czary*, 104–105 • AAL KGL sig. Rep 60 A 43, ff. 342–343
Rogi 1697	Wiślicz, *Regesty spraw*, item 57 • AGAD, Księgi wiejskie Rogi f. 446
Szczerców 1697	Adamczewska, 'Magiczna broń', 10–11 • AGAD, AmSzczerców sig. 2, f. 198
Wyszogród 1697	Olszewski, 'Prześladowanie czarów', 499
Fordon 1698	Pilaszek, *Procesy o czary*, 434 • APBydgoszcz, AmFordon sg. 5 ff. 220
Jadowniki 1698a	Ulanowski, *Acta iudiciorum*, item 4929; Wiślicz, *Regesty spraw*, item 59
Jadowniki 1698b	Ulanowski, *Acta iudiciorum*, items 4930–4939; Wiślicz, *Regesty spraw*, item 59
Kleczew 1698	Wiślicz, 'Township of Kleczew', 86–87; Hajdrych, 'Wizja świata', 162 • BPTPN, ms. 859 ff. 163v–165v
Krowodrza 1698	Ulanowski, *Acta iudiciorum*, items 4364, 4369, 4370; Uruszczak 2012; Wiślicz, *Regesty spraw*, item 60
Lublin 1698	Zakrzewska-Dubasowa, *Procesy o czary w Lublinie*, 66–72 • APLublin, AmLublin sig. 144 ff. 379–381, 391–394
Nowe 1698	Wijaczka, 'Witch and Sorcerer-Hunts', 111–112, 114–115, 117, 121; '*Próba zimnej wody*', 97 • APBydgoszcz, AmNowe sig. 131 f. 8, 31–33
Tomaszów Lubelski 1698	Riabinin, *Jeszcze o czarach*, 6 • APLublin, AmTomaszów sig. D, ff. 107v–108
Wyszogród 1698	Olszewski, 'Prześladowanie czarów', 501

(*Continued*)

(*Continued*)

Trial	Published Source • Archival Source
Żywiec 1698	Komoniecki, *Chronografia*, 267; Wijaczka, '*Próba zimnej wody*', 84
Czukiew 1699	Dysa, *Istoriya z Vid'mamy*, 133 • TsDIA (Lviv), fond 142, op. 1, no. 5, f. 208
Fordon 1699	Pilaszek, *Procesy o czary*, 350 • APBydgoszcz, AmFordon sg. 5 ff. 233–8
Kleczew 1699	Hajdrych, 'Wizja świata', 151 • BPTPN, ms. 859 ff. 63–64
Nowe 1699	Wijaczka, 'Witch and Sorcerer-Hunts', 112, 115, 117–118, 121; Wijaczka, '*Próba zimnej wody*', 91 • APBydgoszcz, AmNowe sig. 131 f. 43–46
Płońsk 1699a	Lasocki, 'Szlachta płońska', 6–7 • AGAD, AmPłońsk sig. 3, ff. 45v–46
Płońsk 1699b	Lasocki, 'Szlachta płońska', 7 • AGAD, AmPłońsk sig. 3, ff. 47v–48
Płońsk 1699c	Lasocki, 'Szlachta płońska', 4–5 • AGAD, AmPłońsk sig. 3, ff. 40–41
Pyzdry 1699	Tripplin, *Tajemnice społeczeństwa*, iii., 267–274; Rosenblatt, *Czarownica powołana*, 14–19 • APPoznań, AmPyzdry sig. 1757 ff. 1–2
Skarszewy 1699a	Wijaczka, 'Procesy o czary przed sądami miejskim i wojewodzińskim' 85–86 • APGdańsk, AmSkarszewy sig. 520/7 ff. 2–4
Skarszewy 1699b	Wijaczka, 'Procesy o czary przed sądami miejskim i wojewodzińskim' 88–90 • APGdańsk, AmSkarszewy sig. 520/7, ff. 9v–11
Skarszewy 1699c	Wijaczka, 'Procesy o czary przed sądami miejskim i wojewodzińskim' 86–88 • APGdańsk, AmSkarszewy sig. 520/7, ff. 4v–9
Fordon 1700	Koranyi, 'Ze studjów nad wierzeniami', 26; Pilaszek, *Procesy o czary*, 345 • APBydgoszcz, AmFordon sg. 5 ff. 246–50
Kamieniec Podolski 1700	Antonovich, *Koldovstvo*, item 1; Dysa, *Istoriya z Vid'mamy*, 55
Kleczew 1700	Wiślicz, 'Township of Kleczew', 90 • BPTPN, ms. 859, ff. 65–66
Lublin 1700	Zakrzewska-Dubasowa, *Procesy o czary w Lublinie*, 72–74 • APLublin, AmLublin sig. 144 ff. 483–487
Łuck 1700	Antonovich, *Koldovstvo*, item 30; Pilaszek, *Procesy o czary*, 362
Nieszawa 1700	Pilaszek, *Procesy o czary*, 352–3 • AGAD, AmNieszawa sig. 18 ff. 96v–97v; sig. 12 ff. 88v–89
Płońsk 1700	Lasocki, 'Szlachta płońska', 8 • AGAD, AmPłońsk sig. 3, ff. 55v–56
Skarszewy 1700a	Wijaczka, 'Procesy o czary przed sądami miejskim i wojewodzińskim' 90–92 • APGdańsk, AmSkarszewy sig. 520/7, ff. 19v–21v
Skarszewy 1700b	Wijaczka, 'Procesy o czary przed sądami miejskim i wojewodzińskim' 92–93 • APGdańsk, AmSkarszewy sig. 520/7, ff. 23v–28v
Słomniki 1700	Siarkowski, *Materiały do etnografii*, 87–90
Wyszogród 1700a	Olszewski, 'Prześladowanie czarów', 500
Wyszogród 1700b	Olszewski, 'Prześladowanie czarów', 493
Fordon 1701	Pilaszek, *Procesy o czary*, 350 • APBydgoszcz, AmFordon sg. 5 ff. 291–7
Kowalewo 1701	Wijaczka, 'Procesy o czary przed sądem sołtysim', 115–116 • APToruń AmKowalewo sig. 8 ff. 3–4
Nowe 1701a	Wijaczka, 'Witch and Sorcerer-Hunts', 108 • APBydgoszcz, AmNowe sig. 130 ff: 265–266

Nowe 1701b	Wijaczka, 'Witch and Sorcerer-Hunts', 112; '*Próba zimnej wody*', 91 • APBydgoszcz, AmNowe sig. 130 ff. 266–267; sig. 131 f. 58
Nowe 1701c	Wijaczka, 'Witch and Sorcerer-Hunts', 109 • APBydgoszcz, AmNowe sig. 13o f. 269, 272
Nowe 1701d	Wijaczka, 'Witch and Sorcerer-Hunts', 127–128 • APBydgoszcz, AmNowe sig. 130 ff. 49–50
Nowe 1701e	Wijaczka, 'Witch and Sorcerer-Hunts', 112, 115, 118; '*Próba zimnej wody*', 95 • APBydgoszcz, AmNowe sig. 131, ff. 67–67
Nowe 1701f	Wijaczka, 'Witch and Sorcerer-Hunts', 109–110 • APBydgoszcz, AmNowe sig. 13o f. 51
Płońsk 1701a	Lasocki, 'Szlachta płońska', 8 • AGAD, AmPłońsk sig. 3, ff. 67–67v
Płońsk 1701b	Lasocki, 'Szlachta płońska', 18–19 • AGAD, AmPłońsk sig. 3, ff. 67–67v
Wyszogród 1701	Olszewski, 'Prześladowanie czarów', 498
Klimkówka 1702a	Łysiak, *Księga sądowa kresu klimkowskiego*, item 1126
Klimkówka 1702b	Łysiak, *Księga sądowa kresu klimkowskiego*, item 1138
Klimkówka 1702c	Łysiak, *Księga sądowa kresu klimkowskiego*, item 1156
Łęczyca 1702	Rafacz, 'Sprawy karne', 568 • ArchGdańsk sig. 717, f. 343
Płońsk 1702	Lasocki, 'Szlachta płońska', 7–8 • AGAD, AmPłońsk sig. 3, ff. 85–87
Żerków 1702	Hajdrych, 'Procesy o czary' • APPoznań, AmŻerków sig. I/3 f. 15
Nowy Wiśnicz 1703	Kaczmarczyk, 'Przyczynki', 330–331
Rzeszów 1703	Dydek, 'Czary w procesie inkwizycyjnym', 386 • APRzeszów, ms. 166 ff. 1001–1008
Szczerców 1703	Adamczewska, 'Magiczna broń', 11 • AGAD, AmSzczerców sig. 2, ff. 267–268
Wyszogród 1703	Olszewski, 'Prześladowanie czarów', 497
Nowe 1704	Wijaczka, 'Witch and Sorcerer-Hunts', 112–113, 118, 121, 122 • APBydgoszcz, AmNowe sig. 131, f. 70–72
Nowe 1704a	Wijaczka, 'Witch and Sorcerer-Hunts', 113 • APBydgoszcz, AmNowe sig. 131 f. 73
Kamieniec Podolski 1705	Dysa, *Istoriya z Vid'mamy*, 225 • TsDIA (Kyiv), fond 39, op. 1, no. 50, f. 267v
Wyszogród 1705	Olszewski, 'Prześladowanie czarów', 506–509
Kowel 1706	Dysa, *Istoriya z Vid'mamy*, 133 • TsDIA (Kyiv), fond 35, op. 1, no. 13, ff. 102–103v
Nowe 1706	Wijaczka, 'Witch and Sorcerer-Hunts', 113, 122, 128 • APBydgoszcz, AmNowe sig. 131, f. 77–78
Płońsk 1706	Lasocki, 'Szlachta płońska', 20–21 • AGAD, AmPłońsk sig. 3, ff. 144–145v
Szczekociny 1706	Siarkowski, *Materiały do etnografii*, 87–92
Grodzisk Wielkopolski 1707a	Mikołajczyk, 'Przestępstwa przeciwko religii', 232 • AGAD, BBaw. sig. 252, ff. 8–8v
Grodzisk Wielkopolski 1707b	Mikołajczyk, 'Przestępstwa przeciwko religii', 232 • AGAD, BBaw. sig. 252, ff. 10v–12v

(*Continued*)

(*Continued*)

Trial	Published Source • Archival Source
Płońsk 1708a	Lasocki, 'Szlachta płońska', 8 • AGAD, AmPłońsk sig. 3, f. 170v
Płońsk 1708b	Lasocki, 'Szlachta płońska', 19 • AGAD, AmPłońsk sig. 3, f. 169
Płońsk 1708c	Lasocki, 'Szlachta płońska', 19 • AGAD, AmPłońsk sig. 3, ff. 173, 183
Poznań 1708	Pilaszek, *Procesy o czary*, 322, 395, 450 • APPoznań, AmPoznań sig. I/647 ff. 167–168v
Wągrowiec 1708	Moeglich, 'Procesy o czary', 58–9 • APPoznań, AmWągrowiec sig. I/25, ff. 39–40
Zbąszyń 1708	Koranyi, 'Ze studjów nad wierzeniami', 29
Fordon 1709	Pilaszek, *Procesy o czary*, 434 • APBydgoszcz, AmFordon sg. 5 f. 314
Nowe 1709a	Wijaczka, 'Witch and Sorcerer-Hunts', 115, 118–119, 121 • APBydgoszcz, AmNowe sig. 130 ff. 85–87
Nowe 1709b	Wijaczka, 'Witch and Sorcerer-Hunts', 109, 113, 118, 121, 129 • APBydgoszcz, AmNowe sig. 130, ff. 81–83
Płońsk 1709a	Lasocki, 'Szlachta płońska', 21 • AGAD, AmPłońsk sig. 3, f. 170v
Płońsk 1709b	Lasocki, 'Szlachta płońska', 21
Płońsk 1709c	Lasocki, 'Szlachta płońska', 21 • AGAD, AmPłońsk sig. 3, ff. 177v–178
Grodzisk Wielkopolski 1710a	Mikołajczyk, 'Przestępstwa przeciwko religii', 232 • AGAD, BBaw. sig. 252, ff. 15–21
Grodzisk Wielkopolski 1710b	Mikołajczyk, 'Przestępstwa przeciwko religii', 232 • AGAD, BBaw. sig. 252, ff. 25–26v
Kamieniec Podolski 1710	Antonovich, *Koldovstvo*, item 11
Kowel 1710	Dysa, *Istoriya z Vid'mamy*, 143 • TsDIA (Kyiv), fond 1237, op. 1, no. 8, ff. 86–86v
Płońsk 1710	Lasocki, 'Szlachta płońska', 20 • AGAD, AmPłońsk sig. 3, f. 215
Rzeszów 1710	Dydek, 'Czary w procesie inkwizycyjnym', 386
Grodzisk Wielkopolski 1712	Mikołajczyk, 'Przestępstwa przeciwko religii', 232 • AGAD, BBaw. sig. 252, f. 30
Nowe 1712a	Wijaczka, 'Witch and Sorcerer-Hunts', 115, 119; '*Próba zimnej wody*', 94 • APBydgoszcz, AmNowe sig. 130, ff. 89, 91, 97
Nowe 1712b	Jacek Wijaczka, personal communication.
Płońsk 1712	Lasocki, 'Szlachta płońska', 20 • AGAD, AmPłońsk sig. 3, ff. 221–224
Toruń 1712	Wijaczka, 'Postępowanie sądowe' • APToruń AmToruń, Catalog II sig. I 3703, ff. 57–120
Wągrowiec 1712	Moeglich, 'Procesy o czary', 59 • APPoznań, AmWągrowiec sig. I/25, f. 40
Kraków 1713	Kracik and Rożek, *Hultaje*, 112 • ANK AmKraków sig. 872 ff. 250–251
Grodzisk Wielkopolski 1714	Mikołajczyk, 'Przestępstwa przeciwko religii', 232 • AGAD, BBaw. sig. 252, ff. 41–42v
Nowe 1714	Wijaczka, 'Witch and Sorcerer-Hunts', 113–115, 119, 121, 132 • APBydgoszcz, AmNowe sig. 131, ff. 105, 107

Brześć Kujawski 1715	Olszewski, 'Prześladowanie czarów', 500
Kraków 1715	Kracik and Rożek, *Hultaje*, 112–113
Satanów 1715	Dysa, *Istoriya z Vid'mamy*, 204 • TsDIA (Kyiv), fond 50, op. 1, no. 1, ff. 128–129
Kamieniec Podolski 1716	Antonovich, *Koldovstvo*, item 22; Dysa, *Istoriya z Vid'mamy*, 45
Kiszkowo 1716	Aleksandrowicz, 'Z badań nad dziejami', 10; Wijaczka, 'Procesy o czary w Polsce', 34
Szczerców 1716	Baranowski and Lewandowski, *Nietolerancja i zabobon*, 201–203 • AGAD, AmSzczerców sig. 2, ff. 134–136
Wyżwa 1716	Antonovich, *Koldovstvo*, item 21; Pilaszek, *Procesy o czary*, 52
Brześć Kujawski 1717	Olszewski, 'Prześladowanie czarów', 502 • APToruń, AmBrześćKuwawski sig. 4, f. 222
Kamieniec Podolski 1717	Antonovich, *Koldovstvo*, item 25; Dysa, *Istoriya z Vid'mamy*, 191
Kraków 1717a	Kracik and Rożek, *Hultaje*, 113
Kraków 1717b	Kracik and Rożek, *Hultaje*, 113
Satanów 1717	Dysa, *Istoriya z Vid'mamy*, 234 • TsDIA (Kyiv), fond 50, op. 1, no. #, f. 156
Wągrowiec 1717	Moeglich, 'Procesy o czary', 59–62 • APPoznań, AmWągrowiec sig. I/25, ff. 41–45
Nieszawa 1718	Pilaszek, *Procesy o czary*, 354 • AGAD, AmNieszawa sig. 12 ff. 111
Nowe 1718	Wijaczka, 'Witch and Sorcerer-Hunts', 114, 119–120 • APBydgoszcz, AmNowe sig. 131, f. 110
Przemyśl 1718	Mikołajczyk, 'O pławieniu czarownic', 128 • APPrzemyśl AmPrzemyśl sig. 85, ff. 9–14
Rzeszów 1718	Dydek, 'Czary w procesie inkwizycyjnym', 393–401 • APRzeszów AmRzeszów sig. 168 vol. 12 ff. 475–488
Wyszogród 1718a	Olszewski, 'Prześladowanie czarów', 496–497
Wyszogród 1718b	Olszewski, 'Prześladowanie czarów', 501
Grodzisk Wielkopolski 1719	Mikołajczyk, 'Przestępstwa przeciwko religii', 232 • AGAD, BBaw. sig. 252, f. 55v
Nieszawa 1719	Pilaszek, *Procesy o czary*, 351 • AGAD, AmNieszawa sig. 19 ff. 287v–288
Nowe 1719a	Wijaczka, '*Próba zimnej wody*', 92 • APBydgoszcz, AmNowe sig. 131 f. 113–114
Nowe 1719b	Wijaczka, 'Witch and Sorcerer-Hunts', 114, 121 • APBydgoszcz, AmNowe sig. 131 ff. 122–123
Pyzdry 1719a	Tripplin, *Tajemnice społeczeństwa*, iii., 278–282; Rosenblatt, *Czarownica powołana*, 12–14 • APPoznań, AmPyzdry sig. 1757 ff. 6–7
Raciąż 1719	Putek, *Mroki średniowiecza*, 240–243 • BTarnowski doc. 6409
Wągrowiec 1719a	Moeglich, 'Procesy o czary', 62• APPoznań, AmWągrowiec sig. I/25 ff. 52–54

(*Continued*)

(*Continued*)

Trial	Published Source • Archival Source
Wągrowiec 1719b	Moeglich, 'Procesy o czary', 62–3, 88 • APPoznań, AmWągrowiec sig. I/25, ff. 46–50
Wągrowiec 1719c	Moeglich, 'Procesy o czary', 63–64 • APPoznań, AmWągrowiec sig. I/25, ff. 50–52
Wągrowiec 1719d	Moeglich, 'Procesy o czary', 64 • APPoznań, AmWągrowiec sig. I/25, ff. 107–109
Krasiłów 1720	Antonovich, *Koldovstvo*, item 30; Pilaszek, *Procesy o czary*, 358
Nieszawa 1720	Pilaszek, *Procesy o czary*, 300, 319, 352, 355 • AGAD, AmNieszawa sig. 19 ff. 267–71
Warta 1720	Adamczewska, 'Magiczna broń', 11 • AGAD, AmWarta sig. 48, ff. 215–216
Nieszawa 1721a	Wawrzeniecki, 'Proces w Nieszawie', 646–654
Nieszawa 1721b	Wawrzeniecki, 'Czary r. 1721' 512–518
Kowel 1722	Dysa, *Istoriya z Vid'mamy*, 149 • TsDIA (Kyiv), fond 35, op. 1, no. 17, f. 105r
Poznań 1722	Berwiński, *Studia o gusłach*, ii., 126; Kolberg, *Dzieła wszystkie*, xv. 15, no. 2, 83–84 • APPoznań, AmPoznań sig. I/648 ff. 1–2
Brześć Kujawski 1723	Olszewski, 'Prześladowanie czarów', 500
Mokrze 1723	Pilaszek, *Procesy o czary*, 309–311 • APToruń, Listy do Rady m. Torunia sig. 3458 ff. 1019–1021
Starogród 1723	Wiślicz, 'Czary przed sądami wiejskimi', 54; Wijaczka, 'Procesy o czary przed sądem zamkowym', 294 • APToruń SDDBC sig. 1 ff. 188–190
Wągrowiec 1723	Moeglich, 'Procesy o czary', 66–7 • APPoznań, AmWągrowiec sig. I/25, ff. 107–109
Dubno 1724	Antonovich, *Koldovstvo*, item 50
Koprzywnica 1724	Guldon and Ruciński, 'Zarys dziejów Koprzywnicy', 116; Wijaczka, 'Procesy o czary w regionie świętokrzyskiego', 62
Starogród 1724	Wijaczka, 'Procesy o czary przed sądem zamkowym', 295–297 • APToruń SDDBC sig. 1 ff. 247–252, 271
Wągrowiec 1725	Moeglich, 'Procesy o czary', 67–9 • APPoznań, AmWągrowiec sig. I/25, ff. 64–81
Lubawa 1726	Wijaczka, 'Procesy o czary w Polsce', 22
Wyżwa 1726	Dysa, *Istoriya z Vid'mamy*, 151 • TsDIA (Kyiv), fond 32, op. 1, no. 5, f. 397r
Czerniewo 1727	*MHDW* v., 30–35; Wijaczka, 'Samosąd', 37–45 • APGdańsk, Akta Krokowskich sig. 999/no. 84, ff. 3–27; APGdańsk, AmSkarszewy sig. 520/10, f. 575
Ołyka 1727	Dysa, *Istoriya z Vid'mamy*, 154–155 • TsDIA (Kyiv), fond 1237, op. 1, no. 8, f. 20
Wągrowiec 1727a	Moeglich, 'Procesy o czary', 69–70 • APPoznań, AmWągrowiec sig. I/25 ff. 85–90
Wągrowiec 1727b	Moeglich, 'Procesy o czary', 70 • APPoznań, AmWągrowiec sig. I/25 ff. 74–76

Wągrowiec 1727c	Moeglich, 'Procesy o czary', 71 • APPoznań, AmWągrowiec sig. I/25 ff. 81–84
Kleczew 1728	Hajdrych, 'Wizja świata', 162, 198 • BPTPN, ms. 859 ff. 125–131
Ołyka 1728a	TsDIA (Kyiv), fond 1237, op. 1, no. 8, ff. 80–80v
Ołyka 1728b	Dysa, *Istoriya z Vid'mamy*, 125 • TsDIA (Kyiv), fond 1237, op. 1, no. 8, f. 86–86v
Wągrowiec 1728	Wijaczka, 'Procesy o czary w Polsce', 35; Moeglich, 'Procesy o czary', 71–4, 86, APPoznań, AmWągrowiec sig. I/25 ff. 93–96
Warta 1728a	Baranowski, 'Posłowie', 211; Wijaczka, 'Procesy o czary w Polsce', 33
Warta 1728b	Adamczewska, 'Magiczna broń', 11–12; Wijaczka, 'Procesy o czary w Polsce', 33
Warta 1728c	Adamczewska, 'Magiczna broń', 12; Wijaczka, 'Procesy o czary w Polsce', 33
Wyżwa 1728	TsDIA (Kyiv), fond 1237, op. 1, no. 8, ff. 91–91v
Kamieniec Podolski 1729	Antonovich, *Koldovstvo*, item 32
Kleczew 1729	Hajdrych, 'Wizja świata', 142, 179, 186 • BPTPN, ms. 859 ff. 291–292
Wyżwa 1729	Dysa, *Istoriya z Vid'mamy*, 135–136 • TsDIA (Kyiv), fond 32, op. 1, no. 5, f. 163
Czukiew 1730	Pilaszek, *Procesy o czary*, 385 • TsDIA (Lviv), fond 142, op. 1, no. 7, ff. 260–262
Kleczew 1730	Hajdrych, 'Wizja świata', 198 • BPTPN, ms. 859, ff. 288–290v
Krzemieniec 1730	Antonovich, *Koldovstvo*, item 34; Dysa, *Istoriya z Vid'mamy*, 45
Ołyka 1730a	TsDIA (Kyiv), fond 1237, op. 1, no. 8, ff. 346–347v
Ołyka 1730b	Dysa, *Istoriya z Vid'mamy*, 132 • TsDIA (Kyiv), fond 1237, op. 1, no. 8, ff. 367v–369v
Satanów 1730	Dysa, *Istoriya z Vid'mamy*, 130 • TsDIA (Kyiv), fond 50, op. 1, no. 3, ff. 123v–126v
Warta 1730	Adamczewska, 'Magiczna broń', 12; Wijaczka, 'Procesy o czary w Polsce', 33–34
Wyżwa 1730	Dysa, *Istoriya z Vid'mamy*, 153–154 • TsDIA (Kyiv), fond 32, op. 1, no. 5, ff. 204 v–206r
Gdańsk 1731	*MHDW* v., 40–79; Wijaczka, 'Procesy o czary w Polsce', 26–29
Inowrocław 1731	*MHDW* v., 37–40; Koranyi, 'Ze studjów nad wierzeniami', 7–8; Baranowski, *Procesy czarownic*, 149–150
Krzemieniec 1731	Antonovich, *Koldovstvo*, item 36
Ołyka 1731a	Dysa, *Istoriya z Vid'mamy*, 132 • TsDIA (Kyiv), fond 1237, op. 1, no. 8, ff. 483–483v
Ołyka 1731b	Dysa, *Istoriya z Vid'mamy*, 194 • TsDIA (Kyiv), fond 1237, op. 1, no. 8, ff. 394–394v
Wągrowiec 1731	Wijaczka, 'Procesy o czary w Polsce', 34; Moeglich, 'Procesy o czary', 74 • APPoznań, AmWągrowiec sig. I/25, ff. 97–98, 102
Pyzdry 1731	*Tripplin, Tajemnice społeczeństwa, iii.*, s. 278–282 • APPoznań, AmPyzdry, *Decreta Criminalia*, f. 6–7

(Continued)

(*Continued*)

Trial	Published Source • Archival Source
Dubno 1732	Antonovich, *Koldovstvo*, item 38
Krzemieniec 1732	Antonovich, *Koldovstvo*, item 37
Lublin 1732	Zakrzewska-Dubasowa, *Procesy o czary w Lublinie*, 75–85 • APLublin, AmLublin sig. 48 ff. 1254–1261, 1281–1288
Ołyka 1732	Dysa, *Istoriya z Vid'mamy*, 224 • TsDIA (Kyiv), fond 1237, op. 1, no. 8, f. 581v
Pyzdry 1732	Tripplin, *Tajemnice społeczeństwa*, iii., 282–283 • APPoznań, AmPyzdry sig. 1757 ff. 8–10
Starogród 1732	Wijaczka, 'Procesy o czary przed sądem zamkowym', 297–298 • APToruń SDDBC sig. 1 f. 437–444
Wyżwa 1732	Dysa, *Istoriya z Vid'mamy*, 131 • TsDIA (Kyiv), fond 32, op. 1, no. 5, ff. 263–263v
Żerków 1732	Hajdrych, 'Procesy o czary' • APPoznań, AmŻerków sig. I/3 ff. 3–9
Kleczew 1734	Hajdrych, 'Wizja świata', 162 • BPTPN, ms. 859 ff. 74r–78v
Barcin 1735	*MHDW* v., 58–59; Koranyi, 'Ze studjów nad wierzeniami', 7
Starogród 1735	Wijaczka, 'Procesy o czary przed sądem zamkowym', 298 • APToruń SDDBC sig. 1 f. 744
Wągrowiec 1735	Wijaczka, 'Procesy o czary w Polsce', 34; Moeglich, 'Procesy o czary', 74–5 • APPoznań, AmWągrowiec sig. I/25, ff. 99–102
Grodzisk Wielkopolski 1737	Mikołajczyk, 'Przestępstwa przeciwko religii', 232 • AGAD, BBaw. sig. 252, ff. 89–92v
Kraków 1737	Rosenblatt, *Czarownica powołana*, 20–22 • ANK AmKraków sig. 876 ff.50–51
Kleczew 1738	Hajdrych, 'Wizja świata', 216 • BPTPN, ms. 859 ff. 91–96v
Wągrowiec 1738	Moeglich, 'Procesy o czary', 75–6 • APPoznań, AmWągrowiec sig. I/25, ff. 75
Lublin 1739	Siarkowski, *Materiały do etnografii*, 105–109
Sambor 1739	Pilaszek, *Procesy o czary*, 300 • BUL sig. 547/III ff. 291–291v
Pyzdry 1740	Rosenblatt, *Czarownica powołana*, 9–12
Pacanów 1741	Wijaczka, 'Procesy o czary w regionie świętokrzyskiego', 58
Przemyśl 1741	Mikołajczyk, 'O pławieniu czarownic', 128; Kowalska-Cichy, 'Proces wróżbity'• APPrzymyśl, AmPrzemyśla sig. 85, ff. 205–214
Wągrowiec 1741	Wijaczka, 'Procesy o czary w Polsce', 34; Moeglich, 'Procesy o czary', 76 • APPoznań, AmWągrowiec sig. I/29, unpaginated
Winnica 1742	Antonovich, *Koldovstvo*, item 49
Kowel 1745	Dysa, *Istoriya z Vid'mamy*, 134 • TsDIA (Kyiv), fond 20, op. 1, no. 3, ff. 83v–84v
Kraków 1745	Pilaszek, *Procesy o czary*, 54, 295 • ANK AMKRAKÓW sig. 878 ff. 229–30
Trembowla 1745	Pilaszek, *Procesy o czary*, 360–62 • LNNBU f. 1 op. 1 sig. 612/II ff. 109–110, 113v–114v, 121–121v

Kraśnik 1746	Zakrzewska-Dubasowa, 'Proces o czary w Kraśniku'; Wijaczka, 'Procesy o czary w Polsce', 37
Krzemieniec 1746a	Antonovich, *Koldovstvo*, item 57
Krzemieniec 1746b	Dysa, *Istoriya z Vid'mamy*, 149 • TsDIA (Kyiv), fond 20, op. 1, no. 4, f. 9v
Krzemieniec 1746c	Antonovich, *Koldovstvo*, item 58
Krzemieniec 1747a	Mikołajczyk, 'O pławieniu czarownic', 129; Dysa, *Istoriya z Vid'mamy*, 46 • AGAD, KcKrzemieniec (mf 18958), ff. 42v–49v
Krzemieniec 1747b	Dysa, *Istoriya z Vid'mamy*, 171 • AGAD, KcKrzemieniec (mf. 18958), ff. 53–55
Nowe 1747	Wijaczka, 'Witch and Sorcerer-Hunts', 107, 109, 114, 120, 122, 132, 135; Ronowska 2016 • APBydgoszcz, AmNowe sig. 131 ff. 125–138
Orneta 1747	Wijaczka, 'Procesy o czary w Polsce', 32–33
Starogród 1747	Wijaczka, 'Procesy o czary przed sądem zamkowym', 298–299 • APToruń SDDBC sig. 1 f. 257
Jazowsko 1748	Grodziski, *Księgi sądowe wiejskie*, item 201
Krzemieniec 1748	Dysa, *Istoriya z Vid'mamy*, 170 • AGAD, KcKrzemieniec (mf 18958), ff. 63–68
Kopanica 1749	Pilaszek, *Procesy o czary*, 359, 365 • APPoznań, AmKopanica sig. I/21 ff. 42–43
Kowalewo 1749	Rafacz, 'Sprawy karne', 568
Ołyka 1749	Antonovich, *Koldovstvo*, item 44; Dysa, *Istoriya z Vid'mamy*, 191
Kraków 1752	Kracik and Rożek, *Hultaje*, 114 • AKMK , Acta Officialia sig. 185 72, ff. 112–116
Oświęcim 1752	Kracik and Rożek, *Hultaje*, 114 • AKMK , Acta Officialia sig. 185 72, ff. 150–151
Gniezno 1753	Karwowski, 'Gniezno', 126–127; Wijaczka, '*Próba zimnej wody*', 95
Krzemieniec 1753	AGAD, KcKrzemieniec (mf 18958), ff. 125–126
Trembowla 1753	Pilaszek, *Procesy o czary*, 65–6 • LNNBU f. 1 op. 1 sig. 612/II ff. 646–647
Braniewo 1755	Pilaszek, *Procesy o czary*, 356 • BPAU/PANK sig. 2797 ff. 81
Krzemieniec 1755	Dysa, *Istoriya z Vid'mamy*, 152 • TsDIA (Kyiv), fond 20, op. 1, no. 5, ff. 84, 85v.
Uście Solne 1760	Wijaczka, 'Procesy o czary w Polsce', 37–38
Kiszkowo 1761	Dydyński, *Wiadomości historyczne*, 101–103
Trembowla 1763	Pazdro, 'Proces o "perepiczkę"', 268–276; Wijaczka, 'Procesy o czary w Polsce', 37–38
Tylicz 1763	Piekosiński, *Akta sądu kryminalnego*, 389–393; Koranyi, 'Ze studjów nad wierzeniami', 22; Wijaczka, 'Procesy o czary w Polsce', 38
Dubno 1767	Antonovich, *Koldovstvo*, item 69
Krzemieniec 1767	Dysa, *Istoriya z Vid'mamy*, 134 • TsDIA (Kyiv), fond 20, op. 1, no. 8, ff. 115–116v

(*Continued*)

(*Continued*)

Trial	Published Source • Archival Source
Krzyżanowice 1772	Siarkowski, *Materiały do etnografii*, 93–94 • ADK sig. II PK-XV/ 2 ff. 454–454v
Bełżyce 1774	Klarner, 'Sprawy o czary', 469
Grabów ca. 1775	X.A.R., 'Relacja'; Michalski, 'Jeszcze o konstytucji', 93–94; Tazbir, 'Z dziejów falszerstw', 104–109 • AGAD, Akta grodzkie Ostrzeszowskie sig. 15 f.458v

References

TEXTS FIRST PUBLISHED BEFORE 1800

Aquinas, Thomas. *Basic Writings of Saint Thomas Aquinas.* Translated by Anton C. Pegis. Edited by Anton C. Pegis. Vol. 1. New York: Random House, 1945.

Augustine of Hippo. *The City of God.* Translated by Henry Bettenson. London: Penguin Classics, 2003 [c. 413].

Białobrzeski, Marcin. *Katechizm ALBO Wizerunk prawey wiary Chrześćiańskiey wedle Nauki Pana Iezusa Chrystusa.* Kraków: No Publisher, 1566.

———. *Postylla ortodoxa [etc.].* 2 vols. Kraków: Drukarnia Łazarzowa, 1581.

Bielski, Marcin. *Kronika tho iesth Historya Swiata na sześć wiekow, a cztery Monarchie, rozdżielona z rozmaitych historykow [etc.]. .* Kraków: M. Siebeneicher, 1564.

Bodin, Jean. *On the Demon Mania of Witches.* Toronto: Centre for Renaissance and Reformation Studies, 1995 [1580].

Brzeżański, Stanisław. *Owczarnia w Dzikim Polu [etc.].* Lwów: Drukarnia Kollegium Lwowskiego Societatis Jesu, 1717.

Caesarius of Heisterbach. *The Dialogue on Miracles.* Translated by H. Von, E. Scott and C.C. Swinton Bland. London: George Routledge & Sons, 1929 [1223–1224].

Cervus, Jan. *Farraginis actionum iuris ciuilis et prouincialis saxonici, municipulisque Maydeburgensis.* Kraków: Officina Ungleriana, 1540.

Chmielowski, Benedykt. *Nowe Ateny, albo Akademia Wszelkiej Sciencyi pełna.* 4 vols. Lwów: Drukarnia JKMci Collegii Societatis Jesu, 1754–1756.

Czarownica powolana, abo krotka nauka y prestroga z strony czarownic Gdańsk: Jan Daniel Stoll, 1714 [1639].

Czartoryski, Kazimierz Florian. *Mandatum pastorale ad universum Clerum et populum Diocesis suae de cautelis in processu contra sagas adhibendis* 1705 [1669].

Dalerac, Francois Paulin. *Memoires du Chevalier de Beaujeu contenant ses divers voyages tant en Polgne, en Allemand, qu'en Hungrie [etc.].* Amsterdam: Les héritiers d'Antoine Schelte, 1700.

Damhouderius, Jodocus. *Praxis rerum criminalium [etc.].* Antwerp: Ioan. Belleri, 1601 [1554].

Del Rio, Martin. *Disquisitionum magicarum libri sex.* Cologne: Petrus Henningius, 1633 [1608].

Facecje polskie z roku 1624. Edited by Aleksander Brückner. Kraków: Akademia Umiejętności 1903 [1624, 1570].

Falimirz, Stefan. *O ziolach y o moczy gich [etc.].* Kraków: F. Ungler, 1534.

Gamalski, Serafin. *Przestrogi Duchowne, Sędziom, Inwestygatorom, y Instygatorom Czarownic.* Poznań: Drukarnia Akademicka, 1742.

Gilowski, Paweł. *Wykład Katechizmu Kościoła Krześćijańskiego, z Pism swiętych dla Wiary prawdżiwey utwierdzenia, a fałszywey się ustrzeżenia.* Kraków: No Publisher, 1579.

Groicki, Bartłomiej. *Artykuły prawa magdeburskiego. Postępek sądów około karania na gardle. Ustawa płacej u sądów.* Edited by Karol Koranyi. Warszawa: Wydawnictwo Prawnicze, 1954 [1558].

———. *Porządek sądów i spraw miejskich prawda magdeburskiego w Koronie Polskiej.* Edited by Karol Koranyi. Warszawa: Wydawnictwo Prawnicze, 1953 [1559].

Haur, Jakub Kazimierz. *Skład Abo Skarbiec Znakomitych Sekretow Oekonomiey Ziemians-kiey*. Kraków: Drukarnia Mikołaia Alexandra Schedla, 1693.

Herburt, Jan. *Statuta Regni Poloniae in ordinem alphabeti digesta*. Kraków: Łazarz Andrysowic, 1563.

Heywood, Thomas. *The Hierarchy of the Blessed Angells: Their Names, Orders and Offices; The Fall of Lucifer With His Angells* London: A. Islip, 1635.

strukcya rzymska, abo postępek prawny, o sądach y processach, Iako maią bydź formowane, y wydawnane przećiw Czarownicom. Kraków: Drukarnia Krzysztofa Domańskiego I.K. M. Typog, 1705 [1688].

Jaskier, Mikołaj. *Juris Provincialis quod Speculum Saxonum vulgo nucupatur libri tres [etc.]* 1535.

Jewłaszewski, Teodor. 'Uspaminy.' In *Pomniki memuarnai literatury Belarusi XVII st.* Minsk: Navuka i Tekhnika, 1983 [c. 1604].

Klonowic, Sebastian Fabian. *Roxolania, czyli ziemie Czerwonej Rusi*. Edited by Mieczys-ław Mejor. Warszawa: Polska Akademia Nauk, 1996 [1584].

Kochanowski, Jan. 'Pieśń świętojańska o sobótce.' In *Dzieła polskie Jana Kochanowskiego*, edited by Julian Krzyżanowski. Warszawa: Państwowy Instytut Wydawniczy, 1952 [c. 1585].

——. *Worek Ivdaszow: to iest Złe nabyćie Máiętności*. Edited by Kazimierz Budzyk. Wrocław: Zakład Narodowy im. Ossolińskich, 1960 [1600].

Kochowski, Wespazjan *Niepróżnujące próżnowanie ojczystym rymem na liryka i epigramata polskie rozdzielone*. Edited by K.J. Turowski. Kraków: Biblioteka Polska, 1859 [1684].

Komoniecki Andrzej. *Chronografia albo Dziejopis żywiecki*. Edited by S. Grodziski and I. Dwornicka. Żywiec: Towarzystwo Miłośników Ziemi Żywieckiej, 1987 [1728].

Institoris, Heinrich. *The Hammer of Witches. A Complete Translation of the Malleus Maleficarum*. Translated by Christopher S. Mackay. New York: Cambridge University Press, 2009 [1487].

Lorencowic, Aleksander. *Kazania na Niedziele Całego Roku*. 2 vols. Kalisz: Drukarnia Kolegium Kaliskiego Soc: Jesu, 1671.

Marchocka, Anna Maria (Mother Teresa). *Żywot y wysokie cnoty W. Matki Teresy od Pana Jezusa Marchockiey*. Edited by Józef Augustynowicz. Lwów: Drukarnia J.K. Mci Societatis Jesu, 1752.

Marcin of Klecko. *Procy na ministry i na wszystkie heretyki z piąćią Dawidowych kamieni w tobole*. Kraków: Wdowa Jak. Siebeneychera, 1607.

Marcin of Urzędów. *Herbarz Polski. To iest o przyrodzeniu Zioł y Drzew Rozmaitych [etc.]*. Kraków: Drukarnia Łazarzowa, 1595.

Nędza z Biedą z Polski idą. In *Antologia literatury sowiźrzalskiej*, edited by Stanisław Grzeszczuk. Wrocław: Zakład Narodowy im. Ossolińskich, 1966 [c.1624].

Opaliński, Krzysztof. *Satyry Albo Przestrogi do Naprawy Rządu Y Obyczajów w Polszcze należące, .* Wrocław: Zakład Narodowy im. Ossolińskich, 1953 [1650].

Opatovius Adam. *Tractatus de Sacramentis in genere et specie*. Cracow: Officina Christoph: Schedelij, 1642.

Otwinowski, Waleryan. *Księgi Metamorphoseon, to iest Przemian*. Kraków: Andrzej Piotr-kowczyk, 1638.

Pasek, Jan Chryzostom z Gocławic. *Tales of the Polish Baroque: the writings of John Chryzostom Pasek*. Translated by Catherine S. Leach. Berkeley: University of California Press, 1976.

Pliny the Elder. *The Natural History.* Translated by John Bostock. London: Taylor and Francis, 1855.

Poklatecki, Stanisław z Gór. *Pogrom. Czarnoksięskie błędy, latowców zdrady i alchemickie fałsze.* Kraków: Jakub Siebeneycher, 1595.

Postępek prawa czartowskiego przeciw narodowi ludzkiemu. edited by Arthur Benis. Kraków: Wydawnictwo Akademii Umiejętności 1891 [1570].

Rej, Mikołaj. *Apocalypsis To iest Dziwna sprawa skrytych taiemnic Pańskich [etc.].* Kraków: Maciej Wirzbięta, 1565.

Rej, Mikołaj. *Świętych słów a spraw Pańskich . kronika albo postylla [etc.].* Kraków: Matys Wirzbięta, 1556.

Rémy, Nicolas. *Demonolatry.* Translated by E.A. Ashwin. London: J. Rodker, 1930 [1595].

Siennik, Marcin. *Herbarz, to iest zioł tutecznych postronnych y zamorskich opisanie co za moc maią [etc.].* Kraków: Mikołaj Szarffenberg, 1568.

Skarga, Piotr. *Żywoty świętych starego i nowego zakonu na każdy dzień przez cały rok.* 12 vols. Kraków: Wł. L. Anczyc i Spółka, 1881–1889 [1579].

———. *The Eucharist.* Translated by Edward J. Doraczyk. Edited by Edward J. Dorczyk. Milwaukee: The Bruce Publishing Company, 1939.

Sowirzalius, Ianuarius [pseud.]. *Sejm piekielny. Satyra obyczajowa.* edited by Aleksander Brückner. Kraków: Wydawnictwo Akademii Umiejętności, 1903 [1622].

Spee, Friedrich von. *Cautio criminalis, seu De processibus contra sagas liber.* Poznań: Albertus Regulus, 1647 [1632].

Starowolski, Szymon. *Arka Testamentu zamykająca w sobie kazania niedzielna całego roku.* Kraków: W drukarniy Krzystofa Schedla, 1648.

Swizralus, Januarius [pseud.]. *Peregrynacja dziadowska.* In *Dramaty Staropolskie. Antologia,* edited by Julian Lewański. Warszawa: Państwowy Instytut Wydawniczy, 1961 [1614].

Synod Klechów Podgórskich. In *Antologia literatury sowiźrzalskiej,* edited by Stanisław Grzeszczuk. Wrocław: Zakład Narodowy im. Ossolińskich, 1985 [1607].

Syreniusz, Szymon. *Zielnik Herbarzem z języka Łacinskiego zowią.* Kraków: W drukarni Bazylego Skalskiego, 1613.

Korczewski, Wit. 'Rozmowy polskie łacińskim językiem przeplatane.' edited by J. Karłowicz. Kraków: Akademia Umiejętności, 1889 [1553].

Szembek, Krzysztof Antoni. 'Edictum ne judices saeculares audeant judicare sagas absque cognitione fori spiritualis.' *Monumenta Historica Dioceseos Wladislaviensis* 5 (1885 [1727]): 15–20.

Szymonowic, Szymon. *Sielanki i pozostałe wierze polskie Szymona Szymonowica.* Edited by Janusz Pelc. Wrocław: Zakład Narodowy im. Ossolińskich, 1964 [1614].

The Book of Enoch. Translated by R.H. Charles. London: Society for Promoting Christian Knowledge, 1917.

The Book of Jubilees. Translated by R.H. Charles. London: Society for Promoting Christian Knowledge, 1917.

The Roman Catechism. Translated by Robert I. Bradley and Eugene Kevone. Boston: St. Paul Edition, 1985.

Uruszczak, Wacław, Stanisław Grodziski, and Irena Dwornicka, eds. *Volumina constitutionum part 1.* Vol. 1–2. Warszawa: Wydawnictwo Sejmowe, 1996–2000.

Virgil. *The Eclogues of Virgil.* Translated by David Ferry. New York: Farrar, Strauss, and Giroux, 1999 [c. 35 BCE].

Volumina legum. 10 vols. Petersburg: Jozafat Ohryzko, 1859–1860 [1732–1782].

Wodka Zelixierem proprietatis Powtornie na poczesne dana [etc.]. no place: no publisher, 1729.

Wujek, Jakub. *Biblia w przekładzie księdza Jakuba Wujka z 1599 r.* Edited by Janusz Frankowski, Prymasowska Seria Biblijna. Warszawa: Vocatio, 2000.

Ząbkowic, Stanisław. *Młot na czarownice. Postępek zwierzchowny w czarach , także sposob uchronienia sie ich, y lekarstwo na nie w dwoch częśćiach zamykaiący.* Kraków: Szymon Kempini, 1614.

——. *Młot na czarownice.* edited by W. Lewandowski. Wrocław: Wyspa, 1992.

Załuski, Józef Jędrzej. *Objaśnienie błędami zabobonów zarażonych, oraz opisanie niegodziwości, która pochodzi z sądzenia przez próbę pławienia w wodzie mniejmanych czarownic.* Berdychów: Drukarnia WW. OO. Karmelitów Bosych, 1766.

TEXTS PUBLISHED AFTER 1800

Adamczewska, G. 'Magiczna broń i jej rola w walce między wsią a dworem w Sieradzkiem w XVI–XVIII w.' *Łódzkie Studia Etnograficzne* 5 (1963).

Adamczyk, Joanna. 'Czary i magia w praktyce sądów kościelnych na ziemiach polskich w późnym średniowieczu (XV–połowa XVI wieku).' In *Karolińscy pokutnicy i polskie średniowieczne czarownice. Konfrontacja doktryny chrześcijańskiej z życiem społeczeństwa średniowiecznego.*, edited by Maria Koczerska. Warszawa: Wydawnictwo DiG, 2007.

Adamczyk, M. 'Zbąszyń. Procesy czarownic w Zbąszyniu.' In *Wczoraj i Dziś Powiatu Nowotomyskiego*, edited by Jan Świerzowicz. Nowy Tomyśl: Powiatowy Komitet Funduszu Obrony Narodowej, 1938.

Albèri, Eugenio, ed. *Le Relazioni degli Abasciatori Veneti al Senato durante il secolo decimosesto.* Six vols. Florence: self-published, 1862.

Aleksandrowicz, M. 'Z badań nad dziejami religijności wiernych na przykładzie archidiakonatu gnieźnieńskiego w początku XVII wieku.' *Roczniki Humanistyczne* 24, no. 2 (1976): 5–34.

Ankarloo, Bengt, and Gustav Henningsen, eds. *Early Modern European Witchcraft. Centres and Perpheries.* Oxford: Oxford University Press, 1993 [1987].

Antonovich V.B., *Koldovstvo. Dokumenty – processy – izsledovanie.* St. Petersburg: V. Kiršbaum, 1877.

Augustyniak, Urszula. *Koncepcje narodu i społeczeństwa w literaturze plebejskiej od końca XVI do końca XVII wieku.* Vol. 332, Rozprawny Uniwersytetu Warszawskiego. Warszawa: Wydawnictwo Uniwersytetu, 1989.

Austen, Ralph A. 'The Moral Economy of Witchcraft. An Essay in Comparative History.' In *Modernity and its Malcontents: Ritual and Power in Postcolonial Africa*, edited by Jean Comaroff and John L. Comaroff. Chicago: University of Chicago Press, 1993.

Baczko, Bronislaw, and Henryk Hinz, eds. *Kalendarz półstuletni 1750–1800. Wybór tekstów.* Warszawa: Państwowy Instytut Wydawniczy, 1975.

Badecki. *Literatura mieszczańska w Polsce XVII w. Monografia bibljograficzna.* Lwów: Zakład Narodowy im. Ossolińskich, 1925.

Baranowski, B., and W. Lewandowski. *Nietolerancja i zabobon w Polsce w wieku XVII i XVIII: wypisy źródłowe*. Warszawa: Książka i Wiedza, 1987 [1950].

Baranowski, B., ed. *Najdawniejsze procesy o czary w Kaliszu*. Vol. 2, Archiwum Etnograficzne. Lublin: Polskie Towarzystwo Ludoznawcze, 1951.

Baranowski, B., W. Lewandowski, and J.S. Piątkowski, eds. *Upadek kultury w Polsce w dobie reakcji katolickiej XVII–XVIII w.* Warszawa: Książka i Wiedza, 1950.

Baranowski, Bohdan. *Kontrreformacja we Polsce XVI–XVII w.* Warszawa: Spółdzielnia Wydawnyczo-Oświatowa "Czytelnik", 1950.

——. *Procesy Czarownic w Polsce w XVII i XVIII wieku*. Łódź: Łódzkie Towarzystwo Naukowe, 1952.

——. 'Wielki proces o czary miłosne w Praszce w 1665 roku.' *Łódzkie Studia Etnograficzne* 4 (1962): 5–14.

——. *Pożegnanie z diabłem i czarownicą*. Łódź: Wydawnictwo Łódzkie, 1965.

——. 'Posłowie.' In *Czarownica. Dzieje procesów o czary*. Warszawa: Polskie Wydawnictwo Naukowe, 1971.

——. *W kręgu upiorów i wilkołaków*. Łódź: Wydawnictwo Łódzkie, 1981.

Barry, Jonathan, and Owen Davies, eds. *Palgrave Advances in Witchcraft HistoriogrAphy*. New York: Palgrave, 2007.

Bartmiński, J., and M. Jasińska-Wojtkowska, eds. *Folklor-Sacrum-Religia*. Lublin: Instytut Europy Środkowo Wschodniej, 1995.

Behringer, Wolfgang. 'Neun Millionen Hexen. Entstehung, Tradition und Kritik eines populären Mythos.' *Geschichte in Wissenschaft und Unterricht* 49, no. 11 (1998): 664–65.

——. *The Shaman of Oberstdorf: Chonrad Stoeckhlin and the Phantoms of the Night*. Translated by H.C. Erik Midelfort. Charlottesville: University Press of Virginia, 1998.

Bem, Kazimierz. 'The Devil Went Down to Oksa: Demonic Visitation and Calvinist Piety in Mid-Seventeenth Century Poland.' *Reformation and Renaissance Review* 23, no. 1 (2021): 48–67.

Berwiński, Ryszard. *Studia o gusłach, czarach, zabobonach i przesądach ludowych*. 2nd ed. 2 vols. Warszawa: Wydawnictwo Artystyczne i Filmowe, 1984 [1862, 1st ed. 1854].

Biskup, Marian, ed. *Ziemia chełmińska w przeszłości. Wybór tekstów źródłowych*. Vol. 1, Prace Popularnonaukowe. Toruń: Towarzystwo Naukowe w Toruniu 1961.

Blécourt, Willem de. 'Witch Doctors, Soothsayers and Preists. On Cunning Folk in European HistoriogrAphy and Tradition.' *Social History* 19 (1994): 285–303.

Bogucka, Maria, and Henryk Samsonowicz. *Dzieje miast i mieszczaństwa w Polsce przedrozbiorowej*. Wrocław: Zakład Narodowy im. Ossolińskich, 1986.

Bogucka, Maria. 'Polish Towns Between the Sixteenth and Eighteenth Centuries.' In *A Republic of Nobles. Studies in Polish History to 1864*, edited by J.K. Fedorowicz. Cambridge: Cambridge University Press, 1982.

——. 'Law and Crime in Poland in Early Modern Times.' *Acta Poloniae Historica* 71 (1995): 175–95.

——. *The Lost World of the 'Sarmatians.' Custom as the Regulator of Social Life in Early Modern Times*. Warszawa: Polska Akademia Nauk, 1996.

——. 'The Centre and Periphery of Witchcraze.' *Acta Poloniae Historica* 75 (1997): 179–88.

——. *Białogłowa w społeczeństwie polskim XVI–XVIII wieku na tle porównawczym*. Warszawa: Wydawnictwo Trio, 1998.

Bojarski, Piotr. 'Nie godzi się, by wisiała. Zabytkową tablicę z antysemickim tekstem usunięto na polecenie abp. Stanisława Gądeckiego.' *Gazeta Wyborcza*, 30 May 2005.

Bossy, John. 'Blood and Baptism. Kinship, Community and Christianity in Western Europe from the 14th to the 17th Centuries.' *Studies in Church History* 10 (1973): 129–43.

———. *Christianity in the West: 1400–1700*. New York: Oxford University Press, 1985.

———. 'Moral Arithmetic. Seven Sins into Ten Commandments.' In *Conscience and Casuistry in Early Modern Europe*, edited by Edmund Leites. Cambridge: Cambridge University Press, 1988.

Bourdieu, Pierre. *Outline of a Theory of Practise*. Translated by Richard Nice. New York: Cambridge University Press, 1977.

Bracha, Krzysztof. 'Latawiec, z katalogu imion rodzimych duchów i demonów w źródłach średniowiecznych.' In *Ludzie-Kościół-Wierzenie. Studia z dziejów kultury i społeczeństwa Europy Środkowej (średniowiecze-wczesna epoka nowożytna)*, edited by W. Iwańczak and S. Kuczyński. Warszawa: Wydawnictwo DiG, 2001.

Brauner, Sigrid. *Fearless Wives and Frightened Shrews. The Construction of the Witch in Early Modern Germany*. Amherst: University of Massachusetts Press, 1995.

Briggs, Katharine. *The Anatomy of Puck: An Examination of Fairy Beliefs among Shakespeare's Contemporaries and Successors*. London: Routledge and Paul, 1959.

———. 'The Fairies and the Realms of the Dead.' *Folklore* 81, no. 2 (1970): 81–96.

Briggs, Robin. 'Women as Victims? Witches, Judges, and the Community.' *French History* 5 (1991): 438–50.

———. *Witches and Neighbours. The Social and Cultural Context of European Witchcraft*. London: Penguin Books, 1996.

Bronikowski, Ksawery. *Pamiętniki polskie*. Przemyśl: Adam Kaczuba, 1883.

Brückner, Aleksander. 'Kazania husyty polskiego.' *Pracy Filologiczne* 4 (1892): 561–86.

———. 'Średniowieczna poezja łacińska w Polsce, II.' *Rozprawy i Sprawozdania posiedzeń Wydziału Filologii Akademii Umiejętności* 22 (1893): 1–62.

———. '"Kazania średniowieczne" part, 2, section 1: "Przesądy i zabobony u ludu polskiego w wieku pietnastym."' *Rozprawy Akademii Umiejętności. Wydział Filologiczny* 24 (1895): 317–49.

———. *Starożytna Litwa. Ludy i bogi. Szkice historyczne i mitologiczne*. Edited by Jan Jaskanis. Olsztyn: Pojezierze, 1979 [1904].

———. *Mitologia polska*. Edited by Stanisław Urbańczyk. Warszawa: Polskie Wydawnictwo Naukowe, 1985 [1924].

Brzezińska, Anna. 'Accusations of Love Magic in the Renaissance Courtly Culture of the Polish-Lithuanian Commonwealth.' *East Central Europe* 20–23, no. 1 (1996): 117–40.

Buczak, Franciszek. 'Śledzenie złoczyńców z pomocą czarów. (Z rachunków miasta Biecza z r. 1600).' *Lud* 16 (1910): 54–56.

Bugaj, Roman. *Nauki tajemne w Polsce w dobie odrodzenia*. Wrocław: Zakład Narodowy im. Ossolińskich, 1976.

Bukowska, Krystyna. 'Proces w prawie miejskim.' In *Historia państwa i prawa Polski*, edited by Julian Bardach, Zdzisław Kaczmarczyk and Bogusław Leśnodorski. Warszawa: polskie Wydawnictwo Naukowe, 1971 [1968].

Bukowska-Gorgoni, Krystyna. 'Procesy o czary i powołanie przez czarownice w orzecznictwie Sądu Wyższego prawa niemieckiego na Zamku Krakowskim.' *Lud* 54 (1970): 156–67.

Burke, Peter. 'The Comparative Approach to European Witchcraft.' In *Early Modern European Witchcraft. Centres and Perpheries*, edited by Bengt Ankarloo and Gustav Henningsen. Oxford: Oxford University Press, 1993.

Bylina, Stanisław. 'Licitum—illicitum. Mikołaj z Jawora o pobożności mazowej i zabobonach.' In *Kultura elitarna a kultura masowa w Polsce późnego średniowiecza*, edited by Bronisław Geremek. Wrocław: Zakład Narodowy im. Ossolińskich, 1978.

——. 'Mesjasz z Gór Świętokrzyskich.' *Odrodzenie i Reformacja w Polsce* 33 (1988): 5–26.

——. 'Magia, czary w Polsce XV i XVI w.' *Odrodzenie i Reformacja w Polsce* 35 (1990): 40–51.

——. *Człowiek i zaświaty. Wizje kar pośmiertnych w Polsce średniowiecznej*. Warszawa: Instytut Historii Polskiej Akademii Nauk, 1992.

——. *Chrystianizacja wsi polskiej u schyłku średniowiecza*. Warszawa: Instytut Historii Polskiej Akademii Nauk, 2002.

Bynum, Caroline Walker. *Holy Feast and Holy Fast: The Religious Significance of Food to Medieval Women*. Berkeley: University of California Press, 1987.

Bystroń, Jan Stanisław. *Polska pieśń ludowa. Wybór*. Chicago: Rada Polonii Amerykańskiej, 1945.

Cavanaugh, William. *Torture and Eucharist: Theology, Politics, and the Body of Christ*. Cambridge, MA: Blackwell, 1998.

Châtellier, L. *The Religion of the Poor. Rural Missions in Europe and the Formation of Modern Catholicism c. 1500–1800*. Cambridge: CUP, 1997.

Cieślak, Stanisław. 'Harfa Duchowna—modlitewnikowy bestseller jezuity Marcina Laterny (1552–1598).' *Nasza Przeszłość* 93 (2000): 23–48.

Clark, Stuart. 'The Rational Witchfinder: Conscience, Demonological Naturalism and Popular Superstitions.' In *Science, Culture and Popular Belief in Renaissance Europe*, edited by Steven Pumfrey et. al. New York: Manchester University Press, 1991.

——. *Thinking with Demons: The Idea of Witchcraft in Early Modern Europe*. New York: Oxford University Press, 1997.

Clough, Paul, and Jon P. Mitchell, eds. *Powers of Good and Evil: Social Transformation and Popular Belief.* New York: Berghahn Books, 2001.

Cohn, Norman. *Europe's Inner Demons. The Demonization of Christians in Medieval Christendom*. revised ed. Chicago: University of Chicago Press, 2000 [1993].

Comaroff, Jean, and John L. Comaroff. 'Occult Economies and the Violence of Abstraction: Notes from the South Africa Postcolony (The Max Gluckman Memorial Lecture, 1998).' *American Ethnologist* 26, no. 2 (1999): 279–303.

Czaykowski, K., and J. Łoś. 'Zabytki augustiańskie.' *Materyały i Prace Komisyi Językowej Akademii Umiejętności w Krakowie* 2, no. 3 (1907): 311–27.

Davidson, Jane P. 'The Myth of the Persecuted Female Healer.' In *The Witchcraft Reader*, edited by Darren Oldridge. New York: Routledge, 2008.

Davis, Natalie Z. *Society and Culture in Early Modern France*. Stanford: Stanford University Press, 1975.

Dillinger, Johannes. 'The Dragon as a Household Spirit: Witchcraft and Economics in Early Modern and Modern Sources.' *Magic, Ritual, and Witchcraft* 17, no. 2 (2022): 212–240.

Drob, Janusz. 'Model człowieka wieku XVII w kazaniach Bernarda Gutowskiego.' *Roczniki Humanistyczne KUL* 29, no. 2 (1981): 75–140.

Dundes, Alan. 'Wet and Dry, the Evil Eye: An Essay in Indo-European and Semitic Worldview.' In *The Evil Eye: A Folklore Casebook*, edited by Alan Dundes. New York: Garland Publishing, 1981.

Dwyer, Graham. *The Divine and the Demonic. Supernatural Affliction and its Treatment in North India.* London: RoutledgeCurzon, 2003.

Dydek, Zbigniew. 'Czary w procesie inkwizycyjnym w Rzeszowie w XVIII wieku.' *Rocznik Wojewówdztwa Rzeszwoskiego* (1968): 383–401.

Dydyński, J., ed. *Wiadomości historyczne o mieście Kłecku.* Gniezno: J.B. Langi, 1858.

Dysa, Kateryna. 'Witchcraft Trials and Beyond: Right-Bank Side Ukrainian Trials of the Seventeenth and Eighteenth Centuries.' Central European University, 2004.

——. *Istoriia z vid'mamy: sudy pro chary v ukraïns'kykh voievodstvakh Rechi Pospolytoï XVII-XVIII stolittia.* Kiev: Kritika, 2008.

——. *Ukrainian Witchcraft Trials. Volhynia, Poodolia and Ruthenia, 17th-18th Centuries.* Budapest: Central European University Press, 2020.

Dżwigoł, Renata. *Polskie ludowe słownictwo mitologiczne.* Kraków: Wydawnictwo Naukowe Akademii Pedagogicznej, 2004.

Erzepki, Bolesław. 'Przyczynki do średniowiecznego słownictwa polskiego I. Glosy polskie wpisane do łacińsko niemieckiego słowniku drukowowanego w roku 1490.' *Rocznik Towarzystwa Przyjaciół Nauk Poznańskiego* 34 (1908): 1–139.

Estes, L.L. 'Incarnations of Evil. Changing Perspectives on the European Witch-craze.' *Clio* 13 (1984): 133–47.

Favret-Saada, Jeanne. 'Unbewitching as Therapy.' *American Ethnologist* 16, no. 1 (1989): 40–56.

Filotas, Bernadette. *Pagan Survivals, Superstitions and Popular Cultures in Early Medieval Pastoral Literature*, Studies and Texts. Toronto: Pontificial Insitutue of Medieval Studies, 2005.

Fischer, Adam. 'Diabeł w wierzeniach ludu polskiego.' In *Studia staropolskie ku czci Aleksandra Brücknera.* Kraków: Krakowska Spółka Wydawnicza, 1926.

——. 'Ryszard Wincenty Berwiński (1819–1879).' *Lud* 37 (1946): 141–59.

Fletcher, Richard. *The Conversion of Europe: From Paganism to Christianity, 371–1386 A.D.* London: HarperCollins Publishers, 1997.

Flint, Valerie. *The Rise of Magic in Early Medieval Europe.* Oxford: Oxford University Press, 1991.

Foster, George M. 'Peasant Society and the Image of the Limited Good.' *American Anthropologist* 67 (1965): 293–315.

——. 'A Second Look at Limited Good.' *Anthropological Quarterly* 45, no. 2 (1972): 57–64.

Frankfurter, David. *Evil Incarnate. Rumors of Demonic Conspiracy and Ritual Abuse in History.* Princeton: Princeton University Press, 2006.

Frazer, James George. *The Golden Bough: A Study of Magic and Religion.* 3rd ed. New York: Macmillan, 1935 [1912].

Gagacki, Ks. 'Widok miasta Koźmina w roku 1772.' *Przyjaciel Ludu* 6, no. 15 (1839): 114–18.

Gansiniec, Ryszard. 'Eucharystia w wierzeniach i praktykach ludu.' *Lud* 44 (1959): 75–117.

Gąsiorowski, Stefan. 'Proces o znieważenie hostii przez Żydów we Lwowie z roku 1636.' *Nasza Przeszłość* 82 (1994): 353–57.

Gąssowski, Jerzy. 'Ośrodek kultu pogańskiego na Łysej Górze.' In *Religia pogańskich Słowian. Sesja naukowa w Kielcach*, edited by A. Oborny and et al. Kielce: Muzeum Świętokrzyskie w Kielcach, 1968.

Gay, David Elton. 'On the Christianity of Incantations.' In *ed., Charms and Charming in Europe*, edited by In J. Roper. New York: Palgrave, 2004.

Geertz, Clifford. *Available Light: Anthropological Reflections on Philosophical Topics*. Princeton: Princeton University Press, 2001.

Geertz, Hildred. 'An Anthropology of History and Magic. Two Views.' *Journal of Interdisciplinary History* 6, no. 1 (1975): 71–90.

Gentilcore, David. *From Bishop to Witch: The System of the Sacred in Early Modern Terra d'Otranto*. New York: Manchester University Press, 1992.

Geschiere, Peter. *The Modernity of Witchcraft: Politics and the Occult in Postcolonial Africa*. Charlottesville: University of Virginia Press, 1997.

Gintel, Jan, ed. *Cudzoziemscy o Polsce. Relacje i opinie*. Vol. 1. Kraków: Wydawnictwo Literackie, 1971.

Ginzburg, Carlo. *The Night Battles. Witchcraft and Agrarian Cults in the Sixteenth and Seventeenth Centuries*. Translated by John and Ann C. Tedeschi. Baltimore: John Hopkins University Press, 1983 [1966].

——. *Ecstasies. Deciphering the Witches' Sabbath*. Translated by Raymond Rosenthal. London: Hutchinson Radius, 1990.

Gloger, Zygmunt. 'Encyklopedia staropolska illustrowana.' Warszawa: Wiedza Poweszechna, 1972 [1900–1903].

Głowacka, Anetta. 'Women in a Small Polish Town in the 16th-18th Centuries.' *Acta Poloniae Historica* 94 (2006): 143–52.

Goffman, Erving. *Interaction Ritual: Essays on Face-to-Face Behavior*. Garden City: Anchor Books, 1967.

Golopentia, Sanda. 'Towards a Typology of Romanian Love Charms.' In *Charms and Charming in Europe*, edited by J. Roper. New York: Palgrave, 2004.

Greengrass, Mark. *The Longman Companion to the European Reformation: 1500–1618*. London: Longman, 1998.

Grochowska, Irena. *Stanisław Antoni Szczuka: jego działalność w ziemi wiskiej 1682–1710*. Warszawa: Polskie Wydawnictwo Naukowe, 1989.

Grodziski , Stanisław, ed. *Księgi sądowe wiejskie klucza jazowskiego 1663–1808*, Starodawne Prawa Polskiego Pomniki, Seria 2, Dział 2, Prawo Wiejskie. Wrocław: Zakład Narodowy im. Ossolińskich, 1967.

Grzeszczuk, Stanisław. *Błażeńskie zwierciadło. Rzecz o humorystyce sowizdrzalskiej XVI i XVII wieku*. Kraków: Wydawnictwo Literackie, 1970.

Guldon, A. 'Proces czarownicy we wsi Staniszewo w 1695 r.' *Studia z dziejów kościoła katolickiego* 2, no. 1 (1962): 150–61.

Guldon, Wojciech. 'Radomska czarownica z drugiej połowy XVI wieku.' *Wieś Radomska* 5 (1997): 169–172.

Guldon, Zenon, and Henryk Ruciński. 'Zarys dziejów Koprzywnicy w szlacheckiej Rzeczypospolitej.' *Almanach Historyczyny* 2 (2000).

Guldon, Zenon, and Jacek Wijaczka. *Procesy o mordy rytualne w Polsce w XVI–XVIII w.* Kielce: Wydawnictwo DCF, 1995.

Guldon, Zenon. 'Straty ludności żydowskiej w Koronie w latach potopu.' In *Rzeczpospolita w latach Potopu*, edited by Jadwiga Muszyńska and Jacek Wijaczka, 289–303. Kielce: Wyższa Szkoła Pedagogiczna im. Jana Kochanowskiego, 1996.

Gunnell, Terry. 'How Elvish Were the Álfar?' In *Constructing Nations, Reconstructing Myth*, edited by A. Wawn, G. Johnson, and J. Walter. Turnhout: Brepols, 2007.

Hajdrych, Łukasz. 'Życiorys Reginy Pawłowej, mieszczanki kleczewskiej, w świetle zachowanych źródeł.' *Kronika Wielkopolski* 155 (2015): 5–8.

——. 'Proces czarownicy Anny z Dębska przed kleczewskim sądem wójtowskim w 1625 roku'. *Kronika Wielkopolski* 162 (2017): 5–12.

——. 'Przemoc wobec kobiet a procesy o czary w Kleczewie w latach 1624–1629.' *Rocznik Leszczyński* 17 (2017): 41–52.

——. 'Procesy o czary przed sądem wójtowskim miasta Żerkowa w pierwszej połowie XVIII wieku.' *Klio* 53 (2020): 247–258.

——. 'Proces o czary w Wąsoszach w 1688 r.: Analiza procesu i problemy interpretacyjne.' *Historyka. Studia Metodologiczne* 51 (2021): 333–350.

——. 'Wizja świata mieszkańców Kleczewa w świetle protokołów z *Księgi sądu wójtowskiego miasta Kleczewa* (1624–1738).' PhD diss, Uniwersytet im. Adama Mickiewicza w Poznaniu, 2022.

Hall, Alaric. 'The Evidence for *Maran*, the Anglo-Saxon "Nightmares".' *Neophilologus* 91 (2007): 299–317.

Henningsen, Gustav. '"The Ladies from Outside." An Archaic Pattern of the Witches' Sabbath.' In *Early Modern European Witchcraft. Centres and Perpheries*, edited by Bengt Ankarloo and Gustav Henningsen. Oxford: Oxford University Press, 1993 [1987].

Herzig, Tamar. 'The Bestselling Demonologist: Heinrich Institoris's *Malleus maleficarum*.' In *The Science of Demons*, edited by Jan Machielsen. New York: Routledge.

Hester, Marianne. 'Who Were the Witches?' *Studies in Sexual Politics* 26–27 (1988): 1–22.

Horsley, Richard. 'Who Were the Witches? The Social Roles of the Accused in the European Witch Trials.' *Journal of Interdisciplinary History* 9 (1979): 689–715.

Hsia Ronald Po-Chia, *Trent 1475: Stories of a Ritual Murder Trial*. New Haven: Yale University Press, 1992.

Hutton, Ronald. 'The Global Context of the Scottish Witch-hunt.' In *The Scottish Witch-hunt in Context*, edited by J. Goodare. New York: Manchester University Press, 2002.

——. *Witches, Druids, and King Arthur*. New York: Hambledon Continuum, 2003.

——. *The Witch: A History of Fear*. New Haven: Yale University Press, 2018.

Ivanits, Linda J. *Russian Folk Belief*. Armonk, New York: M.E. Sharpe, Inc., 1989.

Jackson, Louise. 'Witches, wives, and mothers.' In *The Witchcraft Reader*, edited by Darren Oldridge. New York: Routledge, 2008.

Jackson, Michael. 'The Witch as a Category and as a Person.' In *The Insider/Outsider Problem in the Study of Religion: A Reader*, edited by Russell McCutcheon. London: Cassell, 1999 [1989].

Jaguś, Inga. *Lecznictwo ludowe w Królestwie Polskim na przełomie XIX i XX wieku*. Kielce: Kieleckie Towarzystwo Naukowe, 2002.

Janiszewska Mincer, Barbara. 'Bydgoski proces o czary w 1638 roku.' *Prace Wydziału Nauk Humanistycznych Bydgoskiego Towarzystwa Nauk* 4 (1960): 105–24.

Jarnutowski, J. 'Miasto Wizna.' *Biblioteka Warszawska* 3 (1884): 357–358.

Johnston, Sarah Iles. 'Defining the dreadful: remarks on the Greek child-killing demon.' In *Ancient Magic and Ritual Power*, edited by M. Meyer and P. Mirecki, 361–87. Leiden: E.J. Brill, 1995.

Kaczmarczyk, Kazimierz. 'Proces o czarostwo w r. 1688 i 1689.' *Lud 7* (1901): 302–22.

——. 'Przyczynki do wiary w czary.' *Lud* 13 (1907): 330–32.

——. 'Opisy i notatki z starych aktów: proces o czary w Bochni 1679 roku.' *Lud* 16 (1910): 45–53.

Kamiński, Andrzej Sulima. 'The *szlachta* of the Polish-Lithuanian Commonwealth and their Government.' In *The nobility in Russia and eastern Europe*, edited by Ivo Banac and Paul Bushkovitch. New Haven: Yale University Press, 1983.

——. *Historia Rzezczypospolitej wielu narodów 1505–1795*. Lublin: Instytut Europy Środkowo Wschodniej, 2000.

Kamler, Marcin. 'Rola tortur w polskim sądownictwie miejskim w drugiej połowie XVI i pierwszej połowie XVII w.' *Kwartalnik Historyczny* 95, no. 3 (1988).

——. 'Kary za przestępstwa pospolite w dużych miastach Polski w drugiej połowie XVI i pierwszej połowie XVII wieku.' *Kwartalnik Historyczny* 101, no. 3 (1994).

Karbownik, Henryk. 'Management of Witchcraft Trials in the Light of Synod Resolutions and Bishops' Regulations in Pre-partition Poland.' *Review of Comparative Law* 2 (1988).

Karłowicz, J. 'Czary i czarownice w Polsce.' *Wisła* 1 (1887): 14–20, 56–62, 93–99, 136–43, 72–78, 213–22.

Karpiński, Andrzej. *Kobieta w mieście polskim w drugiej połowie XVI i w XVII wieku*. Warszawa: Instytut Historii Polskiej Akademii Nauk, 1995.

Karwowski, Stanisław. 'Gniezno.' *Rozprawy Poznańskiego Towarzystwa Przyjaciół Nauk* 19 (1892).

Kazańczuk, Mariusz. *Historie dziwne i straszliwe. Jezuickie opowieści z czasów saskich*. Chotomów: Verba, 1991.

Kelly, Raymond C. 'Witchcraft and Sexual Relations. An Exploration in the Social and Semantic Implications of the Structure of Belief.' In *A Reader in the Anthropology of Religion*, edited by Michael Lambek. Malden: Blackwell, 2008 [1976].

Kempf, Wolfgang. 'Ritual, Power, and Colonial Domination: Male Initiation Among the Ngaing of Papua New Guinea.' In *Syncretism/Anti-Syncretism: The Politics of Religious Synthesis*, edited by Charles Stewart and Rosalind Shaw. New York: Routledge, 1994.

Kitowicz, Jędrzej. *Opis obyczajów za panowania Augusta III*. Edited by Maria Dernałowicz. Warszawa: Państwowy Instytut Wydawniczy, 1985 [1840–41].

Kivelson, Valerie. 'Patrolling the Boundaries: Witchcraft Accusations and Household Strife in Seventeenth-Century Muscovy.' *Harvard Ukrainian Studies* 19 (1995): 302–23.

——. *Desperate Magic: The Moral Economy of Witchcraft in Seventeenth-Century Russia*. Ithaca: Cornell University Press, 2013.

Klaniczay, Gábor. 'Shamanistic Elements in Central European Witchcraft.' In *Shamanism in Eurasia*, edited by Mihály Hoppál. Göttingen: Edition Herodot, 1984.

Klarner, S. 'Sprawy o czary w urzędach Bełżyckich w wiekach XVI-XVIII. Z aktów urzędów radzieckiego i wójtowskiego miasta Bełżyc.' *Wisła* 16 (1902): 467–69.

Klint, Paweł. 'Miłość, mężobójstwo i praktyki magiczne: Analiza zeznań i wyroku w sprawie o czary przed sądem miejskim w Sanoku z 1657 r.' *Klio* 53 no. 2 (2020): 183–197.

Kloczowski, Jerzy, *et al*. eds. *Christianity in East Central Europe: Late Middle Ages*. Lublin: Institut Europy Srodkowo-Wschodniej, 1999.

Kloczowski, Jerzy. *A History of Polish Christianity*. Cambridge and New York: Cambridge University Press, 2000.

Köhler, Piotr. 'Nazewnictwo i użytkowania roślin leczniczych na ziemiach polskich w XIX wieku na podstawie ankiety Józefa Rostafińskiego.' In *Historia leków naturalnych, Z historii i etymologii polskich nazw roślin leczniczych*, edited by Barbara Kuźnicka. Warszawa: Polska Akademia Nauk, 1993.

Kolberg, Oskar. *Dzieła wszystkie Oskara Kolberga*. Edited by Julian Krzyżanowski. 68 vols. Wrocław: Polskie Towarzystwo Ludoznawcze/Ludowa Spółdzielnia Wydawnicza, 1961–1990 [1857–1907].

Kolbuszewski, Edmund. 'Materyały do medycyny i wierzeń ludowych według opowiadań Demka Żemeły w Zaborzu w pow. rawskim.' *Lud* 2, no. 2 (1896): 157–63.

Kopczyński, M. *Studia nad rodziną chłopską w Koronie w XVII-XVIII wieku*. Warszawa: Wydawnictwo Krupski i S-ka, 1998.

———. 'Czary i gusła przed sądami kościelnymi w Polsce w XV i pierwszej połowie XVI wieku.' *Lud* 26 (1927): 1–25.

Koranyi, Karol. 'Czary w postępowaniu sądowym. Szkic prawno-etnograficzny.' *Lud* 25 (1926): 7–18.

———. 'Danielis Wisneri *Tractatus brevis de extramagis lamiis, veneficis* a *Czarownica powołana*. Szkic z dziejów polskiej literatury prawniczej.' In *Pamiętnik 30-lecia pracy naukowej Przemysława Dąbkowskiego*, edited by K. Koranyi. Lwów: Kółko Historyczno=Prawne Słuchaczów Uniwersytetu Jana Kazimierza, 1927.

———. 'Wpływ prawa flandryjskiego na polskie w XVI wieku (Damhouder-Groicki).' *Pamiętnik historyczno-prawny* 4, no. 4 (1927).

———. 'Beczka czarownic.' *Lud* 27 (1928): 110–11.

———. 'Łysa Góra.' *Lud* 27 (1928): 57–72.

———. 'Ze studjów nad wierzeniami w historii prawa karnego. I. Beczka czarownic.' *Pamiętnik historyczno-prawny* 5, no. 2 (1928): 401–42.

———. 'Czary w Polsce.' In *Pamiętnik II zjazdu Słowiańskich Geografów i Etnografów*, edited by L. Sawicki. Kraków: Komitet organizacyjny II. Z. S. G. E, 1930.

Kors, A. C., and E. Peters, eds. *Witchcraft in Europe, 400–1700: A Documentary History*. 2nd ed. Philadelphia: University of Pennsylvania Press, 2001.

Korta, Wacław. 'Okres gospodarki folwarczno-pańszczyźnianej XVI–XVIII wieku.' In *Historia chłopów polskich*, edited by Stefan Inglot. Wrocław: Wydawnictwo Uniwersytetu Wrocławskiego., 1992.

Kowalska-Cichy, Magdalena. 'Nieopublikowane fragmenty procesu Reginy Sokołkowej (1660–1662).' In *Czarownice. Studia z kulturowej historii fenomenu*, edited by A. Anczyk, J. Doroszewska, and K. Hess. Katowice: Wydawnictwo Sacrum, 2017.

———. 'Proces wróżbity Bazylego Maksymowicza (1741).' *Rocznik Przemyski* 53 no. 1 (2017): 35–47.

———. *Magia i procesy o czary w staropolskim Lublinie*. Lublin: Wydawnictwo Episteme, 2019.

Kowalski, Waldemar. 'Ludność archidiakonatu sandomierskiego w połowie XVII wieku.' In *Rzeczpospolita W Latach Potopu,*, edited by Jadwiga Muszyńska and Jacek Wijaczka. Kielce: Wyższa Szkoła Pedagogiczna im. Jana Kochanowskiego, 1996.

Kracik, Jan, and Michał Rożek. *Hultaje, złoczyńcy, wszetecznicόw dawnego Krakowa. O marginesie społecznym XVI–XVII wiekόw.* Krakόw: Wydawnictwo Literackie, 1986.

Kracik, Jan. 'Katolicka indoktrynacja doby saskiej w parafiach zachodniej Małopolski.' *Roczniki Teologiczno-Kanoniczne* 20, no. 6 (1973): 13–27.

——. 'Chrzest w staropolskiej kulturze duchowej.' *Nasza Przeszłość* 74 (1990): 181–206.

Krzyczyński, Stanisław. 'Święcenie wody i soli w dawnych czarach mieszczańskich. Wyjątki z kilku rozpraw sądowych 1675–1682.' *Lud* 31 (1932): 109–10.

Krzyżanowski, Julian. *Mądrej głowie dość dwie słowie. trzy centurie przysłόw polskich.* 2 vols. Warszawa: Państwowy Instytut Wydawniczy, 1958.

Kuchowicz, Zbigniew. *Obyczaje staropolskie XVII–XVIII wieku.* Łόdź: Wydawnictwo Łόdzkie, 1975.

Kumor, Bolesław. *Dzieje diecyzji krakowskiej do roku 1995.* 4 vols. Krakόw: Wydawnictwo św. Stanisław BM Archidiecezji Krakowskiej, 1998–2002.

Lambrecht, Karen. *Hexenverfolgung und Zaubereiprozesse in den schlesischen Territorien.* Koln: Bohlau, 1995.

Larner, Christina. *Enemies of God: The Witch-hunt in Scotland.* Baltimore: The John Hopkins University Press, 1981.

——. *Witchcraft and Religion. The Politics of Popular Belief.* London: Blackwell, 1984.

Lasocki, Zygmunt. 'Szlachta płońska w walce z czartem.' *Miesięcznik Heraldyczny* 12, no. 1–3 (1933): 1–8, 18–22, 37–42.

Łaszewski, Ryszard. 'Przestępstwo preciwko religii i dobrym obyczajom w prawie wiejskim Rzeczypospolitej szlacheckiej.' In *Historia Prawa. Historia Kultury. Liber Memorialis Vitoldo Maisel,* edited by E. Borkowska-Bagieńska and H. Olszewski. Poznań: Printer, 1994.

Łaszkiewicz, Hubert, ed. *Churches and Confessions in East Central Europe: Early Modern Times.* Lublin: Instytut Europy Środkowo-Wschodniej, 1999.

Łaszkiewicz, Hubert. 'Sąd wojtowsko-ławniczy w Lublinie a trybunał koronny w drugiej połowie XVII wieku.' *Roczniki Humanistyczne KUL* 36, no. 2 (1988): 161–72.

——. 'Kary wymierzone przez sąd miejski w Lublinie w drugiej połowie XVII wieku.' *Czasopismo Prawno-Historyczne* 41, no. 2 (1989): 139–51.

Lehr, Urszula. 'Wierzenia demonologiczne we wsi Obidza (region sądecki) w świetle badań empirycznych.' *Lud* 66 (1982): 113–49.

Lerner, Berel Dov. 'Magic, religion and secularity among the Azande and Nuer.' In *Indigenous Religions. A Companion,* edited by Graham Harvey. New York: Cassell, 2000.

Levack, Brian. 'State-building and Witch Hunting in Early Modern Europe.' In *The Witchcraft Reader,* edited by Darren Oldridge. New York: Routledge, 2002 [1996].

——. *The Witch Hunt in Early Modern Europe.* 3rd ed. London: Longman, 2006.

——. 'Witch-Hunting in England and Poland: Similarities and Differences.' In *Britain and Poland-Lithuania: Contact and Comparison from the Middle Ages to 1795,* edited by Richard Unger and Jakub Basista. Boston: Brill, 2008.

Lubierska, Joanna. 'Proces o czary w Doruchowie w 1775 r. w świetle nowych źrόdeł.' *Historia Slavorum Occidentis* 12 no. 3 (2022): 30–63.

Łukaszewicz, Jόzef. *Krόtki historyczno-statystyczny opis miast i wsi w dzisiejszym powiecie krotoszyńskim od najdawniejszych czasόw aż po rok 1794.* 2 vols. Poznań: Jan Konstanty Żupański, 1869–1975.

——. *Obraz historyczno-statystyczny miasta Poznania w dawniejszych czasach.* Edited by Jacek Wiesiołowski. 2 vols. Poznań: Wydawnictwo Miejskie, 2000 [1838].

Łysiak, Ludwik, ed. *Księga sądowa kresu klimkowskiego, 1600–1762*, Starodawne Prawa Polskiego Pomniki, Seria 2, Dział 2, Prawo Wiejskie. Wrocław: Zakład Narodowy im. Ossolińskich, 1965.

Łysiak, Ludwik, ed. *Księga sądowa wsi Wary, 1449–1623*, Starodawne Prawa Polskiego Pomniki, Seria 2, Dział 2, Prawo Wiejskie. Wrocław: Zakład Narodowy im. Ossolińskich, 1971.

MacCulloch, J.A. 'The Mingling of Fairy and Witch Beliefs in 16th and 17th Scotland.' *Folklore* 32, no. 4 (1921): 227–44.

Macdonald, Stuart. 'In Search of the Devil in Fife Witchcraft Cases 1560–1705.' In *The Scottish Witch-Hunt in Context*, edited by Julian Goodare. Manchester and New York: Manchester UP, 2002.

——. 'Enemies of God Revisited. Recent Publications on Scottish Witch-hunting.' *Scottish Economic and Social History* 23, no. 2 (2003): 68–84.

MacFarlane, Alan. *Witchcraft in Tudor and Stuart England*. New York: Harper and Row, 1970.

Maclean, Ian. *The Renaissance Notion of Women. A Study in the Fortunes of Scholasticism and Medical Science in European Intellectual Life*. New York: Cambridge University Press, 1987.

Mączak, Antoni. 'Jedyna i nieporównywalna? Kwestia odrębności Rzeczypospolitej w Europie XVI-XVII wieku.' *Kwartalnik Historyczny* 100, no. 4 (1993): 121–36.

——. *Money, Prices and Power in Poland, 16th-17th Centuries. A Comparative Approach*. Brookfield, VT: Variorum, 1995.

——. 'Patron, Client, and the Distribution of Social Revenue. Some Comparative Remarks.' *Studia Historiae Oeconomicae* 23 (1998): 39–49.

Maisel, Witold. *Poznańskie prawo karne do końca XVI wieku*. Poznań: Uniwersytet im. Adama Mickiewicza w Poznaniu, 1963.

Malewski, Z. 'Procesy o czarnoksięstwo i zabobony w Bydgoszczy. Przyczynek do dziejów czarownictwa w Polsce.' *Przegląd Bydgoski* 4, no. 1–2 (1936): 71–81.

Martin, Lauren. 'The Devil and the Domestic: Witchcraft, Quarrels and Women's Work in Scotland.' In *The Scottish Witch-Hunt in Context*, edited by Julian Goodare. Manchester and New York: Manchester UP, 2002.

Maxwell-Stuart, P.G. *Satan's Conspiracy: Magic and Witchcraft in Sixteenth-century Scotland*. East Linton: Tuckwell Press, 2001.

——. *Witchcraft in Europe and the New World, 1400–1800*. New York: Palgrave, 2001.

McNeill, J. T., and Helena M. Garner, eds. *Medieval Handbooks of Penance: A Translation of the Principle Libri Poenitentiales and Selections of Related Documents*. New York: Columbia University Press, 1990 [1938].

Meyer, Birgit. *Translating the Devil: Religion and Modernity Among the Ewe in Ghana*. Edinburgh: Edinburgh University Press, 1999.

Michalski, Jerzy. 'Problem *ius agratiandi* i kary śmierci w Polsce w latach siedemdziesiątych XVIII w.' *Czasopismo Prawno-Historyczne* 10, no. 2 (1958): 175–96.

——. 'Jeszcze o konstytucji sejmu 1776 roku "Konwikcje w sprawach kryminalnych".' *Kwartalnik Historyczny* 103, no. 3 (1996): 89–101.

Michelet, Jules. *Satanism and Witchcraft: A Study in Medieval Superstition*. New York: Citadel Press, 1939 [1862].

Midelfort, H.C. Erik. 'Heartland of the Witchcraze.' In *The Witchcraft Reader*, edited by Darren Oldridge. New York: Routledge, 2002 [1981].

———. 'The Devil and the German People.' In *The Witchcraft Reader*, edited by Darren Oldridge. New York: Routledge, 2002 [1989].

Mikołajczyk, Marian. *Przestępstwo i kara w prawie miast Polski południowej XVI–XVIII wieku*. Katowice: Wydawnictwo Uniwersytetu Śląskiego, 1998.

———. 'O pławieniu czarownic w Gdowie w 1689 r.: Kartka z dziejów miejskiego procesu karnego w Polsce.' *Studia z Dziejów i Prawa Polskiego* 4 (1999): 121–129.

———. 'Przestępstwa przeciwko religii i Kościołowi w prawie miast polskich XVI–XVIII wieku.' *Czasopismo Prawno-Historyczne* 52, no. 1–2 (2000): 225–38.

———. 'Prawo oskarżonego do obrony w praktyce sądów miejskich w Polsce XVI–XVIII wieku.' In *Ustrój i prawo w przeszłości dalszej i bliższej*, edited by Jerzy Malec and Wacław Uruszczak. Kraków: Wydawnictwo Uniwersytetu Jagiellońskiego, 2001.

———. 'Jak obronić oskarżona o czary. Mowy procesowe z 1655 roku w sprawie Gertrudy Zagrodzkiej.' In *Z dziejów kultury prawnej. Studia ofiarowane Profesorowi Juliuszowi Bardachowi w dziewięćdziesięciolecie urodzin*, edited by H. Dziewanowska and K. Dziewanowska Stefanczyk. Warszawa: Liber, 2004.

Milewski, Karol. *Pamiątki historyczne krajowe*. Warszawa: S. Orgelbrand, 1848.

Milis, L. 'La conversion en profondeur: un processus sans fin.' *Revue du Nord* 68 (1986): 487–98.

Misiurek, Jerzy. *Historia i teologia polskiej duchowości katolickiej*. 3 vols. Lublin: Redakcja Wydawnictwo Katolickiego Uniwersytetu Lubelskiego, 1994.

Moeglich, Marcin. 'Procesy o czary przed sądem miejskim wągrowieckim: chronologia i dynamika zjawiska.' *Wangrowieciana Studia et Fontes* 3 (2016): 44–91.

Monter, William. 'Toads and Eucharists: The Male Witches of Normandy, 1564–1660.' *French Historical Studies* 20, no. 4 (1997): 563–95.

Monumenta Historica Dioceseos Wladislaviensis. 25 vols. Włoclawek: Seminarii Dioecesani, 1881–1910.

Moszyński, Kazimierz. *Kultura Ludowa Słowian*. 3 vols. Warszawa: Książka i Wiedza, 1967–1968 [1934].

Muchembled, Robert. *Le roi et la sorcière. L'Europe de bûchers (XVe–XVIIIe siècle)*. Paris: Desclée, 1993.

———. 'Satanic Myths and Cultural Realities.' In *Early Modern European Witchcraft. Centres and Perpheries*, edited by Bengt Ankarloo and Gustav Henningsen. Oxford: Oxford University Press, 1993.

Muszyńska, Jadwiga. 'Straty demograficzne i zniszczenia gospodarzcze w Małopolsce w połowie XVII wieku. Problemy badawcze.' In *Rzeczpospolita w latach Potopu*, edited by Jadwiga Muszyńska and Jacek Wijaczka, 275–88. Kielce: Wyższa Szkoła Pedagogiczna im. Jana Kochanowskiego, 1996.

Muszyński, Michał. 'Glosy, zapiski, i niektóre teksty polskie w starych drukach i rękopisach Biblioteki Kórnickiej do r. 1550 (part 2).' *Pamiętnik Biblioteki Kórnickiej*, no. 9–10 (1968): 154–282.

Narayanan, Vasudha. 'Diglossic Hinduism: Liberation and Lentils.' *Journal of the American Academy of Religion* 68, no. 4 (2000): 761–79.

Nasiorowski, S. *'List pasterski' kard. Bernarda Maciejowskiego*. Lublin: Redakcja Wydawnictw Katolickiego Uniwersytetu Lubelskiego, 1992.

Needham, Rodney. 'Synthetic Images.' In *Primordial Characters*. Charlottesville: University of Virginia Press, 1978.

Niebrzegowska, Stanisława. *Przestrach od przestrachu. Rośliny w ludowych przekazach ustnych*. Lublin: Wydawnictwo Uniwersytetu Marii Curie Skłodowskiej, 2000.

Ochman-Staniszewska, Stefania. 'Od stabilizacji do kryzysu władzy królewskiej: państwo Wazów.' In *Między monarchą a demokracją. Studia z dziejów Polski XV–XVIII wieku*, edited by Sucheni Grabowska and Żarin. Warszawa: Wydawnictwo Sejmowe, 1994.

Okoń, Jan. *Dramat i teatr szkolny. Sceny jezuickie XVII wieku*. Vol. 26, Studia Staropolskie. Wrocław: Zakład Narodowy im. Ossolińskich, 1970.

Oldridge, Darren. *The Devil in Early Modern England*. Phoenix Mill, Gloucestershire: Sutton Publishing, 2000.

Olszewski, F. 'Prześladowanie czarów w dawnej Polsce.' In *Album uczącej się młodzieży polskiej poświęcone J. I. Kraszewskiemu z powodu jubileusza jego pięćdsiesięcioletniej działalności literatckiej*. Lwów: Nakład Czytelni Akademii Lwowskiej, 1879.

Olszewski, Mikołaj. *Świat zabobonów w średniowieczu. Studium kazania O zabobonach Stanisława ze Skarbimierz*. Warszawa: Wydawnictwo Naukowe Semper, 2002.

Ostling, Michael, and Richard Forest. '"Goblins, owles, and sprites": Discerning Early Modern English Preternatural Beings through Collocational Analysis.' *Religion* 44 no. 4 (2014): 547–572.

Ostling, Michael. 'Konstytucja 1543 r. i początki procesów o czary w Polsce.' *Odrodzenie i Reformacja w Polsce* 49 (2005): 93–103.

——. 'Nieznany proces o czary i świętokradztwo w Lublinie, 1643.' *Lud* 89 (2005): 191–204.

——. 'Witches' Herbs on Trial.' *Folklore* 125 no. 2 (2014): 179–201.

——. 'Babyfat and Belladonna: Flight Ointment and the Contestation of Reality.' *Magic, Ritual, & Witchcraft* 11 no. 1 (2016): pp. 30–72.

——. 'Speaking of Love in the Polish Witch Trials.' In *Emotions in the History of Witchcraft*, edited by L. Kounine and M. Ostling. New York: Palgrave Macmillan, 2016.

——. 'Imagined Crimes, Real Victims: Hermeneutical Witches and Jews in Early Modern Poland. In *Ritual Murder in Russia, Eastern Europe, and Beyond: New Histories of an Old Accusation*, edited by W.E.M. Avrutin, J. Dekel-Chen, and R. Weinberg. Bloomington: Indiana University Press, 2017.

——. 'Where've All the Good People Gone?' In *Fairies, Demons and Nature Spirits: Small Gods at the Margins of Christendom*, edited by M. Ostling. New York: Palgrave Macmillan, 2017.

——. '"Accuser of Brothers": A Polish Anti-Demonological Tract and its Self-Defeating Rhetoric.' Reformation and Renaissance Review 22–23 (2020): 218–237.

Partyka, Joanna. 'Książka rękopiśmienna na dworze szlacheckim.' *Odrodzenie i Reformacja w Polsce* 38 (1994): 79–89.

Pazdro, Z. 'Proces o "perepiczkę".' *Lud* 6, no. 268–276 (1900).

Pearl, Jonathan L. *The Crime of Crimes: Demonology and Politics in France, 1560–1620*. Waterloo: Wilfrid Laurier University Press, 1999.

Pełka, Leonard. J. *Polska demonologia ludowa*. Warszawa: Iskry, 1987.

Peters, Edward. *Torture*. Philadelphia: University of Pennsylvania Press, 1996.

Piekosiński, Franciszek, ed. *Akta sądu kryminalnego kresu muszyńskiego, 1647–1765*. Vol. 9, Starodawne Prawa Polskiego Pomniki. Kraków: Akademia Umiejętności, 1889.

'Pierwszy od 300 lat w Polsce proces o czary.' *Gazeta Wyborcza*, 10 March 2004.

Pilaszek, Malgorzata. 'Procesy czarownic w Polsce w XVI–XVIII wieku. Nowe aspekty. Uwagi na marginesie pracy B. Baranowskiego.' *Odrodzenie i Reformacja w Polsce* 42 (1998): 81–103.

——. 'W poszukiwaniu prawdy. O działalności sądów kryminalnych w Koronie XVI–XVIII w.' *Pregląd Historyczyny* 89, no. 3 (1998): 361–81.

——. Litewskie procesy czarownic w XVI–XVIII w.' *Odrodzenie i Reformacja w Polsce* 46 (2002): 7–35.

——. 'Witch-hunts in Poland, 16th-18th Centuries.' *Acta Poloniae Historica* 86 (2002): 103–32.

——. 'Apelacje w polskich procesach czarownic (XVII–XVIII w.).' *Odrodzenie i Reformacja w Polsce* 49 (2005): 113–36.

——. *Procesy o czary w Polsce w wiekach XV–XVIIII*. Kraków: Universitas, 2008.

Płaza, Stanisław, ed. *Księga sądowa wsi Iwkowej, 1581–1809*, Starodawne Prawa Polskiego Pomniki, Seria 2, Dział 2, Prawo Wiejskie. Wrocław: Zakład Narodowy im. Ossolińskich, 1969.

Płaza, Stanisław. *Historia prawa w Polsce na tle porównawczym*. 3 vols. Kraków: Wydawnictwo Naukowe Księgarnia Akadamicka, 1997.

Plezia, M. 'Benedictio Gratiosae. Poznański formularz błogosławieństwa ziół z drugiej połowy XV w.' *Roczniki Humanistyczne* 27, no. 3 (1979): 87–92.

Pócs, Éva. *Between the Living and the Dead. A Perspective on Witches and Seers in the Early Modern Age*. Translated by Szilvia Rédey and Michael Webb. Budapest: Central European University Press, 1999.

——. 'Why Witches are Women.' *Acta Ethnographica Hungarica* 48, no. 3–4 (2003): 367–84.

Podgórski, Marian. *Wola Żarczycka. Streszczona kronika kościelna na zakończenie trzeciego stulecia*. Jasło: L. Stoeger, 1878.

Pol, Zuzanna. 'Nasze dobre złe moce.' *National Geographic Polska* 54, no. 3 (2004): unpaginated.

Polaczkówna, Helena ed. *Najstarsza księga sądowa wsi Trześniowa, 1419–1609*. Lwów: Nakładem Towarzystwa Naukowego, 1923.

Półćwiartek, Józef, ed. *Wybór źródeł rękopiśmiennych do dziejów wsi nad Sanem i Wisłokiem w XVI i XVII wieku*. Rzeszów: Prace Humanistyczne Towarzystwa Naukowego w Rzeszowie, 1980.

Potkowski, Edward. *Czary i czarownice*. Warszawa: Książka i Wiedza, 1970.

Pradelles de Latour, Charles-Henry. 'Witchcraft and the Avoidance of Physical Violence in Cameroon.' *Journal of the Royal Anthropological Institute* 1 (1995): 599–609.

Price, Merall Llewelyn. *Consuming Passions. The Uses of Cannibalism in Late Medieval and Early Modern Europe*. Vol. 20, Studies in Medieval History and Culture. New York: Routledge, 2003.

Purkiss, Diane. *The Witch in History: Early Modern and Twentieth-century Representations*. New York: Routledge, 1996.

Putek, Jerzy. *Mroki średniowiecza. Obyczaje, przesądy, fanatyzm, okrucieństwo i ucisk społeczny w Polsce*. Warszawa: Państwowy Instytut Wydawniczy, 1956 [1935].

Quaife, G.R. *Godly Zeal and Furious Rage. The Witch in Early Modern Europe*. New York: St. Martin's Press, 1987.

Rafacz, Józef. 'Podejrzenie o czary w Krościenku.' *Lud* 18 (1918): 302–03.

——. 'Sprawy karne w sądach miejskich w epoce nowożytnej.' *Kwartalnik Historyczny* 47 (1933): 559–68.

Riabinin, Jan. *Lublin w księgach wójtowsko ławniczych XVII—XVIII w.* Vol. 2, Materiały do Monografii Lublina. Lublin: Wydawnictwo Magistratu m. Lublina, 1928.

——. *Jeszcze o czarach i gusłach w dawnym Lublinie.* Lublin: Głos Lubelski, 1936.

Robbins, Joel. *Becoming Sinners: Christianity and Moral Torment in Papua New Guinea Society.* Berkeley, California: University of California Press, 2004.

Ronowska, Bożena. 'Zbiorowy proces o czary we wsi Morzeszczyn w 1747 roku.' In *Inny – obcy – potwór*, edited by J. Żychlińska and A. Głowacka-Penczyńska. Bydgoszcz: Wydawnictwo Uniwersytetu Kazimierza Wielkiego, 2016.

Roper, Lyndal. *Oedipus and the Devil. Witchcraft, Sexuality and Religion in Early Modern Europe.* New York: Routledge, 1994.

——. *Witchcraze. Terror and Fantasy in Baroque Germany.* New Haven: Yale University Press, 2004.

Rosenblatt, Jósef. *Czarownica powołana. Przyczynek do historii spraw przeciw czarownicom w Polsce*, Biblioteka Umiejętności Prawnych. Warszawa: Wydawnictwo S. Orgelbranda Synów, 1883.

Rostafiński, Józef. *Średniowieczna Historya naturalna w Polsce /Symbola ad historiam medii aevi.* 2 vols. Kraków: Uniwersytet Jagielloński, 1900.

——. 'Wpływ przeżyć chłopięcych Mickiewicza na obrazy ostatnich dwu ksiąg Pana Tadeusza oraz o święceniu ziół na Matkę Boską Zielną.' *Rozprawy polskiej Akademii Umiejętności, Wydział Filologiczny* 61, no. 1 (1922).

Rożek, Michał. *Diabeł w kulturze polskiej. Szkice z dziejów motywu i postaci.* Warszawa: Polska Akademia Nauk, 1993.

Rubin, Miri. *Corpus Christi. The Eucharist in Late Medieval Culture.* New York: Cambridge UP, 1991.

Rubin, Władysław. 'Lud w polskim ustawodawstwie synodalnym do rozbiorów Polski.' *Sacrum Poloniae Millenium* 2 (1955): 131–64.

Ruel, Malcolm. 'Christians as Believers.' In *A Reader in the Anthropology of Religion*, edited by Michael Lambek. Malden: Blackwell, 2008 (1982).

Ryan, W.F. 'The Witchcraft Hysteria in Early Modern Europe. Was Russia an Exception?' *Slavonic and Eastern European Review* 76, no. 1 (1998): 49–84.

——. *The Bathhouse at Midnight. An Historical Survey of Magic and Divination in Russia.* University Park, Pennsylvania: The Pennsylvania State University Press, 1999.

Rybkowski, Mikołaj. 'Dyabeł w wierzeniach ludu polskiego. (Z okolic Biecza).' *Lud* 9 (1903): 212–32.

S.X. 'Kilka słów o czarownicach w Polsce.' *Przyjaciel Ludu* 11, no. 22–23 (1844).

Sabean, D.W. *Power in the Blood. Popular Culture and Village Discourse in Early Modern Germany.* New York: Cambridge University Press, 1985.

Salmonowicz, Stanisław. 'Procesy o czary w Polsce. Próba rozważań modelowych.' In *Prawo wczoraj i dziś. Studia dedykowane Profesor Katarzynie Sójka Zielińskiej*, edited by G. Bałtruszajtis. Warszawa, 2000.

Sawicki, Jakub, ed. *Wybor tekstów źródłowych z historii państwa i prawa polskiego.* Vol. 1, parts 1–2. Warszawa: Polskie Wydawnictwo Naukowe, 1951–1952.

Sawicki, Jakub. 'Z ksiąg Metryki Koronnej. Tekst pierwszych konstytucji sejmowych w języku polskim z r. 1543 w sprawie sądownictwa świeckiego i duchownego.' *Teki Archiwalne* 2 (1954): 51–95.

Scribner, Robert. *Popular Culture and Popular Movements in Reformation Germany.* Ronceverte, West Virginia: The Hambledon Press, 1987.

——. 'The Reformation, Popular Magic, and the "Disenchantment of the World".' *Journal of Interdisciplinary History* 23, no. 3 (1993): 475–94.

——. *Religion and Culture in Germany (1400–1800).* Boston: Brill, 2001.

Semkowicz, Władysław. 'Dwa przyczynki do historyi wierzeń ludowych.' *Lud* 6 (1900): 385–91.

Seweryn, Tadeusz. *Staropolska sztuka ludowa.* Warszawa: Wydawnictwo Sztuka, 1956.

Shuck, Glenn William. 'The Myth of the Burning Times and the Politics of Resistance in Contemporary American Wicca.' *Journal of Religion and Society* 2 (2000).

Siarczyński, Franciszek. *Obraz wieku panowania Zygmunta III,* 2 vols. Poznań: Księgarnia Nowa, 1843.

Siarkowski, Władysław. *Materiały do etnografii ludu polskiego z okolic Kielc.* Kielce: Wydawnictwo Takt, 2000 [1878–1879].

Słomka, Jan. *Pamiętniki włościanina. Od pańszczyzny do dni dzisiejszych.* 2 ed. Kraków: Towarzystwo Szkoły Ludowej, 1929.

Ślusarska, Magdalena, ed. *Dwór, plebania i rodzina chłopska. Szkice z dziejów wsi polskiej XVII i XVIII wieku.* Warszawa: DiG, 1998.

Smith, Jonathan Z. *Imagining Religion. From Babylon to Jonestown.* Chicago: University of Chicago Press, 1982.

——. 'Religion, Religions, Religious.' In *Critical Terms for Religious Studies,* edited by M. Taylor. Chicago: University of Chicago Press, 1998.

Smoleński, Władysław. *Wiara w życiu społeczeństwa polskiego w epoce jezuickiej.* Warszawa: Ludowa Spółdzielnia Wydawnicza, 1951 [1882].

Sójka, Jan. 'Regulus Wojciech.' In *Drukarze dawnej Polski od XV do XVIII wieku,* edited by Alodia Kawecka-Gryczowa, Krystyna Korotajowa and Jan Sójka. Wrocław: Zakład Narodowy im. Ossolińskich, 1977.

Soldan, Wilhelm Gottlieb. *Gesschichte der Hexenprozesse.* Edited by Max Bauer. 2 ed. Munich: Georg Müller, 1911 [1843].

Sollée, Kristen J. *Witches, Sluts, Feminists: Conjuring the Sex Positive.* Berkeley: ThreeL Media, 2017.

Soman, Alfred. *Sorcellerie et justice criminelle: le Parlement de paris, 16e–18e siècles.* Brookfield, Vermont: Variorum, 1992.

Staszków, Michał. 'Sprawy o "zabranie sławy" w sądownictwie wiejskim Małopolski XV–XVIII wieku.' *Lud* 46 (1960): 155–64.

Stephens, Walter. 'Incredible Sex: Witches, Demons, and Giants in the Early Modern Imagination.' In *Monsters in the Italian Literary Imagination,* edited by Keala Jewell. Detroit: Wayne State University Press, 2001.

——. *Demon Lovers, Witchcraft, Sex, and the Crisis of Belief.* Chicago: University of Chicago Press, 2002.

Stewart, Charles. *Demons and the Devil. Moral Imagination in Modern Greek Culture.* Princeton: Princeton University Press, 1991.

Stręciwilk, Janina. 'Męka Pańska w polskiej literaturze barokowej.' In *Męka Chrystusa wczoraj i dziś*, edited by H.D. Wojtyska and J.J. Kopeć. Lublin: Katolicki Uniwersytet Lubelski, 1981.

Surdocki, Marian. 'Pensjonariusze szpitali wielkopolskich w XVII i XVIII wieku.' *Roczniki Humanistyczne KUL* 37, no. 2 (1990): 118–81.

Sygański, Jan. 'Wyroki Ławicy Nowosandeckiej (1652–1684). Kartka z dziejów sądownictwa magdeburskiego w Polsce.' *Przegląd prawa i administracji* 42, no. 11–12 (1917): 421–67.

Szanser, Jan.'Ustrój miasta Kielc na przełomie XVI i XVII wieku.' *Rocznik Muzeum Narodowego w Kielcach* 12 (1982): 27–53.

Szkurłatowski, Krzysztof P. 'Proces inkwizycyjny przeciwko czarownictwu w praktyce sądow sołtysich województwa malborskiego na przełomie XVII i XVIII w. na tle rozwoju europejskiego prawa karnego.' *Rocznik Elbląski* 15 (1997): 44–55.

Szostek, Teresa. 'Exempla i autorytety w kazaniach Jakuba z Paradyża i Mikołaja z Błonia.' In *Kultura Elitarna a Kultura Masowa W Polsce Późnego Średniowiecza*, edited by Bronisław Geremek. Wrocław: Zakład Narodowy im. Ossolińskich, 1978.

Szyszkowski, Władysław. 'Pierwiastek ludowy w poezyi polskiej XV i XVI w (part 1).' *Lud* 19 (1913): 104–52.

Tambiah, Stanley Jeyaraja. 'Form and Meaning of Magical Acts.' In *A Reader in the Anthopology of Religion*, edited by Michael Lambek. Malden: Blackwell, 2008 [1973].

Tazbir, Janusz. 'Z dziejów falszerstw historycznych w Polsce w pierwszej połowie XIX stulecie.' *Przegląd Historyczny* 57, no. 4 (1966).

——. *A State Without Stakes. Polish Religious Toleration in the 16th and 17th Centuries*. Translated by A.T. Jordon. New York: Kosciuszko Foundation, 1973.

——. 'Procesy o czary.' *Odrodzenie i Reformacja w Polsce* 23 (1978): 151–77.

——. *Piotr Skarga: Szermierz kontrreformacji*. Warsaw: Państwowe Wydawnictwo "Wiedza Powszechna", 1978.

——. 'Obraz heretyka i diabła.' In *Szlaki kultury polskiej*. Warszawa: Polskie Wydawnictwo Naukowe, 1986 [1981].

——. *Myśl polska w nowożytnej kulturze europejskiej*. Warszawa: Nasza Księgarnia, 1986.

——. 'Franco de Franco.' In *Reformacja w Polsce. Szkice o ludziach i doktrynie*. Warszawa: Książka i Wiedza, 1993.

——. 'Liczenie wiedźm.' *Polityka* 37 (2001).

——. *Sarmaci i świat (Prace Wybrane)*. Vol. 3. Kraków: Universitas, 2001.

——. *Cudzym piórem. Falsyfikaty historyczno-literackie*. Poznań: Poznańskie Towarzystwo Przyjaciół Nauk, 2002.

Tedeschi, John. 'The Roman Inquisition and Witchcraft: An Early 17th-century "Instruction" on Correct Trial Procedure.' *Revue de l'Historie des Religions* 200, no. 2 (1983): 163–88.

Teter, Magda. *Jews and Heretics in Catholic Poland. A Beleaguered Church in the Post-Reformation Era*. New York: Cambridge University Press, 2006.

——. *Sinners on Trial: Jews and Sacrilege after the Reformation*. Cambridge, Mass.: Harvard University Press, 2011.

Thawer, Tish. *The Witches of BlackBrook*, Fort Collins, Col.: Amber Leaf, 2015.

Thoden van Velzen, Bonno, and Imeka van Wetering. 'Dangerous Creatures and the Enchantment of Modern Life.' In *Powers of Good and Evil: Social Transformation and Popular Belief,* edited by Paul Clough and Jon P. Mitchell. New York: Berghahn Books, 2001.

Thomas, Keith. *Religion and the Decline of Magic.* Harmondsworth: Penguin Books, 1973.

Tokarska-Bakir, Joanna. '*Ganz Andere?* Żyd jako czarownica i czarownica jako Żyd w Polskich i obcych źródłach etnograficznych, czyli jak czytać protokoły przesłuchań.' *Res Publica Nowa* 8, no. 3–32 (2001).

Tomczak, Andrzej. *Zarys dziejów archiwów polskich.* Vol. 2. Toruń: Uniwersytet Mikołaja Kopernika, 1980.

Toon, Francine. 'We are the granddaughters of the witches you couldn't burn.' *Penguin Newsletter,* 2019. Online at https://www.penguin.co.uk/articles/2021/march/francine-toon-pine-inner-witch-violence-against-women.html (Accessed Nov. 5 2022).

Torój, Elżbieta. *Inwentarze księgozbiorów mieszczan lubelskich 1591–1678.* Lublin: Wydawnictwo UMCS, 1997.

———. *Inwentarze książek lubelskich introligatorów z pierwszej połowy XVII wieku.* . Lublin: Wydawnictwo UMCS, 2000.

Tripplin, L. Tassilion, ed. *Tajemnice społeczeństwa wykryte ze spraw kryminalnych krajowych.* 3 vols. Wrocław: Zygmunt Schlettera, 1852.

Udziela, Seweryn. *Świat nadzmysłowy ludu krakowskiego, mieszkającego po prawym brzegu Wisły: wielkoludy, czarownice i czarownicy, choroby.* Warsaw: A. T. Jezierski, 1901.

———. 'Z kronik kościelnych. I. Kronika w Milówce.' *Lud* 16 (1910): 153–59.

Ulanowski, Bolesław, ed. *Acta iudiciorum ecclesiasticorum diocesum gneznensis et poznaniensis (1403–1530),* Monumenta medii aevi res gestas Poloniae illustrantia. Kraków: Akademia Umiejętności, 1902.

Ulanowski, Bolesław, ed. *Księgi sądowe wiejskie,* 2 vols, Starodawne prawa polskiego pomniki. Kraków: Komisja prawnicza Polskiej Akademji Umiejętności, 1921.

Ulanowski, Bolesław. *Wieś polska pod względem prawnym od wieku XVI do XVIII.* Cracow: Księgarnia Spółki Wydawniczej Polskiej, 1894.

Urban, Wacław. *Chłopi wobec reformacji w Małopolsce w drugiej połowie XVI w.* Kraków: Polskie Wydawnictwo Naukowe, 1959.

———. 'Czary i mandragora w Tymbarku.' *Odrodzenie i Reformacja w Polsce* 49 (2005): 181–82.

Urbańczyk, Stanisław et al., eds. *Słownik staropolski.* 10 vols. Wrocław: Wydawnictwo PAN, 1952–2003.

Uruszczak, Wacław, ed. *Acta Maleficorum Wisniciae (1629–1665).* Kraków: Collegium Columbinum, 2003.

Uruszczak, Wacław. 'Proces czarownicy w Nowym Sączu w 1670 roku. Z badań nad miejskim procesem karnym czasów nowożytnych.' In *Historia Prawa. Historia Kultury. Liber Memorialis Vitoldo Maisel,* edited by E. Borkowska-Bagieńska and H. Olszewski. Poznań: Printer, 1994.

———. 'Proces o czary w podkrakowskiej wsi Krowodrza w 1698 roku.' *Studia Iuridica Toruniensia* 10 (2012): 233–241.

Valk, Ülo. *The Black Gentleman: Manifestations of the Devil in Estonian Folk Religion.* Vol. 276, F.F. Communications. Helsinki: Soumalainen Tiedeakatemia, Academia Scientiarum Fennica, 2001.

Van Gent, Jacqueline. *Magic, Body and the Self in Eighteenth-Century Sweden.* Boston: Brill, 2009.

Waite, Gary K. *Eradicating the Devil's Minions: Anabaptists and Witches in Reformation Europe, 1525–1600.* Toronto: University of Toronto Press, 2007.

Wajsblum, Marek. 'Ex Regestro Arianismi. Szkice z dziejów upadku protestantyzmu w Małopolsce.' *Reformacja w Polsce* 9–10 (1939): 89–408.

Warczyńska, Aleksandra. 'Zielarki z Gorzuchowa.' *Wielkopolska Ciekawie* (2019), online at: https://wielkopolskaciekawie.pl/ciekawe-historie/zielarki-z-gorzuchowa-palenie-na-stosie/ (Accessed March 6, 2023).

Wawrzeniecki, Marjan. 'Proces o czary w Nieszawie roku 1721.' *Wisła* 11 (1897): 646–54.

——. 'Proces o czary r. 1721 (part 2).' *Wisła* 13 (1899): 512–18.

——. 'Dwa procesy o czary z 1684.' *Lud* 24 (1925): 170–172.

——. 'Przyczynek do procesów o czary.' *Lud* 24 (1926): 173.

Węgrzynek, Hanna. *'Czarna legenda' Żydów. Procesy o rzekome mordy rytualne w dawnej Polsce.* Warszawa: Wydawnictwo Bellona / Wydawnictwo Fundacji Historia Pro Futuro, 1995.

Wevers, John. *Notes on the Greek Text of Genesis.* Atlanta: Scholars Press, 1993.

Wierzbicki, Andrzej. 'Czarnowidztwo czy apologia? W poszukiwaniu prawdy historycznej.' In *Przewrót Umysłowy W Polsce Wieku Xviii.* Warszawa: Państwowy Instytut Wydawniczy, 1979.

Wiesiołowski, J. 'Funkcjonowanie poznańskiego kultu pątniczego w kościele Bożego Ciała (kon. XV-pocz. XVII wieku).' *Kronika Miasta Poznania*, no. 3/4 (1992): 128–59.

Wijaczka, Jacek. 'Proces o czary w Doruchowie w 1775 roku: Fakt czy mit?' Forthcoming.

——. 'Procesy o czary przed sądami miejskim i wojewodzińskim w Skarszewach w końcu XVII i w pierwszej połowie XVIII wieku.' In *Prusy i Inflanty między średniowieczem a nowożytnością. Państwo—społeczeństwo—kultura*, edited by B. Dybaś and D. Makiłła. Toruń: Wydawnictwo Uniwersytetu Mikołaja Kopernika, 2003.

——. 'Procesy o czary w regionie świętokrzyskiego w XVII–XVIII wieku.' In *Z przeszłości regionu świętokrzyskiego od XVI do XX wieku*, edited by J. Wijaczka. Kielce: Agencja Reklamowo-Wydawnicza "JARD", 2003.

——. 'Mężczyźni jako ofiary procesów o czary przed sądem łobżenickim w drugiej połowie XVII wieku.' *Czasy Nowożytne* 17 (2004): 17–30.

——. 'Proces o czary we wsi Młotkowo w 1692 roku. Przyczynek do polowania na czarownice w Rzeczypospolitej w XVII wieku.' *Odrodzenie i Reformacja w Polsce* 48 (2004): 161–70.

——. 'Procesy o czary przed sądem zamkowym w Starogrodzie w pierwszej połowie XVIII wieku.' In *Cała historia to dzieje ludzi. Studia z historii społecznej ofiarowane profesorowi Andrzejowi Wyczańskiemu*, edited by Cl Kukla and P. Guzowski. Białystok: Wydawnictwo Uniwersytetu w Białymstoku, 2004.

——. 'Procesy o czary w Polsce w dobie Oświecenia. Zarys problematyki.' *Klio* 17 (2005): 17–62.

——. 'Men standing trial for witchcraft at the Łobżenica court in the second half of the 17th century.' *Acta Poloniae Historica* 93 (2006): 69–85.

——. 'Postępowanie sądowe w sprawie o czary w Toruniu w 1712 roku.' *Odrodzenie i Reformacja we Polsce* 51 (2007): 199–212.

——. *Procesy o czary w Prusach Książęcych / Brandenburskich w XVI–XVIII wieku.* Toruń: Wydawnictwo Uniwersytetu Mikołaja Kopernika, 2007.

——. 'Witch and Sorcerer-Hunts in the Town of Nowe, the 17th and the 1st half of the 18th century.' *Acta Poloniae Historica* 98 (2008): 103–33.

——. 'Procesy o czary przed sądem miejskim w Grudziądzu w XVI–XVII wieku.' *Rocznik Grudziądzki* 18 (2009): 87–101.

——. 'Samosąd w sprawie o czary w Czerniewie (dawny powiat tczewski).' *Rocznik Gdański* 69–70 (2009–10): 37–45.

——. 'Proces o czary we wsi Osowo z 1686 roku.' *Czasy Nowożytne* 24 (2011): 221–230.

——. *Kościół wobec czarów w Rzeczypospolitej w XVI–XVIII wieku (na tle europejskim)*, Warsaw: Neriton, 2016.

——. 'Oskarżenia i procesy o czary w Koźminie w XVII–XVIII wieku.' *Roczniki Historyczne* 82 (2016): 197–219.

——. 'Próba zimnej wody (pławienie) w oskarżeniach I procesach o czary w państwie polsko-litewskim w XVI–XVIII wieku.' *Odrodzenie i Reformacja w Polsce* 60 (2016): 73–110.

——. 'Procesy o czary przed sądem sołtysim Kowalewa (Pomorskiego) w XVII–XVIII wieku.' *Zapiski Historyczne* 82 no. 2 (2017): 101–119.

——. 'Jak się pozbyć matki, która bije? Dziecięcy process o czary w Gnieźnie w 1689 r.' *Przegląd Historyczny* 111 no. 3 (2020): 539–555.

Wilby, Emma. 'The Witch's Familiar and the Fairy in Early Modern England and Scotland.' *Folklore* 111, no. 2 (2000): 283–305.

——. *Cunning Folk and Familiar Spirits. Shamanistic Visionary Traditions in Early Modern British Witchcraft and Magic.* Brighton: Sussex Academic Press, 2005.

Willis, Deborah. *Malevolent Nurture. Witch-hunting and Maternal Power in Early Modern England.* Ithaca: Cornell University Press, 1995.

Wilson, Stephen. *The Magical Universe. Everyday Ritual and Magic in Pre-Modern Europe.* New York: Hambledon and London, 2000.

Wiślicz, Tomasz, ed. 'Regesty spraw o czary przed sądami wiejskimi w Koronie XV–XVIII w.' *Collectanea ad historiam plebanorum*, online at https://plebeanorum.wordpress.com. (Accessed June 10, 2022).

Wiślicz, Tomasz. 'Czary przed sądami wiejskimi w Polsce XVI–XVIII wieku.' *Czasopismo Prawno-Historyczne* 49, no. 1–2 (1997): 47–63.

——. '"Miejsca cudowne" w Małopolsce w XVI–XVIII wieku.' *Kwartalnik Historii Kultury Materialnej* 47, no. 3–4 (1999): 335–48.

——. *Zarobić na duszne zbawienie. Religijność chłopów małopolskich od połowy XVI do końca XVIII w.* Warszawa: Wydawnictwo Neriton / Instytut Historii Polskiej Akademii Nauk, 2001.

——. 'Religijność wiejska w Rzeczypospolitej szlacheckiej. Problemy i trzy przybliżenia.' *Barok* 11, no. 2 (2004): 97–118.

——. 'Społeczeństwo Kleczewa i okolic w walce z czartem (1624–1700).' *Kwartalnik Historyczny* 111, no. 2 (2004): 37–60.

——. 'The Township of Kleczew and its Neighborhood Fighting the Devil (1624–1700).' *Acta Poloniae Historica* 89 (2004): 65–95.

Wisner, Henryk. 'Jurysdykcja duchowna skażona.' In *Rozróżnieni w wierze. Szkice z dziejów Rzeczypospolitej schyłku XVI i połowy XVII wieku.* Warszawa: Książka i Wiedza, 1982.

Wiśniewska, Halina. *Świat płci żeńskiej baroku zaklęty w słowach*. Lublin: Wydawnictwo UMCS, 2003.

Witkowska, Aleksandra. *Kulty pątnicze pietnastowiecznego Krakowa. Z badań nad miejską kulturą religijną*. Lublin: Wydawnictwo Towarzystwa Naukowego Katolickiego Uniwersytetu Lubelskiego, 1984.

Wójcicki, Kazimierz W. *Zarysy domowe*. 4 vols. Warszawa: M. Chmielewski, 1842.

Wojcieszak, Bogumił. *Opalenickie procesy czarownic w XVII wieku*. Opelanica: Miejsko-Gminny Ośrodek Kultury, 1987.

Wojtyska, Henryk Damian. 'Męka Chrystusa w religijności polskiej XVI-XVII wieku.' In *Męka Chrystusa wczoraj i dziś*, edited by H.D. Wojtyska and J.J. Kopeć. Lublin: Katolicki Uniwersytet Lubelski, 1981.

Worobec, Christine D. *Possessed. Women, Witches and Demons in Imperial Russia*. De Kalb, Illinois: Northern Illinois University Press, 2001.

Woronczak, Jerzy. 'Procesy o czary przed poznańskim sądem miejskim w XVI wieku.' *Literatura Ludowa* 16, no. 3 (1972): 49–58.

Woźniakowa, Maria. *Sąd Asesorski Koronny 1537–1795. Jego organizacja, funkcjonowanie i rola w dziejach prawa chełmińskiego i magdeburskiego w Polsce*. Warszawa: Naczelna Dyrekcja Archiwów Państwowych, 1990.

Wróbel, Elżbieta Elena. *Chrześcijańska rodzina w Polsce XVI–XVII wieku. Między ideałem a rzeczywistością*. Kraków: Wydawnictwo Naukowe Papieskiej Akademii Teologicznej, 2002.

Wyczański, Andrzej. *Polska Rzeczą Pospolitą szlachecką*. Warszawa1991.

Wyporska, Wanda. 'Witchcraft, Arson and Murder–the Turek Trial of 1652.' *Central Europe* 1, no. 1 (2003): 41–54.

Wyporska, Wanda. *Witchcraft in Early Modern Poland, 1500–1800*. New York: Palgrave Macmillan, 2013.

X.A.R. 'Relacja naocznego świadka o straceniu razem 14 tu mniemanych czarownic w drugiej połowie 18 go wieku.' *Przyjaciel Ludu* 2, no. 16–18 (1835): 126–27, 34–35, 38–39.

Zakrzewska-Dubasowa, Mirosława, ed. *Procesy o czary w Lublinie w XVII i XVIII w.* Lublin: Nakład. Polskiego Towarzystwa Ludoznawczego, 1947.

Zakrzewska-Dubasowa, Mirosława. 'Proces o czary w Kraśniku z r. 1746.' In *Z dziejów powiatu kraśnickiego. Materiały sesji naukowej*, edited by J.R. Szaflik and K. Miśliński. Lublin: Wydawnictwo Lubelskie, 1963.

Zakrzewski, A. *W kręgu kultu maryjnego. Jasna Góra w kulturze staropolskiej*. Częstochowa: Wydawnictwo WSP, 1995.

Zand, Andrzej. *Z dziejów dawnej Łodzi*. Łódź: Towarzystwo Bibljofilów w Łodzi, 1929.

Zaremska, Hanna. 'Procesje Bożego Ciała w Krakowie w XIV–XVI wieku.' In *Kultura elitarna a kultura masowa w Polsce późnego średniowiecza*, edited by Bronisław Geremek. Wrocław: Zakład Narodowy im. Ossolińskich, 1978.

——. *Niegodne rzemiosło. Kat w społeczeństwie Polski XIV–XVI w.* Warsaw: Wydawnictwo Naukowe PWN, 1986.

Zdrójkowski, Zbigniew. *'Praktyka kryminalna' Jakuba Czechowicza. Jej źródła i system na tle rozwoju współczesnego prawa karnego zachodniej Europy*, Roczniki Towarzystwa Naukowego w Toruniu Toruń: Towarzystwo Naukowe w Toruniu, 1949.

Zguta, Russell. 'The Ordeal by Water (Swimming of Witches) in the East Slavic World.' *Slavic Review* 36, no. 2 (1977): 220–30.

Zielińska, Ewa. 'Kraśnika sprawy z katem.' In *Drogą historii. Studia ofiarowane profesorowi Józefowi Szymańskiemu w siedemdziesiątą rocznicę urodzin,* edited by P. Dymmel, K. Skupieński, and B. Trelińska. Lublin: Wydawnictwo Uniwersytetu Marii Curie-Skłodowskiej, 2001.

Zika, Charles. *The Appearance of Witchcraft. Print and Visual Culture in Sixteenth-Century Europe* New York: Routledge, 2007.

Zwissler, Laurel. 'Witches Tears: Spiritual Feminism, Epistemology, and Witch Hunt Horror Stories.' *The Pomegranate* 18 no. 2 (2016): 176–204.

Index